D1453525

# The Intellectual
# Enterprise

ANNA BOSCHETTI

# The Intellectual Enterprise

SARTRE AND *LES TEMPS MODERNES*

*Translated by*

RICHARD C. McCLEARY

NORTHWESTERN UNIVERSITY PRESS

EVANSTON, IL

Northwestern University Press
Evanston, IL

Originally published in Italian under the title *L'impresa intelletuale, Sartre e Les Temps Modernes*, copyright © 1985, Edizioni Dedalo. This translation is based on the edition published in French under the title *Sartre et "les Temps Modernes": une enterprise intellectuale*, copyright © 1985 by Les Editions Minuit.

Library of Congress Cataloging-in-Publication Data

Boschetti, Anna.
    The intellectual enterprise.

    Translation of: L'impresa intellettuale.
    Includes index.
    1. Sartre, Jean Paul, 1905–1980—Criticism and interpretation.
2. Temps modernes. 3. French periodicals—History—20th century.
4. France—Intellectual life—20th century. I. Title.
PQ2637.A82Z58213 1987          848'.91409          87–24767
ISBN 0–8101–0755–4
ISBN 0–8108–0756–2 (pbk.)

# Contents

Raymond Aron, Simone de Beauvoir, Jean-Marie Domenach, André Gorz, Claude Lefort, Pierre Naville, Jean Piel, Jean Pouillon, Roger Stéphane, and Alain Touraine all are actors who held representative positions within the field analyzed in this book. Thanks to them, a reconstruction of that field based solely on documents and subject to an outsider's misperceptions has gotten inside confirmation.

# Introduction

Sartre's enterprise is undeniably one of the most extraordinary successes in French cultural history. During the fifteen years which followed the Liberation, he held undivided sway over the entire realm of French intellectual life as no one has since. To find comparable dominion, we must go back to Hugo, or even to Voltaire. Even after Sartre had been dethroned by new intellectual fashions, he kept drawing attention to himself by additional feats: the *Critique of Dialectical Reason, The Words* and the Nobel Prize, *The Family Idiot*, his political battles. The fifty thousand people who crowd in the wake of his funeral train; the articles, translations, recollections, and efforts to sum up his works which keep piling up; all show that Sartre has never ceased to be the most famous contemporary French intellectual in the world.

Because Sartre's domination encompasses every dimension of the intellectual life of an entire epoch, explaining it requires analyzing the development and function of the intellectual field as a whole throughout a period which reaches beyond the stage of his crowning success. The conditions of his success and subsequent decline must be sought in the history which precedes and follows them.

My reference to "the intellectual field" indicates the main theoretical and methodological orientation of my analysis: the works of Pierre Bourdieu and all those influenced by his approach, in which the concept of "field" plays a key part. Although I cannot claim to sum up the various aspects of this vast productive undertaking, I will set forth briefly the principles which most directly govern my work.

Bourdieu has often gone back over the road which, beginning with the first consciously decisive formative influence, the relational mode of thinking developed by Cassirer, led him to rework and synthesize the contributions of apparently antagonistic traditions stemming from the founders of his discipline—Marx, Durkheim, and Weber.[1] What made this synthesis possible was the fact that these three authors agreed on one fundamental point: the symbolic does not originate and function in relation to a priori forms of human understanding, as the Kantian and neo-Kantian traditions assume, but in relation to society. What Bourdieu sees in Marx's concept of "class," Weber's concept of "standing," and the socially produced "elementary forms of classification"

1

which Durkheim takes to be the basic categories of human understanding are three different forms of social class existence which become mutually compatible once social classes are understood as systems whose structures and structurings are inseparably economic, symbolic, and logicognoseological.

Bourdieu particularly acknowledges the importance of Weber's insight, in respect to religion, into a phenomenon we must take into account if we wish to avoid the "short circuit" characteristic of the best-known Marxist sociologists of culture: Lukács, Adorno, and Goldmann. Shackled by a "theory of reflection" which reduces culture directly to class structure, they are unable to account for the variety of forms taken on in a given epoch by the cultural products of one and the same social class. Weber showed that the production and management of "religious goods" came historically to be monopolized by a body of specialists that was relatively autonomous in respect to established economic and political powers. Bourdieu sees this autonomy as the essential condition of a "symbolic economy" characterized by a specific functional logic of its own. The basic determinant is social demand, but its effects combine with those of the field's internal demand. Thus the nature of the field is always doubly "in-formed." But the greater its autonomy, the greater the need to seek explanations for practices in the structure and function of the field itself. Even those practices which seem the most disinterested—and are lived as such—may be understood as "strategies": that is to say as ways of acting governed by objective relationships between the resources which individual actors command and the opportunities which the field structure offers. The actors' "habitus," or set of socially acquired dispositions, functions as a "practical sense" which shapes their strategies. The conflicts and alliances within the field determine its development: they form a dynamic structure of interrelations within which a legitimating hierarchy of all aspects of the field is itself objectively formed. (In the case of an intellectual field, a hierarchy of authors; of those ruling bodies of specialists whose judgments reproduce and consecrate intellectual life; of disciplines, styles, themes, and theories.)

Since intellectual legitimacy comes from recognition by the field, its value is symbolic. It excludes commercial logic, the search for economic gain (although it may result in economic gain), and even the search for symbolic gain: the dispositions of the most legitimate agents are in such perfect accord with existing requirements for success that they can respond without calculation and can thus seem to others, and to themselves, to be wholly disinterested. As a result of their scorn for the commercial logic which treats cultural goods as commodities, producers who aspire to autonomy tend to contrast their work to the products of mass culture, and to form instead a narrow circle of legitimate creators.

The concept of field can apply to a very broad reality, such as the cultural field as a whole, as well as to a small group such as the editors of a magazine. A field is any system of social relations which functions according to a logic of its own that must be taken into account in explaining its development. The more specific concept of cultural field[2] does not always have the national scope it takes on in French society, where the process of cultural unification and centralization is so ancient and advanced. In other cultures it would perhaps be better to map out a system of regional fields than one single one. But it is precisely the Parisian focus of French culture which makes it an ideal observatory for viewing, in a magnified and concentrated form, the laws which govern changing trends in the growth and function of a highly complex, institutionalized intellectual field. And there will be no paradox in studying this field through the particular case of Sartre if it can be shown that Sartre is a "perfect" product of that culture, and that the course of his career provides a complete list of the questions raised by any study of intellectuals and their practices. The very structure of this book should make it clear that I am not trying, as Sartre is in his biographies, "to reveal the whole man." I have only considered that period of Sartre's life in which he personifies intellectual legitimacy, and only those aspects of it which raise interesting questions.

I thought it was important to show the contribution that the sociology of culture could make to literary and philosophical criticism once it had rid itself of the misunderstood Marxism which had led it to look for all of its answers directly and essentially in the material interests of a given class or (I'm thinking of Escarpit's approach) in the strictly economic sanctions of the market. When literary criticism, even in its most sophisticated semiological versions, claims to establish value criteria intrinsic to literary works themselves, it condemns itself to endless discussions of their "literariness" and, more generally, of their worth and fortunes. Sartre's case makes it clear that legitimacy is a result of recognition by already established legitimating bodies: the narrow circle of producers, critics, editors, and journals which has the power to consecrate others because it is itself consecrated. It also makes clear the mechanisms through which demand tends to shape not just a work's aims and readers, but its most narrowly technical characteristics and the way in which it is read. And it shows too how developments in an author's relationship to the field govern developments in his creative project, and how much the fluctuations in that project's recognition and success depend on the fluctuations in the established values of the field.

Since Sartre is both a writer and a philosopher, he leads us to ask ourselves about the relationships between two types of intellectuals, the professors and the "creators," who in the history of the field have held separate and antagonistic positions, but in him have become one. For our part, comparing his trajectory with others in relation to which it is defined enables us to test a series of hypotheses as to what distinguishes a success like his from both the difficult life of the avant-gardes and the short-lived and much-scorned commercial success of the "best-sellers."

Sartre's different strategies must be understood in terms of the changing balance he establishes between adaptation and innovation, material and symbolic profits, the long run of the classics and the short run of current events, the circle of established legitimating bodies and the general public, and the university and journalism, as well as in terms of those changing combinations of independence and interaction, of conflict and cooperation, in respect to which the boundaries between these different sets of interacting elements are ceaselessly drawn and redrawn.

On the other hand, reconstructing the role of *Les Temps Modernes*, its position in the field of intellectual journals, and its evolution can help us understand an institution whose function and specific properties have not yet been adequately investigated. We can see that for Sartre it is a decisive instrument which reinforces his position and transforms it into a collective enterprise, a new "school of thought": "existentialism."

The case of Sartre, who up until the war is part of an artistic cult closer to Flaubert than to Marx, but who subsequently becomes the committed intellectual and fellow traveler incarnate, raises the question of the political choices of intellectuals. More specifically, it forces us to ask ourselves about the relation between "art for art's sake" and political prophetism, as well as about the ties between intellectuals and the Communist Party and Marxism. Bourdieu's conception of the intellectual field and its function makes it possible to avoid the polemical alternatives of left and right to which the sociology of intellectuals seems to be doomed when it deals with these themes. In Sartre's case, the alternatives are represented by the conflict between Aron, who reduces Marxism to an "opiate of the intellectuals," and Sartre himself, who denounces the intellectual "watchdogs" of the Establishment. In order to explain the political opinions of intellectuals, we must be aware that they arise not just from social demand but from symbolic profits that different symbolic choices offer and from "professional deformities"— that is to say, from the perceptual and evaluative frameworks which these "specialists in intelligence" acquire from their training and from the conditions under which they practice their calling.

Sartre's case lends itself particularly well to the study of ideological mechanisms: existentialism, as a philosophy which in attributing to man the power and duty to achieve complete lucidity carries the illusion of transparent consciousness to the extreme, elevates autobiography to an unprecedented state of dignity. Thanks to the abundance of letters, memoirs, recollections, and interviews, Sartre's life has become public property as no other intellectual's life ever has. It is an invaluable source not only for developing an anthropology of intellectuals but for understanding what Sartrean man, the one embodied in his characters as ontology's universal man, owes to Sartre's particular way of imagining the social world.

Finally, dealing with Sartre's case in terms of field contributes to the general history of a period which is poorly understood as a whole. The state of existing research offers a macroscopic and therefore particularly clear example of field effect. In the first place, the boundaries between different disciplines within the field have produced, in reproducing themselves in the distribution of objects of investigation, parallel histories which never meet: literary histories, histories of philosophy, and histories of the politics of intellectuals (usually subdivided in turn into leftist politics and rightist politics). The shortcomings of such isolated studies become evident in the case of an object of investigation like Sartre: his success is essentially a result of his having occupied several positions at the same time, yet in the entire bibliography of Sartre there is not one single analysis which systematically considers the interdependence of these different dimensions. You may say that Sartre is an exceptional case. But you need only think of the relation between literature and literary criticism, or between academic criticism and journalistic criticism, or between author and public, to be persuaded that even the "purest" work refers to the system of relationships it sustains with other fields.

It is significant that attempts at general historical reconstruction are so rare and so frequently mediocre: they are either scholarly texts or essays, very few of which are sufficiently rigorous and informed to be usable. This situation is perhaps in part a result of the antipositivist bias which those who seek to analyze the historical interrelationships of philosophy and literature run up against, above all when they try to reconstruct broad outlines instead of studying an author or a text in depth. Such obstacles dissuade specialists who do have the necessary competence from investing it in this sort of task.

This study in no way claims to be exhaustive, but it can provide a relevant map of the positions and interrelationships between positions which counted the most in Sartre's success. By simply substituting for the names of individual agents and groups the characteristics which distinguished their position from that of Sartre and his journal, we can bring out the objective bases of his supremacy. Nizan, Aron, Camus,

Merleau-Ponty, Bataille, and Mounier lose their air of mere friends and familiars of Sartre to become competitors whose distance from his success is measured by the extent to which their symbolic capital is objectively inferior to his in both degree and kind.

Having arrived at the end of my analysis, I have some hesitation in reporting the results. I know how likely it is that the meaning of this undertaking will be distorted. The task I set for myself was to help clarify the history and function of the intellectual field by throwing light on the conditions of Sartre's success. Properly understood, scientific analysis must be a labor of objectification. But I cannot forget that today the role of the intellectual as Sartre embodied it is the stake of a struggle, and that one need only read my investigation as a value judgment to turn it into a weapon. In an effort to obliterate a public figure—and above all a public role—which is troublesome to them, some are sure to use this study to speak of Sartre's powerlessness and imposture, to reduce his strategy to cynical calculation, and to discredit thereby the whole idea of the committed intellectual. Certainly the example of Sartre shows the ideological temptations which threaten the intellectual as a consequence of his habits of thought and the interests associated with his position in the field. But Sartre's enterprise also shows that the reason why this social role can be sustained—and effectively sustained—is that it is based on an autonomous worldview which is itself based in an autonomous field. At the same time, Sartre's enterprise shows that this role confronts every intellectual as a possibility and a responsibility which he cannot escape. And that's not all. As a "total intellectual,"[3] Sartre is the symbol of a conception of the intellectual's task which today may seem outmoded. The gap between literature, philosophy, and the human sciences is tending to widen. But in his ambition to master and synthesize everything, Sartre embodied a demand for the unity of knowledge which is still "the ruling aim and aspiration of the intellectual calling."

# PART ONE

# The Conditions of Sartre's Success at the Liberation

"So that, without having planned it, what we launched early that fall turned out to be an 'Existentialist offensive.' In the weeks following the publication of my novel, *The Age of Reason* and *The Reprieve* appeared, as well as the first numbers of *Les Temps Modernes*. Sartre gave a lecture—'Is Existentialism a Humanism?'—and I gave one at the Club Maintenant on the novel and metaphysics. *Les Bouches inutiles* opened. We were astonished by the furor we caused. Suddenly, in much the same way as one sees the picture in certain films breaking out of its frame and spreading to fill a wider screen, my life overflowed its old boundaries. I was pushed out into the limelight. My own baggage weighed very little, but Sartre was now hurled brutally into the arena of celebrity, and my name was associated with his. A week never passed without the newspapers discussing us. *Combat* printed favorable comments on everything that came from our mouths or our pens. *Terre des hommes*, a weekly started by Pierre Herbart and destined to survive only a few months, devoted numerous friendly or bittersweet columns to us in every number. Gossip about us and about our books appeared everywhere. In the streets, photographers fired away at us, and strangers rushed up to speak to us. At the Flore, people stared at us and whispered. When Sartre gave his lecture, so many people turned up that they couldn't all get into the lecture hall; there was a frenzied crush and some women fainted."[1]

These words of Simone de Beauvoir recall vividly the change in Sartre's position which occurred at the Liberation: a lightning breakout from a little pocket of admiring peers into the broad public realm of fame. Sartre becomes, as he himself often said, a "public monument," the object of a devotion which even at the time was in some respects too exceptional to seem no more than a passing fancy.

The whole intellectual field is involved. Sartre commands the attention of the philosophical world and the literary world, the world of high culture and that of the leading dailies, and thereby crosses the two frontiers which have historically marked the functioning of the field: the dividing line between the philosophical circuit and the literary circuit, and the line between legitimate success and popular fame. He unifies a polycentric system by becoming the single reference point in relation to which the other sectors must define—or redefine—themselves. So much so that we need only reconstruct Sartre's position at war's end by running the range of comments about him to be able to reconstruct the whole field. Not a single voice which counts fails to answer up in one way or another.

Among writers, and considering only a few representative names, we can mention Gide, the personification of the between-the-wars model whom Sartre dethroned, and Sartre's rivals in his own generation: Camus, Bataille, Maurice Blanchot.

In the December 8, 1945, issue of *Terres des hommes*, a weekly Gide sponsored (and that is why Simone de Beauvoir considers it so important), Gide himself comments in an article, "Existentialism." Referring to Sartre's Introduction in the first issue of *Les Temps Modernes*, he speaks of "a step towards barbarism" and conjures up the specter of Party art in the U.S.S.R. But we can get a better idea of the alarmed attention Gide pays to Sartre's success by considering the amount of space his weekly gives to Sartre. Look especially at Justin Saget's "billet-doux" in issue number 7, which goes so far as to apply to Sartre the label "leading contemporary" created by Mauriac for Gide in the era when Gide reigned as literary pope. An obvious symbolic recognition that Sartre has succeeded Gide as lord of the literary field. And Saget writes in number 8: "Although Sartre speaks of committing himself to our times, it is our times which are committed through him."

Albert Camus had paid careful attention to Sartre ever since the publication of *Nausea*, at which time he had spoken of "unlimited talents."[2] A flattering review of *The Wall*,[3] a meeting at the premiere of *The Flies*, and subsequently a close friendship are steps which draw the two men together and at the Liberation make Camus and his newspaper, *Combat*, one of the positions linked most closely to Sartre in a relationship of constant exchange and collaboration with the staff of *Les Temps Modernes*—a relationship which will subsequently deteriorate progressively up to the complete break following publication of *The Rebel*.

A rival's concern also shows through Maurice Blanchot's close attention to Sartre's career. Blanchot is one of the first to notice *Nausea*.[4]

And he reviews *The Age of Reason* and *The Reprieve* at length when they come out.[5] As for the attitude of Bataille and the journal, *Critique*, which he founds in 1946, we shall examine it below in Part Two, Chapter 8.

And we could add to these all the other well-known writers still holding center stage, from Mauriac[6] to Céline.[7]

Among philosophers, we see former members of the avant-garde such as Jean Wahl,[8] who had introduced "philosophies of existence" to the Sorbonne, and current competitors such as Gabriel Marcel[9] and Maurice Merleau-Ponty.[10] And then there are those propagators of existentialism, the "thinking masters" at the most prestigious prep schools for the elite: Jean Beaufret[11] at Henri-IV and Ferdinand Alquié[12] at Louis-le-Grand.

The literary critics for journals spawned by the war—Georges Blin (*Fontaine*),[13] Gaëtan Picon (*Confluences*),[14] Maurice Nadeau (*Combat*)[15]—and critics such as Emile Henriot (*le Monde*),[16] André Billy[17] and André Rousseaux (*le Figaro*),[18] who write for the major Parisian dailies, all answer the call to arms. Representatives of "militant" culture and its main tendencies at the time are among Sartre's most assiduous commentators. In the Catholic camp, it is *Etudes*[19] and, above all, *Esprit*[20] which respond: although E. Mounier[21] and Béguin[22] keep their distance, fellow members of their staff such as Francis Jeanson[23] and Claude-Edmonde Magny[24] become Sartre's rapt disciples. Among hostile critics, Boutang[25] and Thierry Maulnier[26] stand out on the "right." But they are outdone by Communist Party intellectuals. From the best-known ones such as Roger Garaudy[27] and Henri Lefebvre,[28] to the young recruits such as J. Kanapa[29] and Henri Mougin,[30] their furious attacks on Sartre attest to and strengthen his central position.

Sartre's conduct at the time bears witness to his undisputed supremacy: he quickly stops paying any attention to his competitors. The essays and articles he writes about his contemporaries are chiefly prefaces for works written by friends or followers. The intensity of the reactions he provokes further heightens his dominance. He astonishes, irritates, shocks, enraptures, fascinates, and concerns, forcing even university critics to abandon the neutral tone which academic debate seeks to establish.

The responses form around a twin axis which reflects the essential duality of a success that marries the recognition of the initiate to the infatuation of the profane. Debate moves from a strictly intellectual discussion to a political or moral evaluation of Sartre's works and very self. He is attacked or praised, both for the technical characteristics of his work and as the prophet of commitment or the teacher of a new morality. For some he is heroic. For others he is depraved: the direct source of Saint-Germain-des-Prés's nocturnal practices, crimes, and "existentialist" suicides. The image the initiates have of Sartre does not simply coexist with that of the outsiders; it is strongly conditioned by it. The lecture Simone de Beauvoir refers to above is an intellectual operation, carried out in "an atmosphere of plebiscite and riot,"[31] which shows Sartre's worldwide impact.[32] Merleau-Ponty even goes so far as to publish in the *Figaro* a stalwart defense of the morality of Sartre's works and life.[33]

Sartre's later success makes it clear that this widespread, tumultuous recognition of his supremacy cannot be explained simply in terms of a particular conjunction of circumstances at the Liberation. Yet in order to show that his supremacy is neither mysterious nor accidental, but is based on an extraordinary correspondence between his position and the demands of the "market" he is subject to, we must reconstruct the conditions which make that supremacy possible. It is not just Sartre's works which are exemplary, but their development; not just his intellectual practices but all the characteristic traits of his personality, his worldview, and his lifestyle.

# CHAPTER 1
# Professor and Creator

When Sartre finishes his studies, he has earned the titles of graduate of the Ecole normale supérieure and *agrégé* in philosophy. To understand the importance of these titles in the French society of the thirties—and the consequences of holding them—we must consider how the Ecole normale, the *agrégation*, and philosophy itself are ranked at this time in the French school system's hierarchically structured universe. Between the wars, the Ecole polytechnique and the Ecole normale supérieure (E.N.S.) are still the two schools which are considered the testing ground of the "elites," the former as the school of future powerholders, the latter as the royal road to the professional aristocracy. The grants these institutions offer seem to guarantee opportunity to even those among the best and brightest in each generation who are the least privileged by birth and geographic provenance.[1]

The title which caps off the academic career of students at the Ecole normale is the *agrégation* in philosophy. In the thirties, it is still the most prestigious in the French university system, especially for those preparing the ground for future work in the theory of knowledge and ontology.

And Sartre has even more signs that he is one of the elite of this elite: the Ecole normale ranks him second in his class; his classmates consider him the greatest genius among so many alleged geniuses.[2] They look forward to his coming examination for the *agrégation* as a major event, and when he fails at his first try, take it to be an obvious error on the jury's part. When he tries again the following year he is ranked number one.

Sartre's success in his academic work earns him the most charismatic marks of excellence the Ecole normale has to offer. To begin with, recognition by the members of his "corps." The graduates of the school—those ultimate aristocrats of intelligence from whose ranks the chief protagonists of French intellectual life will spring—are both his public, his rivals, and his judges—the only ones who have the authority to decree his success. This explains the important role that his friends and competitors at the Ecole—such as Nizan and Aron—end up playing in the subsequent course of his life.

In the canon of professional excellence—philosophy, essays, and literary criticism—Sartre wins a reputation comparable at least to Bergson's, who already seemed to have raised the worldly prestige of philosophy professors as high as it could go.[3] But what is unprecedented about Sartre is that he simultaneously wins recognition as a writer. This dual success, which the prior history of the field seemed to show was impossible, explains the effect Sartre produces of being a prodigious anomaly. It is not just that no one before has ever accomplished such a feat, and accomplished it so brilliantly; it is a feat beyond the reach of public imagination, which has been led by a succession of clear constrasts embodied in a host of famous predecessors to distinguish writers and professors.

It is during the time of the Dreyfus Affair that this contrast first bursts into view: it is through this violent battle, in which the very definition of the intellectual is at stake, that the noun, "intellectual," comes into common parlance. Originally applied in a pejorative way to the "intellectual's party," the Dreyfusards, the professors, it ends up being adopted voluntarily by the latter.[4] This is not really a mere terminological matter. The imposition of a term and its connotation is often the stake in a power struggle. At the end of the last century in France, defining the social role of the intellectual is an issue which involves the different sectors of the intellectual and political fields. In the context of a crucial confrontation between the still shaky Republican regime and the Orleanist reaction, the support of prestigious intellectuals can be an effective legitimating factor for the parties in the lists. The Republican bloc has a special interest in winning their support, because it has found powerful allies among the Dreyfusards and, in their slogans (the defense of truth and justice, "scientific" and secular management of society), a combative ideology fit for a regime depicting itself as on the side of progress in opposition to adversaries upholding tradition and the past.

At the same time, this confrontation marks the appearance in the literary field of a movement hostile to professors, a movement tied to the changed social position of this group. The status of university professors has considerably improved in the previous century as a result of the Republican policy of expanding the teaching corps.[5] The aggressive attitude toward professors which, particularly from the time of the Dreyfus Affair, is abundantly attested to by literature seems to be above all a result of their increased prestige and power as intellectuals. As critics who frequent the literary salons, they write for the most influential periodicals of the day and control access to the Académie française; as adversaries or rivals in the political struggle, they have become an encumbrance to the writers and threaten their vital interests.

In the parlance which has become common since the Dreyfus Affair, writers are stereotyped as bourgeois, conservative "heirs," and professors as petit bourgeois, progressive "scholarship boys." Professors are viewed as having the institutional virtues required to get ahead in a meritocracy—discipline, diligence, and precision; creative writers as having "personal gifts," a gratuitous, inexplicable natural "genius" which those who have not had it from birth can never hope to have. These clichés never fully correspond to empirical reality. The actual characteristics of the positions of writers and professors are constituted by the specific relations linking each individual agent and sector of the intellectual and political fields to all the others.

Zola, the most famous case, became the herald of the Dreyfusards, the "intellectuals' party" or professors' party. Zola hates this classification and describes it ferociously: "Anyone who has been dipped in the waters of the Ecole normale is drenched with them for lfe. His brain exudes a bland and musty odor of the lecture hall. He is stamped forever and in spite of himself with the crabbed attitudes, the self-punishing need for discipline, and the dull impotent longings of old bachelors who could never get a wife. When these gay dogs are witty and bold, when they come up with new ideas, as they occasionally do, they chop them up into such tiny pieces or stretch them so much out of shape with their pedagogical frame of mind as to render them lifeless. They are not, they cannot be, original, because they have been cultivated in a very special fertilizer. If you sow professors, you will never reap creators. . . ."[6]

Although Zola's apparently paradoxical political choice can only be explained by establishing the objective bases of his position in the literary field and in the logic of Dreyfusism,[7] these clichés are nevertheless significant: up until Sartre they are based on actual differential tendencies of social (and thus educational) origin—objectively established values and political penchants, alliances, and functions—which may be explained in terms of the social conditions of literary success. Literature during this whole period is still a risky, long-term investment whose burden those who have not already won uncontested consecration cannot successfully assume unless they are socially privileged individuals who enjoy an independent income or at least the connections and dispositions (such as the feeling of being one of the chosen few and completely dedicated to one's "calling") which being well-born facilitates.[8] The uncertainty of a writing career, in contrast to the bureaucratic certitudes of academic life, bolsters the charismatic image of writers by perpetuating the Romantic myth of creative individuality. Writers themselves help shape this image in works which drip scorn and resentment for professors. Professors are embittered or ridiculous men of frustrated ambition, and, as poor teachers who in the name of knowledge lead their disciples to ruin, abound in the works of Bourget, Barrès, and Zola.[9]

Contrary to what a superficial reading might suggest, writers' polemics against intellectuals and science in the Dreyfus era do not mark the beginnings of self-criticism. The anti-intellectualism of the day is always an attack on the professors mounted from within the range of objective motives for conflict or aversion which are inherent in the structural relations between the apparently incompatible careers of teacher and writer. The writers' relationship to the academy and its professors is often as wretched as that of the professors' to creative writing. Although creative ability does not seem to be one of the requisite virtues for academic success, more than one creative writer has suffered failure during the long, methodical, and narrowly programmed period of austere self-denial needed to succeed in the competitive examinations, a failure which casts a permanent shadow of doubt on the literary calling and literary success. Zola flunks his *baccalauréat* twice; Barrès, son of a graduate of the Ecole centrale des arts et manufactures, barely earns his B.A., as does Bourget, even though his father is a graduate of the Ecole normale. Their demeaning of the teaching profession can be seen as a dialectical transformation of failure suffered into actively chosen renunciation.

Another very lively source of resentment of professors is the power they have as reviewers to produce or destroy the literary fame of writers.

Two illustrations are Lemaître and Brunetière, who in the Dreyfus era acquire all the authority available to those whose job it is to crown writers with fame. Each is a graduate of the Ecole normale and a member of the Académie française, and each holds sway over one of the most influential journals and one of the most influential salons of the day. If we consider the role played by similar somebodies in the resounding failure of Zola, who is rejected twenty-four times as a candidate for the Académie, either by rivals (Brunetière is chosen over him in 1893; Lemaître in 1895) or by influential opponents, we can see that these objective reasons for being bitter have an influence on Zola's depiction of Ecole normale professors as puffed up literary critics and failed writers.[10]

The contrasts and rivalries between writers and professors are also fed by the difference in their habitus and heightened by the time's political struggles. If professors are not considered outright political adversaries, they are at least considered spokesmen for competing parties.

Since Barrès keeps every one of these motives for animosity in his heart, it is all the easier to understand the particularly violent attack on professors, science, and rationalist culture found in his works. In them the mere B.A.'s need for revenge, the nationalistic ideologue's rancor toward Republican and Dreyfusard professors, the dependence of a writer who at the time of the Affair is not yet sure of being anointed on Ecole normale graduates who monopolize the power to anoint, and the rivalry with some of them, such as Lemaître and Brunetière, come together in the service of a single ideology.[11]

But the only reason writers can have such success in vaunting creative power over scholarship is that professors have soaked up from their schooling a conception of culture which has led them to exalt creativity themselves. The academy does respect erudition, the proof that those who attain the goals it sets for them have merit. Yet what it admires most of all is originality, a virtue which not only cannot be acquired through effort but which seems incompatible with erudition, as the frequent failures of professors who try to write creatively suggest.

The social characteristics of those who are undoubtedly the outstanding representatives of these two categories prior to Sartre's generation show that the traditional contrast between teacher and writer is still in force.

Gide, Proust, and Paul Valéry fit the image of the creator as much by their social characteristics as by the leisurely pace of their careers. They come from bourgeois or big bourgeois families which, in the case of Proust and Gide, possess cultural capital as well as independent income. (Gide's father is a law school professor, Proust's an *agrégé* in medicine.) Although Valéry has no economic capital, his family circle and connections give him great social capital. None of the three is an especially brilliant student. All begin very early to frequent the literary salons, which continue to be the decisive way for writers to get to know one another and become a success.

Among the professors, three exemplary names may be mentioned: Brunschvicg, Bergson, and Alain. They represent respectively three peaks of the teaching career: the first, domination within the university; the second, a member of the Collège de France since 1910, secular fame; and the third, pedagogical perfection. All three are professors shaped by their social origin (petit bourgeois or bourgeois-intellectual), by their schooling (E.N.S., *agrégation*), and by the kind of success they have.

It is true that the popular and international notoriety Bergson wins is rare among philosophy professors. From the beginning of this century until the thirties, he is the thinking master of successive generations of French intellectuals. Péguy, Proust, Thibaudet, and Mounier are among those who recognize him as their most influential teacher. And we know that thanks to the time it takes fashions to filter down to schools, Bergson is still for the schoolboy Sartre the great discovery which draws him toward philosophy. Bergson is without doubt the sign of a change in the previous definition of a philosophy professor as more of a tutor than an author of original works.[12] For Sartre he sets a precedent by his very success, which goes beyond the confines of the University: he wins the Nobel Prize in 1928. The motley crowd that even squeezes up beneath the windows of his Collège de France classroom to hear him, and the snobbish aspect of the charm he holds for them, irresistably evoke the tumultuous public which will so clamorously welcome the "pope of existentialism" in 1945. But Bergson does not venture into literature. He remains a philosopher who inspires literature, interprets it, and influences its interpretation; he does not produce it.

The political commitments of these writers and philosophers also correspond to the traditional distinction between these two objective social categories. Proust's solidarity with the dominant class, although implicit, is undeniable. Valéry is openly reactionary at the time of the Dreyfus Affair: in contrast to Gide and Proust, he speaks out publicly against Dreyfus. As for Gide, it takes the special conjuncture of the Popular Front and the politicization of the literary field to get him to examine his class ties. The framework for Alain's choices, on the other hand, during the time he is a fervent Dreyfusard and the subsequent period in which he is theoretician of radicalism, and for the more indirect choices of Bergson and Brunschvicg (both active in the cultural section of the League of Nations), is the progressive Republicanism first linked to the category of university professors at the time of the Dreyfus Affair and subsequently established as the legitimate form of relationship between university and state.

Although Gide's pontificate clearly reflects its traditional bases, it also marks the beginning of a profound change which is merging the careers of professor and writer. The expansion of education on both the secondary and university levels, the development of publishing, and a series of related phenomena are transforming the mechanisms of literary consecration as well as the relationships between professors and writers. As a consequence of the increased length of required studies, the new generations of writers tend increasingly to have the same academic program, the same education, and thus the same habitus as the professors. On the other hand, changes in the academic market increase the status of professors.[13] The two categories, writers and professors, become more and more alike in the way that they are recruited and in the social characteristics which define them, as is shown by a phenomenon such as the "Décades de Pontigny," a series of meetings begun in 1910 by Paul Desjardin, which bring writers and academics together each summer for an intellectual retreat. As a result of the opportunity they give members of the two worlds to get to know one another and exchange ideas under the aegis of Gide and the *Nouvelle Revue française* (*N.R.F.*), these meetings are more than just a symbol of togetherness. They are the place in which a new definition of the relationships between literature and philosophy, as well as a new image of the intellectual, is being forged and reinforced.[14]

On the other hand, the democratization of education is producing a new cultured and anonymous public which enhances the increasing autonomy of the literary field. This public is the basis for the development of properly cultural ruling bodies whose judgments play a decisive role in the process of literary consecration. They replace the Académie française and the salons of the Parisian big bourgeoisie—that is, the apparatus by means of which the dominant class has previously been able to control literature—and they make possible a new kind of creative writer who is no longer directly dependent on the material and symbolic support and influence of those who hold economic and social power. Moreover, big publishing houses such as Grasset and Gallimard begin to subsidize writers, thereby depriving patrimony of its previous discriminatory power.[15] Journals such as, above all, the *N.R.F.* become the judges of legitimacy.

Prior to Sartre, there are already signs of an active transformation of the relationship between academics and writers. Ecole normale graduates become writers more often: Romain Rolland, Jules Romains, Giraudoux, and Nizan are the most famous ones. There is no Sartrean synthesis yet, only a movement from field to field: literature is taking philosophy's place. Besides, Giraudoux is the only one of these fugitives to win complete legitimacy.

Although Romain Rolland and Jules Romains become famous and make an impact on a very broad reading public, their writing lacks many of the essential characteristics of the dominant model. Their literary practice is a far cry from Gide's "subtle and reticent" art. Their theoretical principles are also far removed from those which govern the prevailing model, the aesthetics of the *N.R.F.*, which extols (and this is no accident) the characteristic values of every "pure" aesthetics: "taste," "decorum," "subtlety," "fear of spontaneity," "terror of inspiration," "balance," and "reserve." Their themes show a precocious sensitivity to the century's traumatic upheavals: Romain Rolland's pacifist humanism and Romains's unanism share a concern for the destiny of European society, whereas the *N.R.F.* reflects the indifference of a bourgeoisie which will remain walled up in its privilege until the twenties. Rolland, like Zola much discussed and famous, rediscovers political prophetism in a period, following the Dreyfusian interregnum, when "art for art's sake" is once again the undisputed champion in the literary field. In 1919, the contrast bursts forth. In a manifesto, Rolland and Henri Barbusse brand as irresponsible all intellectuals who did not oppose the "right-wing war." The *N.R.F.* hits back in October 1919, in an article by Jacques Rivière, "A Defense of French Intelligence." For the first time in its history, the journal explicitly asks itself about the social responsibility of culture: "Is intelligence a private matter or is it social property?" But it answers by lining up pretty narrowly with the equation of France and culture, and thus of nationalism and the defense of civilization, which has been the typical right-wing position since the time of Dreyfus: "We are the only ones in the world, and I say this dispassionately, who still know how to think. Only what we say concerning philosophy, literature, and art really matters." This is the position which Henri Massis and the other nationalistic ideologues writing in *L'honneur de servir* take in response to Rolland.

It is significant that Giraudoux is the author whom Nizan and Sartre like most during the period in which, as Ecole normale students avid for glory, they find that they are bound together by a literary "calling" which they live as an alternative to the academic life they detest[16]: "Teaching was a way of life which disgusted us. Because for me and Nizan, teaching was just a job. Not like art. We wanted to write. . . . Teaching disgusted us. We said to each other: 'O.K. So we'll teach in the sticks for twenty years, marry a woman from the sticks. . . .' We invented a little lyrical drama for ourselves so that we could bemoan our fate. It was only later, when we had learned that some professors had still written books, that we changed. But we really were not happy at the thought of being teachers."[17]

They read as apprentices read, looking for lessons and confirmations in their discoveries. And what they seem to like in Giraudoux is that he is an Ecole normale graduate whose success reassures them by proxy that their ambition is realistic.

It is true that Giraudoux too seems to emphasize the need to choose between literature and philosophy, between formal elegance and conceptual rigor. And Nizan, who begins to publish and make himself known before Sartre does, not only turns away from philosophy but is far from making the total commitment to the literary project which is necessary to succeed. Yet his efforts are important because he is Sartre's alter ego during the years they are fellow students, when they have so many common characteristics that they are, as Sartre will write, "indistinguishable."[18] Nizan helps Sartre see that his own project has a certain sociological probability, that it falls within the line of development of a generation of *lectores* whose avant-garde members at least are on the way to breaking through the historical barrier which separates them from *auctores*. Another indication Sartre has that his project is possible is the recruiting of *N.R.F.* writers: Rivière, Paulhan, and Parain are all fugitives from the academy. And Alain, the professor par excellence, writes regularly for the journal.

Although the synthesis of philosophy and literature is thus not only wished for but possible, Sartre alone fully realizes it. The reason why it has been necessary to recount this long history of antagonism and separation, of the prestige of literature, and of its fascination for philosophy professors is to make us able to appreciate the extraordinary novelty of Sartre's accomplishment.

Sartre's 1939 article on Husserl's concept of intentionality can be seen as a compact manifesto in which he stresses the revolutionary nature of his enterprise.[19] Its author is a graduate of the Ecole normale. But he has already gotten himself noticed as a writer and philosopher.[20] And now he hails this new way of thinking which makes it possible to break down the traditional barriers between philosophy and "the world of artists and prophets." He leads this esoteric and avant-garde philosophy out from the inner sanctum of university seminars into the open. And what is more, he proclaims it in the emotional, metaphorical language which is the traditional intent and mark of "literariness." He performs, in short, a dizzying high-wire crossing coruscating with glimpses of a reconciliation unprecedented in the entire history of the field.

The history of French culture since Sartre shows that this was no irreversible change. None of the "major" intellectuals who succeeded him as the representative of intellectual excellence managed to duplicate his accomplishment. Literature and philosophy once again went their separate ways. The structural changes we have been considering are necessary to make Sartre's enterprise possible; they are not sufficient to explain it. Conjunctural factors are also decisive in understanding its uniqueness. They can be situated either in reference to the particular demand of a society which in suffering through the Depression, the War, the Occupation, the colonial wars, and the Cold War is tragically discovering history and favoring a philosophical culture capable of articulating and making sense out of these unprecedented experiences, or in reference to the growing convergence of philosophy and literature. By analyzing the state of the two fields at the moment Sartre makes his appearance in them, we can begin to see the first fruits of his model in a clearly emerging process of partial assimilation.

Since Blanchot is also a candidate for the role of "metaphysical novelist," he is in a good position to see as early as 1945 that this convergence is one of the conditions of Sartre's enterprise: "It is of course possible to maintain that Sartre's capacity to write simultaneously such different kinds of works as important philosophical investigations and no less important novels, plays and critical essays is peculiar to him and shows nothing more than the diversity of his individual talents. Yet the fact of the matter is that this joining together of an equally excellent philosopher and writer in one man is a result of the possibility philosophy and literature offered him of joining them together in himself."[21]

Sartre's phenomenological descriptions and existential analyses, to the extent that they reject conceptual abstraction and bring the events of everyday life into philosophical discourse, end up taking on the functions and effects of literature. Furthermore, they make free use of linguistic resources and literary texts. And in this respect they are the converse of the writings of the man who in the thirties is the young hope of the *N.R.F.*, a man who writes a "metaphysical" literature whose aim is not so much to make formal innovations as to express a "worldview"— the man named Malraux.

The chief novelty in the role Sartre creates is his dual career in two distinct fields which are separated from one another by profoundly different histories. And if we do not recognize that paradoxically his revolution was less a matter of subverting models which were already established or were being established than it was of uniting them, we cannot explain his success. The reason why Sartre is able to make use of what seem to be the most radical of innovations to produce an effect of unparalleled legitimacy is that each of his practices deeply respects the logic of the specific position he adopts. In so doing, he only carries to extremes the combination of conformity and difference which intellectual success always requires. If one must introduce a "spread" to distinguish oneself from already existing positions, one must also reproduce the already legitimated forms which the field is prepared to recognize as marks of competence and as values. Sartre's literary and philosophical practices are directed toward different markets, different juries of persons who are competent in their respective fields, and different publics; they are judged according to different criteria of competence; and they are deeply conditioned by these different jurisdictions.

This is especially true of the works Sartre writes prior to 1945. No one at that time respects the rules of the game more than he does, spontaneously; no one points himself as unfailingly as he toward the most legitimate choices; no one knows better how to adapt himself constantly as a model heir must. Not only is he far from being the *"écrivant,"* the instant ideologist he has ended up being reduced to in an image drawn too hastily from the Sartre of political manifestos; during this entire phase his basic concerns are technical. He is preoccupied with the intense labor of achieving acceptable form, work that must be done if one is to get oneself recognized by a cultural field which thanks to its already long-standing autonomy can establish as criteria of legitimacy distinctive, purely technical values that can only be truly judged by those who have already mastered the techniques, the producers themselves.

Sartre acts as if he were unconsciously following and carrying through to completion a program for producing, in accordance with established forms and in the requisite order, the literature and philosophy which the French literary and philosophical fields of the time demand. It is not enough to recognize that Sartre's works are woven out of other sources, influences, and imitations, as has already been recognized for his literary and theatrical output (although not sufficiently yet for his philosophical texts, concerning which the tradition of reading works for their intrinsic worth is more tenacious). His practices must be related to the pertinent systems of reference: the definitions of literary and philosophical excellence which were in force when he made his debut. Then what we shall see emerging is a sort of *summa* of all that is legitimate in the two fields. That is why it is necessary to consider separately the two parallel careers by means of which, between the time he graduated from the Ecole normale and 1945, Sartre won absolute dominion over the entire intellectual field. Nothing is more misleading in trying to explain the characteristics and the fortunes of an oeuvre which was so profoundly shaped by its conditions of production and recognition than claiming to read it without taking this division into account, as do those who lump Sartre's philosophy and his literary works together in the fuzzy category of *"écriture."*

The effects of working in both domains must also be emphasized. There can be no doubting the basic importance of being able to bring to bear in each sector of production resources drawn from outside the sector. This means not just transfering symbolic capital but making it interact. There are not just exchanges of prestige between the writer and the philosopher; there are exchanges of experiments and procedures. But these exchanges can only be specified in relation to the possibilities and contributions characteristic of each field.

# CHAPTER 2
# Literary Debut

## 1. THE RELATION BETWEEN WORK AND FIELD

The relation between work and field is never unimportant. Even the apparently most original and singular work owes something to this relation. At the very least, the field establishes the conditions that a work must meet to be literary, and gives rise to a notion of the literary work which the author cannot help reckoning with, if only to resist it. All this is clear in Sartre's case: few works are bound as closely as his are to the demands of the current literary market.

Geneviève Idt's Preface to the Pléiade edition of Sartre's *Œuvres romanesques* provides a significant indication of this relationship. Significant because of Geneviève Idt's position as one of the eminent Sartre specialists. Significant too because of its solemn setting: the monumental edition which shortly after Sartre's death inaugurates his posthumous career.

In a text which we have every reason to believe is meant to reestablish Sartre's importance, the balance sheet Geneviève Idt draws up is a courageous one. She has no hesitation in speaking of a "sonorous echo" which "speaks for its time . . . and dies out with it," and of a "top student" who by "extending to their limits the rules of good writing handed down through half a century of pedagogical drills . . . plays in the 20th century, in the eyes of a public which has for the most part gone through the same schooling, the role Hugo played in a century which had just learned to read."

What is even more striking in this Preface than declarations like these is that the current importance of Sartre's work is salvaged only at the cost of radically rejecting the image of it which Sartre himself offered at the height of his fame in *What Is Literature?* His conception

24

of literature as a "search for communication," "a laborious, didactic, almost scholarly quest for meaning and truth in works of fiction" is rejected as what makes the work "classic" (that is, out of date) "to the detriment of its originality."

Geneviève Idt asks us to look elsewhere for Sartre's singularity, and even for the explanation of his success: "in the versatility with which he masters and mixes available modes of discourse," the virtuosity which makes his works a vast palimpsest, an entirely second-order literature held together by pasteups and props, unacknowledged quotes and plagiarisms, tacit references and unconscious reminiscences, pastiches and parodies." She goes so far as to say: "Every statement Sartre makes, except in those rare instances of real feeling, seems to be written in quotes followed by ironic pauses, like a telegram, or like a host parasitically inhabited by alien voices." Although it seems paradoxical, Idt sees this exaggerated diversion of mainstream forms as not just the secret of the "disturbing familiarity," that "powerful sense of something read before yet somehow new," which may be the source of Sartre's fascination for his contemporaries, but also the key to his modernity: "re-read through the works which have followed, from the Nouveau Roman to the carnavalesques, Sartre's novels have taken on a different charm . . .: they now invite us to their play of language and imagination."

This line of interpretation, which is based on a very close and very thorough reading of Sartre's works, and can in no way be considered hostile or hasty, marks a shift in relation to the phase of Sartre's great success. A shift in consensus and a shift in reading. It shows that today these works can only hope for a different, and more restricted, legitimacy. But it does not give the system of reference—the evolution of the intellectual field—which could make this shift intelligible. The image of the prodigious imitator of forms explains neither the extent of Sartre's recognition nor its subsequent decline. Nor does the fact that in the immediate postwar period, Sartre (lying to himself) claimed to write only for his own time justify Idt's claim that "Sartre's works expressed his times and died with them—as he foresaw and wished." It remains to be explained why in these present times "modernity" rejects the search for truth in works of fiction and cherishes instead the "baroque" and the "carnavalesque." It is only in relation to the hierarchy of positions discernible in the literary field during Sartre's formative years that we can measure the legitimacy of the figure he cut—and in so doing understand how the overthrow of that hierarchy casts doubt on this figure.

A sense of the opportune—which is undoubtedly spontaneous and due to the accord between demand and dispositions—seems to govern each aspect of Sartre's career. Going from novels to plays and essays, from esoteric works informed by all the avant-gardes which the *N.R.F.* is currently setting forth as models to more traditional solutions, from recognition by Paulhan and Gide to recognition by the wider intellectual public which frequents Parisian theaters (teachers, students, and the cultured bourgeoisie), from primarily aesthetic concerns to the chiefly moral and political concerns of commitment, and from a stress on contingency and solitude to a stress on freedom and collective history, Sartre meets the most important structural and conjunctural requirements established by the evolving field. One of the structural conditions of the legitimate path to success is that consecration by the more restricted public of productive intellectuals (who alone are authorized to consecrate) precede public fame. And the course which leads from absurdity to commitment, and from the primacy of form to the primacy of communication, coincides exactly with the field's shift from the *N.R.F.* model to the prophetic model. Thus Sartre can seem at the War's end to be the most perfect expression of the new order which is replacing the overthrown pre-War order.

According to Sartre's personal mythology, the literary ideas and models passed on to him by his professor-grandfather and reinforced by academic teachings, and the skill at imitating rather than inventing which he acquired from having learned through books how to live, were handicaps; but in the light of the logic of the field, they can be seen to have a positive function. For these received ideas—of writing to fulfill a mission, of trying (in conformity with the entire rhetorical tradition) "to express *the* ideas in a beautiful form only,"[1] of mixing philosophy and art, and of following the rules of nineteenth-century realism and basing narrative art on observation and description—are all in perfect accord with one or another of the formative influences dominating French literature at the time Sartre starts to write: the recent experiments of British and American novelists, the even more recent discovery of Kafka, the phenomenological method which gives new weight to description by granting it the power to intuit essence, and the socialist realism Sartre learns about from Nizan. Even the wholly second-order relation to literature which first seems such an obvious shortcoming in a field where originality is the basic attribute of excellence is actually only an exaggerated version of the sort of competence which is tending to become the very condition of originality in contemporary art, in which innovation is defined in relation to the overall history of the field, and thus presupposes a mastery of it.

Giving an adequate idea of everything that the nature and reception of Sartre's literary work owe to effects of the field necessitates a diachronic reconstruction which reveals Sartre's constant, spontaneous adaptation of his position to the field's demands, and his progressive accumulation of symbolic capital right up to the time of his crowning consecration. It is precisely because Sartre is just the opposite of an autodidact and perfect lector that even if we wanted to we could never track down all the references and models for his work. But we do not want to: we are only concerned with those which best show how the intellectual field affects his project and his works.

## 2. THE ADOLESCENT PROJECT

The earliest version of Sartre's literary project can be reconstructed from his adolescent writings and biographical sketches. In this prehistory, as in an embryonic matrix, we can already make out the fantasy world which underlies Sartre's future works and constitutes the hidden source of the irresistible echo they awaken in the intellectuals who read them (as if in becoming embodied in the life story of a model intellectual hero, it realized the group's archetypal myth, the primordial form of their shared fantasies).

The reconstruction must begin with ancient products such as the "novel," *Jesus the Owl*, and the story, "The Angel of Morbidity." These documents, written just before Sartre entered the university, are very revealing: they show clearly the expressive interest Sartre's creative project originally had before the covert violence of that all-encompassing pedagogical apparatus, the *khâgne* and the Ecole normale, so radically repressed and transposed it that it seemed to have been wiped out completely. Although only a lycée graduate, the youthful Sartre nevertheless has the courage to write about his obsessions. Through the protagonists of these first stories, and in a typical and obvious way, he exorcises the possibility of failing as a writer. He stages incarnations of a fate he dreads: frustrated, "mediocre" professors who, incapable of writing and unable to live, are trapped in mournful marriages and problems of bourgeois respectability. These are negative possibilities for someone who sees writing as an exceptional calling which—even though its successes are always uncertain and must first be won and then defended—offers a way of escaping the fate of insignificance, the sum of whose horrors is the life of a provincial teacher amidst the invariably smug small-mindedness of the provincial bourgeoisie.

This interpretation of the way the subjects chosen by the apprentice writer function to protect him against the risks of his calling is reinforced by the violence with which he condemns his wretched heroes—an aggressiveness which reveals the intensity of the anguish tied to the projection—and by the special fury of his attack on one vice, the illusion of grandeur, which would not be so repugnant to him if it were not the danger he feared the most.[2] It is no accident that these characters seem straight out of the "laments" handed down at the Ecole normale, which underneath their superficial appearance of disabused, cynical descriptions of the likely future course of things are really ritual incantations.[3] And it is no accident either that they remind us of the creatures of other failed (or miraculously saved) professors in French literature: Barrès' "Bouteiller," Bourget's "Sixte" and "Monneron," and Louis Guilloux's "Cripure."

Similar comparisons would suggest that even the imaginary world Sartre expresses as an adolescent is far from naive. The texts written by this child brought up to live for the sake of writing, and to learn to write by reading, are already *exercices de style*, reworkings of other texts. Not just the restricted models in the family library but the various more or less "legitimate" readings of the omnivorous, famished reader produced by that childhood. Although the basic guidelines for his writing are the rules governing nineteenth-century fictional realism which Sartre with his childhood habitus spontaneously found to be in the nature of things, recognizable shoots gleaned from other sources are grafted onto them. The title of Sartre's early "novel," and its aim of laying bare a sordid and perverse reality, come from *Jésus-la-Caille*, written in 1914 by Francis Carco, who at the time was very much in fashion and admired by the young writer. But Sartre's evident relish for evoking "atmospheres" and "souls" of countrysides or towns springs from a style of the day common to the idols he recently had as a lycée student, the contemporary writers Nizan had told him about: Barrès, Valéry Larbaud, Paul Morand, Gide, and Proust.[4] And it would be easy to show that these are not the only authors Sartre's adolescent writings bring to mind.

# 3. THE INFLUENCE OF SCHOOL

In the objective aims Sartre had in view when he began in 1931 to write *Nausea*, the work that he hoped would earn him access to a literary career, we can still see the traits we saw in the writing he did at eighteen: the autobiographical nucleus whose focus is a "calling," the narrative models, and, implicitly, the concept of literature. But we must also take into account the effects of the pedagogical treatment Sartre had been subjected to in the interim.

His evolution as a writer could serve to illustrate the power of academic programs, especially the programs of a system based on academic competitions. Although Sartre keeps on reading contemporary writers (a rare practice for students in classes which are meant to prepare them for competitive examinations, and which tend to result in complete absorption in the disciplines and authors stressed by the program), his literary efforts at this time retain no more than a few traces of these incursions into modern work. One has the impression of a veritable censorship in favor of the "classical" canons and models inculcated by the school. For example, we need only think of the sovereignty which the culture of the Ecole normale grants to philosophy to account for the most important new development in Sartre's project during his student days there: without giving up literature, he enlarges the scope of his ambition to include philosophy. Connect Stendhal and Spinoza,[5] connect art and truth, "express *the* ideas in a beautiful form only": here we see formulated the essential aim of Sartre's work, which throughout his many twists and turns he never really abandoned.

This aim is the most natural one in the program Sartre is following, in which all the precedents that the students and professors endlessly reread, take apart, comment on, paraphrase, and imitate show that reconciling the True, the Good, and the Beautiful has always tended to define excellence for the man of letters, and especially for teachers, whose pedagogical concerns and social class dispositions incline them to reject every form of "art for art's sake," every purely formal aesthetic unconcerned with the ethical and cognitive functions of art. In addition to this ideal, Sartre finds in academic culture legitimate solutions to his literary problems: "the Platonic myth, the medieval allegory, the Cartesian meditation, the philosophical tale, the post-Romantic epic."[6] The apprentice who heretofore has only concentrated on the art of narration thus gets a glimpse of clearly demarcated new aims to pursue. He must try to appropriate the models of one genre, philosophical literature, which in accordance with the aim of philosophy seeks to express the universal, but appropriate them as literature does, in the form of the singular instance. He must preserve for the philosophical procedures of abstracting and generalizing the charm of a concrete, unique experience. In short, he must come to understand the resources and secrets of metaphor, symbol, and myth.

It is in relation to this unformulated program that Sartre's trial writings between his graduation from the lycée and his first teaching job take on a meaning. It is as if his efforts were governed by two imperatives. First, go from that still unmediated and transparent questioning of your individual destiny, which takes the form of personifying and staging your own failure, to its transposed philosophical form of meditating on man's fate. Second, put philosophical messages in the mouths of mythical or historical speakers, in order to be able to remain faithful to that earliest literary expression of the philosophical calling, the tale.

Very early in this process of conversion to philosophy, the lycée student comes to see one single concept as the exact translation of the truth it is his mission to convey: the concept of the contingency of human existence. For the "unjustifiable" child whom *The Words* will evoke, there is nothing abstract about this metaphysical concept: it has the resonance and tangibility of immediate experience.[7] Yet even in this idea which in Sartre's eyes constitutes the originality of his philosophical project we can see the influence of school. The whole history of French idealism is shot through with an insistence on contingency which serves as a defense against the deterministic claims of rival doctrines and disciplines. This preoccupation is all the more pressing for the philosophy of Sartre's day, which is threatened by its competitors, Marxism and the human sciences. The dissertation topics for the competitive examinations for admission to the Ecole normale and the *agrégation* are an important sign of this. They faithfully reflect changes in approach to problems which are occurring with changes in the historical epoch during the years Sartre is being initiated to philosophy, yet the questions around which they revolve seem to the Ecole normale student to be the upshot of a wholly personal itinerary. It is thus no accident that for the written exam at the *agrégation*, Sartre is assigned precisely the topic which could be the title of his complete philosophical works: *Freedom and Contingency.*

A dual, apparently paradoxical movement can be seen in Sartre's literary and philosophical efforts during his days at the Ecole normale. It is as if the more he stripped his stories of their obvious realistic traits and autobiographical elements, the more courage he acquired to openly broaden their intellectual sweep. Universalized as truth or myth, everything can be said; even unbounded ambition no longer seems dangerous.

The first story Sartre writes at this time still has much in common with his adolescent productions; it is still a "novel," and its protagonist, Nietzsche, who is a philosopher-writer and almost a contemporary, is obviously a projection. And also a not insignificant precedent: according to Aron, it was during a talk entitled "Is Nietzsche a Philosopher?" that Sartre for the first time in his years at the Ecole normale formulated his own ideas about contingency.[8] But Sartre takes good care not to emphasize the respects in which he identifies with his character. He prudently stresses instead the worldly failure (the ill-starred love for Cosima Wagner) which is the price of the hero's superiority, even taking the precaution of stating this message in the title, *A Defeat*. But the second title he gives to this novel, *Empedocles*, foreshadows successive works—*Er the Armenian*, the play *Epimetheus*, and *The Legend of Truth*—which under the protective screen of myth fearlessly celebrate the mission of the intellectual. The formula is still "loser wins." What makes all these new characters great is their denunciation of commonplace illusions about existence. Their superiority to other men is unmistakable. This is especially true of *The Legend of Truth*, and this is no accident. This text, which was written during Sartre's military service after the completion of his studies, recapitulates and terminates the changes that the Ecole normale made in his literary project. Modeled on Platonic myths, it shows Sartre's new ideal (to unite philosophy and literature), the form in which this ideal is expressed (the symbolic narrative), the philosophical theme (contingency) which has replaced the earlier autobiographical nucleus, and the positive figure (the lucid and solitary intellectual hero) who has replaced the fantasies of failure.

# 4. FROM SCHOOL TO LITERATURE: *NAUSEA*

These are the characteristics of *The Legend of Truth*, which can be considered the starting point for the work which was begun in 1931 and ended up as *Nausea*: "In its very first draft the new [factum] was still very much like *The Legend of Truth*, being a lengthy, abstract dissertation on contingency."[9] But between the last narrative Sartre wrote as a student and the final version of *Nausea*, a radical transformation takes place, and we cannot understand it if we simply consider the intrinsic demands of his project, biographical data, and collective events. For it is from *The Legend of Truth*'s[10] flop that Sartre learns that a formal solution modeled after the classics of an academic course of studies cannot meet the demands of the work's real audience and judge, the contemporary literary field. And from this point on, objective conditions lead him to establish a new goal: to adapt the product to the tastes of his market. And he is ideally situated to make out the weaknesses of his model. As one of the small group of recently licensed *agrégés* from whose ranks the new protagonists of the intellectual scene will spring, he has among his closest friends (who like him are stamped from a common mold and committed to breaking out of it to become the writers of their time) competent and demanding readers whose tastes give him an exact idea of the preferences of that public of equals—publishers and readers in publishing houses, critics, other authors—upon whom recognition depends. In addition to Simone de Beauvoir, whose *imprimatur* Sartre will seek for everything he writes, it is natural that Nizan, having blazed the trail, should be very important for him. Nizan not only publishes *Aden, Arabie* and *The Watchdogs* at just this time, but having managed before Sartre has to size up his work in terms of the demands of the current literary field, he can point out to Sartre the imperative with which it confronts two graduates of the Ecole normale soaked in classicism: master the technical arsenal of problems and solutions which makes writing modern.[11]

All the work Sartre does to move from the "factum" to *Nausea* could be boiled down to an intense apprenticeship in modern literary form. Yet he hangs onto the points of his "program" which have been approved of by his friends and have become constituent aspects of his habitus. In Sartre's development, as in an idealistic dialectic, each stage is preserved and ends up being essential to his success. His academic course of studies is not enough to make a writer of him, but this will not handicap him at all. His philosophical ambitions, his metaphysical themes, and his recognized competence to fulfill these ambitions will constitute the decisive difference between him and his rivals in an age which demands that literature provide metaphysical and moral messages. Furthermore, his decision to narrate almost exclusively "internal" experiences, "facts of consciousness," corresponds to one of the main upshots of contemporary literature's characteristic rejection of the events and actions of plot.

## 4.1 *The work of reconversion*

When *Nausea* is published, it still has its original structure of a Cartesian journal which tells in first person the story of an intellectual revelation, the discovery of contingency. But we know that Sartre also had in mind recent prestigious models of spiritual autobiography which certainly helped persuade him that the Cartesian meditation could be given a contemporary form. One of these models is *Monsieur Teste*, in which Valéry had deliberately set out to combine autobiography and the *Discourse on Method*, "to write the life of a theory as one writes the life of a passion." Contrary to what a few superficial differences might lead one to think, this work of Valéry's, because of its intellectualism, was a very important guide for Sartre.[12] The other model, as Sartre himself points out, is *The Notebooks of Malte Laurids Brigge*. Rilke's work had struck a deep sympathetic chord in Sartre in his days at the Ecole normale, and has an important influence on *Nausea*.[13]

It is easy to see that the Cartesian format lends itself to modernization. Its initiation to truth, and to the search for meaning or true identity, is the timeless plot of religion, myth, and story. And it is the form of plot which, more refined, best survives in the contemporary novel. Although the fiction of someone else's journal is a scarcely original literary device which goes back as far as the eighteenth century, it too plays a part in the transformation of the factum. In adopting this genre, in splitting himself into an openly fictive "I," Sartre unconsciously lays the foundation for the simplest transition to a series of concerns which are crucial for the avant-gardes of that time. Before he is even fully conscious of what he is doing, he challenges the point of view of the omniscient narrator, establishes distance between author and narrative, and abandons hierarchical and causal order in fiction.[14]

Furthermore, this strategy is well-suited to the first big change Sartre decides to make. "I insisted that Sartre should give Roquentin's discovery some fictional depth, and infuse his narrative with a little of that suspense which we enjoyed in detective novels." Accepting Simone de Beauvoir's advice, Sartre transposes Roquentin's meditation into what Barthes baptized the "hermeneutic code": he makes it the progressive unveiling of an enigma.[15]

In getting inspiration from the detective story, Sartre has recourse to a common "strategy" for making innovations in literature: the techniques of a genre which is not yet legitimate or discussed are introduced into an established genre. This technique brings good returns because it produces an effect of novelty and daring (which is especially highlighted in this case, in which the enigma is a metaphysical idea), and because it corresponds to tendencies which are already evident in the French intellectual field during the thirties. The grafting of inventions—subjects and forms—culled from anomalous fields—language games and ethnology, psychoanalysis and black humor—is one of the basic keys to the scandal of surrealism. And the taste for the British and American detective story which is just becoming fashionable at this time among the Parisian intelligentsia predisposes this genre to be a source of inspiration for writers like Sartre and Simone de Beauvoir, who are so much a part of the milieu.[16]

But *Nausea* draws on all the cultural models of the day. By borrowing ideas from them, or simply alluding to them, the factum takes on, in the eyes of the contemporary public, a contemporary look. Clear echoes of movies have been identified in Roquentin's agonizing Bouville: settings out of Carné and Renoir[17]; techniques for making things nonsensical and unreal (metamorphoses of objects) inspired by surrealism and American comedies, especially the Marx Brothers.[18] And it is Sartre's passion for jazz, the music hall, and American Negro songs which explains why in *Nausea* a ragtime tune can play (as both imitation and parody) the role that the "short passage from Vinteuil" plays in Proust.[19]

## 4.2 *The lessons of the avant-garde*

What produces the key change in Sartre's manuscript is his falling in step with the literary avant-gardes which are just at the point of being recognized. Models which matter invariably get recognized, and there is nothing mysterious about this. They are designated and delimited with great precision by the multitude of signals sent out from the different sources of legitimacy: editors, critics, literary awards, competent members of the reading public, literary magazines. Sartre gets reliable guidance from all these sources: from his friends' introductions, from the established publishers he has chosen (Grasset, Gallimard), from the literary magazines he diligently reads (*Europe, les Nouvelles littéraires* and, above all, the *N.R.F.*), and from the inner-circle bookstores where Adrienne Monnier and Sylvia Beach first display for French intellectuals the treasures of contemporary English and American literature.[20] So it is not at all surprising that he is so perfectly oriented in this seemingly disoriented landscape of modernity.

Among the important sources of the lessons Sartre learns about adapting his work in progress, his reading of *Journey to the End of the Night* is chronologically the first, and (although this is not evident) it is also of lasting importance. But there is no need to search for elements Sartre borrowed or derived from Céline. Although Sartre does see Bardamu as a brother to Roquentin (and that is the main point of Nausea's epigraph from Céline), he does not need to imitate: the resemblance springs from a shared feeling characteristic of the time, and its chief value for Sartre is that it reassures him about his own work. In their ideological stance, construction, syntax, and vocabulary, the two books are clearly different. As Contat and Rybalka show, Céline "gave Sartre license to dare." Before, they point out, all of Sartre's texts were immured in academic "good writing." "Thanks to Céline, everything becomes legitimate: the walls of proper language fall and all words, even the most obscene, are offered the keys to the kingdom of literature. This brusque expansion of vocabulary simultaneously opens up new possibilities for the field of the novel itself: from now on anything may be openly discussed. By liberating vocabulary and loosening up syntax, Céline let the body appear in a French novelistic tradition which had previously been dominated by the soul. Céline gave *Nausea* the chance to rush behind him out through the breach he had opened into liberated territory."[21]

Simone de Beauvoir gives us a revealing account of Céline's revolutionary importance for Sartre: "But the book of the year for us was Céline's *Journey to the End of the Night*: we knew whole passages of it by heart, and his type of anarchism seemed very close to ours. . . . He attacked war, colonialism, the cult of mediocrity, platitudes, and society generally in a style and tone which we found enchanting. Céline had forged a new instrument: a way of writing that was as vivid as the spoken word. What a relief after the marmoreal phrases of Gide and Alain and Valéry! Sartre was strongly influenced by it; he finally abandoned the starchy verbiage he had still been using in *The Legend of Truth*."[22]

Joyce's *Ulysses*, like *Journey to the End of the Night*, leads Sartre to another key breakthrough, although its influence is seldom noticed: in *Nausea* there are no visible signs of it, not even of the inner monologue which Sartre had certainly pondered.[23] As Geneviève Idt notes, Roquentin's monologue is never presented as a transcript of the stream of consciousness: it is always stylized, or at least quoted, so as to call attention to the fact that it is a representation.[24] But as Céline makes even the crudest commonplace fair game, Joyce shows what a writer soaked in culture can do. Insofar as his novel, with its combinations of different ways of playing with the forms of language and literature, is an extreme case of transtextuality, it forms a perfect model for allowing Sartre to turn his imitativeness and encumbering academicisms into assets. Joyce shows Sartre that one can be original without throwing away one's books, that one can on the contrary pour them all into one's writing—but only after having first made use of travesties and transformations, sacrilegious interminglings, caricatures and paradoxes to strip them of their learned mystery. Surrealist experiments and, more generally, the pervasive aesthetic of the collage suggest this same tack. But it is Joyce who explores its most varied possibilities, and who is, moreover, already so well-known that he guarantees the legitimacy of this solution. When Sartre reads in the *N.R.F.* in 1932 that Proust, Joyce, and Kafka are the century's three greatest novelists, the names of Proust and Joyce do not surprise him in the least, but Kafka's does: "If this Kafka person had really been a great writer, we could hardly have failed to know about him. . . ."[25] *Ulysses*, on the contrary, is an already familiar precedent which justifies a whole string of *Nausea*'s features: if Homer can be transformed, then one can certainly parody Descartes and pile up in one's plot centuries of annotated knowledge orchestrated in a polyphony of registers and styles. Whereas Céline's lesson led Sartre to go from lofty language to an everyday register in which we can hear in a stylized form the deliberately brutal slang of intellectuals, Joyce's authorized him to break up the monotony of discourse. Abounding in allusions and quotations which are often packed one inside the other like Russian dolls (a page from Balzac and magazine articles, Flaubert and Conrad, Valéry and Proust, Barbusse and Gide, Stendhal and Malraux . . .), and shuffling different kinds of writing together (naturalism and reporting, inner monologues and tales of the fantastic, conversational commonplaces and hagiography, philosophical meditation and surrealistic hallucination, tragic novella and phenomenological description, Dos Passos and Hemingway), *Nausea* coruscates with the knowing winks which are essential to the cultivated reader's pleasure.

In 1934, when Sartre does read "The Metamorphosis" (in the *N.R.F.*) and *The Trial*, he not only recognizes the greatness he has heard about but sees a profound affinity between Kafka's work and his own project. It undoubtedly leads him to rethink the strange inner adventures he has attributed to his character. They no longer seem to him to be just a playful way of challenging reality inspired by a contemporary taste for what he sees as shared by the Marx Brothers, surrealist painters, and even Faulkner. He discovers in Kafka and in his own book a new genre of fantasy,[26] an "upside-down world" whose transformations are made horrible by the reversal of relationships between ends and means, mind and body. Simone de Beauvoir clearly suggests that for Sartre, Kafka's work is above all a mirror in which the sense of his undertaking becomes clear and justified as the most up-to-date image of man's fate: "K's story differed considerably from that of Antoine Roquentin, being far more drastic and despairing; but in both cases the hero found himself so remote from the context of his familiar surroundings that as far as he was concerned all rational order vanished, and he wandered alone and benighted through a strange shadowy wilderness. We conceived an immediate and deep-rooted admiration for Kafka; without being quite sure why, we felt that his work had personal significance for us. . . . Kafka described *ourselves* to us. . . ."[27]

Reading Kafka changes not just Sartre's conception of his novel but the novel itself. It clearly prompts him to develop and accentuate its "fantastic" aspects, those disturbing contaminations of the human by the natural, of the user by his utensils, which give rise to Roquentin's "nausea." Furthermore, by stressing the unusualness of these reversals, Sartre puts the key to reading the text in the text itself: "Objects should not *touch* because they are not alive. You use them, put them back in place, you live among them: they are useful, nothing more. But they touch me, it is unbearable."[28] "Things—you might have called them thoughts which stopped halfway, which were forgotten, which forgot what they wanted to think and which stayed like that, hanging about with an odd little sense which was beyond them."[29]

It is thus understandable that Paulhan has no hesitation in speaking of Kafka's writing as the only writing *Nausea* can possibly be compared

to[30]: it is the only resemblance Sartre sets forth expressly, through un-
equivocal symbols, in his text. Of course this is not a matter of an
imitation but of an elective affinity which reveals Sartre to himself and
reassures him of the worth of what he is writing. For is not Kafka at
this time, for those who are in the know, the most recent great discovery,
the model whom other interesting young writers of the time—Camus,
Blanchot—would like to equal in France? Sartre will give these rivals'
works a careful reading in 1943, denying that they have any real affinity
to Kafka's works.[31] Between the lines, he will thus claim this true affinity
for himself, with all the authority of one who in publishing *Being and
Nothingness* has recently added to his already brilliant image as a writer
and playwright that of a major thinker. So there is justification in seeing
an allusion to Kafka in the insert Sartre wrote for the first edition of
*Nausea*: "Now Roquentin is losing his past drop by drop: every day he
sinks more deeply into a strange and suspicious present. . . . It is then
that his real adventure—an insinuating, softly horrible metamorphosis
of all his sensations—begins. . . ."[32]

Another acquisition which is essential for Sartre's legitimation is the
technical secrets of American novelists. Gallimard is beginning to make
these writers known by publishing translations of their works introduced, preferably, by well-known French authors. (Malraux and Valéry
Larbaud, for example, write prefaces to Faulkner's works.) Thanks to
his readings of Joyce, Virginia Woolf, and others, Sartre has already
realized that he must abandon "the pseudo-objectivity of the realist
novel." But it is above all in his reading of the works of Dos Passos,
Hemingway, and Faulkner that he gives close, meticulous attention to
the procedures and solutions of the contemporary Anglo-Saxon novel.

The effects of this study are not as clear in *Nausea* as in later works.
Sartre does not change the novel's initial journalistic structure—which
even though it is not characteristic of his later models does not follow
the traditional canons of realism either—as if for the time being he
would rather not take a chance with skills he has not yet fully mastered.
Besides, the new requirements are in some respects so perfectly matched
to Sartre's original intentions that they seem to flow naturally from them.
The American masters' most characteristic aim of imitating the lived
time, uncertainties, and gaps of perception and memory by hiding (beneath an apparently monotonous and arbitrary adding on of instant after
instant) the design which actually governs each representation seems
to coincide with the oldest, most essential aim of Sartre's project. Staging contingency means rendering with unbearable clarity the formless,
senseless flow of existence in its permanent contrast to the hoped-for
strict order of which art gives us a glimpse. In the eternal and eternally
crumbling present without past or future which Faulkner has created,

in the meticulous descriptions which are the secret of Hemingway's power to give a feeling of "the resistance of things" and the "majestic course" of time, and in the care with which Dos Passos removes every sign of causal explanation, Sartre thinks he has found the literary technique which corresponds to his metaphysics. A decisive experience, which inclines him to erect the relationship of technique and metaphysic into a principle for explaining and evaluating art.

In addition to these general directions, we can already glimpse here and there specific stylistic imitations. Although Roquentin's visit to the Bouville museum is a real *topos* in which a host of cultural and biographical allusions intersect, the power of its sarcasm is due to a technique Sartre took from Dos Passos[33]: the shifting point of view which alternates between that of the characters themselves and the pompous image of them which that "sententious and accomplice" chorus, public opinion, might yield. It is this solemn voice which, by commenting on the portraits of Bouville's first citizens, crystallizes their stupid pride into destiny and transforms them into *"salauds."* The stress on the meaningless details of daily life which helps give the factum the solidity of history comes from Hemingway.[34] And it is from Faulkner in particular that Sartre gets the nerve to speak the unspeakable violence of Roquentin's fantasies, including even the "soft, criminal desire to rape" which bursts forth while he is reading a news item.[35] In its audaciousness, this treatment of sexuality seems to carry on and surpass that of Proust and Gide, who had made it an aspect of the image—and the fame—of the true writer.

Sartre's technique of including the theory of the narrative in the narrative to show that every narrative necessarily betrays reality by establishing an order which is alien to actual existence is undoubtedly meant to be another show of skill.[36] This expedient has a number of functions. It makes the book's metaphysical message clear: existence is completely anarchic; only art can give it meaning. It asks us to see the narrative form of confused, incomplete, unrelated notes in which Roquentin records his groping search as a deliberate device for simulating actual experiencing. It shows that the author is well aware of the theoretical approach of the century's avant-garde, and that he is claiming to surpass it by condemning the inevitable fictiveness of its attempts to eliminate the author from fiction (the same ironic condemnation which is found at the opening of the book in the Editor's Note and the Undated Pages). And finally, this expedient places *Nausea* in the tradition of the antinovel, which has already been legitimated in France by Gide's *Paludes* and *The Counterfeiters*, but which has not yet lost its originality, as it will after the Nouveau Roman.[37]

## 4.3 *The philosophical base*

The sources we have pointed out—and they are only the most obvious signs of literary distinction to be seen in *Nausea*—are in themselves sufficient to account for the impression of prowess and certain success that Sartre's debut made in the circle of those competent to judge. By the mere fact that he brings all of these current models of excellence together in a single position, Sartre seems to set out from the results achieved by a whole century of literary efforts and then surpass them all. No other French author, whether already established or simply a newcomer, can rival this polyphonic virtuosity which makes every other success seem less than complete, if not downright naive and provincial. When *Nausea* is published, André Thérive, one of the most influential critics of the day, writes: "If *Nausea* had come out thirty years ago, what a turmoil it would have caused in the world of letters, and no doubt what an outcry too! Today the book seems perfectly normal; what is important about it (not to speak of its author's talent, which already seems beyond compare) is that it sums up many tendencies in contemporary literature and psychology."[38]

But to ignore the literary effects which the philosophical development that accompanies the labor of writing has on the work and its reception would be to neglect its most striking and decisive difference from its competitors. One of the advantages Sartre derives from this development is a theoretical habitus which enables him to conceptualize and justify his literary practice. The concept of limit-situation (*Grenzsituation*) already seems to play this role in 1927, when Sartre picks it up from Jaspers, by encouraging him to look for literary ideas in the realm of social pathology—news items, madness—which interests him so much. But the philosophical experience which has far the greatest weight for *Nausea* is Sartre's encounter with phenomenology. This is understandable: the changes in the novel that we have described so far all take place during Sartre's stay in Berlin, where he divides his time between studying Husserl and making a second revision of his manuscript. And phenomenology is not only the key experience in the growth of Sartre's philosophy (it can be said to give form to it as during the same period the literary avant-gardes shape the metamorphosis of the factum); it is a conception of philosophy which seems to bring to their logical conclusion the aims and techniques to which his literary education is leading him at this time. Phenomenology seems to legitimate Sartre's ambition to unite philosophy and literature and show that his literary project has a logically necessary order. More than that, it is a total experience which seems to him to combine and justify in one coherent system not only his intellectual investigations but his entire life, including even his most private fantasies. In other words, phenomenology for Sartre has the function of an ethicoreligious conversion.

In this respect, the religious and emotional language of the key article on the concept of intentionality which appears in the *N.R.F.* in 1939, and images in that article such as the tree root which condense Sartre's most characteristic obsessions, are very revealing. Phenomenological description of objects seems to bring out all their subjective connotations: it gives the tree the attraction and repulsion of a fetish which reawakens Sartre's first, childish image of his calling, as well as all the philosophicoreligious overtones it has subsequently acquired, to the point of making it, with its "pointless proliferation," the best symbol for Sartre of human contingency.[39]

Geneviève Idt has shown that meditation on a tree is already at the end of the nineteenth century one of the favorite writing exercises French lycée students are asked to do, and is still in use when Sartre is a schoolboy, although Sartre certainly finds precedents for it later in Proust, Valéry, and Husserl after it has become a philosophicoliterary commonplace.[40] Thus it is the model which comes naturally to Sartre's grandfather-professor when he gives writing lessons to "Poulou": " 'Ah!' my grandfather would say, 'it's not enough to have eyes. You must learn to use them. Do you know what Flaubert did when de Maupassant was a little boy? He sat him down in front of a tree and gave him two hours to describe it.' "[41] But it is not just a lagging habitus which makes the tree theme persist so in Sartre's works. It is because the tree has the power to evoke all the fantasies associated with the child's writing exercise that it becomes the adult's most adequate symbol of a personal myth.

Sartre sees the concept of intentionality ("'consciousness' necessary existence as consciousness of something other than itself": if "consciousness could ever take complete possession of itself, become wholly one with itself, all nice and cosy in its little tight-shut room, it would simply disappear"[42]) as the metaphysical justification for a character like Roquentin. As a character who has no past, no social situation (he is writing a history book, he thinks and talks like an intellectual, at times in fact like a philosopher, but he has no profession, as if that did not matter), and no psychological traits other than those which can be deduced from the gestures, words, and thoughts recorded in his journal, Roquentin seems to be the pure and empty consciousness of the phenomenological "ego" incarnate.

To understand the importance Sartre accords this philosophical base, we must recognize that the metaphysics of *Nausea*, its truth, its coherence, and the adequacy of its expressive form seem to him to be the criteria of literary success. It is in having realized a spontaneously Husserlian novel in accordance with what he considers to be a revolutionary philosophical conception of man that Sartre claims he has "surpassed" all competing models, including the most consecrated ones. As he puts it in a revealing word, Husserl "liberated" him from Proust: "So now hate, love, fear, sympathy, all these famous 'subjective' reactions swimming in Spirit's foul-smelling brine break suddenly free; they are no more than ways of discovering the world. . . . And we are liberated from Proust. Liberated too from the 'inner life': to seek as Amiel sought, like a baby snuggling in its mother's arms, the soothing consolations of our own intimate life, would be vain, since everything ultimately is outside us, everything, including ourselves: outside, in the world, among others."[43]

Roquentin's progressive relinquishing of illusory ways of existing—as adventurer, scholar, and lover—can thus be read as a metaphor of the phenomenological "method" of reduction, which claims to put the psychology of the empirical ego in parentheses. This reading is further confirmed by the impersonal consciousness which replaces the "I" in the final pages of the novel: it is the realization of the *epoche*[44]: "Now when I say 'I,' it seems hollow to me. I can't manage to feel myself very well, I am so forgotten. The only real thing left in me is existence which feels it exists. . . . A little while ago someone said 'me,' said *my* consciousness. Who? . . . Now nothing is left but anonymous . . . consciousness. . . . There is . . . consciousness of a face. . . . There is a consciousness of this body. . . . There is knowledge of the consciousness. It sees through itself, peaceful and empty between the walls, freed from the man who inhabited it, monstrous because empty. . . . [There is] consciousness of suffering. . . ."[45]

Some of the essential traits *Nausea* has taken on in the course of its development also seem to be dictated by and based directly on this phenomenological metaphysic: for example, the representation of time as a sequence of instants which Sartre got from American writers; or the "world from the wrong side" which so many authors, from the Surrealists to Kafka, taught him to see and show. The phenomenological linking of perceiving to the intrinsic properties of things perceived ("things suddenly show themselves as hateful, sympathetic, horrible, lovable"[46]) makes the looking-glass world of *Nausea*, in which man and things or animals interchange characteristics, the truth of existence for a subject able to "put himself in parentheses." We can thus see a token of Sartre's gratitude in his fervent declaration: "Husserl has restored the horror and charm of things. He has reinstated the world of artists and prophets, a frightening, hostile, dangerous world with havens of grace and love."[47]

Although Sartre sharply condemns slipping interpretations in between descriptive lines,[48] in *Nausea* he does it all the time himself. One way he does is by writing into the book's images norms for interpreting them; the more implicit they are, the more effective they are. We can see why a philosophical reading manages to produce (in a literary context) the effect of being without precedent which played an important part in making the book seem original.

Thus, in a review which Contat and Rybalka say "greatly helped establish *Nausea's* reputation," E. Jaloux writes: "It is a book of the future whose life will be long. It will undoubtedly fail to fit traditional categories because it is profoundly original. It has no echoes but is wholly new; the metaphysical experiences to which Antoine Roquentin has been condemned will not recall a single literary voice. It will perhaps be said that it is not a novel. But what is a novel above all but a form of fiction which contains wide experience?"[49]

It is worth adding the thank-you letter Sartre sent M. Jaloux, because it clearly shows how much he wanted *Nausea* to be read philosophically: "Dear Sir, let me tell you how grateful I am for the two remarkable articles you have written about *Nausea*. Among all the critics who have been kind enough to talk about my books, you, Sir, are the only one who has analyzed it as a phenomenological experiment, a work of fiction which gives insight into essence. I have been concerned for some time that a misunderstanding might separate me from those who read this work on the basis of what critics have said about it. It seems to me now, Sir, that thanks to you I need no longer worry about such a misunderstanding, and you can imagine how pleased I am to have been so perfectly understood. I beg you, Sir, to accept my highest regards. J.-P. Sartre."[50]

## 4.4 *Publishers' revisions*

One last important transformation separates the manuscript from the published work: the changes that the publisher, Gallimard, ordered by way of two of his most prestigious writers, Jean Paulhan and Brice Parain. This is the stage at which the demand of the literary market most clearly shows its power to control the literary work.

"Once the manuscript is accepted, Brice Parain at Gallimard is assigned the task of readying it for publication, and he begins by asking Sartre to make rather extensive revisions in order to cut out the most daring passages and the crudest words. . . . Reluctantly, but conscious of having written at too great length, Sartre accepts Brice Parain's suggestions and cuts out fifty pages. . . . These cuts or changes have to do chiefly with the book's populist and erotic aspects. . . . *Although* Nausea *is a profoundly personal and original work, it is also, paradoxically, one of Sartre's texts which owes the most to what others have to say about it.*

"Others even choose the title that the novel will ultimately have. *Melancholia* having been judged unsatisfactory . . . Gaston Gallimard finally (in Oct. 1937) hits on the title which will make Sartre famous and which to this day is the one most closely associated with his name."[51]

Judging by the revisions, we can say that the publisher's almost total elimination of the most "naturalistic" sections of the book tends to remove any doubts as to its genre by putting an evident stress on its fantasy-metaphysical aspect. It points up the affinity on which there is the most objective reason to bank, the resemblance to Kafka. Among all the images of literary excellence which are currently coming to the fore, this model is the one which *Nausea* is being readied to evoke most readily. Substituting "Nausea" for a title as murky and thick with esoteric traces as "Melancholia"[52] does not sully this image (Roquentin's nausea, like the anguish of Kafka's characters, has a metaphysical root), but by association it does add a new mark of distinction: an aggressive violence which puts Sartre on the side of the great rebels, particularly the latest Parisian find, Céline.

## 4.5 *Sartre's self-interpretation of his work*

The publication of the book opens a new chapter in its exchanges with the field: the give-and-take of views between the author and his critics which weaves the work's established image. At this stage it is even easier to see how Sartre's philosophical capital promotes his work of self-interpretation. Of course Sartre is not the only writer who has to do this work. The older the tradition within which the literary practice of any writer is inscribed and defined, and the greater its autonomy with respect to the broader economy, the more necessary it is for him to investigate and articulate theoretically what it is that specifically distinguishes his creative project from those of his contemporaries and predecessors. Since the "worth" of works is determined by the judgments of those considered competent to judge, any producer must face up to the image he receives from publishers, critics, and other authors. In speaking of his work or the works of others, they constantly call upon him to take a stand, to accept, reject, or modify their objectification of his undertaking by explicating and systematizing his own way of conceiving of it. But no other author at this time has in such a high degree the competencies—the entitlements and professional habitus—Sartre has to produce and impose a veritable literary code in terms of which he can turn the representation of his work which he has formulated through his complex interactions with the field into a precise image of literary excellence.

Looked upon as an instruction manual, the insert for *Nausea* may be considered the first act in establishing this code of literary excellence. It is important to see how much the view of the novel which is presented there owes to the many compromises which were involved in the revision and publication of the book, and above all to the final important intervention of its publisher. The aspects Sartre stresses—Roquentin's solitude "among ferociously good people"; his miserable life as an antihero; his "metamorphosis," which has to do with perception; and the wholly intellectual nature of his "adventure," "nausea" at "existence revealing itself"—clearly reflect the combination of Kafka, Husserl, and Céline that Gallimard is asking the public to recognize in *Nausea*.

Sartre goes ahead with the work of building his image through interviews, reviews, or, indirectly, the series of articles on contemporary authors he writes between the publication of *Nausea* and *What Is Literature?* This way of intervening through short essays published in leading literary journals is characteristic of the Sartre of this period. Subsequently, Sartre's literary criticism will oscillate between monumental biography and the intense work of prefacing books which is expected of France's most famous intellectual. These essays are on the contrary minor skirmishes mapped out objectively according to the strategic requirements of a precise stage of Sartre's career. The writers they are devoted to hold key positions in the literary panorama of the day: masters the young writer makes use of (Faulkner, Dos Passos); authors of his own age whom he challenges (Camus, Blanchot, his friend Nizan); and more or less talked about, famous, and influential elders (Mauriac and Giraudoux, Ponge and Parain, Drieu la Rochelle and Charles Morgan). These are objects which promise big symbolic returns for a newcomer if he can seem capable of revealing the truth of their work by relating it to a worldview which illuminates each of its aspects. These critical incursions are thus no waste of time, as Simone de Beauvoir feared.[53] They are a powerful tool with which Sartre clears the field around him and at the same time works to define and legitimate his position in it. Of course he does not consciously plan this; what he is consciously seeking to do through these analyses is to articulate and organize a theory of the literary fact.

C. Chonez reports: "At the same time, J.-P. Sartre felt the need to make clear his ideas about the novel, a genre he considered to be narrowly defined and governed by *precise laws*: a novel must be constructed in terms of the concept of duration, and also of the unforeseen, which requires constant attention from the reader. This is the basis of his harsh criticism of the naturalistic novel's determinism. It will also be the source of the 'tongue-lashing' he plans to give Mauriac in a coming issue of the *N.R.F.*, criticizing him for depicting his characters from 'God's standpoint' and robbing them of those subtle mechanisms which produce their resistance to their author and their serendipitous complicity with their readers—robbing them, that is, of their true freedom."[54]

The fact is that Sartre's theorizing alone is enough to set him apart in a field in which no one else at the time is capable of presenting an alternative theory to challenge him. His recourse to "precise laws" especially helps give resounding authority to the verdicts which abound in his essays, and give the appearance of objectivity to a beginner's insolent criticisms of famous authors. This is especially evident in his article against Mauriac, a famous but traditional writer who forms a perfect target for Sartre's ringing—and self-serving—attack:

". . . He once wrote that the novelist is to his own creatures what God is to His. And that explains all the oddities of his technique. He takes God's standpoint on his characters. God sees the inside and the outside, the depths of body and soul, the whole universe at once. In like manner, M. Mauriac is omniscient about everything relating to his little world. What he says about his characters is Gospel. He explains them, categorizes them and condemns them without appeal. . . .The time has come to say that the novelist is not God. . . . [What] I maintain is precisely the fact that *he has no right to make these absolute judgments. A novel is an action related from various points of view.* . . . It is, in short, the testimony of a participant and should reveal the man who testifies, as well as the event to which he testifies. It should arouse our impatience (will it be confirmed or denied by events?), and thus give us a feeling of the dragging of time. Thus, each point of view is relative, and the best one will be that which makes the reader feel most acutely the dragging of time. The participants' interpretations and explanations will all be hypothetical. . . . In any case, the introduction of absolute truth or of God's standpoint constitutes a twofold error of technique. . . . But there is something even more serious. The definitive judgments with which M. Mauriac is always ready to intersperse the narrative prove that he does not conceive his characters as he ought. . . . Fictional beings *have their laws, the most rigorous of which is the following*: the novelist may be either their witness or their accomplice, *but never both at the same time.* . . .

"*La Fin de la Nuit* is not a novel. . . . If it is true that a novel is a thing, like a painting or architectural structure, if it is true that a novel is made with time and free minds, as a picture is painted with oil and pigments, then *La Fin de la Nuit* is not a novel. It is, at most, a collection of signs and intentions. *M. Mauriac is not a novelist.*"[55]

The effects of this particular sally into the literary field can give us an idea of the multiple functions such critical activity performs. It stirs up a clamorous polemic which puts Sartre at the center of attention at the most opportune moment, just at the time *The Wall* is coming out, and only a year after the publication of *Nausea*. André Rousseaux, in the eyes of the general public an influential critic, is shocked by Sartre's essay and replies to it in the *Revue universelle*.[56] The editors of the *N.R.F* come to Sartre's defense in their own journal.[57] The essay wrecks Mauriac's career as a novelist. In 1969, he admits that Sartre has been responsible for his long silence: "Sartre's attack wounded me. He tore one of my novels, *La fin de la nuit*, to shreds. He was not only a very young author at that time; he was also the hero of his entire generation. I won't say that his attack completely demoralized me, but just the same it gave me a lot to think about."[58]

The axiom upon which the "theory" Sartre is formulating is more and more explicitly and peremptorily based—"A fictional technique always relates back to the novelist's metaphysics. The critic's task is to define the latter before evaluating the former"[59]—enhances the value of Sartre's symbolic capital by investing his literary judgment with his philosophical holdings. It is true that the inconsistency and ambiguity of the principle to which he is appealing become evident once a few independent statements are compared to one another. At times Sartre seems to be arguing that literary technique is engendered and explained by the author's metaphysics (as, for example, in the case of Dos Passos, Faulkner, Nizan). At times that it depends on the author himself: Sartre accuses Mauriac of failing to adapt his technique to an idea of man which his own Christian religion articulates and which is particularly well-suited to the novel ("man is free"). At times Sartre argues that the very incoherence of an author's worldview may serve his art ("Dos Passos' world—like those of Faulkner, Kafka and Stendhal—is impossible because it is contradictory. But therein lies its beauty. Beauty is a veiled contradiction"[60]). At times that only a philosophy of freedom is suited to the novel: "Do you want your characters to live? See to it that they are free"[61]; ". . .a novel is made of time and free minds, as a picture is painted with oil and pigments."[62] And it has been shown that Sartre's own practice does not always follow his strict principles[63]: "Fictional beings have their laws, the most rigorous of which is the following: the novelist may be either their witness or their accomplice, but never both at the same time"[64]; "In a novel, you must tell all or keep quiet;

above all, you must not omit or skip anything."[65] But in the immediate situation, Sartre's confident tone, his philosophical titles, and the rigor which taken singly his analyses seem to have as a result of the apparently systematic nature of a way of speaking which draws on the most consumate philosophical rhetoric all work together to discourage any effective counteroffensive from a weak-willed literary world. These essays thus play objectively a decisive role in the construction and the consecration of the image of Sartre the author. They are so many opportune raids on the articulate based on a typical philosophical strategy of which Sartre is a past master: the strategy of radical breakthrough. Applied to prestigious positions, it allows Sartre to seize for himself the recognition which was theirs, and the honor of having moved beyond them.

# 5. THE REDEFINITION OF THE PROJECT: FROM STORIES OF CONTINGENCY TO AN EPIC OF FREEDOM

The self-interpretation which begins with the publication of *Nausea* does not simply look back to the earlier stories. New developments in his project which are an evident effect of his response to new demands of the field begin to take shape. Not just his response to the reactions to his published work which come from within the field, but also to the many signs that the field itself has reached a major turning point: as international and domestic tensions mount, politics invades literature. The profound impression which the defeat of the Spanish Republicans, the Austrian Anschluss, the Munich pact, and (in France) the demise of the Popular Front and the growing violence of fascist organizations make on Sartre and his friends,[66] and the "excitement that far outstripped any purely literary emotion"[67] with which they read Malraux's *Man's Hope*, are feelings they share with all left intellectuals of the day. This collective atmosphere calls writers' attention dramatically to the individual's relation to society and history. Sartre feels the pressure in two ways: directly, through his everyday experience, and retranslated already into a series of strictly literary signals. The success of books such as *Man's Hope*, Bernanos's *Les grands cimetières sous la lune* (and *Verdun, Dialogue with Death, Wind, Sand and Stars*—the works to which Sartre will subsequently attribute an important role in shaping his "ethics"[68]); the political commitment which resounds from France's most illustrious writers during the Popular Front years; and even the meaning which certain critical reviews ask him to see in *Nausea* all work together to wean Sartre from the solipsism of his early characters.

The commentators who see most clearly that this possibility is already present in *Nausea* are two committed intellectuals, one Communist and the other Catholic. Nizan ends his review for *Ce Soir* as follows: "As a result of its closing pages, *Nausea* is not a book with no exit. M. Jean-Paul Sartre, who the whole length of his book paints the picture of a large bourgeois city (which for me is Le Havre) with such a fierce humor and violent sense of social caricature, has novelistic talents which are too precise and too cruel not to issue forth into the full light of reality."[69] And Jean Daniélou writes in *Etudes*: "The final pages seem to show that . . . Sartre . . . will take a place in the tradition of Valéry or Proust among the writers for writing's sake. And this alone is a sign of his greatness. Yet to me, Antoine Roquentin's disgust seems to point ahead, because the only way Sartre can really transcend it is by taking the difficult path of reinventing the need for man himself. If he keeps going down this road, his work will certainly take on a completely different meaning."[70]

The first effects of Sartre's new concerns are already visible in "The Childhood of a Leader," the only one of the stories collected in *The Wall* which was written after the publication of *Nausea*.[71] It shows an unmistakable development in relation to the four stories which precede it. These earlier stories, which Sartre began writing in 1935 after his stay in Berlin, seem in every respect to complement *Nausea*. They are contemporary with the final rewriting of the factum, and express the same intentions derived from the same literary apprenticeship. They have the same "metaphysical" thesis: to "look existence in the face" by showing, through a gallery of unsuccessful evasions, the futility of all efforts to escape it.[72] The only difference is that in these stories Sartre seems to make things more thematically and technically complex, as if, before launching out on a large-scale work (as he will with *The Roads to Freedom*), he wanted to try out, in the laboratory of micronovels, the whole gamut of possible narratives he had in mind.

The variety of characters, surroundings, situations, linguistic registers, and formal procedures he makes use of seems to show that he wants to enlarge his repertoire. He seems especially to want to venture in the directions his American masters have pointed out to him: temporal effects, multiple points of view, dissimulation of the causal order of things. Although the oldest stories—"Erostratus" and "The Wall"—are written in first person from a single point of view, one or more subjects in third person appear in subsequent stories. Furthermore, he draws away from *Nausea's* scarcely disguised autobiography and present-tense narrative by establishing a social distance between author and characters, and by playing with verb tenses. He pushes to their limits his imitative and parodic virtuosity, his demythologizing crudity concerning sex and physiological functions, and his artful reversals, contaminations of the human by the nonhuman, seeming enigma, and derision.[73]

As for themes, Sartre significantly repudiates an early source of inspiration—exoticism—found in trial efforts which do not appear in the collection.[74] Although many epigones following Barrès, Morand, Larbaud, and Gide took up exoticism again, it would seem to be outdated, even in the disenchanted version of it sketched out in "Dépaysement." *The Wall* will only include themes which were completely up-to-date in 1939, such as the war in Spain, madness, and more generally, pathological situations, in which the interest of intellectuals had been aroused by the vogue for Surrealism which was then at its height. (The Surrealist Exposition was held in 1938.) We need only think of the praise of crime and madness in Surrealist manifestos, of Breton's interest in Freud, and of his book, *Nadja*, which from 1928 on made the social definition of madness and the function of asylums a subject of discussion. We need only recall the attention paid to the crime of the Papin sisters (1933), who were greeted by the Surrealists as "heroines . . . sprung fully armed from a song of Maldoror," who were the subject of one of Lacan's first articles ("Motifs du crime paranoiaque: le crime des soeurs Papin," *Minotaure*, 1933), and who were later the inspiration for Genet's *The Maids*. Or the interest Bataille and other "surrealizers" at the Collège de sociologie had for the "shadow realm" of human existence. If we recall these things, then the intense interest with which Sartre and de Beauvoir begin at the outset of the thirties to follow news items in *Detective* and *Paris-Soir* (and especially the crime of the Papin sisters), and to explore the problem of madness, will no longer seem unusual. (We know that in 1935 Sartre had his former fellow student Lagache, a psychiatrist who was to become an eminent psychoanalyst, give him a shot of mescaline, which made him depressed and gave him hallucinations. And in 1936, Sartre visited a psychiatric ward in Rouen, where he seemed to be struck especially by the way in which institutionalization seemed to make madness incurable.)[75]

In sum, the difference between the first four stories in *The Wall* and *Nausea* seems to consist above all in Sartre's increased mastery of the play of forms and themes which distinguishes the avant-garde. They do not herald a new departure, but they do put into practice—and demonstrate—all the things Sartre had learned during his intense *aggiornamento*. Above all, their characters are still conceived of as phenomenological consciousnesses who are the subject not of histories but of meticulous snapshots in one of those limit-situations all of which reveal the same essential truth about existence.

It is in just this respect that the change introduced by "The Childhood of a Leader" is striking: not only is the individual set in a more precise social and historical context, his life is followed through diachronically to show how the adult is fashioned by early childhood experiences. The article Sartre writes on Dos Passos gives us an invaluable indication of the new sources orientating this new departure: since it was published in 1938, it lets us know what preoccupied Sartre while he was writing the story.

". . . [How] I hate Dos Passos' men! I am given a fleeting glimpse of their minds, just enough to see that they are living animals. Then, they begin to unwind their endless tissue of ritual statements and sacred gestures. For them, there is no break between inside and outside, between body and consciousness, but only between the stammerings of an individual's timid, intermittent, fumbling thinking and the messy world of collective representations. What a simple process this is, and how effective. All one need do is use American journalistic technique in telling the story of a life, and like the Salzburg reed, *a life crystallizes into the Social, and the problem of the transition to the typical—stumbling-block of the social novel—is thereby resolved. There is no further need to present a working man type, to compose (as Nizan does in Antoine Bloyé)* an existence which represents the exact average of thousands of existences. Dos Passos, on the contrary, can give all his attention to rendering *a single life's special character. Each of his characters is unique*; what happens to him could happen to no one else. What does it matter, since Society has marked him more deeply than could any special circumstance, since *he is* Society? Thus, we get a glimpse of an order beyond the accidents of fate or the contingency of detail, an order more supple than Zola's physiological necessity or Proust's psychological mechanism, a soft and insinuating constraint which seems to release its victims, letting them go only to take possession of them again without their suspecting, in other words, a statistical determinism. These men, submerged in their own existences, live as they can. They struggle; what comes their way is not determined in advance. And yet, neither their efforts, their faults, nor their most extreme violence can interfere with the regularity of births, marriages, and suicides."[76]

We find here not only a deep interest in the problem of representing the relation between the individual and society, which is new in Sartre, but also a very indicative choice of models to contrast to Dos Passos—Zola, Proust, and Nizan. They show the new tradition Sartre is taking up in his effort to outdistance his predecessors, the tradition of what he calls here the "social novel." The fact that the first, and only current, work he compares to his own is Nizan's *Antoine Bloyé* is particularly revealing, if we consider the book's characteristics and Nizan's position in relation to Sartre. We might think that this friend-rival who has gained some literary visibility before Sartre has is, as a result of his political commitment, one of the concrete mediations which communicate to Sartre most intimately the urgency of making room for the social and historical. And as a matter of fact, *Antoine Bloyé* (1933), a biographical novel and the first French attempt to transpose Marx and Freud into literature,[77] does help point up this new direction in Sartre's project by showing the weight of class determinants in the course of an individual life. In drawing away from his earlier phenomenological inspiration toward showing in "The Childhood of a Leader" "a single life's special character" as it "crystallizes into the Social," Sartre does indeed end up with an aim very close to Nizan's. This is a decisive transformation of his project: it is with this aim that he will approach each character, real and imagined, in all his subsequent works, from the hero of his novelistic cycle to his ultimate effort, *The Family Idiot*. And we can already see the focus in which he will henceforth regard his approach to biography as different from the Marxist and psychoanalytic ones: deny determinism, show that beneath the chains of social necessity each life is "unique" and free. Yet "The Childhood of a Leader," by constantly returning to psychoanalytic and Marxist approaches even as it parodies them, proves that Sartre is more influenced than he is willing to admit by the theories from which Nizan draws inspiration, and by the possibilities opened up by transferring them to literature.

Concerning the decisive importance which this dual reference to Marxism and psychoanalysis takes on in Sartre's literary work with "The Childhood of a Leader," a 1970 interview shows that Sartre himself saw the advent of these two systems of thought as a dividing line in contemporary literature. After Marx and Freud, Sartre argues, only two kinds of novel are possible: those which seek to be "naive" and decide "consciously to ignore Marxist and psychoanalytic methods of interpretation, and in so doing necessarily become less naive," and the "pseudo novels" such as those of Gombrowicz. Sartre sees Gombrowicz's "infernal machines . . . objects which self-destruct in the very process of being constructed," as "the model for what a simultaneously analytic and materialist novel could be" (*Situations* 9, 123). G. Idt is right in pointing out that " 'The Childhood of a Leader' already falls into the second category," and that "like Gombrowicz, Sartre maintains a skeptical attitude toward psychoanalysis and Marxism."[78] Even without quoting here the innumerable subsequent confirmations provided by Sartre's works and available biographical data, we can see that the indications we have mentioned (above all the story's construction) are sufficient to show that it constitutes a real turning point in Sartre's project, whose chief aim now becomes to write a novel which will be an answer to Marx and Freud. This is not the place for an extensive analysis of the story, but it is clear that among the many aims which must be understood if its form is to be explained, its basic aim is still to contrast its own categories of bad faith and choice to Freud's concept of the unconscious and Marx's concept of class in reconstructing the role that experience and social milieu play in shaping an individual life. And the claim that during this period Marxism and psychoanalysis become two of Sartre's chief concerns is further confirmed by their being at the forefront of his concurrent philosophical production (see Chapter 3).

We can understand, then, the sense of novelty we have in reading the essays and proclamations Sartre began to write in 1938: the philosophical message he puts at the heart of his future novels is no longer contingency but the positive power to transform it, human freedom.[79] Creating free yet historical and socially determined characters has become for Sartre the project which combines his formal and philosophical concerns and his new need to show how the freedom of the individual can be reconciled with history's "insinuating constraints"—a need which is his first form of commitment, his response to the pressure that events are putting on literature. Putting such a program into operation really seems to guarantee the coherence of technique and metaphysics which literature and history seem to presuppose. And no one more than Sartre seems to have the dual competence required to do it. This is what explains that in his reviews of Mauriac and other representatives of the French novel Sartre makes this task the ultimate aim and sign of worth of the contemporary writer, and that he feels that he is the one who has been chosen to carry it out. The fact that he conceives of *The Roads to Freedom* during the time he is finishing "The Childhood of a Leader" is thus no mere chronological coincidence. The "conversion" to history which began with this story of a liberty which failed henceforth requires that Sartre "oppose construction to demolition and a reason for living to the nausea of existing."[80]

To understand the new intention we can see in *The Roads to Freedom*, therefore, we must consider the ideological development taking place in the field. But that is not enough. There is another, parallel development which surely counts in this new turn, this "veritable resurrection from nausea to ardor"[81] expressed by the contrast between Roquentin and the new heroes Sartre projects: his journey from the difficult years in Le Havre, that concentrate of the as-yet-unexorcised horrors of being an obscure provincial teacher, to the first flatterings of recognition heightened by the knowledge that his years of exile to the provinces are over. "And then, at that precise moment, when I was at the nadir—so miserable that on several occasions I contemplated death with indifference; feeling old, fallen, finished; convinced, through a misunderstanding, that *Nausea* had been rejected by the *N.R.F.*, I met T., I got a teaching post in Paris. All of a sudden I felt full of a tremendous, intense youthfulness; I was happy and found my life beautiful."[82]

When *Nausea* comes out, it arouses the interest and admiration of almost all the influential critics. To this is added the esteem of prestigious peers such as Paulhan and Gide,[83] the imminent publication of the stories collected in *The Wall*, and the image and reflections fed by Sartre's intense critical activity.

Sartre's new position also helps explain another characteristic of his project: the great technical ambition it shows. We can see in its idea of staging a group of characters and following their ups and downs Sartre's tacit intention to try pens with a long line of illustrious forerunners, above all with *The Counterfeiters*. (And before Sartre did, Nizan too must surely have had this book in mind when he conceived of *La conspiration*: Gide's novel is the first important effort the French novel makes to open up to the modern novel.) In thinking about writing an epic in several volumes which will unfold against the background of "great historical events," Sartre is also competing implicitly with famous undertakings still under way: Jules Romains's *Men of Good Will*, Roger Martin du Gard's *The Thibault*, and Aragon's *Le monde réel*. Although Sartre's hesitant and rebellious petit bourgeois mock heroes, stumbling ahead through their mistakes, stand in sharp contrast to the solemn and often edifying characters of these grand "summae," and remind us instead, through having lucidity as their sole virtue, of Gide's characters, Sartre aims to surpass all previous models technically—including the complex orchestration of different points of view which Gide has achieved—thanks in particular to the importation of American techniques.[84]

# 6. 1939–45. CHAMPION OF A COMMITTED LITERATURE

In completing the first two volumes of *The Roads to Freedom*, Sartre subjects the philosophical message and technical ambition that originally distinguish his project to a different fate. He seems to focus more and more on the first aspect—which he unceasingly elaborates, deepens, and stresses, to the point of making it the main, distinctive thrust of his entire literary enterprise—at the expense of the second. His technical feats, innovative as they surely are in relation to French literature of the time, add nothing new of importance to the objectives he had already mapped out during his apprenticeship. In *The Age of Reason*, he limits himself in substance to applying the "rules" he learned from Hemingway: the "subjective realism" which requires that the author "coincide" without mediation with his characters' consciousness, and in so doing reflect the individual's consciousness of time, making it felt in its entirety "with no shortcuts." And as Michel Contat rightly points out, Sartre's basic technique remains unchanged in *The Reprieve*, although the characters multiply, the narrative rhythm speeds up, the spatiotemporal context expands, the montage technique is perfected, and the kaleidoscopic play of different literary models and registers which began with *Nausea* bursts forth in full frenzy, as if the rule of construction being followed were to exploit to the limit all resources at hand.[85] What is different, and beginning in 1945, strikingly different, is that the ideological functions of communication and prophesying win out over formal considerations. Tackled originally as a literary problem, the expression of historicity becomes a primarily moral problem.

The standard explanation of this development gives decisive weight to Sartre's wartime experience and is based on suggestions he himself makes in his autobiographical writings as to the significance of his mobilization, captivity, life in Occupied Paris, and role in the Resistance (the beginning of commitment for many an intellectual). Yet in order to account for the particular forms that Sartre's "conversion" took, it is also necessary to consider the new changes in his position which occur between 1940 and 1945. They seem to have two principal determinants.

The first is that the logic of his success leads him to move into the foreground of his literary work its content, "philosophy," whose previous role in his success had been important but subordinate to the role played by winning strictly literary marks of legitimacy. Having made himself a reputation in the eyes of the experts, Sartre can now shoot for a wider audience. He addresses his works to a new audience which historical trends have produced, an audience of cultured bourgeois and lycée students and teachers who lack the specialized knowledge required to appreciate the technical aspects of his writing and are inclined to judge it by its message alone.

Nothing better expresses this need to "popularize" his project in order to reach a wider public than the playwright's career Sartre sets out on at this time. He has always thought of theater as less exalted than literature, a minor genre which falls between entertainment and the rostrum that a writer who has achieved consecration and the maturity of his powers can mount to reach a new public. This is the image of theatre which has been passed down to him by a long line of predecessors, from Giraudoux and Gide (the closest ones) to Voltaire and Hugo, remote ancestors he is coming more and more to resemble by the variety of genres in which he writes and by his prophetic attitude.

Sartre's entire theatrical production bears witness to this perspective by its manifestation on a larger scale of tendencies which have already surfaced in the cycle of novels. In starting out in the theater, he does not even consider the possibility of setting out in an experimental, innovative direction like the one which is suggested, for example, by Artaud's position. Definitely shooting for effectiveness, he does not hesitate to use the most predictable gimmicks and theatricalities of just the sort of play that bourgeois audiences want to see. It is significant that Sartre's theatrical debut and principles owe much to a man of the trade, a consummate actor like Dullin. "My dialogue was wordy. Dullin, without reproaching me for it or even advising cuts at first, made me understand by simply talking to the actors that a play should be just the opposite of an orgy of eloquence—that is, the smallest possible number of words cemented irresistibly by an irreversible action and a restless passion."[86] And it is evident that Sartre is concerned from the start with communicating a philosophical way of dealing with problems. *Bariona* and *The Flies* are calls to resist; *No Exit* illustrates the relationship to the Other which is set forth in *Being and Nothingness*.

The other chief determinant of the existential "ethics" which comes to the fore in the novel Sartre is writing and in his plays is his philosophical conversion, between 1939 and 1940, from Husserlian disciple to "Heideggerian zealot." This conversion is a fundamental structural principle, as Sartre's notebooks and letters from the front make clear, and as Sartre himself explicitly recognizes in his entry for February 1, 1940: "This influence [of Heidegger] has in recent times sometimes struck me as providential, since it supervened to teach me authenticity and historicity just at the very moment when war was about to make these notions indispensable to me. If I try to imagine what I'd have made of my thought without those tools, I am gripped by retrospective fear."[87] In Heidegger's thought, which like his own expresses a tragic conjuncture in human history and (in a sublimated form) an ontology which is wholly political and shot through with appeals to the emotions,[88] Sartre finds an extaordinarily apt model for thinking through and articulating what is happening to him. The philosophy we see coming to birth almost from day to day in his letters and notebooks is still much closer to a rewriting of *Being and Time* than to an outline of the ethic implicit in *Being and Nothingness*.

The concepts, language, and themes are very recognizable: man, who is free but "thrown into the human condition," is "responsible" and must "authentically" assume his own historicity, "living and thinking through this war on the horizon," in an epoch whose whole meaning springs from man's "being-for-the-war."[89]

Sartre himself is aware of this: "I have read over my five notebooks and they did not please me as I had anticipated. It seemed to me that much of it was vague and pretty, and that the clearest ideas were regurgitations of Heidegger—in short, that all I had done since September, with the stuff about 'my' war, etc., was to develop in a labored way what Heidegger says about historicity in only ten pages."[90]

It is from this ethic conceived in Heidegger's furrow that Sartre's concept of the social responsibility of the writer springs. It is in his Introduction to *Les Temps Modernes*, in 1945, that Sartre will lay solemn claim to this concept, but it is here that it is actually established, in this encounter of a future "novelist-philosopher" with Heidegger and war, and it already produces a major change in the work in progress. When Sartre reads over the proofs of *The Age of Reason* in April 1940, it seems to him to have an essential flaw: "It's a Husserlian work."

". . . From my current standpoint, I wanted my novel to give the feeling that we are living in a fundamentally important era. . . . But in the first volume, none of that comes through—and that's sad. This is not the result of any technical shortcomings, but solely of my being so fouled up when the war broke out. It is a Husserlian work, and that's a bit disgusting when one has become a Heideggerian zealot. My novel also disgusts me a bit. I'll try to put as much of this as I can into Mathieu's monologue, which I have to rewrite, but I'm afraid that the novel as a whole won't be existential at all. Luckily it's finished. . . . As dissatisfied with it as I am, there's no question of not publishing the factum since I've completed it. And it's funny because I'll let it be published with an essential flaw, whereas I would never let it come out with a technical flaw."[91]

The main concern governing the sequel, *The Reprieve*, and the interpretation which Sartre already begins to suggest in it, is to express this new outlook, to make palpable, in the clouded perceptions of individual consciousnesses, the inseparability of their own destinies and the unfathomable historical totality which is taking shape in them, sustaining them, orienting them, and imbuing them with its meaning: "A hundred million free consciousnesses, each aware of walls, the glowing stump of a cigar, familiar faces, and each constructing its destiny on its own responsibility. And yet each of those consciousnesses, by imperceptible contacts and insensible changes, realizes its existence as a cell in a gigantic and invisible coral. War: everyone is free, and yet the die is cast. It is there, it is everywhere, it is the totality of all my thoughts, of all Hitler's words, of all Gomez's acts; but no one is there to add it up."[92]

Yet to get at the public significance the work acquires when it comes out in 1945, when Sartre first bursts into fame, we have to recall the multitude of signals which combine to form his new and increasingly explicit and systematic image. It is not simply a matter of noting what Sartre and his commentators say and write. We must also consider the dual metamorphosis—the passage to high consecration and to prophecy—which characterizes the course of his wartime development. It becomes impossible to separate the individual outlines of his various activities from the set of distinctions his overall position is accumulating. On the one hand, the specificity of different aspects of his work tends objectively to lessen to the extent that his prophetic aim comes to dominate them all. On the other hand, thanks to his notoriety everything which has to do with him blends together in the image of a commanding public figure. His multiple activities color one another, and they are themselves colored by the lurid tales evoked not only by his works but by the nonconformist lifestyle that the public gets a glimpse of through the scandalizing aura with which his daring themes and language, the hubbub of admiring or indignant critics, and the polemics he stirs up surround him. From now on, what people see behind his novels as behind his plays and his literary and philosophical essays is a public figure who, be he corrupter of the young or moral leader, cannot possibly be ignored.

It is in this context that we can evaluate the growing effectiveness of Sartre's work of defining his position and making it explicit, work, it should be noted, which plays an increasingly important role in his post-1943 activities, when thanks to the theater, both his fame and everything enticing him to take some public stand increase.

In looking for the conditions which explain not just the effect this public discourse has on Sartre's works but the characteristics of the works themselves, we must not overlook the way the Occupation welds literary legitimacy to the cause of the Resistance. Everything in that period encourages a Manichaean ideology which by making political commitment a criterion of aesthetic discrimination turns the mission of condemning writers who collaborated and the mission of expunging them from literature into one single solitary crusade. The first text in which Sartre expresses this orientation in saying that writers who collaborate cannot possibly have talent (*"La littérature, cette liberté"*) appears, significantly, in *les Lettres françaises*, the underground organ of the *Comité national des écrivains*: "Literature is not an innocent and facile lyric capable of accommodating itself to any sort of regime, but by its very nature confronts us with the political problem: to write is to demand that all men be free, and if a work is not the act of a freedom which wants to get itself recognized by other freedoms, it is nothing but infamous gossip."[93]

Sartre's subordination of literary success to moral worth becomes increasingly clear. In a December 1944 interview, he goes so far as to say: "My main interest now is what it has always been—ethics. . . . I have scarcely been concerned with the beautiful. When I write a book I don't want people to say it's beautiful; I want them to say it exists. . . . What is important is to tell about what exists."[94] And in the only interview Sartre granted at the time the first two volumes of *The Roads to Freedom* came out, he speaks exclusively of the novel's philosophical and moral content.[95]

In this process of self-interpretation, the Introduction to *Les Temps Modernes*, the review Sartre starts in 1945, deserves special attention. Sartre is not content with simply proclaiming that literature has a moral and political function; he proudly stresses the point that such a conception of literature constitutes a radical break with the entire literary tradition, and he claims that he is forcing others to recognize that it is the only legitmate conception, the point of view from which the past must be reread and (harshly) judged. Voltaire, Zola, and the Gide of *Voyage to the Congo* (the only ones he does not condemn) are the rare forerunners in whom he sees himself, the prefigurations of a model he alone has been able to perfect, because he alone is able to give it its true basis.

As a matter of fact, Sartre's revolution is less radical than he makes it seem: he never discusses the autonomy of literature.[96] But his insistence on art's social function is already an unforgivable heresy in a field in which the dominant conception of art has always been (as Gide puts it in his *Pretexts*) that "it must be sufficient unto itself, an end unto itself, and its own best argument for its existence." Thus Sartre's Introduction is a spectacular show of strength whose language reveals a typical pretender's manifesto. With the confidence of his accumulated titles, Sartre claims that his position is not only novel but the best. But this incisive gesture cuts two ways. Although it is essential that the author establish his own image of his project, in so doing he rigidifies it and inhibits its subsequent development. A lasting eclipse of Sartre's fame will be necessary before his image of himself as champion of committed literature can be questioned, and the aspects of his writing which make possible today's different ways of reading it can be discovered and evaluated.

# CHAPTER 3
# Philosophical Legitimacy

## 1. THE REDEFINITION OF EXCELLENCE IN FRENCH PHILOSOPHY TOWARD 1930

"In 1925, while I was studying at the Sorbonne, whose traditional teaching was steeped in Kant, the new dominant philosophy was Bergson's."[1] This is how Jean Hyppolite, a contemporary of Sartre's who enrolled one year after he did, defined the ruling philosophy of their university days. And there is no denying that Bergson and Brunschvicg, a neo-Kantian to whom Hyppolite's recollection alludes, are the two most prestigious French philosophical figures of the day. The former is a worldly, charismatic hero presiding at the Collège de France. The latter is the undisputed eminence of academic philosophy, the founder of the *Revue de métaphysique et de morale* (the most authoritative academic organ of the day), a member of the Académie, and the leading arbiter of the Societé française de philosophie and other governing bodies (chairs, special series at publishing houses, national and international meetings) which hold the power to consecrate.

These two different embodiments of philosophical excellence have one essential trait in common: their philosophies are philosophies of the subject—philosophies of knowledge or philosophies of mind—which are at bottom the sort of spiritualist philosophy that dominates the entire French philosophical tradition. Sartre's generation confronts "the primacy of the spiritual"[2] as an objective condition of its philosophical existence, an unstated assumption orienting its way of thinking even when it seems to be thinking in direct opposition to its teachers. Consider, for example, Georges Politzer amd Nizan. By the end of the twenties they are beginning to attack their professors in the name of Marx,[3] but they use the language and the arguments these same professors have taught them. To legitimate Marxism, the first thing they

59

have to show is that it upholds human freedom and the human spirit. No one has evoked this primacy of the spiritual better than Sartre himself has in the famous pages of his *Search for a Method* in which he depicts the inescapable "idealism" of his youth.[4] This is the attitude which emerges from all the works of this era as one of its basic coordinates.[5]

The persistence of this tradition in France cannot be explained by an academic tendency toward cultural lag. It must be understood in terms of a culture which is organized in such a way as to make use of powerful institutions to uphold in the highest degree the prestige and independent status of its spiritual experts. This independent status in turn inclines professional thinkers to underestimate the importance of the material determinants of existence, the body, and society (as the evident primacy of spiritualism in the history of philosophy shows). In short, the defense of human freedom and the human spirit is philosophy's point of honor in its rivalry with other disciplines.

There is no doubt that the rise of science dangerously threatens philosophy's prestige and very reason for being. Not just the natural sciences, whose independence and progress increasingly undermine philosophy's ancient pretension to oversee the conditions and consequences of knowledge: since the turn of the century, the human sciences, especially sociology and psychology, compete with philosophy on its own grounds. Furthermore, as departments of the school of liberal arts, they challenge philosophy's traditional power as it is measured by numbers of chairs, places on university committees, and career opportunities.

In the thirties, it is true, sociology may seem to have lost face as a rival. From the time of Durkheim's death, its school has progressively lost ground until it leads a shadowy existence shrouded by negative prejudices which can only discourage new students from following it as their calling.[6] The work of Granet, Simiand, and Halbwachs is ignored. C. Bouglé, the head of the sociology department at the Ecole normale, is cut off from the rest of the school,[7] and few students take his courses.[8] As for ethnology, it is developing in positions which are barely institutionalized, marginal, or even alien in respect to the academic field: positions centering in Mauss—at the Ecole pratique des hautes études— and in Paul Rivet, head of the Musée ethnographique. This marginal position undoubtedly helps make the work of Durkheim's followers more fruitful than that of the historicosociological branch of ethnography established in the liberal arts faculty, but it also helps turn Ecole normale students away from a discipline which would be a step down in relation to the prestige and opportunities for advancement the University offers its most brilliant sons. The disciples of Mauss and Rivet are chiefly drawn instead from the period's most unsettled, unconventional literary avant-gardes in Surrealist and Collège de sociologie circles.[9]

The science which becomes a formidable competitor of philosophy at this time is psychology: less the henceforth outdated experimental psychology of Dumas than behaviorist psychology, Gestalt psychology, and above all psychoanalysis. We can see a sign of philosophy's reaction, in an effort to win back lost ground, in the direction taken by Sartre's generation itself, whose promising young philosophers, such as Sartre, Merleau-Ponty, and Politzer, begin their philosophical thinking with psychology. The special interest psychoanalysis arouses is shown by a series of works which refer expressly to Freudian ideas: in addition to Politzer's *Critique des fondements de la psychologie* (1928), there is Bachelard's psychoanalysis of the elements and Dalbiez's book, *La méthode psychoanalytique et la doctrine freudienne* (1936), which preserves Freud's method in rejecting his doctrine, an approach similar to the one Sartre will adopt under the influence of the same need to reestablish philosophy's theoretical superiority to science.

Although Marxism is still far from being the main concern of these philosophies of mind, it does confront them with a problem they can no longer ignore. The already cited pages of *Search for a Method* set forth in a most plausible fashion the conditions which define the problem for Sartre and his comrades. It is not Marx's writings, almost unknown then among the French intelligentsia, which make Marxism important; it is, in Sartre's famous words, "the *reality* of Marxism," the "heavy presence of . . . the masses of workers" who see it as their doctrine, "the Proletariat as the incarnation and vehicle of an idea." It is a society in which, with the Popular Front, Marxist organizations suddenly manifest their importance. It is the growing attractiveness for intellectuals of these forces which seem to be history's new motor.

Around 1930, there are many signs that the definition of philosophical legitimacy embodied in Bergson and Brunschvicg is threatened. The works by which these two seek almost simultaneously to reestablish their dominance—*Two Sources of Morality and Religion* (1932) and *The Ages of Intelligence* (1934), respectively—seem already outdated as soon as they appear. In a French culture permeated by Marx and Freud, any thinking which has persisted in ignoring both is immediately dated pre-Marxist and pre-Freudian. It is further dated by the sense of a historic break with the past and uncertainty about the future that is spreading throughout France and other countries—Germany, Spain—which are being sorely tried by economic and political crises. To the "spirit of 1930," the optimistic philosophies of "creative evolution" and "the progress of consciousness in Western philosophy," as well as their characteristic ways of speaking and thinking, are so much wreckage from the past. The demand for a more "concrete" way of thinking which will make room for individual and collective experience of conflict and anguish seems to characterize all that Sartre's generation sees and does. As is often the case in generational conflict, the young's rejection of the old is not unrelated to their desire to succeed, any more than their "tragic sense of life"[10] is unrelated to a feeling of personal insecurity of young people who are still unknown. But this mood of the younger generation is reinforced and legitimized by its reflection in the mood of the whole era and, above all, in the new existential and phenomenological philosophies which have all it takes to embody the new legitimacy. They are the same old spiritualist philosophies that the field's rigid tradition has always demanded, but for France they are new, decked out with the prestige of their German philosophical origins, and well suited to give lofty expression to the new pathos of everyday life. Their way of understanding philosophy as a "concrete," preconceptual comprehension of "things themselves" also makes them seem to be the very means of overcoming the academic segregation of philosophy that the younger generation is looking for: a total philosophy which can lay claim to dominion over all other realms of intellect because it comprehends all truths and reconciles literature, science, and common sense.

It is in its encounter with this new German thinking that French Existentialism takes shape: its early forms all flow directly from this source. Slowly, in a hit-or-miss fashion, Frenchmen begin to read, to write about, and to translate works of the new German thinkers and their most important predecessors, Kierkegaard and Heidegger, previously unknown in France. From now on, furthermore, the apprenticeship of newly licensed philosophers is not complete without a trip to Germany to study Husserl, Scheler, and Heidegger. And a decisive role in their initiation to the philosophical profession is played by the lecture courses which are now being offered by important émigrés, whose influence in Parisian avant-garde circles is extraordinary. Kojève's famous course on Hegel is by no means the unique event, the absolute origin, which numerous reconstructions of those days have made it out to be.[11] It rises from a broader stream of exotic imports brought by the primarily Russian and German political exiles who flood Paris between the Russian Revolution and the Second World War.

We may begin with the case of Bernard Groethuysen, who reached Paris before World War I. Having become the "*éminence grise* of the *N.R.F.*, Paulhan's adviser, Gide's close friend and the one who piques his curiosity about the Soviet experiment,"[12] Groethuysen makes use of this influence he has gained, and of the intellectual openness which his many-sided and truly European training has no doubt helped give him, to play a key role in putting ideas from abroad in circulation in France. He was a friend of Scheler's and an admirer of Heidegger and Dilthey. A Communist supporter and expert on the thought of Marx, he wrote "Hegel's Conception of the State and German Political Philosophy" in 1924,[13] when Hegel was almost unknown in France. His *Introduction à la pensée allemande depuis Nietzsche* was one of the first works to familiarize France with contemporary German thought. He was one of the first to interest *N.R.F.* circles in Kafka, in Freud ("about whom he was careful to speak with the ironic grace which was customary in such circles"[14]), and in Weber. ("At this time the *N.R.F.* people scorned sociology. Groethuysen made it seem a discipline which, although queer, was nevertheless worthy of interest."[15]) And he himself wrote an original sociological study, *Les origines de l'esprit bourgeois en France*. It can be said of Groethuysen that he brought together in an astonishing symbiosis all the main stimuli to which the young generation of intellectuals responded. At least in this sense, if not in a strict sense, Jean Wahl is right in saying, "[He] launched . . . the career of Sartre as well as of many others."[16]

Certain Russian émigrés—the best known being Berdiaev and Chestov—who had fled what seemed to them a cataclysm for the whole of Western civilization provide another important link. Berdiaev's *Un nouveau Moyen Age* (1926) attracts a large following in certain intellectual circles. He helps crystallize in France, where the Russian Revolution makes itself felt somewhat later than in other countries, the apocalyptic, anguished mood of the "crisis culture" which has become widespread in Europe between the two wars, and which existentialism in some ways expresses. Furthermore, the Franco-Russian Studio, one of whose leading lights was Berdiaev, is one of the first inner circles to revive Kierkegaard, a basic source of the new existential thinking.

The role played by the émigré philosophers at *Recherches philosophiques*, a journal which is an essential link between French existentialism and its immediate antecedents, must also be stressed. The journal's founder, Alexandre Koyré, was Husserl's student. And although Kojève, with his protoexistentialist reading of Hegel, was not the sole inventor of a line which was to shape Hegel interpretation in France for a long time to come, he nevertheless heralds the return to Hegel which Dilthey initiated in Germany at the turn of the century. What this rediscovery of Hegel stresses is not his system but his dramatic sense of existence and history, preferring not his *Logic* but his *Phenomenology of Mind* and the youthful works which preceded it (and which had been published by Nohl in 1907). The fact that these mediators had been brought up on the new German philosophy and bred to its approach and favorite themes accounts for the precision with which *Recherches philosophiques* lines up with the dominant tendencies on the other side of the Rhine, both in terms of the forerunners it offers and discloses (in addition to the young Hegel, Kierkegaard, Husserl, and Heidegger) and the investigations it undertakes and welcomes in its pages. It is here that the works of Jean Wahl which have such repercussions for Sartre and his comrades first appear: *Les malheurs de la conscience dans la "Phénoménologie de l'esprit" de Hegel* (1929), *Towards the Concrete* (1932), and *Etudes kierkegaardiennes* (1938).

The effects of this emigré influence can also be seen in the case of Gabriel Marcel, the other Frenchman who (with his 1928 *Metaphysical Journal*) ushers in a French existentialism. In addition to writing for *Recherches philosophiques*, he is a member of the Berdiaev circle. And this collective labor rooted in an imported train of thought is an important basis for Sartre's thinking, as is suggested by the fact that *The Transcendence of the Ego*, that first sketch of Sartre's basic themes, is published in *Recherches philosophiques*.

We can even catch a glimpse of an early contact with recent German thinking in the academic theses of Lévinas (1930)[17] and Elbert (1931),[18] the first French works about Husserl (which explains the big jump in discovering phenomenology that these two had on Sartre himself: Lévinas' work is published two years before a conversation with Aron arouses Sartre's interest in Husserl, and is the first source Sartre turns to while he is waiting to go to Berlin[19]). Lévinas teaches at Strasbourg's school of liberal arts, and Elbert at Nancy's, both universities at which phenomenology has probably become influential through the new German theology inspired by Husserl and introduced at Strasbourg by professors in the school of Protestant theology. Another new direction in German theology, that of Barth, which is basic to German existentialism and the rediscovery of Kierkegaard, explains why Protestant theologians (Denis de Rougemont, in *Hic et nunc*) are from 1932 on the first professors in France to set forth Kierkegaard's thinking in a systematic way along with Barth's. And the study sessions which the Thomist Society devotes to phenomenology in 1932[20] are a reply to the competition that this new German Protestant theology offers.

The other episodes so often cited as what set French existentialism going are also encounters with German philosophy. Husserl's lectures at the Sorbonne in 1929, his first formulation of *Cartesian Meditations*. The public lectures, also given at the Sorbonne (in 1928, 1929, and 1930), by another émigré, Gurvitch, who is also the author of the book,

*Tendances actuelles de la philosophie allemande* (1930), which Jean Wahl considers "the first authoritative book on German philosophy, particularly phenomenology."[21] And finally, the translations of German philosophy: Sartre, for example, first encountered Jaspers in 1927 when he and Nizan were revising a translation of *General Psychopathology*.

It is important to stress these collective labors, for they show that French existentialism is a second-order thinking whose concerns, language, and choice of predecessors are deeply influenced by foreign works.

These new tendencies in French philosophy are so marked that by 1933 a well-placed observer like Nizan can already notice them and see in them the new direction which will probably replace the "official philosophy": "The younger generation of the bourgeoisie is standing up to its fossil fathers. It would be naive to think that this is making them any less bourgeois. But bourgeois sons are shaking their ancestral tree. They are on the scene; they want to 'live' and to know that they count for something. Their fathers have already lived long enough to make plain all the things they have not been able to do. The time has come for the young to stand guard against the proletarians: if they do not reach their posts in time, everything will crumble. They are ready with their new politics, their economics, and their moralities. They want to relieve the old guard—if need be, violently. . . . Martin Heidegger's philosophy can provide theoretical justification for a fascist doctrine. . . . The philosophy of anguish and the catharsis of nothingness are infiltrating France; J. Wahl is introducing Kierkegaardian meditations into French thinking. The philosophical journals themselves are beginning to discover Phenomenology. Perhaps tomorrow these new themes will provide the skillful arguments which official philosophy cannot readily produce."[22]

All evidence confirms the growing legitimacy of the new doctrines. To begin with, an undertaking like *Recherches philosophiques* which—and this is important—has the support of Sorbonne professors. And then the direction taken by other philosophers (Le Senne, Lavelle) who, like Jean Wahl, belong to the unfortunate generation between Bergson and Sartre who were born between 1880 and 1890 and called up and cut down during World War I. They barely manage to lure a certain audience away from the preceding generation when the following generation is ready to move beyond them. Even their "philosophy of mind" is protoexistentialist in its approach, if not in its sources and its language. As for Sartre's generation, the surest signs of its alignment with the new thinking are the affinities to it which are evident in those who are most clearly moving away from it. The most critical group, at the *Revue marxiste*, manifest a consensus of their time in reading Marx in a way which, in spite of the fact that his youthful works are still unknown, emphasizes the humanist and utopian Marx, the theorist of alienation and its revolutionary transcendence. Even students of Brunschvicg like Aron, Cavaillès, and Canguilhem, who are clearly headed in different directions, are to a certain extent caught up in the spreading fad for German thinking. *Introduction to the Philosophy of History*, the doctoral thesis with which Aron makes his entry on scene in 1938, conceives of history as having no objective rhyme nor reason, but only the meaning and rational order that man gives it through his decisions, a view which today seems astonishing in the theorist of the end of ideology. In his posthumous book, *Sur la logique et la théorie de la science* (1947), Cavaillès reflects on the relationships between logical objectivity and Husserl's transcendental subjectivity. Canguilhem investigates teleology and mechanistic determinism in biological theory. And another brilliant member of Sartre's class, Lagache, long tries to reconcile Freud and the new philosophies of mind.

This way of thinking seems to be the natural ground on which the most promising recruits to the new philosophical field and the avant-gardes of the literary field can meet and exchange ideas. The makeup of Kojève's audiences clearly shows this. Recalling Kojève's course, Queneau spills out pell mell as its most faithful attendants Koyré and another exile, Eric Weil, Doctor Jacques Lacan, still unknown, future Ecole normale students such as Aron, Merleau-Ponty, and Fessard, and finally Surrealists and surrealizers: in addition to Queneau himself, Breton, Klossowski, and Bataille.[23]

# 2. SARTRE'S TITLES

Having grown up in the esoteric world in which the dominant philosophy is being elaborated; having been in contact with its institutions, its concerns, and its most important agents; and having been imbued with its expectations and endowed with the dispositions needed to fulfill them, Sartre is able from the start to head spontaneously toward a position which could have been expressly designed to combine all the aspects and perform all the functions that characterize the new legitimacy. This is surely no conscious project, but it is a "program" which objectively governs the young Sartre's philosophy: it accounts for the extraordinary coherence it appears to have.

## 2.1 *A spiritualist* malgré lui

Although Sartre always meant to make a clean break with spiritualism, his position is recognizably a form of it, in the broad sense of tending to make consciousness the highest good, if not the sole reality. To begin with, consciousness, its activities, and its ontological status are the guiding thread of the whole first phase of his thinking, whose successive topics are imagination, the transcendent power of consciousness, emotion, and intentionality. Sartre lays the groundwork for *Being and Nothingness*, which is itself an ontology of consciousness-in-the-world, in a systematic work of phenomenological psychology.[24] In this work he gives a privileged position to the freedom and creative power to transcend which are the prerogatives of consciousness and prove its irreducible difference from, and superiority to, "physical facts." This difference and superiority are implicit in the very polar opposition which structures Sartre's ontology. Seven hundred pages of ever-changing epiphanies illustrate the conflict between consciousness and "things." It is true that the "negative" spirit of the times and the logical—and terminological—differences by which Sartre distinguishes himself from his predecessors result in an evident reversal of signs: consciousness is baptized "Nothingness" and the world "Being." But this transparent mask does not conceal the fact that "Nothingness" is the positive pole, the freedom which "gives birth to" meaning and value, and that Being is "facticity," passivity, meaninglessness, a threat. Sartre reserves a negative, sometimes openly phobic description for everything "material" or "biological."

In his works on imagination, the main thing Sartre wants to show is that it is imagining consciousness (which is radically different from perceptual consciousness of "things") that alone produces images, and in so doing reveals the power to transcend which constitutes its greatness in the world.[25] But Sartre also reveals his own deep-seated feeling of repulsion for the "world" when he goes so far as to say: "To posit an image is to construct an object on the fringe of the whole of reality, which means therefore to hold the real at a distance, to free oneself from it, in a word to deny it."[26] "When the imaginary is not posited as a fact, the surpassing and the nullifying of the [existent] are swallowed up in the [existent]; the surpassing and the freedom *are there* but are not revealed; the person is crushed in the world, run through by the real, he is closest to the thing."[27]

Sartre's essay on the emotions is dominated by the same concern to show that psychological phenomena have particular characteristics of their own which cannot be reduced to empirically observed ones. And in *The Transcendence of the Ego*, the reason why he makes consciousness' unreflected activity its supreme function is that he considers such activity to be the loftiest expression of the subject's power to create: "Thus each instant of our conscious life reveals to us a creation *ex nihilo*. Not a new *arrangement*, but a new existence. . . . At this level man has the impression of ceaselessly escaping from himself, of overflowing himself, of being surprised by riches which are always unexpected."[28]

Sartre's gut feeling of repugnance for the body, which makes spiritualism an unbeatable option for him—less an intellectual position than a deep-seated disposition—becomes strikingly evident in *Being and Nothingness*, where it constantly surfaces and finally bursts forth in the concluding chapter's famous analysis of the "slimy" and the "hole."

Sartre's spiritualism gives him the essential characteristic required of all true heirs to the great tradition of French philosophy. But in order to understand the particular success his enterprise has in meeting this general requirement, we must consider the specific form his spiritualism takes. It is as if the main characteristics of his position were fashioned so as to meet all the current requirements for being a legitimate heir. Thus he aims a main thrust of his efforts at the formerly dominant thinkers he must dethrone: more against Brunschvicg's philosophy of knowledge and Dumas' experimental psychology than against Bergson. For since the latter has retired long ago from teaching and public life, he is a far less important target for this young *agrégé* who is not slated to abandon his orientation toward a university career until the Liberation. Since Sartre's first philosophical writings are psychological, it is natural that he should also move to the attack against behaviorism, Gestalt psychology, and above all psychoanalysis—the imported doctrines competing with philosophy. Nor can he ignore the questions of society and history raised by Marxism. Yet the most difficult and imposing task which confronts the new champion of French philosophy is to challenge the new German philosophy.

## 2.2 *Sartre's critique of philosophies of knowledge and empirical psychologies*

Phenomenology offers Sartre a ready-made weapon for his attack on an epistemology which reduces philosophy to a reflection on scientific knowledge and on a psychology which claims to be an empirical science (both of which, for a man for whom philosophy is the queen of the sciences, are ways of subordinating philosophy to science), for phenomenology was developed to meet similar needs. Sartre's own development of a phenomenological counterpoint to neo-Kantian epistemology and empirical psychologies constitutes one of the main thrusts of the philosophical texts he writes at this time.

The foremost reason for Sartre's enthusiasm for Husserl in the aforementioned article on the concept of intentionality is that this concept liberates thinking from the "digestive philosophy" which "[after] a hundred years of academicism" still reduces the problem of the relationships between consciousness and the world to an assimilation "of things to ideas, of ideas by ideas, of minds by minds." "Against the digestive philosophy of empirico-criticism, of neo-Kantianism, against all, 'psychologism,' Husserl persistently affirmed that one cannot dissolve things in consciousness" (p. 1 of the Joseph P. Fell translation). In his *War Diaries*, Sartre recognizes the extent to which his early works depended on Husserl: "It took me four years to exhaust Husserl. I wrote a whole book (apart from the final chapters) under his inspiration: *[The Psychology of Imagination]*. Against him, granted—but just insofar as a disciple can write against his master. I also wrote an article against him: *[The Transcendence of the Ego: an Existentialist Theory of Consciousness].*"[29]

Sartre's essays on imagination and emotion could be considered phenomenological refutations of empirical psychological analyses of the same subjects. Thus the aim of *The Psychology of Imagination* is to show that, contrary to "the naive metaphysics of images" which makes "[the] image . . . into a copy of the thing, existing as a thing,"[30] "[only] a phenomenology of consciousness and Being was capable of taking up the problem of imagination from scratch and making an *existential* distinction between the 'imaged' and the perceived object."[31]

These same targets also explain the tendency to devaluate conceptual reasoning and the empirical which is apparent from the very first in Sartre's philosophical writings. One of the traditional weapons philosophy uses against the sciences—above all in reference to psychological phenomena—is to claim that philosophy has its own peculiar kind of understanding which is different from scientific knowledge and superior to it in its adequation to its object and in its consciousness of its own ontological foundations. Like "intuition" in Bergson's thinking, phenomenological "comprehension" in Sartre's thinking becomes the only form of understanding which can grasp the total human being in the activity of consciousness. But Sartre goes farther than Bergson: Bergson too insisted on the limitations of scientific knowledge, but he did not contrast the mere "probability" of scientific hypotheses to the "certainty" of philosophy's a priori intuitions, nor did he lump together in the category of the "probable" scientific theories based on experimental investigations and philosophical conclusions arrived at through the philosopher's observation of his own states of consciousness.

This downgrading of reflection to a "secondary" mode of consciousness which is bound to fail in its efforts to conceptualize the concrete stream of unreflected conscious life that only "comprehension" can grasp is already foreshadowed in *The Transcendence of the Ego*, where it is directed openly at Kantian philosophies of knowledge, and is also the starting point of a critique of Husserl's tendency to "weight down" consciousness with a transcendental ego.

In *The Emotions: Outline of a Theory* and *The Psychology of Imagination*, it is the empirical which is downgraded, since what Sartre is attacking in these works is all forms of empirical psychology: "[Psychology], insofar as it claims to be a science, can furnish only a sum of miscellaneous facts, most of which have no connection with the others," we read in Sartre's essay on the emotions.[32] And though Sartre says that "the facticity of human existence" makes the "a priori intuition" of "pure phenomenology" inadequate, and "necessitates systematic recourse to the empirical," the "empirical" he takes into account is not that of experimental psychology; it is the product of the new version of traditional introspective psychology which phenomenology basically offers. This facticity of human existence, furthermore, "in all likelihood, will prevent psychological regression and phenomenological progression from ever coming together"[33]: in comparison to the philosopher's "pure" intuition of essence, empirical knowledge will always be alien and inferior. And the same distinction recurs in *The Psychology of Imagination*, even justifying the book's division into two sections: "The Certain" (the philosopher's "immediate" certainty) and "The Probable" (the fruit of his observations).

In *Being and Nothingness*, there is an even more explicit affirmation of the impotence of "intellectualist analysis" and the "illusoriness" of idealist gnoseology: ". . . by a radical reversal of the idealist position, knowledge is reabsorbed into being. It is neither an attribute nor a function nor an accident of being; but *there is* only being. From this point of view it appears necessary to abandon the idealist position entirely, and in particular it becomes possible to hold that the relation of the For-itself to the In-itself is a fundamental ontological relation . . . *representation*, as a psychic event, is a pure invention of philosophers" (216–17).

In contrast to the "impure" reflection of empirical psychologies, Sartre distinguishes a "pure" reflexive consciousness which alone "can discover the For-itself reflected-on in its reality" (163), for "[its] knowledge is a totality; it is a lightning intuition without relief, without point of departure, and without point of arrival. Everything is given at once in a sort of absolute proximity" (155). Whereas it is a "shadow of being, *[a]* necessary and constant correlate of impure reflection that the psychologist studies under the name of *psychic fact*" (161).

"There is only intuitive knowledge" (172), Sartre reaches the point of writing in the chapter he devotes to knowledge. He repeats the language and arguments that twentieth-century philosophy keeps using to assert its superiority to science. The problems of science, its theoretical disagreements, the analyses of Poincaré (134–35), de Broglie, Heisenberg, and Einstein (307–308) which cast doubt on the very concepts of absolute knowledge and physical determinism are for Sartre only pretexts for proclaiming the uncertainty of the results of scientific investigation, if not, like Husserl, "the crisis of the sciences" themselves.

## 2.3 *The "refutation" of psychoanalysis*

*The Emotions: Outline of a Theory* already gives psychoanalysis a special place among the rival psychologies that Sartre aims to refute. One sentence in particular shows how much he is preoccupied with this psychology which he cannot simply dismiss as vulgar "scientism": "The truth is that what makes an exhaustive refutation of psychoanalysis difficult is that the psychoanalyst does not consider signification as being conferred on consciousness from without. For him there is always an internal analogy between the conscious fact and the desire which it expresses, since the *conscious fact symbolizes with the complex which is expressed.*"[34] We already see here a first sketch of the tactic Sartre will develop more fully in *Being and Nothingness:* grant that certain consequences of certain insights are justified, but only if they are detached from their psychological theory, which you then proceed to show is based on a "causalism" that reduces consciousness to a "thing." But it is in his ontology that we can see much more clearly how important it is for him to win a showdown with Freud. His "existential psychoanalysis" reveals an elaborate counterpoint whose basic strategy is typical of the one philosophy employs in its relationship to competing positions. As Bergson did in respect to biology, Sartre opposes psychoanalysis with a "transcendence" which enables him to salvage its accomplishments and merits while "correcting" it on the level of principles.

"What ontology can teach psychoanalysis is first of all the *true* origin of the meanings of things and their *true* relation to human reality. Ontology alone in fact can take its place on the plane of transcendence and from a single viewpoint apprehend being-in-the-world with its two terms, because ontology alone has its place originally in the perspective of the *cogito*" (*B.N.*, 603).[35]

The contrasts which structure the book's discourse show the tension between Sartre's incorporation and rejection of Freud: the contrast and tension between Freud's "empiricist," "thinglike," and "determinist" psychoanalysis and a psychoanalysis which is "conscious of its principles" and safeguards the freedom and singularity of the individual; between Freud's "unconscious" and "libido" and Sartre's "bad faith" and "choice."

"The Childhood of a Leader," which Sartre wrote in 1938, can be seen as not just a superficial parody of psychoanalysis but a sort of practical verification of the origins of this Sartrean counterpsychoanalysis. It is already clear that the Freudian model dominates Sartre's thinking. His emphases on childhood, dreams, relationships with parents, and sexuality all make Lucien's story a countercase which demands to be interpreted as the reconstruction of the successive choices in bad faith through which "a member of the ruling class" becomes a "leader" and "*salaud.*"

Of course Sartre grants that the "existential psychoanalysis" he is thinking about has much in common with Freudian psychoanalysis (*B.N.*, 569–71). But he treats Freud's contribution as a "first outline" for an ontologically based psychoanalysis which "has not yet found its Freud" (575). Tacitly assuming that it is his job to provide this new psychoanalysis, Sartre sets forth the a priori conditions it will have to meet. His formulation of these conditions makes sizable concessions to the empirical and conceptual knowledge he has elsewhere proclaimed to be illusory: "The *goal* of psychoanalysis is to *decipher* the empirical behavior patterns of man; that is to bring out in the open the revelations which each one of them contains and to fix them conceptually. Its *point of departure* is *experience*. . ." (568). Yet Sartre steers clear of Freud's "empirical psychoanalysis" and presents a summary, mechanistic view of it which he can easily refute. If the unconscious is defined as "a censor, conceived as a line of demarcation with customs, passport division, currency control, etc." (50), then it is hard to deny "the language and the materialistic mythology of psychoanalysis" (52). Similarly, Sartre need only state that "in spite of everything," the acts of the subject are for Freud "only a result of the past" (458) to reduce the Freudian concept of psychological life to a "vertical determinism" (458ff), in contrast to the heroic image of human freedom which his ontology offers. He need only speak of an "environment [which] acts mechanically" (572) or, concerning the concept of the libido, of a "psycho-biological residue"

(571) to convince us of the superiority of a theory which makes "choice" the basis of behavior.

The standards Sartre defends against the threat of Freud are in fact the traditional standards philosophy upholds in its opposition to science. In Kantian fashion, he contrasts causal explanation to explanation in terms of *ends*, the only kind, he says, that is capable of accounting for human conduct (477). He reproaches science's "abstract and general laws" for their inability to account for the individual in his concrete and irreplaceable singularity (557ff).

Understanding the weight psychoanalysis in general has for Sartre enables us to understand the particular pains he takes to refute Bachelard's psychoanalysis. In this case too, it is by appealing to principles that Sartre is able to stigmatize Bachelard's "psychoanalysis of things" as merely empirical, based on experimental results or postulates instead of on ontology. Sartre's verdict concerning Bachelard ("his psychoanalysis seems more sure of its method than of its principles" [602]) makes use of the same formula he used on Freud (574–75). But here his tone becomes condescending. Bachelard poses no threat as a rival: this former Post Office employee from Bar-sur-Aube—a self-taught philosopher who was over fifty when in 1940 he won a chair at the Sorbonne with works which were original but were completely blocked off from the main philosophical currents of the time and destined to win attention and recognition only after the War—is far from having the legitimate academic and philosophical profile Sartre has.

". . .Thus M. Bachelard's study of water, which abounds in *ingenious and profound* insights, will be for us a *set* of suggestions, a *precious collection of materials* which should now be utilized by a psychoanalysis which is aware of its own principles" (603ff—my italics). Beneath this damning with faint praise we see Sartre's characteristic reduction of empirical psychology to the positivistic "labors of a collector" which cannot "[discover] the meaning of that synthetic totality which one calls world," but can "furnish only a sum of miscellaneous facts."[36]

We need only think of the rigid distinction which Sartre's philosophy of consciousness and freedom makes between human reality and "things" to understand why he is so dead set on attacking the concept of "material imagination" which Bachelard uses to suggest that the meanings we give to things are unconscious projections (*B.N.*, 600ff). For a man who has devoted his first philosophical work to insisting on the difference between perceiving and imagining, between representing things and transcending them, such a "contamination" is unbearable.

This concern with opposing Bachelard accounts for a surprising theme in a philosopher who makes the subject the source of meaning and value:

"psychoanalysis will not look for images but rather will seek to explain the meaning which really belongs to things. . . . [It is a matter of] applying not *to the subject* but to things a method of objective interpretation which does not suppose any previous reference to the subject" (600).

The examples Sartre chooses to illustrate this "method of objective interpretation" of the "objective meaning of things" enables us to show how the phenomenologist, in reviving the ancient philosophical claim to reach "pure" truth by introspection alone, unintentionally opens himself up to taking his subjective view of the world for an "irreducible" and "universal" truth: that is to say, to falling into precisely the Bachelardian projection whose possibility he peremptorily denies. All the examples Sartre gives in his analyses of the "hole" and the "slimy" in the final chapter of *Being and Nothingness* bring out very clearly the network of associations which link his ontological categories to his imagination of the world. In attributing to Being itself all the negative and threatening characteristics which popular imagination attributes to women, Sartre shows that for him Being-in-itself, matter, nature, and the female sex form a single constellation, that "unnameable and unthinkable *residuum*" (482) from which the For-itself-mind-consciousness-virility must ceaselessly struggle to tear itself free. This also explains why one form of being seems especially repugnant to Sartre: that of the "substance in between two states" (607). It is the symbol of a fusion whose horribleness is expressed by the terms Sartre uses to describe it: the For-itself compromises its "primacy," it is "absorbed," "possessed," "held," "trapped," "swallowed," it risks being "diluted," "lost," undergoing the most "horrible" of "metamorphoses"; the "slimy" is "shady," "flaccid," and "docile," but with the "supreme docility of the possessed, the fidelity of a dog who *gives himself* even when one does not want him any longer, and in another sense there is underneath this docility a surreptitious appropriation of the possessor by the possessed." The "slimy" shows that "there exists a poisonous possession." It "absorbs," it "sucks," it "is like a leech sucking me." "Slime is the revenge of the In-itself. A sickly-sweet, feminine revenge." The "slimy offers a horrible image; it is horrible in itself for a consciousness to *become slimy*" (604ff, passim).

## 2.4 *An anti-Marxist philosophy*

The direct allusions to Marxism in *Being and Nothingness* are rare. But the attention of the book pays not so much to Marx's own thinking as to the realities of society, history, class, and revolution which Marx makes us think about can by no means be reduced to these traces. When Sartre's ontology comes down out of the rarified air of "ipseity" to start describing man's relation to the world, one of its main concerns is to reply to "materialism."

To understand Sartre's position, we must recognize the objective ambivalence of its governing intentions. There is a gap between his announced aims and the unconscious attitudes with which he confronts the historical and social dimension of reality. The attitude he means to take was already set forth in the conclusion of *The Transcendence of the Ego:* to show that philosophy has no need of this "absurdity which is metaphysical materialism" to establish "its bases in reality."[37]

Considered as a project which aims to set out from the Cogito and recuperate the world, the ontology of *Being and Nothingness* shows what seems to be a strangely preponderant realist tension. But if we read this apparent monument to the world as an actual ritual exorcism, its monumental scope shows the extent of the concern that the world unceasingly causes Sartre. For him as for the entire spiritualist tradition, the social is at bottom a troublesome reality. Together with the body and matter, it is the negative principle which threatens the transparent purity—the freedom—of consciousness. For the philosopher who sees his role—and worth—as consisting in his strictly individual search for "pure" truth—in his possibility of making himself a disembodied view (*theoria*), without a past or point of view, and of putting the world in parentheses in defiance of all mundane opinion—horror of the social, fed by a gut feeling of repugnance, becomes almost a professional ideology. The body, the past, and society seem to block his path; the historical and social perspective which ties each individual to collective events and social class determinants seems to be off the path. Yet is is Sartre's way of conceiving and carrying out philosophy's mission as a quest for ontological foundations which is actually the supreme form of theoretical illusion: the project of describing the general and absolute modes and conditions of being by deducing them from the irreducible certainties of consciousness as truths which owe nothing to the empirical and are indeed, in strict logic, prior to any observation of phenomena, since they are their basis. *Being and Nothingness* presents itself as a phenomenological description of "essences" and, as this conception of philosophy prescribes, puts the establishment of "principles" ahead of the analysis of the "modes" of empirically existing realities. The impression of realism which certain of its famous examples give is a result of factors which have nothing to do with sociological precision. Sartre's examples are undeniably abstract, and for the most part reduced to a single characteristic: "a woman who has come to her first meeting with a lover," "a homosexual," "a café waiter." The effect of concreteness such examples produce is tied to surreptitious factors: to the sense of transgression which is produced by introducing into ontology subjects such as sex which the philosophical tradition censors, or trivial subjects such as a café waiter's job; to the autobiographical truth Sartre projects into the phenomenological ego of his imaginary instances in lending them a lived intellectual life; and to the air of truth such a representation of social reality can take on in the eyes of an intellectual public already inclined by affinities of habitus and experiencing to perceive the world in the same way.

Sartre's way of talking about the social shows how repulsive it is for him as a reality which, like the body, suggests the power that the ontologically inferior has over its superior (it was for the same reason that Plato identified evil with mixtures). Like physical reality, the temporal and collective dimension of existence is for Sartre an obstacle to be overcome; it is a threat to human freedom and has value only as freedom's necessary condition, freedom being able to exist only in negating it (*B.N.*, 361ff). We can recognize here the attitude which "pure" philosophies par excellence, like Kant's or Maine de Biran's, characteristically adopt in the face of similar obstacles.

This attitude explains the position Sartre adopts in opposition to "what Comte called *materialism*; that is, . . . explaining the higher by the lower" (562). For Sartre, taking account of the conditions and conditionings of existence means holding them at a distance while showing that freedom *always* can and always *should* transcend them (478). For him, the "given" and the "situation" can never condition consciousness. Their meaning is always determined by the subject's choice (*B.N.*, 435ff).

It is as if collective history and the individual past cannot and do not have for Sartre any intrinsic meaning, but only take on meaning in the eyes of someone who is contemplating them: "If human societies are historical, this does not stem simply from the fact that they have a past but from the fact that they reassume the past by making it a *memorial*. . . . [The] historian is himself *historical*; that is, . . . he historicizes himself by illuminating 'history' in the light of his projects and of those of his society. Thus it is necessary to say that the meaning of the social past is perpetually 'in suspense.' " Sartre's horror at all forms of inertia leads him in the end to the most complete subjectivism: "The perpetual historization of the For-itself is the perpetual affirmation of its freedom" (500–501); man has "the permanent possibility of effecting a rupture with [his] own past, of wrenching [himself] away from [his] past . . . so as to be able to confer on it the meaning which it *has* in terms of the project of a meaning which it *does not have"* (436). If it is man who from moment to moment creates and changes the meaning of reality, facts and actions lose all objectivity, and their continuity depends on the subject's voluntary, continuing, yet indefinite choosing and re-choosing of himself as committed to an ongoing project, or on his renouncing his freedom by choosing a way of existing in bad faith which reduces him to, and gives him the permanence of, an object.

What proves that Marxism is the specific target of such affirmations are the special efforts Sartre makes to challenge any objectivist conception of class and history, the crucial aspects of the Marxist philosophy of history. It is not the conditions of existence, Sartre says, which produce class consciousness, but the objectifying look of a "Third": that of the "capitalist" for the proletariat; that of the proletariat, when it revolts, for the capitalist. What determines revolutionary action is not exploitation but an individual awareness on the part of the exploited that revolution is possible. Conceptualized in this way as an aggregate of individual consciousnesses, social class as such can never become a subject except in an illusory way through the individual project of the "leader" who pulls the class along after him, and of the individual class member who follows the leader by *choosing* to "[lose] himself in this object-ness" (422). As Merleau-Ponty will subsequently point out,[38] Sartre can only think about social reality by reducing it to a confrontation between individual consciousnesses, to the war between onlookers that he takes intersubjectivity to be.

"It is not the hard work, the low living standard, or the privations endured which will constitute the oppressed collectivity as a class [: . . .] the primary fact is that the member of the oppressed collectivity . . . apprehends his condition and that of other members of this collectivity as looked-at and thought about by consciousnesses which escape him. The 'master,' the 'feudal lord,' the 'bourgeois,' the 'capitalist' all appear not only as powerful people who command but in addition and above all as *Thirds*; that is, as those who are outside the oppressed community and *for whom* this community exists. It is therefore *for* them and *in their freedom* that the reality of the oppressed class is going to exist. They cause it to be born by their look" (*B.N.*, 420–21).

It is on this basis that Sartre can find in the freedom Descartes attributes to God his own idea of human freedom as a freedom which only its own decisions constrain (608ff); and he praises Descartes for having been able "in an authoritarian age" to articulate, if only as a "divine prerogative," the sole adequate concept of freedom.[39] For a consistent spiritualism, the only alternative to strict voluntarism is strict determinism: "two solutions and only two are possible: either man is wholly determined (which is inadmissible, especially because a determined consciousness—i.e., a consciousness externally motivated—becomes itself pure exteriority and ceases to be consciousness) or else man is wholly free" (*B.N.*, 442).

We need only spell out some of the corollaries of this position to see that objectively it is at odds with Sartre's political choice of solidarity with the oppressed. He says for example that freedom is the "pure and simple negation of the given" (478), a "being-without-support and without-springboard," and consequently, "the project in order to be must be constantly renewed" (480). Or he says: "I choose myself perpetually and can never be merely by virtue of having-been-chosen; otherwise I should fall into the pure and simple existence of the in-itself" (ibid.). Or again: " 'to be free' " means " 'by oneself to determine oneself to wish' (in the broad sense of choosing)" and "success is not important to freedom" (483). We thus understand why any recognition of objective determinants of class and action comes to seem to Sartre a derelection which plunges the proletariat into passivity, freezes it as a class-thing. He calls every effort "revolutionaries" make to consolidate gains by means of a permanent doctrine and organization "serious," which for him is synonymous with "bad faith": "revolutionaries are serious. They come to know themselves first in terms of the world which oppresses them. . . . [All] serious thought is thickened by the world; it coagulates; it is a dismissal of human reality in favor of the world" (580).

It is hard to deny the elitism implicit in the intransigent ethic of responsibility to which Sartre's insistence on "unconditional" freedom leads. "Therefore there is no privileged situation . . . no situation in which the *given* would crush beneath its weight the freedom which constitutes it as such—and conversely . . . there is no situation in which the for-itself would be *more* free than others" (549). Each man "carries the weight of the whole world on his shoulders; he is responsible for the world and for himself as a way of being" (553). "Whatever our being may be, it is a choice; and it depends on us to choose ourselves as 'great' or 'noble' or 'base' and 'humiliated' " (472). "I am always equal to what happens to me *qua* man, for what happens to a man through other men and through himself can only be human [: . . .] there is no non-human situation. It is only through fear, flight, and recourse to magical types of conduct that I shall decide on the non-human, but this decision is human, and I shall carry the entire responsibility for it" (554). If "struggling free of the world" or remaining imprisoned in it is no longer a matter of anything but individual choice, the resignation of proletarians who do not "choose" to be "revolutionary" becomes their own fault. Sartre's aggravated ethical voluntarism justifies an aristocratic morality (553, 554, 625ff). Furthermore, its conception of a freedom independent of consequences, of a transformation of the world which is condemned to be no more than a conceptual revolution because it degrades itself as soon as it seeks to be an actual one, justifies quietist attitudes which its author never meant to justify.

Sartre never did understand these implications of his thought. The dual way of talking about the world which weaves together the explicit and implicit meanings of his anthropology is ambiguous. But it is also unintended. Only a reading which makes it objective makes it evident: its underlying, unstated message is so censored that its author can ignore it. Yet the message is essential. It is precisely the ambivalence of Sartre's tribute to the Marxist approach that makes it the perfect premise for a philosophy of "commitment" whose watchword is "sympathize, but don't join." It contradicts stereotypes which refer unequivocally to Marxist thought, without ever itself mentioning this unmentionable philosophy. While seeming to open the world up at last to philosophy, it continues to hold it at arm's length. It combines a real sympathy for the proletariat with the philosopher's traditional horror of the "masses." It lines up on the side of revolution while from moment it proclaims "all human activities . . . equivalent . . . and . . . doomed to failure" (626), it judges revolution absurd and impossible.

## 2.5 *Philosophical nobility*

Sartre's passage from the specialized topics of his early works to a full-blown ontology fits the profile of an exemplary career in philosophy. After a philosophical debut in which he has subjected himself as the rules required to erudite refutations of current academic doctrine (as in *The Psychology of Imagination* and the first part of his essay on the emotions), and with the confidence that his atypical prestige as a "creator" gives him, Sartre can now dare the supreme and most profitable (if riskiest) undertaking: constructing a philosophical system of his own. By its scope, by its encyclopedic design, by its almost total absence of notes, quotes, and explicit sources, and by its infrequent use of specific authors, *Being and Nothingness* is an open challenge to the official representatives of philosophy's illustrious tradition of synoptic systems. Husserl and Heidegger are the only living authors Sartre openly and systematically confronts, because they are the only ones he recognizes as competitors. The other names he mentions are those of the famous dead, either undying ones such as Descartes and Kant, or ones such as Hegel and Kierkegaard who are currently being resurrected. Other important points of reference such as neo-Kantianism, empirical psychology, and Marx are sparsely quoted or no more than alluded to. This is not simply a matter of Sartre's adopting a strategy which will distinguish him from others. According to the field's implicit logic, Husserl and Heidegger are the two positions it is necessary and sufficient to "go beyond" in order to win out over every other position. This is the task which every candidate who seeks to rule the philosophical field must tackle: question your own masters, the very definition of excellence, whose authority has made them both your leaders and supporters during your apprentice years. Sartre spontaneously finds the philosophical tradition's characteristic strategy for succession and ends up replicating a process which (to take someone near at hand) we can see illustrated in many ways in Heidegger himself. But Sartre is far from denying the philosophical worth of those he attacks, since doing so would undermine his own legitimacy. Instead he tends objectively to make them out to contain a partial truth which is inadequate because it is insufficiently developed and "founded": to be no more than premises which foreshadow and call for his own thinking as the way to overcome their limitations by incorporating them in a new synthesis. This approach allows him when necessary to make use of famous forebears such as Hegel, Kant, and Descartes, thereby adding the authority associated with their names to the permanent values stored up by tradition.

To fully illustrate Sartre's ontological aim of solving the problem of the relationship between subject and object, consciousness and the world, we must consider the functional logic of the philosophical field. This problem, as formulated by Kant, is the one which all subsequent philosophies—including phenomenology—must confront, the decisive grounds on which any would-be heir to the tradition must battle for legitimacy. The expository order Sartre follows—from defining "foundations" to "existential analysis," from Cogito to action—is equally in accordance with a tacit norm of philosophical nobility. Similarly, his way of establishing his own positions concerning canonical topics of major philosophical systems (particularly topics which have been most obviously taken up again by Hegel, Husserl, and Heidegger, the rising philosophers he acknowledges) accords with the traditional conception of philosophy as progressively realizing the truth through century after century of repeated attempts to rethink what has previously been thought about perennial topics. Sartre presents his theses as if he were reaching the finish line of a race in which Husserl corrects Descartes, Heidegger (thanks to hints from Hegel and Kierkegaard) moves past Husserl, but Sartre alone reveals the full meaning and significance of the original insight by carrying it to its final conclusion.

"Now the *cogito* never gives out anything other than what we ask of it. Descartes questioned it concerning its functional aspect—'*I doubt, I think.*' And because he wished to pass without a conducting thread from this functional aspect to existential dialectic, he fell into the error of substance. Husserl, warned by this error, remained timidly on the plane of functional description. Due to this fact he never passed beyond the pure description of the appearance as such; he has shut himself up inside the *cogito* and deserves—in spite of his denial—to be called a phenomenalist rather than a phenomenologist. His phenomenalism at every moment borders on Kantian idealism. Heidegger, wishing to avoid that descriptive phenomenalism which leads to the Megarian, anti-dialectic isolation of essences, begins with the existential analytic without going through the *cogito*. But since the *Dasein* has from the start been deprived of the dimension of consciousness, it can never regain this dimension" (73).

This is a revealing paragraph because it sums up the essential tradition *Being and Nothingness* associates itself with, as well as the main arguments Sartre gives against Husserl and Heidegger. To put it briefly, Sartre reduces their positions to the basic oppositions of post-Kantian philosophy: subjective idealism or realism without a transcendental ego. And he takes credit for having realized phenomenology's aim of surpassing these alternatives by having accomplished in a single philosophy the two aims which Husserl and Heidegger accomplished separately: maintaining the transcendence of the subject by basing it on the Cogito, and incorporating "things themselves" into philosophy.

The ideological effect of Sartre's philosophical interpretation of the history of philosophy is to toss history out of philosophy: philosophical concepts are transformed into absolute ideas unrelated to the historical conditions which produced them. This is particularly clear in the role played by a Hegel reinterpreted in terms of Wahl and Kojève. It is from Hegel that Sartre draws the basic elements that his system must have in order to be distinguished from those of Husserl and Heidegger: his definition of consciousness as nothingness—pure transcendence—and his tragic conception of intersubjectivity. This Hegel is obviously Kojève's protoexistentialist Hegel who defines mind as the power to negate and a lack, and defines the relationship to the Other as a "flight to the death." Sartre passes over this link with Hegel in silence. Yet it is essential not only to his interpretation of Hegel but to our understanding of how Hegel, whom Sartre discovered and read after Husserl and Heidegger, and interpreted in the light of phenomenology, can seem to him to be post-Husserlian. Sartre himself reminds us that philosophical discourse can situate itself in "a sort of non-temporal dialectic" which allows us to ignore chronology: "If now instead of observing the rules of chronological succession, we are guided by those of a sort of non-temporal dialectic, we shall find that in the solution which Hegel gives to the problem in the first volume of *The Phenomenology of Mind*, he has made significant progress over Husserl" (235).

The effectiveness of this timeless reading is also evident in the anachronistic comparisons and verdicts that it enables Sartre to reach. Through it, the philosopher becomes a judge dispensing praise and blame, error and truth. "In this sense Hegel is right rather than Heidegger when he states that Mind is the negative" (18–19). "Descartes's concept and Bergson's can be dismissed side by side because they are both subject to the same objection" (110). "Husserl and Descartes . . . demand that the *cogito* release to them *a truth as essence*. . . . But if in consciousness its existence must precede its essence, then both Descartes and Husserl have committed an error" (438–39).

Sartre's mastery of the field's rules and resources is never so evident as it is in his showdown with Heidegger. This is the most important test, because Heidegger, in addition to being the philosopher of the day and the model who replaced Husserl in the growth of Sartre's system, is a virtuoso in the art of philosophical discourse. He is thus Sartre's most formidable adversary, the one who more than any other dares Sartre to meet him on his own grounds.

The weight Sartre gives to "refuting" Heidegger (in the chapter he devotes to the key points of the "existential" approach to philosophy[40]) is especially evident in the care with which he examines Heideggerian concepts and in the nature of his objections to them, which invariably tend to stress two aspects that for a philosopher are the most serious weaknesses: the lack of rigor and the holes in Heidegger's thinking. It is in this fashion, for example, that Sartre undermines Heidegger's "theory of death," which is the Archimedean point of a philosophy that defines human reality (the *"Dasein"*) as *"Sein zum Tode"*: "The sleight of hand introduced by Heidegger is easy enough to detect. He begins by individualizing the death of each one of us, by pointing out to us that it is the death of a *person*, of an individual, the 'only thing which nobody can do for me.' Then this incomparable individuality which he has conferred upon death in terms of the *Dasein*, he uses to individualize the *Dasein* itself . . . . But there is a circle here. How indeed can one prove that death has this individuality and the power of conferring it? . . . [It] is perfectly gratuitous to say that 'to die is the only thing which nobody can do for me.' Or rather there is evident bad faith in the reasoning" (533–34).

This paradoxical reversal—which turns back against Heidegger the strategy of beating one's opponent at his own game that Heidegger is himself a master of—and the consummate skill with which Sartre has learned to use this strategy produce particularly biting effects when it is Heidegger's own most characteristic categories and *distinguos* which provide the arguments for Sartre's critique. As Heidegger attacked the neo-Kantians in the name of Kant, Sartre refutes Heidegger in the name of Heidegger. In rejecting Heidegger's concept of *"Mitsein,"* for example, Sartre accuses it of not respecting the distinction between "ontological" and "ontic," the verbal distinction Heidegger himself used to establish a metaphysical distinction between the order of principles and the empirical order (244–49). Now this is an essential distinction for a philosophy like Heidegger's which bases its superiority to "ordinary" thinking on the fact that it first establishes its foundation in Being before analyzing any phenomena. In a similar way, Sartre develops the key definition of his philosophical anthropology, consciousness as nothingness, by radicalizing Heidegger's own position concerning "transcendence." Profiting from the lessons of the master, Sartre promotes transcendence from a "negating activity" to an "original structure" of the for-itself (16ff).

The tactic Sartre adopts of confronting Heidegger not with a different model but with a perfected version of his own which has been reduced to its barest outlines becomes even more evident when we consider the other characteristic stamp of Heidegger's philosophical revolution: treating daring topics in a philosophically irreproachable style. Sartre does not stop with taking up again in Heidegger's wake the *pathos* of the Kierkegaardian themes of anguish, fear, and forlornness which Heidegger has elevated to philosophical dignity by transmuting them from empirical categories into attributes of being. He systematically extends Heidegger's procedure, as is illustrated by his chapter on sexuality, a subject Heidegger passes over in silence. Sartre does not hesitate to stress the seriousness of such a mutilation of the *Dasein;* and in order to show how necessary it is to make the subject a part of the "existential analytic," he falls back on Heidegger's own crowning argument: to ennoble sexuality, he makes it a "permanent possibility" of the for-itself (406ff).

## 3. RECOGNITION BY PEERS

These summary remarks do not exhaust the multilayered richness of intentions and effects in Sartre's ontology. But they do suggest how beneath its appearance of completely independent thinking, the work is strictly governed by specific tasks that the times impose upon philosophy. It is on this basis that we can understand how a work expressing so many interests which were urgent and vital for its author and its readers can seem so extraordinarily multifaceted, and how specifically it can immediately win the recognition by the most authoritative judges which is essential to legitimation. Witness a collective work (published in 1950) by the most famous names in the French academic philosophy of the day (Wahl, Brehier, Lalande, Le Senne, Lavelle).[41] Not only is Sartre the author who is most frequently and fully quoted (as the index shows); Jean Wahl, who does the overview, writes about existentialism at length and calmly admits: "[Existentialism] took on its specifically [French] form during the Occupation, with the publication of Sartre's *Being and Nothingness*."[42] As a consequence of his position, Wahl may be considered representative of the element at the Sorbonne who are closest to Sartre—and his closest rivals. Now even though Wahl is better equipped than anyone else to point out Sartre's antecedents and borrowings, he greets *Being and Nothingness* instead as the realization of a "form"—French Existentialism—which has been the common project of an entire generation. A form which retrospectively reduces his own attempts to pale foreshadowings.

To this indication of Sartre's recognition by his peers we can add the response of Merleau-Ponty, who having already published two original phenomenological works is by 1945 Sartre's closest rival among philosophers of the same age. In a commentary published at the time in *Les Temps Modernes*, Merleau-Ponty is far from criticizing the direction in which Sartre's enterprise is heading.[43] His complaint that Sartre has not completely resolved subject-object dualism is to be expected in a philosopher who considers this task of developing a nondualistic ontology to be *the* central problem with which contemporary philosophy confronts its most ambitious heirs. In short, although their position as competitors prevents Sartre's peers from expressing unreserved admiration, there is no doubt that they see him as the principal embodiment of a view of philosophy's tasks which they share.

# 4. THE COMPLEX CHARM OF AN ONTOLOGY

The strictly philosophical merits of *Being and Nothingness* cannot explain its power to attract a following among a wider public who, although lacking the titles of Sartre and his peers, ecstatically acclaim the book from the time it first comes out—and thereby contribute not a little to its becoming widely known. Of course these readers of lesser rank do take the recognition Sartre's peers give to his book as a sure sign of its greatness. (As a result, noticing and appreciating Sartre's *summa* becomes a trial rite which confers a sort of election on those who survive it). But there are additional factors which account for the favor Sartre wins in the eyes of a wider intellectual public, factors which can be illuminated by analyzing certain responses which are significant because of the position those who make them hold in the field.

The reactions of Beaufret, Havet, and Campbell, all of them philosophy professors in lycées, make clear the reason for a favorable consensus among a class of readers for whom Sartre is not a rival but an inspiration.[44] These professors, who clearly want to improve their own status (they do not simply teach but give lectures and publish articles and books), hail Sartre (who up till 1945 himself teaches philosophy in lycées) as one of their own who makes their most sanguine dreams seem realistic by not only realizing but surpassing them. Not to mention the revenge on university philosophy symbolized by the success that this lycée professor has in giving philosophy a new life and an unprecedented supremacy in every corner of the intellectual field.

In "irreverently" attacking the " 'digestive' philosophies" that French universities hold dear, in bringing metaphysics down into the cafés, Sartre seems to establish "the chance to rise above the stagnant antitheses between the philosophy of academic people and that of the society people" (Havet), to wrest philosophy free from the monopoly of academicians and give it back to the world. As a "method ready to seize upon lived experience," which makes it possible "to clean up the world of things and the world of ideas by placing each problem in its right perspective" (Havet), "existential philosophy" brings philosophy back to life. Moreover, by "[easily showing philosophy's] great logical superiority" to psychoanalysis, empirical psychology, and science in general (Campbell), *Being and Nothingness* realizes philosophy's perennial aspiration to dominion over all other forms of knowledge. The feat which best expresses and fulfills this philosophical imperialism, and which best sums up the power Sartre has won for philosophy, is his "literary and philosophical success" (Campbell), which is symbolized by the publisher he chooses: not Alcan, the traditional publisher of philosophical works, but Gallimard, the publisher of Gide and the *Nouvelle Revue française*. Sartre's accomplishment is thus not just revenge against philosophy's mandarins but a victory for the "scholarship boys" over the "coupon clippers" who ruled literature until Sartre came along. We can thus understand why for these disciples "the text which best represents

Sartre's talent" (Beaufret), the one which by clearly conveying existentialism's atmosphere of "intellectual exaltation" allows us to "understand the strange fascination the movement has since had for the public" (Havet), is the article on Husserl which Sartre published in 1939 in the *Nouvelle Revue française:* it is because of the image of philosophy twice triumphant which Sartre evokes in praising Husserl. And although all this makes Sartre's system seem "completely new" (Havet)—an essential characteristic of excellence—its "technical difficulties" guarantee that it is also "demanding," that is to say that its revolution in thinking, its "sensitivity," and its good writing are all achieved with the most irreproachable philosophical distinction.

What Michel Tournier, Claude-Edmonde Magny, and André Gorz say brings out the needs that Sartre's philosophy meets for another class of readers: young writers, journalists, literary critics, and essayists.[45] These needs show through the recurrent motives for admiration found in their comments: *Being and Nothingness* is an *"extraordinary" event* (like "the founding of a city . . ., an Alp, a menhir," Magny); *unexpected and unique* ("a dazzling fall into the desert of French philosophy," Magny; "a book fell on our desks . . . which for a moment dazed us," Tournier); *a difficult 'system'* ("a long rumination," Tournier; "without understanding much of anything at first," Gorz); *"superbly technical,"* and thus *dazzling, original, and new* ("seven hundred pages without a single footnote, reference, or aphorism," Magny); *massive and compact* ("this great lava flow, this great single block of stone . . . which must be wholly accepted or wholly rejected," Magny); *an exhaustive system* ("an encyclopedia which, since it tackles everything, must have an answer for everything," Gorz); a "system *which must be lived as much as understood"* (because it lays the "foundations" for "an ethic, a theory of value, a literary criticism . . . , a marvelous key to current literature," Magny). For this group of intellectuals most lacking in status and authority in the field, "Sartre's system—which can look like an absolute creation to unspecialized readers because they are not even able to recognize its implicit sources—offers a "total" response: it is a "major" philosophy which is simultaneously a key to understanding experience, a critical method, and a morality—which is, in short, that rationalization of all existence which religions provide. And the intensity of their adherence is indeed religious ("Starting at the end of '43, Morel had dethroned all other gods before him. . . . He took on the image of a demiurge," Gorz; in the presence of *Being and Nothingness*, "one had the urge to give oneself up to lyric enthusiasm and, instead of criticizing, celebrating . . . ; a work to be provisionally accepted or rejected in its entirety, without haggling or discriminating," Magny). An attitude found again in a more censored form in the "intellectual exaltation" Havet recalls, and in the mystical language ("revealed," "initiation," "sudden insight," "wished-for enlightenment") of Beaufret, who concludes his essay as follows: "Some think that (Sartre's) calling man back to what is best in him must be seen as an 'aestheticism,' as no more than the shabby answer of those who are disillusioned with answers. Let us hear in it instead the ringing matinals which wake us from the dead, and let us put our trust in Jean-Paul Sartre. Orestes' hour is coming on apace with giant strides."[46]

This adherence is certainly a result of the characteristics of Sartre's philosophy—of its seeming to be a "total" system which manages to combine loftiness with a closeness to everyday life—as well as of other characteristics of his position: the combination of titles he has accumulated and the effectiveness his philosophical ideas acquire by being embodied in theatrical or novelistic characters. But we would be neglecting the essential if we did not consider the main, most hidden function of Sartre's oeuvre, the aspects of it which make it an irresistible ideology for intellectuals.

# CHAPTER 4
# An Intellectual Worldview

The imaginary social world of Sartre's early works is unconscious, and is expressed in an unrestrained and particularly rich, intense way. But it is hidden by the formulations and retranslations imposed on it by the different "genres" Sartre adopts: euphemistically transfigured in novelistic contexts, no more than implicit in awakening reflections on writers and literature, even less recognizable in the ethereal dress of conceptual systems. In order to understand not just the ideological functions and consequences of Sartre's works but their formal properties, we must make clear the perception of the social world and of the writer's place within it which structures these works' various achievements.

## 1. "SOLITARY MAN"

Sartre has analyzed, and theorized about, the work of literature as a beautified expression of a metaphysics. In *Nausea* and his short stories, he considers contingency to be the heart of his narratives: "Every existing thing is born without reason, prolongs itself out of weakness, and dies by chance . . . existence is a fullness which man can never abandon," he writes in *Nausea*.[1] And in the insert which sums up the significance of his short stories: "No one wants to look Existence in the face. Here are five little failures—tragic or comic—confronting it, five lives. . . . All these efforts to escape are blocked by a wall; to flee Existence is still to exist. Existence is a fullness which man can never abandon."[2]

The effect that this interpretation has on the reading public shows the power Sartre's discourse has to establish an image of his works. All the commentaries consider it self-evident that the nucleus, the starting point, of Sartre's novels is a philosophy—no matter how enriched with nonphilosophical intentions and meanings it may be as a result of its transposition into literature—and that this philosophy is a philosophy of despair, from which the narratives' pessimistic view of society derives. Sartre's commentators agree, in sum, that in the development of his works, his metaphysical concept of contingency precedes his image of society. And following Sartre's own suggestion, they tend to think that the generative principle of the view of man embodied in his narratives and plays is set forth explicitly in *Being and Nothingness*' view of man. The mutilated demigod who can only endlessly transcend the inertia and opacity of an immutable, unintelligible world, this tragic paradox, this "useless passion," seems to lay bare the absolute, ontological pessimism which the book's conclusion so clearly formulates: ". . . all human activities are equivalent . . . on principle doomed to failure. Thus it amounts to the same thing whether one gets drunk alone or is a leader of nations." But the commentators forget that Sartre adds: "If one of these activities is superior to the other, this will not be because of its real goal but because of the degree of consciousness which it possesses of its ideal goal, and in this case it will be the quietism of the solitary drunkard which is superior to the vain agitation of the leader of nations."[3]

This proviso already introduces a distinction whose meaning becomes more precise when we consider the human world displayed in the literary works which Sartre publishes at the same time as his ontology. This world is never an undifferentiated one; it is always grouped into categories which, if we look closely, are always social categories arranged in an implicit hierarchy. And it can be shown that the basis of this order is not a metaphysical concept but a writer's representation of society's structure and the writer's place—his eminent place—within it.

It may seem strange that this representation is nowhere so insistently, so fully expressed as it is in Sartre's early works—*The Legend of Truth, Nausea, The Wall*—the works whose matrix Sartre has been most anxious to insist is philosophical. But we must consider that at this stage between the completion of his studies and the beginning of his consecration, when Sartre doubted that he would succeed,[4] it was important for him to transform his suffering into a sign of election by fictionally depicting the this-worldly solitude and exile of the intellectual as both condition and proof of his superiority to all other social groups. And it is for this reason too that although the historical context in the subsequent *Roads to Freedom* becomes broader and more precise, their representation of society is narrowed decisively to concentrate on one single group, the intellectuals. The bourgeoisie and the proletariat fade into an indistinct background from which they intermittently make a few fleeting appearances. The main characters are intellectuals, as is shown by their style of thought and life, and by their paradoxical lack of any explicit social or professional characteristics. The reason Sartre thinks—as in Roquentin's case—that there is no need to give these characters a line of work is that he conceives of them as he conceives of intellectuals: as indeterminate, set apart from all social classes, and irreducible to class determinations. To a by now self-assured writer, it is no longer important to confirm his calling by showing what distinguishes it from bourgeois smugness and proletarian brutishness. His problem is already a different one, the one which sums up the chief focus and concern of the philosophy of commitment: to justify the freedom of the intellectual in relation to the discipline and dogma of the Communist Party. That is why it is to Sartre's earlier works that we must look for the fullest projection of his imaginary social world.

*The Legend of Truth* gives us an early reflection of this imaginary world, and its naive symbolism makes it an especially limpid one. It is a veritable classification of society: to define the intellectual's position, Sartre must represent the overall social structure, particularly the sectors of the dominant class which embody the different forms of economic and political power on which the intellectual has turned his back. In the *Legend*'s social space, the "solitary men" (those social outcasts—artists, writers, and thinkers—who are society's "thaumaturges" because they alone have access to the truth) stand in contrast to social formations whose limitations are a result of the limitations of the classes which dominate them. Aristocratic society disdains universality and prefers the "probable" concepts of abstract philosophy; bourgeois society arises from commerce and, considering citizens interchangeable units, postulates commonsense truths and produces science.

In a less transparent way, Sartre's social fantasies also structure Roquentin's worldview in *Nausea*. The world of gestures, objects, words, and habits which unfolds beneath the hero's savage eye is filled with minutely noted, clearly classified, or classifiable marks of social class and status. Here too the space of Sartre's imagination is dominated by the class he is obsessed with, the "bourgeoisie." For this young professor, who has been reared and educated by professors, and whose emotional ties are limited to just a little chosen circle of peers and disciples, the "people" are still a remote, rather mysterious entity. His way of thinking of them is ambiguous, divided between pity for their suffering and scorn for their acceptance of it. To describe them, Sartre falls back spontaneously on already established artistic and literary images which are a part of his experience and are perfectly suited to his expressive needs because they too are ambivalent and constructed from a comparable structurally ambiguous viewpoint of artists who brood over the "people" in solidarity and horror. The dark and silent Sunday crowd which moves toward Bouville is straight out of expressionist paintings. Indistinct, both painful and menacing to behold, it mirrors all the tensions of a schizoid glance which not only caricatures the bourgeoisie but unconsciously projects Sartre's own uncertain and conflicting feelings: "In all the suburbs, between the interminable walls of factories, long black processions have started walking, they are slowly advancing toward the centre of the town. To receive them, the streets have taken on the look they have when trouble is expected, all the stores, except the ones on the rue Tournebride, have lowered their iron shutters. Soon, silently, these black columns are going to invade the death-shamming streets. . . . Soon the Sunday crowd will be born, between bolted shops and closed doors" (41).

The rare faces which stand out individually in the crowd exhume clichés worthy of nineteenth-century literature. For example Lucie, the charwoman at the Hotel Printania, is a stylized evocation of naturalism's hapless charwomen. Her function is to be a personal symbol of the people, of their misfortunes and their inability to suffer them nobly. Plaintive, always dirty, "[she] has an unhappy home life" (her husband "drinks"; he is probably "tubercular"), "she is able neither to console herself nor abandon herself to her suffering. She thinks about it a little bit, a very little bit, now and again she passes it on. . . . She suffers as a miser. She must be miserly with her pleasures, as well" (11). If she seems for an instant to suffer "with a frenzied generosity" when she unexpectedly meets Roquentin on the Boulevard Noir, outside the daily setting of her life, it is not "from herself that she draws the strength to suffer. It comes to her from the outside" (27), from the surroundings. In describing the Boulevard Noir—which in Bouville's geography, where each sector is linked explicitly to a segment of society, is the topographical equivalent of the people—Sartre gives away the formula which governs his social vision: the "people" are "simply the reverse side," the reverse side of the "bourgeoisie," but equally "inhuman": "The Boulevard Noir does not have the indecent look of bourgeois streets, offering their regrets to the passers-by. No one has bothered to adorn it: it is *simply the reverse side*. The reverse side of the Rue Jeanne-Berthe Coeuroy, of the Avenue Galvani. . . . [It] rushes straight ahead, *blindly*, bumping finally into the Avenue Galvani. The town has forgotten it. . . .The Boulevard Noir is *inhuman*. Like a *mineral*. Like a triangle" (26, my italics).

*The Legend of Truth*'s objective aim of celebrating the distinctiveness and superiority of that penniless, powerless, unsuccessful "bourgeois"—the intellectual—in comparison to all forms of "bourgeois" success is taken up again and carried to completion in *Nausea*, whose literary structure, a although more complex, is still based on the contrast between the intellectual and all the positions of the dominant class. To show Roquentin being stripped bare of all earthly possessions, Sartre must make him triumph over a whole gamut of worldly temptations.

But this requirement is not enough to explain the sociologically relevant and quasi-systematic representation of the bourgeois world which Sartre manages to provide—in contrast to his vague, conventional sketch of the people. In the case of the bourgeoisie, all he has to do to be complete and concrete is reproduce his own experience of the social world as it is structured and animated by his relationship to his own class. His lengthy, close, and pitiless observation of the different ways of being bourgeois allows him to orchestrate skillfully—as Roquentin's rootless life in hotel, restaurant, and café allows him to display—a broad sampling of the few physical and moral traits needed to distinguish the old bourgeoisie from the new, and both from the petit bourgeoisie of shopkeepers, traveling salesmen, and stockbrokers.

Of course, the only reason why Sartre pays so much attention to social hierarchies is to be better able to mock them, as his way of constructing a Sunday in Bouville makes clear. It is only after he has made the different categories of "owners" pass in review, by contrasting them systematically and singly to one another, that Sartre-Roquentin can blur them all together in the symbolic afternoon stroll along the seaside: "I . . . joined the crowd streaming towards the sea. There was more of a mixture than in the morning. It seemed as though all these men no longer had strength to sustain this fine social hierarchy they were so proud of before luncheon. Businessmen and officials walked side by side; they let themselves be elbowed, even jostled out of the way by shabby employees. Aristocrats, élite, and professional groups had melted into the warm crowd. Only scattered men were left who were not representative" (51).

It is in terms of this logic, which requires that the hierarchy be shown in order to be challenged, that we can understand the necessity of the chapter on the visit to the museum, which would otherwise seem out of place.[5] It is this logic which requires that Sartre paint a particularly detailed and atrocious portrait of the highest caste, the one which holds economic and political power and embodies the attributes—and the horror—of the entire class. And in taking leave of its "leaders" ["Farewell, beautiful lilies, elegant in your painted little sanctuaries, . . . goodbye, you bastards!" (94)], Sartre is taking leave of the entire bourgeois world.

It is not immediately evident that Sartre's depiction of the bourgeoisie sustains a relationship of contrast whose other term is the intellectual, since the intellectual is only defined as the negation of the bourgeois.

Whereas the bourgeios is identified by who he is and what he has—by his properties, roles, titles, and honors—the stigmata of the intellectual are what he has lost or has never had—his failure in this world—transformed into a voluntary renunciation. These stigmata are the price and proof of the freedom from social conditioning which is the condition of the one true virtue, lucidity. Only he who refuses to take any stand can escape the inevitable limitations of doing so and arrive at a truth beyond all standpoints. In admitting total defeat, Roquentin actually proclaims his victory over the *salauds:* "I lost the whole game. At the same time, I learned that you always lose. Only the rascals think they win" (157). To challenge a hierarchy based on worldly goods, Sartre almost inevitably has recourse to the paradoxical reversal which is the ideological weapon par excellence that the intellectual uses to proclaim his superiority to the other segments of the dominant class.

Defined as indefinite, the intellectual is the most evanescent of heroes. As nothing but a purely contemplative view of things, he slips so far into the shadows of the world he shows us that we forget him. Roquentin "is losing his past drop by drop,"[6] to the point that he is stripped in the most radical way possible of all worldly ties (including not just worldly ambitions but also the most ennobling, disinterested commitments: adventure, science, love)—to the point of becoming an impersonal consciousness. He lends himself so well to embodying the phenomenological ego because the same intellectualist utopia of absolute lucidity which engendered phenomenology engenders him.

Actually, there is not a single image of social reality in *Nausea* which is not at least implicitly contrasted to this vanishing presence, or which does not, to be more precise, help celebrate—through its depiction of the blindness and absurdity of the successful—the solitary individual who has failed in everything, and is bereft of everything, except his power to "look Existence in the face." We need only compare Roquentin's attributes and actions to those of other social categories to see the outlines of a coherent system of contrasts in which Roquentin's superior worth is evident. But he who cannot define his social importance without referring to other positions, if only to deny them, is still in spite of everything determined by the very determinants from which he claims to be free.

This is why we need only reverse the Bastard's formula—"I have the right to exist, therefore I have the right not to think" (101)—to obtain Roquentin's—"But I *know.* I don't look like much, but I know I exist and that they exist" (111).

Whereas others seek out one another's company, tend to live in groups and as a herd, because "[in] order to exist, they must consort with others" (6), Roquentin does not need anyone, he makes his solitude a matter of his own choosing: "I live alone, entirely alone. I never speak to anyone, never; I receive nothing, I give nothing" (6). "I am alone in the midst of these happy, reasonable voices. All these creatures spend their time explaining, realizing happily that they agree with each other. In Heaven's name, why is it so important to think the same things all together?" (8)

"I felt the afternoon all through my heavy body. Not my afternoon, but theirs, the one a hundred thousand Bouvillois were going to live in common. At this same time, after the long and copious Sunday meal, they were getting up from the table, *for them* something had died" (50, my italics). Solitude, which ordinary human beings feel condemned to, becomes the intellectual's badge of honor: " I was no lamb" (88). "I don't want to be integrated" (118).

Whole scenes are orchestrated in an almost systematic counterpoint of serial contrasts. The Sunday crowd strolls down to the seaside "slow-ly," it is "lukewarm," inert, incapable of strong feelings. Obliged to rest on Sunday to be able to "start anew on Monday morning," it never has the time to really live: "[These] people were neither sad nor gay: they were at rest. Their wide-open, staring eyes passively reflected sea and sky. . . . [They] wanted to live with the least expenditure, economize words, gestures, thoughts, float: they had only one day in which to smooth out their wrinkles, their crow's feet, the bitter lines made by a hard week's work. . . . [Only] their breathing, deep and regular as that of sleepers, still testified that they were alive" (50, passim). Roquentin, on the contrary, is *quick, active, vigorous, hard,* and has so much time he does not know what to do with it: "I walked stealthily, I didn't know what to do with my hard, vigorous body in the midst of this tragic, relaxed crowd" (52–53). He feels his heart "swell with a great feeling of adventure" (54), and thinks: "[For] me there is neither Monday nor Sunday: there are days which pass in disorder, and then, sudden light-ning like this one" (54).

The inhabitants of Bouville keep everything, all their objects and all their memories: their lives are cluttered up with things, the prisoners of things: "They live in the midst of legacies, gifts, each piece of fur-niture holds a memory. Clocks, medallions, portraits, shells, paper-weights, screens, shawls. They have closets full of bottles, stuffs, old clothes, newspapers; they have kept everything. The past is a landlord's luxury."

Not wanting to own anything, Roquentin even refuses to have a past: "Where shall I keep mine? You don't put your past in your pocket; you have to have a house. I have only my body: a man entirely alone, with his lonely body, cannot indulge in memories; they pass through him. I shouldn't complain: all I wanted was to be free" (65).

Roquentin's feeling of being different from others sometimes openly reveals his scorn for them: "I feel so far away from them, on the top of this hill. It seems as though I belong to another species. They come out of their offices after their day of work, they look at the houses and the squares with satisfaction, they think it is *their* city, a good, solid, bourgeois city. They aren't afraid, they feel at home. . . . Idiots. It is repugnant to me to think that I am going to see their thick, self-satisfied faces. They make laws, they write popular novels, they get married, they are fools enough to have children" (158).

The metaphor par excellence for this relation between the intellectual and the world is looking. It is thus wholly symbolic that Roquentin, when he reaches the end of his stay and his spiritual exercises, *looks out over* Bouville *from on high* and is the only one in *the "good, solid, bourgeois city"* who sees *the horrible truth its inhabitants do not see*: nature invading it in a meaningless proliferation which marks the triumph of contingency, the Bouvillois' surrender to the inhuman: "And all this time, great, vague nature has slipped into their city, it has infiltrated everywhere, in their house, in their office, in themselves. It doesn't move, it stays quietly and they are full of it inside, they breathe it, and they don't see it, they imagine it to be outside, twenty miles from the city. I *see* it, I *see* this nature. . ." (158). "How *natural* the city looks despite all its geometries, how crushed it looks in the evening. It's so . . . so evident, from here; could I be the only one to see it?" (160)

The contrapuntal relationship between bourgeois and intellectual is more invisible than ever in Sartre's stories, because they have no characters who could be called intellectuals. But it can be seen implicitly in the author's own relationship to his characters. The marionettes ("tragic or comic") who snap and jerk about, clumsily trying to solve that insoluble problem, life, draw our attention imperiously to the creator who is pulling their strings, who knows the plot of this dumb show they are too dumb to know they are acting out. And here, too, the target is the bourgeoisie. It is at their expense that the author manifests his power from on high by unmasking their representatives—from the little seamstress for whom living like the bourgeoisie is no more than a dream after which she models her life to the leaders for whom it is their right. In *The Wall*, which won the Populist Prize, the people are only present as supernumeraries, a faceless crowd.

To appreciate the significance of these social fantasies, we must look at them as the very source of Sartre's ontology. By breaking away from the philosophical reading Sartre has urged us to make, we can see the many signs which show that his philosophy is actually based on what it claims to be the basis of: that it is not philosophical concepts which explain his political ideas, but projections and transfigurations of social groups and classes which produce his metaphysical categories, that the Sartrean "being-in-the-world" is the philosophical form of a particular view of the social world—an intellectual's view.

It is indicative, to begin with, that in order to define the very contrast between the for-itself and the in-itself which structures his ontology, Sartre has recourse to his fictional formulations of the relation between the intellectual and society. The for-itself does not correspond to the general run of human beings in his narratives, but exclusively to the intellectual heroes: to the "solitary men" of the *Legend*, to Roquentin. It is to these heroes alone that Sartre's purportedly universal definitions of the following terms actually apply: "nothingness," "lack of being," "lack," "empty consciousness," "absolute lucidity," "unjustifiable freedom," "infinite transcendence"; "the being-which-is-not-what-it-is and which-is-what-it-is-not, which chooses, as its ideal of being, being-what-it-is-not and not-being-what-it-is," which "thus chooses not to get itself together but to flee itself, not to become one with itself but to remain always separated from itself"; but which is also *"the being through whom values exist"* (*B.N.*, 627).

Conversely, the characteristics of the in-itself are those of Bouville's bourgeois or its resigned proletarians: "[Being] is opaque to itself precisely because it is filled with itself. . . . *[Being] is what it is.* . . . [It] is *solid.* . . . It is what it is. This means that by itself it can not even be what it is not. . . It is full positivity. It knows no otherness . . ." (*B.N.*, lxv–lxvi).

What defines the *salauds* in *Nausea*, and Lucien Fleurier and M. Darbédat, is the renunciation of thinking implicit in equating oneself with what one is, adhering to one's own (social class) existence, perceiving one's existence as a right—the complacency of the person who identifies himself wholly with a place, a title, or a function and who lacks nothing and aspires for nothing. "[How] happy one must be to be nothing more than a Legion of Honour and a moustache and no one sees the rest, he sees the two pointed ends of his moustache on both sides of the nose; I do not think, therefore I am a moustache. . . .He has the Legion of Honour, the bastards have the right to exist: 'I exist because it is my right,' I have the right to exist, therefore I have the right not to think . . ." (*Nausea*, 101).

"I feel them so far from me . . .They are comfortable, they look with assurance at the yellow walls, the people, and they find the world pleasant as it is just as it is, and each one of them, temporarily, draws life from the life of the other. Soon the two of them will make a single life, a slow, tepid life which will have no sense at all—but they won't notice it" (107).

The petit bourgeois and the proletarians depicted in *Nausea* are equally inhuman because they are equally incapable of putting their sorry destinies in perspective by thinking about them. Lucie "seems turned to stone" (27). At the Museum, Roquentin is equally scornful of the taxpayer, the voter, and "the humble right to honour which twenty years of obedience confers on an employee" (86). And at the restaurant, this is the way he contrasts himself to the other clients: "I glance around the room. What a comedy! All these people sitting there, looking serious, eating. No, they aren't eating: they are recuperating in order to successfully finish their tasks. Each one of them has his little personal difficulty which keeps him from noticing that he exists; there isn't one of them who doesn't believe himself indispensable to something or someone" (111).

Roquentin, on the contrary, is the only one who insists on setting himself apart from all the rest—even from his memories and his own ideas—and who renounces everything, is alien to everything, is nowhere at home, feels he is unjustified and unjustifiable, yet succeeds in being free, in seeing, in knowing: "I had always realized it; I hadn't the right to exist" (84). "[If] I exist, it is because I am horrified at existing" (99–100). "My existence began to worry me seriously. Was I not a simple spectre?" (86). "I want to leave, go to some place where I will be really in my own niche, where I will fit in. . . .But my place is nowhere; I am unwanted, *de trop*" (122).

This relationship between the empirical (Sartre's experience of the world) and the ontological surfaces more clearly when Sartre makes a direct transition from social categories to metaphysical categories: "The bourgeois who call themselves 'respectable citizens' do not become respectable as the result of contemplating moral values. Rather from the moment of their arising in the world they are thrown into a pattern of behavior the meaning of which is respectability. Thus respectability acquires *a being*; it is not put into question" (*B.N.*, 38, my italics).

"[It] is true that among the thousands of ways which the for-itself has of trying to wrench itself away from its original contingency, there is one which consists in trying to make itself recognized by the Other as *an existence by right*. We insist on our individual rights only within the compass of a vast project which would tend to confer existence on us in terms of the function which we fulfill" (*B.N.*, 485, my italics). "Any member of the ruling class is a man of divine right. Born into a class of leaders, he is convinced from childhood that he is born *to* command and, in a certain sense, this is true, since his parents, who do command, have brought him into the world to carry on after them. A certain social function, into which he will slip as soon as he is of age, *the metaphysical reality, as it were,* of his person, awaits him. Thus, in his own eyes, he is a person, an a priori synthesis of legal right and of fact."[7]

Sartre's metaphysics condemns not just the bourgeoisie but the people and their representatives, the Communists, as guilty (for different reasons) of the same crime, the crime of taking the world seriously (which is unforgivable for an intellectual like Sartre whose spiritual point of honor is to live detached from the world). This is shown by one paragraph of *Being and Nothingness* in which the continuity between "social reality" and the "world" of ontology is clear: "It is not by chance that materialism is serious; it is not by chance that it is found at all times and all places as the preferred doctrine of the revolutionary. This is because revolutionaries are serious. They come to know themselves first in terms of the world, which oppresses them, and they wish to change this world. In this one respect they are in agreement with their ancient adversaries, the possessors, who also come to know themselves and appreciate themselves in terms of their position in the world. Thus all serious thought is thickened by the world; it coagulates; it is a dismissal of human realtiy in favor of the world. The serious man is 'of the world' and has no resource in himself. He does not even imagine any longer the possibility of *getting out of* the world, for he has given himself the type of existence of the rock, the consistency, the inertia, the opacity of being-in-the-midst-of-the-world. . . . Marx proposed the original dogma of the serious when he asserted the priority of object over subject. Man is serious when he takes himself for an object" (*B.N.*, 580).

Now we can see why *Being and Nothingness*, that ponderous philosophical tract with its "superbly technical" air, can evoke the emotional identification evident in so many reviews and memoirs. The man whose tragic grandeur it so feelingly, untiringly celebrates is not man in general. He is a particular instance, the intellectual, or more precisely, the intellectual as Sartre sees him: a sublime pariah, free and impotent, lucid and pitiable. The philosopher's pretentious treatment of his own "certainties" as unconditional truth inevitably leads him to universalize the representation of the world which he has derived from his particular experience. Thus Sartre's conception of the for-itself, "a nothing which makes value come into the world," is only a translation into philosophical terminology of his image of the intellectual. And it is in this sublimated, unrecognizable form that the book's message, far from losing its effectiveness, acquires its supreme legitimacy. By elevating the idealized characteristics of the intellectual to the level of human essence, by transforming into a universal anthropological structure the intellectual's alleged capacity to hold the world—and first of all himself—at a distance, Sartre imparts the authority of metaphysical truth to an arrogant ideology which relegates all other social categories to the realm of the inhuman. By identifying itself with this heroic and solitary "nothing," the exclusively intellectual public which reads *Being and Nothingness* avenges itself by proxy for its exclusion from the privileges of the mindless power of the "bourgeois," who are only what they are and nothing more.

It is perfectly comprehensible that one human activity, art, enjoys a special status in *Nausea* and *Being and Nothingness*. Art wins a victory over "contingency," if only in "the mode of the imaginary": "in the aesthetic intuition, I apprehend an imaginary object across an imaginary realization of myself as a totality in-itself and for-itself" (*B.N.*, 195). Art constitutes the one "slender possibility of self-acceptance" (*O.R.*, 1695) which Roquentin salvages at the end of his spiritual exercises. Art is the triumph of the omnipotent impotence which at this time Sartre attributes to the intellectual: beauty represents "the impossible and perpetually called for fusion of essence and existence," an "ideal state of the world, correlative with an ideal realization of the for-itself; in this realization the essence and the existence of things are revealed as identity to a being who, in this very revelation, would be merged with himself in the absolute unity of the in-itself" (*B.N.*, 194–95). It is only in the imaginary mode of art that man's fundamental, "useless passion," "the desire to be God," is realized (*B.N.*, 615). And it is precisely because this power is imaginary that it justifies the artist's existence as a human being who transcends the world's contingency in making it visible, transforming it into a spectacle, and at the same time recognizes that it cannot be transcended and holds it at a distance. If "the idea of God is contradictory," and man is "a *dieu manqué*," a "nothingness" who dreams of being everything but loses himself as soon as he tries to "be," then art, the imaginary unity of thought and power, of intellectual lucidity and bourgeois completeness, is the only truly human activity.

## 2. CONDITIONS AND VARIANTS OF MANDARIN IDEOLOGY

The image of the intellectual celebrated by the early Sartre is in fact no private fantasy or isolated historical accident. The cumulative history of the field prepares the ground for it. Its main traits can already be seen in the ideology of creator and creation which is developed and established in the nineteenth century by, for example, the initiates of the cult of "art for art's sake" (although as a result of differences in field conditions and dispositions of agents, these traits are combined and expressed in a different way).

To show that this is so, we need only cite one representative instance, Flaubert. Through a whole range of comparable aspects, his position shows a striking similarity to Sartre's.[8] The same pessimism concerning the world and the same optimism concerning the writer's capacity to transcend the world. An analogous contrast between life, with its irremediable finitude and vanity, and art, which justifies life because it renounces it and surmounts its limits through the omnipotence of writing. The same pretense of gaining freedom from all social determination—distance from the common ties and "commonplaces" of everyday existence—by renouncing all worldly success, and in so doing gaining insight, the faculty which underlies the writer's superiority to the world, his possibility of transforming it into a spectacle which he contemplates and reveals from on high. And finally, as a product and discovery of this position, the same basic way of expressing absurdity by restricting oneself almost entirely to piling up descriptions.

It is no accident that this common intellectual worldview leads both writers to adopt a chiasmatic rhetorical structure: the technique par excellence for neutralizing and deriding is to proceed by way of antitheses and paradoxical reversals of situations, ideas, and trajectories without ever taking a stand of one's own. The contraposed stereotypes of the proprietress and the charwoman of the Hotel Printania offer a typical example of this technique: "The proprietress spoke with difficulty, using short sentences, because she had not put in her false teeth; she was almost naked, in a pink dressing gown and Turkish slippers. Lucie was dirty, as usual; from time to time she stopped rubbing and straightened up on her knees to look at the proprietress. She spoke without pausing, reasonably" (*Nausea*, 20).

One of the pregnant instances of this method of bringing contraries together to create distance is the conversation in the Restaurant Bottanet between Roquentin and the Self-Taught Man. Geneviève Idt has pointed this out.[9] As she shows, not only does the author take no stand of his own in the discussion between Roquentin, who claims to write for the sake of writing, and the Self-Taught Man, who asks, "Doesn't one always write to be read?"; the theme of the passage itself, since it is a classical subject for compositions in aesthetics, laces their discussion with a parodical allusion to those fake scholastic debates in which one character embodies the pro and the other the con.

Geneviève Idt also brings out the kinship that Sartre's way of dealing with "commonplaces" has to Flaubert's: "the commonplace is 'represented' here by being held at an ironic distance, without the subject of the statement, the one who signed the text, taking any explicit stand on the substance of discussion."[10] But she does not bring out the ideology which is implicit in this pretense of unmasking all ideologies by rejecting them all, "discrediting one along with the other" by lumping them all together, as Flaubert did, in a universal *"bêtise"* from which we can save ourselves only by abstaining from "drawing any conclusions."

In the short stories, where the tactics of representation are more clearly recognizable because they have been condensed to fit the narrow scope of the narrative, this technique of structuring through antitheses and reversals is particularly evident. First of all, in the plot structure. Pablo's farcical confession, which he believes will bring on his own death and save his friend, but which through an unforeseen coincidence produces the opposite result: it spares him and condemns his friend. "The Room," in which the "normal" and the "insane" are two contrasting roles—one as unacceptable as the other—two ways of being trapped in the same farce. The crime Paul Hilbert dreams of committing loses all meaning once it is actually carried out. In "Intimacy," Lulu's ideas about love and happiness turn out to be stereotypes which lead her to misunderstand all her desires. It is Lucien Fleurier's passive following of others which enables him to become a "leader," to ready himself for his social role as a member of the ruling class who is convinced he has the right to rule. And to this must be added the reversals of meaning, the farces transformed into tragedies, the parodical blending of the sublime and the ridiculous, and the constant mocking of edifying sentiments by brusque, crude references to the needs of the body, a machine built to evacuate repugnant secretions.

It is not through imitation that Sartre, in his obsession with setting himself apart from all established positions, and in his manner of expressing his obsession, seems to recapture Flaubert's position and carry it to extremes, even to the point of producing its philosophical equivalent. The affinity is clearly as spontaneous as it is profound, and can only be accounted for by referring to the structural conditions which made it possible for the mandarin ideology to develop in the nineteenth century. The essence of these conditions is summed up in a single phenomenon: the increasing relative autonomy of intellectual production through the combined effect of such important transformations as the introduction of mass instruction and the development of publishing houses and other institutions (journals, academies, circles) governing the dissemination and consecration of the intellectual product.[11] The structural ambiguity of the relationship which ties intellectual producers to the dominant class is reinforced by the anonymity and unpredictability of the new bourgeois public which the school system has created. Intellectuals, who are members of the "bourgeoisie" by lifestyle if not by birth, yet are like the people excluded from economic and political power, are condemned to an uncertain and unstable class consciousness, fluctuating between identification with the dominators and solidarity with the dominated. And the difficulty they have identifying themselves socially increases with the ambiguity of their relation to the symbolic market—that is to say, with their desire and disdain for the recognition that the bourgeois public offers them. A sense of belonging settles on the writers who owe their fame and material advantages to the support of the salons. And a sense of exclusion can push the more marginal and indigent writers who are objectively closer to the people over toward their side. That is why it is financially independent producers like Flaubert who can claim to turn their backs on not just the market and the bourgeoisie but the whole of society. It is they who uphold "art for art's sake" and build the image of the "*artiste maudit*," socially rootless and misunderstood by his contemporaries, and at the same time one of the chosen few who cannot be reduced to any given condition or class, or to any of the limits associated with a distinct social identity, and who above all cannot be reduced to that most intolerable of all limits, already established, limited ideas—"*idées reçues.*" The fury of Flaubert's attack on "*bêtise*" implies a will to set himself apart from all ideas, whose source is this illusion of not being socially determined—an illusion *which is itself socially determined.*

It is thanks to a series of historical changes that this image of the intellectual reaches its apotheosis in Sartre's epoch. To begin with, the changes in the social recruiting and training of new producers. Existentialists such as Camus, Nizan, and Malraux (an influential precedent) are an elite produced by the French school system. For the most part supported since adolescence by the state, first as "scholarship boys" and then as civil servants, these intellectuals are freed from the economic and emotional bonds, and from the ethos, which would never let the writers of the previous generation forget that they belonged to the dominant class. All this makes these new intellectuals feel that they are remote from, and superior to, the social world. And all the more so if, as in Sartre's case, they come from an intellectual family which already has these same characteristic dispositions. But what they have to say can be heard only because there has also been a change in their public, where professors and students of liberal arts and philosophy, who are related to them by social origin, habitus, and aspirations, increasingly prevail over the "cultured upper classes" who were still the main readers of the *N.R.F.* between the wars.

There is no doubt that Sartre's conversion to "commitment" constitutes a new departure in respect to *Nausea*'s "solitary man." But it does not involve any abandonment of the mandarin ideology. It is as if he had successively rediscovered the two basic political attitudes which the whole history of the field shows that this ideology can produce. To begin with, by rejecting society as a whole and saving art alone, Sartre takes up the position which tends to prevail among legitimate writers from the mid-nineteenth century on. Then he hooks onto the prophetic variant which characterizes certain specific phases of this position: the Romantic era, the period of the Dreyfus Affair, and the Popular Front years. What links these two at first blush so apparently unrelated models of the uninvolved spectator and the moral guide is their charismatic image of the writer. What actually makes both models seem correct to their authors is the ambiguous class consciousness and the feeling of belonging to a special caste which being intellectuals gives them. An aristocracy of intelligence is free to live apart, as it is free to attribute to itself a sort of authority to enlighten its fellows.

These swings of position, sometimes within the course of a single life history (Sartre's was preceded by the even more clamorous conversion of Gide, the champion of pure art who finds himself in 1935 a "fellow traveler"), are for the most part too obviously sincere and collective to be reduced to mere opportunism. They are never isolated choices but always concern shifts in whole sectors of the field. They have to do with significant changes in the basic relation which governs all cultural practices, their relation to the field of power. More precisely, all the acute phases of intellectual participation in public life seem to correspond to periods of social and political crisis in which power relations among classes are at stake. It is in such periods that, for some of the conflicting sectors, the support of intellectuals may become a valuable source of legitimacy.

Thus to understand the dimensions of the violent turn taken by the turn-of-the-century battle over a court case, we must consider what is really at stake in the struggle: the entire political regime of the Third Republic. The Republican front finds in the Dreyfusard movement a decisive ally which restores its unity and strength.

In the period of the Popular Front, the mobilization of intellectuals occurs at an acute stage of social and political conflict: on the eve of the elections which, by bringing the socialists to power, seem to mark a real upheaval in the social order. In this instance too the support of intellectuals is solicited by the organizations most in need of legitimacy, and most of all by the Communist Party, which opposition propaganda likes to portray as the enemy of France and French culture.

## 3. THE DOCTRINE OF COMMITMENT

The weight of the conjuncture of historical forces is even more evident in the Sartrean philosophy of commitment than it is in these earlier periods of political prophetism. More than ever before, the social conditions in France show the correlation between crisis and prophecy. But to explain the specific form which prophetism takes in Sartre's doctrine of commitment, we must consider some of the characteristics of its context which the intellectuals themselves pointed out in what they said at the time or recalled later. These eyewitness accounts of an age have been so often cited that they have become part of the stock account of the climate at the Liberation. But they still bear rereading, so that we can see how they converge.

### 3.1  *The conjunctural conditions: intellectuals and the political field at the Liberation*

The basic feeling expressed in these eyewitness accounts—the sense of a radical break in history—is characteristic of prophetic times. The pre-War social and political order, and with it its principles and values, seems to have been swept away. The intellectuals, including those who are least suspect of extremism, share the common sense that a really revolutionary process is underway, even if it is to be (as in September of 1944 the president of the Conseil national de la Résistance, Georges Bidault, hopes it will be) a "lawful" process. *Combat* takes as its motto, "From Resistance to Revolution"; and Mounier can write in February of 1945: "We do not call ourselves revolutionaries out of a passion for words or a taste for theater. We do so because an honest analysis of the French situation shows that it is revolutionary."[12] In this context, the existentialists' attitude can be seen to be no more than a sign of the times and perfectly compatible with the mood of the entire intellectual Establishment: "Through the C.N.R. Charter, France was taking the path of socialism. We believed that the country had been shaken deeply enough to permit a radical remodeling of its structure without new convulsions."[13]

This unanimity is attested to by the radical restructuring of the political field which is evident in the elections of 1945. In the face of the eclipse of the right and the collapse of the Radical Party, the symbol of the Third Republic, the Communist Party, with its five million votes, becomes the leading party in France. Many other signs—the purges, the law governing the press, the beginning of a planned economy—help sustain an expectation of a true resurrection of society, which in turn gives birth to millenarian hopes. People dream of a new France emerging from Resistance struggles fully united, open, and cleansed of the old evils of the oligarchy of the bankers, the powerlessness of the politicians, and the subjugation of the press. Revolution seems to be in "circumstances," as Simone de Beauvoir recollects in *Force of Circumstance* (a volume whose title expresses the discovery of the weight of "facts" which sums up the lesson that an entire generation of intellectuals learned from the War): "These pleasant dreams were engendered by the Resistance, which had revealed history to us but had also concealed the class struggle. It seemed that all reactionary influences had been politically liquidated along with Nazism; only that fraction of the bourgeoisie which had cooperated with the Resistance was now participating in public life and accepted the charter of the C.N.R. On their side, the Communists supported the government with 'national unanimity.' Thorez came back from the U.S.S.R. and told the workers it was their duty to revive our industries, to work, to be patient, and to refrain for the time being from all claims. No one spoke of putting back the clock; reformists and revolutionaries were taking the same paths into the future. In this atmosphere, all antagonisms became blurred. That Camus was hostile to the Communists seemed a subjective trait of little importance, since in his struggle to bring the charter of the C.N.R. into effect he was defending exactly the same positions they were. Sartre, a Communist sympathizer, nevertheless approved of *Combat's* policy enough to write an editorial for it. Gaullists, Communists, Catholics, and Marxists fraternized. All the newpapers expressed the same ideas. Sartre gave an interview to *Carrefour*. Mauriac wrote for *Les Lettres Françaises*; we all sang in chorus our hymn of the future."[14]

One of the most eloquent and decisive "circumstances" establishing this mood is certainly the electoral triumph of the Communist Party. Never before in France has the notion of a mission of the proletariat, as the universal class, and of an inevitable triumph of the Communist Party, as the precise and necessary expression of the proletariat, seemed so close to being verified historically. To the Communists' new political power must be added the extraordinary prestige they have won by their meritorious service in the Resistance. For intellectuals such as Sartre and Simone de Beauvoir, whose structural opposition to the "bourgeoisie" strengthens their feeling of solidarity with the subject classes, the

Communist Party is the sense of history incarnate. To be against it is to be against history—or what is worse, outside of history. This seductive power of "Objective Spirit," coupled with the honest feeling of guilt aroused by the image of the "disinherited" marching forward behind the "Party," is all it takes to account for the practical taboo against anti-Communism which sets in among the "sympathizers" of the day. It is not until the end of 1949 that *Esprit* and *Les Temps Modernes* begin to break the prevailing rule of Communist untouchability. That this relationship to the Communist Party was assumed to be unquestionably correct is attested to by the scarcely less explicit language of many revealing accounts, such as this passage from Edgar Morin: "In 1944 the Resistance denounced anti-Sovietism and anti-Communism. Stalinist Communism, the martyr and the winner of the War, shone forth like the sun in its splendor. Those who dared to challenge this view were doomed to be scorned or ignored."[15] There is no doubt that what sets off the philosophy of commitment for Sartre and other intellectuals like him who are just getting involved in politics is the War and the dramatic choices the Occupation has forced people to make. But from the Liberation on, the basic factor which conditions and specifies the direction their commitment takes is the new legitimacy that the Communist Party has achieved concretely through election returns.

Yet we need only compare the salient characteristics of the French Communist Party and the established values of the French intellectual field to see that the relationships between the two camps cannot help being problematical. Although it may seem absolutely inevitable to intellectuals that they should ally themselves with the party of the subject classes, the fact is that everything keeps them from giving that party their unqualified support. The discipline of an unusually rigid political organization is unacceptable to those for whom freedom of thought is a professional point of honor. Identifying oneself with a mass party is difficult for one who believes that the worth of a human being lies in being a subject who cannot be reduced to a process and a class. And for these representatives of legitimate culture, it is unthinkable to convert to the doctrine of the Communist Party, Marxism, which is a materialist philosophy banished from academic philosophy and at this time presented in its most dogmatic form by the philosophers of a French C.P. which is just turning toward a politics of cultural *dirigisme*.

## 3.2 Sartre's position

Sartre's position condemns him to live this necessary and impossible relationship with maximum intensity and ambivalence. No one is more preoccupied with the relationship than this man who has become France's leading intellectual. That is why no one since the War has thought more deeply than he about the responsibility of the writer.

Sartre's constant search for the undiscoverable role of the intellectual in respect to the Party, the masses, and the revolution has a contingent origin. We see this better in Simone de Beauvoir's reminiscences than in Sartre's works, in which the contingent origin is already transfigured into the eternal struggle between individual morality and historical necessity: "Sartre's relations with the Communist resistants had been perfectly friendly. Now that the Germans were gone, he had every intention of maintaining this accord. Rightist ideologists have explained his alliance with the Communist Party by psychoanalytical jargon; they have imputed it to inferiority or rejection complexes, to repressed aggression, to infantilism, and to nostalgia for a church. What nonsense! The masses were behind the Communist Party; socialism could triumph only through the Party. Furthermore Sartre was now aware that his connection with the proletariat entailed a radical reconsideration of his whole existence. He had always supposed the proletariat to be the universal class. But as long as he believed he could attain the absolute by literary creation, his relation to others (*être pour autrui*) had remained of secondary importance. With his historicity he had discovered his dependence; no more eternity, no more absolute. The universality to which, as a bourgeois intellectual, he aspired could now be bestowed on him only by the men who incarnated it on earth. He was already thinking what he later expressed[16]: the true perspective is that of the most disinherited; the hangman can remain ignorant of what he does; the victim experiences his suffering and his death irrecusably; the truth of oppression is the oppressed. It was through the eyes of the exploited that Sartre was to learn what he was. If they rejected him, he would find himself imprisoned in his petit bourgeois individualism."[17]

Simone de Beauvoir immediately—and significantly—follows this revealing analysis with an allusion to the "serious ideological differences" which kept their sympathy from becoming adhesion. It is as if it is not possible for her to describe this relationship without expressing the ambivalent movement which defines it. The same legitimacy conferred on Sartre by his relationship to the Communist Party is by its very definition the quintessence of what prevents intellectuals from joining the Party; for he owes his authority chiefly to a philosophical system inspired by Husserl and Heidegger and based on a celebration of the subject, of freedom, and of choice. "There were no reservations in our friendship for the U.S.S.R.; the sacrifices of the Russian people had proved that its leaders embodied its true wishes. It was therefore easy, on every level, to cooperate with the Communist Party. Sartre did not contemplate becoming a member. For one thing he was too independent; but above all, there were serious ideological divergences between him and the Marxists. The Marxist dialectic, as he understood it then, suppressed his as an individual; he believed in the phenomenological intuition which affords objects immediately 'in flesh and blood.' Although he adhered to the idea of *praxis*, he had not given up his old, persisting project of writing an *ethics*. He still aspired to *being*; to live morally was, according to him, to attain an absolutely meaningful mode of existence. He did not wish to abandon—and indeed, never has abandoned—the concepts of negativity, of interiority, of existence and of freedom elaborated in *Being and Nothingness*. In opposition to the brand of Marxism expressed by the Communist Party, he was determined to preserve man's human dimension."[18]

Implicitly, Simone de Beauvoir's account shows that the philosophical concept of commitment is no more than a sanction for the objective relations between Sartre's position and that of the Communist Party. Yet though the political legitimacy of the French C.P. is sufficiently imposing to draw a profession of revolutionary faith from the most legitimate of intellectuals, Sartre has all the intellectual competence and authority he needs to invent a way of squaring himself with the revolution not only without joining the Communist Party or making the slightest concession to it, but while stealing a march on it.

This search to come to terms with the revolution without joining the Party is what structures all the forms that Sartre's commitment takes during the first two years after the Liberation. The chief objective function of a whole series of statements he makes during this period is to establish his philosophical distance from Marxism. This is the thread which ties together his 1944 "A More Precise Characterization of Existentialism,"[19] the October of 1945 Introduction to *Les Temps Modernes*, the lecture, *Existentialism Is a Humanism*, and the book, *Materialism and Revolution*, which crowned this first phase of Sartre's confrontation with Marxism.

In the 1940s this confrontation is not for the champion of legitimate philosophy the weighty task it will become in the period of the *Critique*. The position of Marxism in the French philosophical field is still so weak that Sartre can claim to refute it on the basis of very summary knowledge and arguments. As a matter of fact, Sartre seems to be referring more to what Party philosophers such as Lefebvre and Garaudy are beginning to say than he is to Marx's own thinking. And he limits himself to developing objections already implicit in *Being and Nothingness*: an objectivistic materialism is incapable of providing a basis for a revolutionary movement. All he has to do in short is muster up the tried and true weapons of philosophical terrorism: repeat basic principles, cast doubt on determinism.

Though Sartre limits himself in "A More Precise Characterization of Existentialism" to a condescending self-defense, in introducing *Les Temps Modernes* he writes: ". . . Marxism does not yet have the synthesizing psychology that its totalizing concept of class requires." And he presents his own philosophy as one which, in contrast to Marxism, has already met this need: "As for us, we refuse to let ourselves be torn between thesis and antithesis. We have no problem understanding how man can be totally conditioned by his situation yet remain an irreducible center of indeterminacy . . . ."[20] The text of his 1945 lecture is even more explicit: "this theory [existentialism] is the only one which gives man dignity, the only one which does not reduce him to an object. The effect of all materialism is to treat all men, including the one philosophizing, as objects, that is, as an ensemble of determined reactions in no way distinguished from the ensemble of qualities and phenomena which constitute a table or a chair or a stone. We definitely wish to establish the human realm as an ensemble of values distinct from the material realm."[21]

Constituting oneself a transcendental consciousness which alone is capable of theoretically articulating the reality of the proletariat and the revolution not only makes it possible to be a revolutionary without being a Communist, it also neutralizes one of the strong points of the Party's power to make intellectuals feel guilty: the dogma of action. Consecrated by the Resistance, this dogma deeply disturbs all who put intellectual activity above everything else and put everything into it. Thanks to his authority, Sartre can overthrow it in a magisterial way: he can maintain that thinking and writing are not only themselves action, but the highest form of action. The intellectual's action of revealing the world is not just necessary to change the world, it is sufficient to change it. This theme, which was foreshadowed in some of Sartre's wartime writings, shapes the first manifesto of commitment, the Introduction to *Les Temps Modernes*, and continues to be one of the main directions his thinking takes from 1945 to 1947. It culminates and is systematized in *What Is Literature?*

This theme in no way involves the subordination of literature to politics which the dismayed and scandalized Gide and the other advocates of "pure" literature saw in it. On the contrary, it is an impassioned defense of literature against politics. Sartre's reason for so vehemently repudiating irresponsibility and gratuity is not so much to oppose the devotees of formalism, who are hardly fearsome competitors at this prophetic conjuncture, as to rid literature of suspicion and establish its absolute self-sufficiency. Proclaiming that literature is already intrinsically political is the best way of freeing it from the narrow sense of the political to which others would like to bind it.

It is useless to try to find any statement in the Introduction to *Les Temps Modernes* which justifies the impression of quasi-Zhdanovism it aroused in the literary milieu of the time. But we have to recognize that Sartre does view his position as a radical break with the past, and tends objectively through the inherent characteristics of his writing to produce the same view in the eyes of his readers. The structural design of this Introduction—"It has been said . . . but I say to you"—its scourging moralizing, its claim to herald an ethical revolution, its inspired tone, and its irreverent language ("payment in kind," "profit," "money in the bank") are all characteristics of the prophetic challenge, and encourage its readers to take its message as just such a challenge.

In reality, Sartre's underlying concern is defensive. Having set out from the contemporary writer's uneasiness and uncertainty about his role, from his "inferiority complex in relation to workers," Sartre states: "We do not want to be ashamed of writing." This is the objective aim of the whole Introduction. Sartre is concerned to rehabilitate literature before the bar of the advancing revolution, which suspects that literature is useless. In a real, symbolic *coup de force*, Sartre legitimates literature by simply giving it a new definition which seems to him to be, and which he presents as being, its true essence finally brought to light through an age-old process: ". . . And we do not want to write nonsense. Even if we wanted to, moreover, we would not succeed. No one can succeed. All writing has meaning, even if this meaning is far from the one the author dreamed of giving it."[22] Writing not only always has meaning; it is always an act. "Were we as mute and silent as stones, our very passivity would be an act. . . . All speech has repercussions. And all silence."[23] From this stems the writer's *responsibility* to assume a specific mission which is of capital importance to society: "It is our task as writers to give you a glimpse of the eternal values which are involved in these social and political debates."[24] Although every man is "a singular and absolute project," action for the writer consists in writing; the writer is not required to act as ordinary men are, to get into politics, to join a party. "Our review will take a stand on each issue. But not *politically*; it will not serve any party; . . . it will try to bring out the conception of man governing current theses, and it will judge these conceptions according to its own."[25]

## 3.3 *The models*

This first formulation of the doctrine of commitment is not as unprecedented as it might seem. It reproduces familiar patterns sketched out between the wars by others, because it is a response to a similar situation. Discrediting Marxism as a mechanistic materialism which does not recognize human freedom is a typical strategy of European anti-Marxist philosophy. As for the famous views of the function of literature which have become the symbol of Sartre's commitment, they reproduce the position which is already recognizable in the Surrealists and in most of the writers close to the Communist Party in the period of the Popular Front.

This is the position that true art is always revolutionary, that the demands of literature harmonize spontaneously with the demands of revolution. This notion springs from the apparent homology linking the position of artists and intellectuals to the position of the proletariat through their common domination by the dominant class. It is an assumption which characterizes the history of intellectuals' relationships to socialism. Yet it is belied by the conflicts, incomprehensions, and fallings-out with which this very history is spotted. For the fact of the matter is that the more autonomous the intellectual field, and the more opposed its values to the utilitarian criteria governing the cultural directives of political organizations, the greater the tendency of the supply of cultural avant-gardes and the demand of political avant-gardes to diverge.

It is no accident that Sartre's assertions specifically recall the optimistic statements about the revolutionary function of literature which can be found in Nizan's writings: "The writer is he whose function it is to define and reveal to men their highest values and most far-reaching ambitions: he brings out the values which their lives no more than suggest and gives them justifications which all can accept because they point toward human greatness and the realization of human potentialities."[26]

The analogy between the two men's positions is explained, to begin with, by the affinity between their dispositions, which were shaped by the same education, as well as by their common literary project. Furthermore, they have the same relations with the Communist Party. It is true that Nizan, unlike Sartre, is a Party member. But in 1935 the Party is still far from the cultural *dirigisme* of "its" intellectuals which it will adopt in 1947. Nizan can still delude himself into thinking that for the Communist writer the demands of the revolution and those of his own ambition are one and the same. At the Liberation, Sartre sets forth this claim in the much more elevated form of a theory based on a prophetic authority which Nizan was far from having in 1935, and without the mortgage which being a Party member involves.

Even Gide's career played a role in Sartre's commitment, as the final interviews with Simone de Beauvoir show. Gide's notion that the dedicated writer ends up involved in politics provided a model for Sartre: "Very early on I got the idea that this is the way a man's life ought to develop: he is not political to begin with, and then towards fifty he becomes political, like Zola, for example, who got into politics at the time of the Dreyfus Affair. . . . This is the way I saw my life: I was going to land in politics. Gide did the same: in his last period he went to the U.S.S.R. and Chad, and at the end of the War he had all sorts of connections with politics. . . . Or Victor Hugo, who went into exile on his island and condemned the Second Empire from there. . . ."[27]

## 3.4 *The function of Sartrean prophetism*

To understand the success which Sartre's attitude had, we must consider all the expectations which, without meaning to and simply by facing up to the problems posed by the existing political conjuncture, it opportunely fulfilled for a public faced with the same problems. In substance, the "doctrine" of commitment allows intellectuals to ease their conscience not only without joining the Communist Party or giving in to its pressures, but while reaffirming in an extreme form their pre-destined calling as the chosen few.

For in putting the intellectual at the service of the proletariat in 1945, Sartre is far from renouncing the elitism of his youth. He still thinks that the perfected model of humanity is the committed intellectual, who is able as a free man to help the masses free themselves. The committed intellectual alone seems able to take on the crushing responsibility Sartre preaches, that "writer's morality," as he himself subsequently characterizes it: ". . . our responsibility is much greater than we might have supposed, because it involves all mankind. . . . I am . . . responsible for myself and for everyone else. I am creating a certain image of man of my own choosing. In choosing myself, I choose man."[28]

But in contrast to Roquentin—the first Sartrian personification of the intellectual hero, who is satisfied to hold reality at arm's length—the committed intellectual acquires a form of power over the world by explicitly considering himself a demiurge: ". . .we mean to try to make certain changes in the world around us."[29]

What Sartre does, in short, is lend legitimacy to the intellectual's characteristic aim of taking a stand and acting politically—in times which call for politics and action—in a direct, first-person way which delegates no powers to others, in a way, that is, and from a point of view which are fittingly intellectual. In other words, he establishes the political prophetism of intellectuals as an indispensable component of excellence.

That Sartre remained the constant spokesman for this pretension throughout the apparent transformations of his political position is shown by the fact that his rare attempts to involve himself in organized politics all have the common characteristic of being undertakings promoted and carried out by intellectuals. This is true of his first but very typical attempt, *Socialisme et liberté*. (The solution Sartre immediately looks for once he gets home from prison camp is to form a group of intellectuls independent of the C.P., a group whose title alone expresses its project and reason for being: to reconcile *socialism*, which history demands, and *freedom*, which the intellectual cannot renounce.) The same is true of his involvement with the R.D.R. (Rassemblement démocratique révolutionnaire), the movement he starts in 1948 with David Rousset, where in the midst of the Cold War he chases after the same utopian dream of political action by intellectuals who are independent of all political parties. And in May of 1968 he will see the "Maoists" as the reincarnation of this dream.

It is symbolic that the two manifestos of commitment—the Introduction to *Les Temps Modernes* and the lecture on existential humanism—follow one another at an interval of only a few days in October of 1945, so that the beginning of *Les Temps Modernes* is accompanied by the outburst of the rage for existentialism: nothing better illustrates the prophetic function which the existentialism found in the pages of *Les Temps Modernes* performs for intellectuals.

But the success of this prophetic discourse cannot be explained simply by the authority of the prophet and the tenor of his message; the decisive factor is that it is couched in a seductive mythology of overblown Romantic verbal gestures from tormented heroes who are unfailingly clear-headed and alone: "A man is the whole earth. He is everywhere present, acts everywhere, is responsible for everything, and finds his destiny is at stake in every place: in Paris, Potsdam, Vladivostok,"[30] we read in the Introduction. Or again: "This is man as we conceive of him: total man. Totally bound and totally free. And yet it is this free man who must be liberated, by increasing his possibilities of choice."[31] At the heart of this pathos lies the path of "ennoblement through suffering" characteristic of religious prophecy, which always stresses the difficulty and risk of the ideal ethic it propounds: " . . . Freedom might seem to be a curse; it is a curse. But it is also the sole source of human grandeur."[32] Sartre's first committed hero can be seen in Orestes, about whom he writes: "Orestes will go down that road of his, unjustifiable, without excuses, without recourse, alone. Like a hero. Like anybody."[33] And Orestes' brothers are all the desperately free intellectuals—"*sans foi ni loi,*" "*sans attaches ni racines,*" in search of a free commitment— who henceforth become the protagonists of Sartre's literary and theatrical works, beginning with Mathieu, about whom Sartre says: "He is like Orestes at the outset of *The Flies,* weightless, rootless, with no connections with the world."[34]

A series of important analogies to the conditions and functioning of religious prophetism shows that the position which Sartre inaugurates in this way and gets ready to develop—above all through his plays and the review, which is an incomparable tool for accomplishing that direct and timely intervention into current events on all fronts that his model requires—is an ideological position insofar as it as discourse which claims to be universal but actually expresses and favors the interests of a particular social stratum.

As in Hebraic prophetism,[35] in Sartre's too there is a relatively autonomous field of production endowed with institutions of its own which reproduce and legitimate it. (What corresponds to the role of the church in this case is the school system, with sanctuaries such as the Ecole normale supérieure, and the other established legitimating bodies such as academies, publishing houses, and already consecrated journals.) There is an established corps of specialists: the professors, whose title as *agrégés* consecrates them as high priests of culture. There is the emergence of a new clientele: the neo-intellectuals produced by mass education. There is a situation of acute social crisis which established institutional doctrine seems incapable of understanding. And there are the prophets themselves, institutional deserters fitted with the dispositions which the role demands.

Existentialism is characterized by a dramatic sense of the weight of history and events, to the point that the wall between culture and politics so tenaciously guarded by the whole lofty tradition of philosophy falls, and politics becomes "thinkable," a legitimate subject for philosophy. This sense seems characteristic of all periods of crisis. Politics and the social world invade individual life and impose a historical way of thinking and historical things to be thought about which the discourse of normal times excludes; and prophetic discourse is only an extreme expression of this irruption of historicity. In the face of an intolerable and incomprehensible present, historical reflection takes the form of a movement toward the future, a thinking about change, a relativization of an existing world which can only become rational in the perspective of what the world may become.

The audience for prophecy—and the prophets—generally come from the social groups who, although they do not suffer materially, are as a result of their training most likely to make a problem out of the meaning of existence, and especially out of the meaning of their own existence and all the modes which are socially inherent in it. In intellectuals, a habitus shot through with rationality creates a need to understand and predict history in terms of means and ends; to articulate as a system of explicit norms the *ethos* or unarticulated standards of value and conduct governing practice: in short, to turn the *ethos* into an ethics.

It is understandable that at the Liberation the intellectuals find existential humanism to be the ethics they are looking for, the language for thinking about the radical breaks, the tensions, and the dilemmas of an apparently unprecedented situation. The invention of a politics for intellectuals, in an epoch which forces intellectuals to think about politics, corresponds to the ideal of "general culture"—a power of thought capable of mastering all that is human—which is embodied in the entire *paideia* of the West, and which lives on in the model of excellence expressed in the Ecole normale. The "total" intellectual is simply the earthly apotheosis of this model. He exists only in relation to the new kind of agents, public, and producers who emerge with existentialism: that is, only in relation to intellectuals fostered by the French school system and brought close to him by the common training they have received in this system. And as in religious prophecy, the initiates to the cult are recruited above all from the minor clergy whose tasks are those of simple reproduction.

In this latter respect, the contrast between the interest existentialism arouses in the most famous *khâgne* professors of the day and the critical distance stubbornly maintained by the most prestigious exponents of academic philosophy and by that elite of university students, the students at the Ecole normale, is significant.

In addition to the aforementioned examples of Beaufret and Alquié, we could cite other famous *khâgne* teachers who in criticizing or opposing existentialism continue to be concerned with it and in doing so contribute to its success: men such as E. Borne, professor at the lycée Louis-le-Grand and key figure of the Centre Catholique des Intellectuels Français (at the time a center of Catholic intellectual life), or Jean Lacroix, who as we shall see plays a key role in the dominant group at *Esprit*.

In contrast, the attitude of professors such as Gueroult and Canguilhem, who represent the quest for rigor in the academic philosophy of the time, is rather reserved. Although Vuillemin has an appreciation for Merleau-Ponty and is his friend (as is Gueroult), and is thanks to this friendship one of those who write for *Les Temps Modernes* as long as Merleau-Ponty stays with it, he is a stranger to the existentialists' way of formulating and dealing with problems. And it is no accident that the emigré philosophers from Russia and Germany who play a leading role in the development of the French philosophy of the day— Koyré, Kojève, Eric Weil—all write for *Critique* rather than for *Les Temps Modernes*.

As for contemporary Ecole normale students, they show in an interview which Paul Guth had with a group of them (*Figaro littéraire*, May 17, 1946) their general suspicion of a philosophy they consider to be a drawing-room fad.

The analogy between existential and religious prophetism may be extended to the producers as well. Sartre combines the marks of a radical break with institutions—which make his discourse seem to be the pure fruit of a "personal grace" or "charisma" that apparently owes nothing to institutions—with an "institutional grace": the titles and merits of a model child of institutions. Prophets and heresiarchs come chiefly from the ranks of those who are fugitives from the sacerdotal hierarchy. They are trained in the church. Although they challenge it, they do not renounce its values but claim to realize them in a more authentic, purer way. The reason why Sartre's planetary prophetism—his aspiration to think about everything, the big questions and the most insignificant personal matters—can seem to be such a legitimate ambition is that it unites and surpasses all established images of intellectual greatness. It is thanks to his unassailable authority that his works can so rapidly seem to be "classics," and can be read in classrooms without first having had to spend the time waiting out in the hall which the school makes the works of his contemporaries spend before it admits them to its programs.

But even all these merits would not suffice to make such an exemplary prophet of Sartre if his breaks with tradition were not so shattering. He introduces taboo subjects into philosophy. He speaks outside the canonical fortress of the university. He speaks to a broad intellectual public instead of to specialists. And finally, but no less importantly, his lifestyle is an almost systematic violation of all the norms of academic propriety. Unmarried, childless, without professional obligations, homeless (he lives and works in hotels, cafés, and restaurants), and siding with all who are socially outcast, Sartre is a living symbol of ethical liberation. As is the case with all prophecies, the anticonformist morality preached by a "scandalous author" would not have been so attractive and influential if it had not been so perfectly embodied in his style of life.

This combination of life and prophecy seems to owe its effectiveness to effects which also come into play in religious prophecy. It flatters the uninitiated public because it seems to give them access to a typically esoteric and distinctive kind of knowledge. At the same time, it is precisely because it directs this knowledge to a new audience, and in a profane place, that it produces an essential effect—the effect of being unheard-of—and like heresies, whose "generative principle is always a more or less radical challenge to the sacerdotal hierarchy,"[36] can also seem to suit an antihierarchical temper.

# CHAPTER 5
# A Fitting Habitus

## 1. THE "CALLING"

One condition of Sartre's success that we must not forget is his home and school life, all of whose aspects seem to work in concert to produce a model intellectual habitus.

Sartre himself has analyzed this history in what is apparently such a clear, complete way that it might seem superfluous to go over it again. We have seen how, beginning in 1939 and following a series of personal and collective events, his main expressive interest is redirected: having moved beyond the problem of settling on and settling into a calling which was his chief concern in his youthful works, he is now haunted by new questions concerning the reasons for choosing to be a writer and the social function of the intellectual. It is this concern, expressed differently in different genres, which underlies everything he subsequently produces—novels or plays, essays or philosophy. And it is because autobiography is the genre which best suits this basic concern that it starts out as no more than a projection through biographies of other writers, from Baudelaire to Flaubert, and ends up invading and taking over the other genres. How does one become (how have I become) a writer? This question is invariably the source of all Sartre's biographies.

The scope of this self-analysis is limited by a prior choice. As we know, what leads Sartre to adopt a biographical perspective beginning with "The Childhood of a Leader" is the combined pressure of psychoanalysis and Marxism.[1] The Marxian and Freudian conception of man as conditioned by his family and class makes the philosopher of freedom focus on the individual's relationship to society and history.

Marxism especially challenges Sartre's charismatic image of the writer as uncreated creator whose art redeems the world's disorder. From now on, he will never stop coming back to the question of the explanation and the justification for that suspect calling, the life of a writer. And yet he only takes historical and social determinants into account in order to show that the individual cannot be reduced to them, and above all to safeguard the freedom and singularity of the creative subject.

In his first biographies—*Baudelaire,* "Mallarmé," *Saint Genet*—Sartre does no more than put into practice the principles of "existential psychoanalysis" which he set forth in *Being and Nothingness,* without yet claiming, as he will with *Search for a Method,* to integrate Marx and Freud. Yet even his vertiginous accumulation of "data" in his final undertaking, *The Family Idiot,* does not alter his basic assumption. Whether he is writing about Genet, himself, or Flaubert, Sartre the biographer means to show that one's calling always transcends one's "situation," and is anchored in one's fundamental choice of one's existence. We can see here the same "original project" which *Being and Nothingness* already made the "irreducible goal" of the investigations of "existential psychoanalysis": "a method destined to bring to light, in a strictly objective form, the subjective choice by which each living person makes himself a person."[2]

Of course Sartre does grant that man "makes himself" throughout his life, but the form of his project is fundamentally determined by the choice he makes in his youth. There is always in particular one certain moment which is represented as a decisive, wholly inward ordeal upon which the whole meaning of the subject's existence depends, and upon which each of Sartre's biographies dramatically turns.

In *The Words,* it is Sartre's conversation with his grandfather which transubstantiates a destiny foreshadowed throughout his childhood into a "project" which seems to transcend not just what his grandfather hopes to teach him but even what he could be objectively expected to learn. The decisive moment for Flaubert is the "night of Pont-l'Evêque" about which the first two volumes of *The Family Idiot* turn. This moment is clearly for Sartre a "conversion in the religious sense of the term"[3] which reveals to Gustave "the rules of the game, of *his* game: loser takes all"[4]: "We shall see that the road from Deauville to Rouen was in a certain sense his road to Damascus," the "darkest and longest night of his life . . . an extraordinary moment when he finally becomes free to choose his neurosis, and his neurosis, in the very act of overwhelming him, becomes his freedom."[5] When a calling is presented in this way as an epic triumph over one's objectively probable future as a member of a social class, it can also seem to be a mysterious "call": "Flaubert had to be both he who seeks in fear and trembling, knowing there is nothing to be found, and he to whom a mute inaudible voice calls out: 'Thou wouldst not have sought me hadst thou not found me.' "[6]

Sartre never produced any better articulation and defense of his personal myth than he did in *The Words*, his most radical attempt to criticize and expunge it. Everything about this text gives it the air of a perfect denunciation. At first sight it seems that no one so forcefully resists the characteristic temptation of the genre (a famous writer's autobiography): viewing one's own childhood retrospectively as the herald of one's predestined greatness. On the contrary, Sartre's aim seems to be to demolish the very concept of a calling by reducing it to its social truth: the education which made it possible. And yet a whole series of tactics neutralizes and gives the lie to this reduction. To begin with, the narrative is structured in terms of the concept of "fundamental choice" as a self-contained and compact drama, each of whose episodes is a stage in the developing project and as such already interpreted when it appears, and thus discourages any alternative interpretation. This sense of strict necessity is further reinforced by the effect of rhetorical virtuosity which Sartre deliberately sought to achieve in his so-called farewell to literature.

SARTRE: . . . *The Words* is heavily worked over. It contains some of the most worked-over phrases I've ever written. And I spent a lot of time over it. I wanted there to be hints, implications in every phrase, one or two implications, so that it would strike people at one level or another. And then I wanted to present each thing, each character in a particular manner. It's heavily worked over, *The Words*. . . . It was full of tricks, of clever dodges, of the art of writing, almost of plays on words.
DE BEAUVOIR: That is to say that the desire to charm the reader by words, by the turn of phrase, is greater than in any other of your works?
SARTRE: That's it.[7]

But it is above all Sartre's way of presenting his characters in the mode of sanctifying sacrilege which puts the finishing touches on his transfiguration of the "family comedy" into a singular and unforgettable saga. The ostentatious statement of their social characteristics which he makes at the beginning of the book ("Around 1850, in Alsace, a schoolteacher with more children than he could afford was willing to become a grocer"[8]) means little, since in what follows he does not relate his characters to the common characteristics of social groups but instead depicts them by means of obviously mythological techniques such as referring constantly to literary archetypes which are loaded with symbolic connotations: Moses, Ariadne, Griselda.

To see what Sartre's denunciation hides, we must look at the childhood which he denounces as a particular instance of the typical childhood of an intellectual. As a Parisian and a second-generation intellectual,[9] Sartre combines the social and geographical origins which are statistically most propitious for success. The early education described in *The Words* carries to the extreme the pedagogical model which is almost a corollary of such origins: when the objective basis for a family's wealth is its cultural capital, it is hard for books and reading not to be the center of its life.

Other aspects of Sartre's early education confirm its exemplary character. Sartre's family not only makes him familiar with culture, bubut through its constant encouragement and expectations gives him a sense of being one of the elect—two essential bases for success as an intellectual. His early schooling is in its very irregularity so in keeping with an elitist education that as Geneviève Idt points out, it "represents a condensed version of all the modes of primary education open to a young bourgeois at the beginning of the twentieth century: elementary classes in lycées, private school, neighborhood schools but only on condition that the gentleman's son be kept apart from his schoolmates, education at home by tutors or his mother." In any case, he escapes the routine of "mass education"[10] and its possible influences. Leading a sort of *in vitro* life, "alone between an old man and two women"[11] up to the age of ten (when he enters that "school for leading citizens," the lycée), he is shaped entirely by his family.

It might seem that the contrast and conflict between the teachings of Sartre's grandfather and those of the two women contradicts this view of the coherence of his education. Sartre certainly makes it the keystone of *The Words*. It is what enables the subject in its freedom to slip through the determining links which bind it: the play of alternative possibilities which frees Sartre's calling from the realm of necessity and turns it into a "choice." And yet this conflict between contrasting models may be seen instead as a division of educational labor which helps perfect Sartre's habitus.

As a "living instruction manual,"[12] a personification of the pedagogical model which dominates French secondary education at the time, Sartre's grandfather looks on him from early childhood as a potential lycée student. He readies his grandson to be a model recipient of high culture, the academic culture to which Sartre will have constant recourse, at first by imitating it and then (when he must distinguish himself from it in order to become a writer) by exaggerating its rules to the point of distortion.

Geneviève Idt, quoting *Nausea*, shows that Sartre is always dominated by these rules and can challenge them only by extending them. The subjects of his chapters are those suggested by a textbook of the day: "What one sees from the window," "A dinner, a street, a dining room of an inn, a garden," "At the museum," "Twilight in the city," "A food shop," "The Sunday strollers (show precisely which part of town it is whose strollers you are describing)" . . . . The Self-Taught Man offers Roquentin typical dissertation topics such as "Doesn't one always write to be read?" or "[Travel] is the best school. Is that your opinion, Monsieur?" Sartre apes methodical description to the point of demonstrating that its object's imperviousness to description makes methodical description impossible. He applies the rules of *dispositio* and *elocutio*, as they have been adapted from classical rhetoric by the school, to the point of shattering the contradiction between the aspiration to be realistic by finding the *"mot juste"* and the quest for stylistic elegance through metaphor. Metaphor proliferates in *Nausea* to the point of producing the "upside-down world" which Sartre sees as the modern source of the "fantastic."[13]

Through his precepts, his library, his tastes, and his scorn for readings which are produced by women or encouraged by women, Charles Schweitzer conveys to his grandson a sense of the contrast and conflict between high culture and popular culture, between the models offered by the school for imitation and the impure delights of forbidden fruits. As Geneviève Idt shows, his direct or implied suggestions, and his rules for good writing, faithfully follow secondary-school composition teaching, its exercises in observation and description, and its ambiguous criteria of verisimilitude and originality.[14]

As *The Words* makes clear, moreover, the idea of excellence governing the education Sartre received from his grandfather is based on two concepts—talent and merit—which as we have seen are the two legitimating values of the academy's system of perception and evaluation. This academic worldview is an ambiguous ideology which combines faith in hard work and admiration for "natural gifts": brilliance, quickness, originality.[15] And the social destiny it offers the child comes down to the only conceivable choice the academic system of values can offer, the choice between the two possible embodiments of intellectual excellence, becoming a professor of liberal arts or becoming a writer.

The assumption in terms of which the academy seeks to overcome the contradictory values of its legitimating ideology is the belief that grace is earned through hard work—the belief in meritocracy. Significantly, it is just this synthesis of talent and merit which is achieved by the concept of election Sartre uses to sum up his grandfather's message: "In any case, as the minister of the cult would whisper to me, genius is only a loan: it must be merited by great suffering, tested by ordeals that must be accepted modestly and firmly. One ends by hearing voices and writes at their dictation. . . . My grandfather had slyly hoped to disgust me with writers, those intermediaries. He achieved the opposite result: I merged talent with merit."[16]

This message has never really been rejected by the famous adult who writes: "It's true that I'm not a gifted writer. I've been told so, I've been called labored. So I am; my books reek of sweat and effort; I grant that they stink in the nostrils of our aristocrats. . . . But the fact is this: apart from a few old men who dip their pens in eau de Cologne and little dandies who write like butchers, all writers have to sweat."[17]

Although this meritocratic elitism is described in *The Words* as "ideas that had been current under Louis Philippe" and as "a handicap of eighty years," it is in fact the spontaneous ideology of the schools in which the child in *The Words* will complete his education. It guides and legitimates the dispositions which will enable him to be a model student in them. His academic career (toward which he was also pointed by his grandfather) is not really the myopic, pathetic plan about which the writer who believes that he has fulfilled his destiny *in spite of it* so ironically speaks: ". . . I would take the royal road: in my person, martyred Alsace would enter the Ecole Normale Supérieure, would pass the teaching examination with flying colors, and would become that prince, a liberal arts professor."[18] This strategy was, a posteriori, the best Sartre could adopt in respect to the objective possibilities open to someone who came from such a childhood.

What lets Sartre build something more on this groundwork than the teaching career his grandfather envisages are the things he learns from the essential way that it is reworked by women. The influence of women helps fashion and encourage a more daring version of his calling—writing—as well as the fantasy life which sustains it. The child's first "novels" try to prolong and reproduce the half-hidden pleasures of the readings his mother brings him ("Was that reading? No, but it was death by ecstasy"[19]) and of the movies they regularly go to see together. This writing given up to fantasy and plagiarism is very different from the "exercises" his grandfather suggests: letters in verse and observation's "dismal and disappointing game." "I was spending a vacation in a brothel but did not forget that my truth had remained in the temple. . . . I peacefully continued my double life. It has never ended. Even now, I read the 'Série Noire' more readily than I do Wittgenstein."[20] As Geneviève Idt suggests,[21] the characteristic movement of Sartre's writing—its tension between "conveying the truth" and "the play of language and imagination"—springs from this "double life" of his childhood. By interpreting "Poulou" 's novels as "signs" of his "calling," his female public—his mother, his grandmother, Madame Picard—transform the "mandate" he has received from his grandfather's prudent aspirations for him into the goal of becoming a writer, which in the objective situation of the day is the most brilliant success that the grandson of a *clerc* can possibly achieve. And faith, as we know, is essential to the successful fulfillment of prophecy.

There is one characteristic of Sartre's childhood, brought out in *The Words*, which seems completely personal, the result of a singular conjunction of circumstances: the sense of gratuitousness which is the first form of his concept of contingency. Sartre gives it a major role in the explanation of his "mental illness": his need to justify his existence led him to make writing an absolute. And yet this apparently singular sense of gratuitousness is a recognizably typical component of the worldview of intellectuals. This anxious need for justification and this search for an identity are the other side of the illusion of being absolutely free, of being able to stand apart from everything. And the biographical circumstances to which Sartre attributes his problems of identity—the dual culture (French and German), the dual religion (Catholic and Protestant), the lack of any inheritance, and above all the "very unresolved 'Oedipus complex' " of a fatherless child "feminized by maternal tenderness, dulled by the absence of the stern Moses who had begotten [him], puffed with pride by [his] grandfather's adoration"[22]—are not actually exceptional circumstances but "necessary accidents." They are among the secondary determinants most commonly associated with the intellectual calling as specific mediations tending to produce favorable dispositions. Sartre's case is different only in the high degree of his competence, including even secondary factors which all seem suited, and at times more than suited, to the requirements of the intellectual habitus.

The limitations of any interpretation which does not try to situate Sartre's case sociologically are even more clear in the narrowly psychoanalytic readings of Sartre's "personality," as is shown a fortiori by Josette Pacaly's attempt, which is the most rigorous and complete analysis of its kind.[23] We need not discuss her clinical "diagnosis," with its four hundred pages of supporting documents and indexes: an unresolved Oedipus complex which manifests itself in an easily identifiable constellation whose most prominent symptoms are latent homosexuality, narcissism, and an inordinate ambition which—out of castration anxiety—assumes the guise of an apparent renunciation of all worldly ambitions. There may be some justification in seeing this psychological makeup as the primary source of the "rule" of "loser wins" and other characteristically Sartrian reversals: the pretense of being no different from anyone and different from everyone (the conclusion reached by *The Words*) which conceals the refusal to be reduced to anything definite,[24] the horror at the thought of being "superfluous" which expresses the wish to be "indispensable to the Universe."[25] But it is arbitrary to make Sartre's specific vocation and his strictly intellectual expressive interests stem directly and exclusively from this general syndrome. When psychoanalysis ties basic experiences to sexual and emotional relations without recognizing that they are also socially structured forms which in turn structure society's imaginary world, it denies itself the means of mediating between neuroses and the practices in which they are embodied. It cannot explain why Sartre invests his dream of omnipotence in the specific practice of writing unless it considers a sociological characteristic of his family: its making a fetish out of books and culture.

It is significant in this respect that Josette Pacaly has to keep introducing social factors into her interpretation, especially in order to account for Sartre's precocious sense of the contrast and conflict between the bourgeois and the intellectual. Sartre finds an actual embodiment of this contrast and conflict in the two men who are the successive heads of his family: his grandfather, who is a professor of liberal arts, and his stepfather, who is an engineering-school graduate and company head. And there is no doubt that the ideological contrast and conflict between the lofty but scorned intellectual and the bourgeois *chef* and *salaud* which will later form the heart of Sartre's social philosophy is first formed during his adolescent years. Between 1916 and 1920, establishing the intellectual's superiority to a social hierarchy which ranks engineers higher than men of letters and implies that teaching is a loser's profession becomes a pressing concern for a young lycée student who is destined to be a *clerc* like his grandfather but has suddenly fallen "under the thumb of a graduate of the Ecole Polytechnique."[26]

Sartre must have really been tormented by doubt about his calling to come back to it again in *The Family Idiot* for one final settlement of his own accounts by way of Flaubert. Of course the choice of writing as a calling is described there as the failure of a bourgeois to live up to his class potential: "The choice of a mutilation imposed on him,"[27] "the revenge of a castrated man,"[28] of "a man without qualities,"[29] "a stacked deck. . . . Could Art be no more than the humble pastime of *minus habentes* who aren't smart enough to become 'doers'? . . . Literature is the haven of subhumans who are unconscious of their subhumanity or are deceiving themselves so as not to recognize it."[30] But it would be naive to take this "sociological reduction" of an indisputable success like Flaubert seriously: this is only one more instance of the paradoxical reversal by which the intellectual likes to take his revenge.

Yet it does make particularly clear the inconveniences of a method which makes psychoanalysis a universal key to understanding. Even though Josette Pacaly has caught a glimpse of the role society plays in structuring Sartre's childhood experience, she hastens to tie everything to her Oedipal analysis by reducing Sartre's hatred for the bourgeois to his horror of socially indeterminate boundaries, his desire to be everything, and his castration anxiety.[31] In this way she represses the very factor which links Sartre's emotional frustration to his political orientation. The reason why Sartre's hatred of the bourgeois antedates his discovery of the proletariat and produces a political passion to which he is extraordinarily faithful up till the day he dies is that it is an overdetermined hatred shaped by the greatest conflict there is: an adolescent's twin rivalry with an engineering-school graduate who simultaneously threatens his "calm possession" of his mother and his dreamed-of eminence in the role he is preparing to play. If it is true that the scorn intellectuals have for the bourgeoisie is a transfigured expression of the resentment which, as the dominated sector of the dominant class, they feel for the powerholders, then it is this incurable adolescent wound which predisposes Sartre to be an exemplary intellectual even in his ideology.

In a sociological perspective, we can wonder whether this "mental illness" itself (which the psychoanalytic interpretation, by isolating Sartre's case, ends up presenting as peculiar to him)—this total investment in writing which subordinates life to the demands of the oeuvre—is not a type of mental illness especially suited to literary success. Think of all the great writers who have been "enslaved to writing" who could have adopted as their own (as Sartre did) Chateaubriand's phrase: "I quite realize that I am only a machine which makes books."[32] It is striking, moreover, that as Josette Pacaly herself shows, Sartre finds a relation to literature and even a psychological structure very much like his own in all the writers whose life he analyzes in depth—Baudelaire, Mallarmé, Genet, Flaubert. Of course, his interpretations involve projection, but projection based on objective affinities. The "mental illness" which leads people to transform their lives into literature, the refusal to accept limitations and insignificance which transforms literature into an absolute, may be necessary bases of literary success. Although this generalization does not hold for all times and all cultures, it does seem to be true at least for the French cultural field since the beginning of Romanticism, as the increasing autonomy of the producers of literature has created the conditions for an increasing subordination of the artist's life to the demands of the oeuvre.[33]

## 2. SCHOOL

For anyone whose aim is to retrace the steps by which a habitus is formed, the shortcoming of psychoanalytic reconstruction and of self-analysis alike is their lack of concern for the consequences of school and university. This omission is perfectly consistent with Freudian analysis, which traces neuroses to early childhood conditioning by the family. As for the silence of Sartrean self-analysis about this matter, there seem to be several contributing factors. To begin with, the example of psychoanalysis itself, which we know played a very important role in the development of "existential psychoanalysis." The fact is that beginning with his first biography, "The Childhood of a Leader," which although imaginary is rich in autobiographical revelations, Sartre gives special stress to the same materials Freud does: child-parent relationships and the dreams or memories which bear on them. A second factor to consider is Sartre's thesis that it is one's "original project" which, independently of all conditioning, determines one's calling. To show that the subject is capable from the outset of surmounting all determining factors, Sartre must show that his project takes shape in early childhood. And since the effects of the pedagogical and institutional labors of a paradigmatic academic career seem more difficult to reduce to a choice than those of the family, we may assume a resistance on Sartre's part to tackling this subsequent stage of his development.

It is thus no accident that Sartre's autobiography ends with his childhood and that, as he states in 1969 in an interview, a sequel to *The Words* holds no interest for him: "I do not think that a sequel to *Les Mots* would be of much interest. The reason why I produced *Les Mots* is the reason why I have studied Genet or Flaubert: how does a man become someone who writes, who wants to speak of the imaginary? This is what I sought to answer in my own case, as I sought it in that of others. What could there be to say of my existence since 1939? How I became the writer who produced the particular works I have signed. But the reason why I wrote *La Nausée* rather than some other book is of little importance. It is the birth of the decision to write that is of interest."[34]

Sartre's omission of his school years has been perpetuated by his commentators, who respect Sartre's protective silence concerning the role school played in his education. Yet as we shall see, this role is far from being "of no interest."

What another heir, Alain Touraine, says about his own itinerary[35] could be said of the schools Sartre attended: "Nothing marginal in all that." Except for the one in La Rochelle, the schools which channeled Sartre to the rue d'Ulm are the most prestigious of all: Henri-IV, where he received his *baccalauréat*, and Louis-le-Grand, where he prepped for L'Ecole normale, are the two Parisian establishments which (measured by the chance they give students to be admitted to the foremost schools) crown the summit of the hierarchy of lycées. And as a model student,

Sartre is a perfect illustration of the pedagogical and symbolic consequences of such a course of studies.

Some of these consequences have already been pointed out in our analysis of the contents, skills, techniques, rules, and models of Sartre's works. We have seen how forcefully the school censors the underlying expressive impulse of Sartre's youthful literary project by saddling it with aesthetic canons, choices of genre, and norms of composition and writing which Sartre will succeed in distorting and deriding but never wholly forgetting. And traces of teachings from his preparatory classes can also be found in his philosophical works. *Being and Nothingness*, for example, frequently reminds us of the approach that dissertation writers are traditionally advised to take (one in which the even more traditional medieval *disputatio* lives on): the three-pronged attack of two contrasting theses and a conclusion which takes up both again and goes beyond them. Indeed, we can say that this is the way Sartre presents the key concepts of his entire philosophical system. Through a discussion of the positions of Hegel and Heidegger, the concept of "nothingness" is defined as a synthesis which eliminates the errors and incorporates the positive contributions of each (*B.N.*, 12ff). And remember the passage on the Cogito in which Sartre seems to move beyond Husserl and Heidegger, who are reduced to the typical alternatives of post-Kantian philosophy: subjective idealism and objective realism (*B.N.*, 233ff). Or the chapter on freedom, which opens with a "discussion" that is meant to show that "two solutions and only two are possible: either man is wholly determined . . . or else man is wholly free" (*B.N.*, 442). And finally, many examples of what are called in prep-school slang "*topos*"—units of discourse preconstructed to lend themselves to multiple uses—are embedded in some of Sartre's wholly unsupported "demonstrations": for example in the famous bravura pieces about the "hole" and the "slimy," the first draft of which goes back to the *War Diaries* written during the "*drôle de guerre.*"[36]

But we would be neglecting what is most essential if we were to forget the effects of the educational system that is involved in Sartre's apprenticeship, especially during the very strictly organized and controlled stage of preparatory classes.[37] For the fact is that simply through its mode of operation—above all in the "*khâgnes*"—this system inculcates a conception of culture, of intellectual work, and of the intellectual's social role. Thus even though a synoptic aspiration to total synthesis is inherent in the whole philosophical tradition, it is certainly reinforced by an educational system whose aim is to impart "general culture" in the most effective way possible—a system which even today is the basis of academic programs designed to prepare candidates for competitive examinations. And this culture for the sake of competitive success encourages an instrumental, pragmatic conception of intellectual work which prefers speed and quantity of information to precision and depth, brilliant theoretical syntheses to the slow labors of empirical research, and the resources of already established knowledge to the risks of invention.

Now this training leaves an unmistakable mark on Sartre's literary and philosophical practice. It is reflected, for example, in his conception of philosophy as the sovereign discipline which should encompass all aspects of life and thought and hold dominion over all the special sciences: either by contrasting philosophy's ontology and phenomenological "comprehension" to scientific reason and empirical knowledge or by setting itself up as the transcendent legitimating body which judges and justifies all sciences without practicing any. Although certain aspects of Sartre's writing—such as his rare use of quotations and footnotes, and his vague, implicit sources—stem from this conception of philosophy, they may also have some relation to prep-school teaching. Because such teaching is obsessed by productivity and production delays, it encourages students to acquire hurried information—if need be from manuals and anthologies—rather than real erudition. The paradoxical fruit of this pedagogy is the work which achieves originality by carrying to extremes the academic art of assimilating, embroidering on, and patching together already established models.

We must not forget that among the best hidden and most important effects of the elite schools is their effect on their students' way of imagining society, on the way they see themselves and their place and worth in the world and, by extension, the social function of culture and the intellectual. To understand the power that school has to impose its image of the individual and his calling on Sartre, we need only recognize that the effectiveness of teaching is directly proportional to its consistency. The image that the school imposes, moreover, extends and reinforces the two factors which *The Words* shows are already at work throughout Sartre's childhood: the assurance of being one of the chosen few and the sense of indeterminacy which for Sartre are the chief explanations of his "mental illness."

In the French system of select schools for training ruling elites, the educational process performs the additional function of providing charismatic consecration. It is a veritable "rite of passage" which transforms the elect into an elite—not just in the eyes of others but more importantly, as far as explaining their habitus is concerned, in their own eyes. In this perspective, pedagogical operations and means of acculturation are aspects of a ritual which seems explicitly designed to produce a sense of belonging to a caste set apart from ordinary mortals. The selection made by competitive examination is at the same time a statutory election: in granting those chosen a social rank and status, it differentiates them from the mass of university students who failed—a distinction which the effect of "noblesse oblige" helps solidify. This effect is further heightened by a number of characteristic aspects of the elitist course of studies, such as the initiatory hazing of beginners by the upper classmen, the change in lifestyle and asceticism required by the furious pace of preparatory classes, the constant testing required by the institution, and the rich mythology of *esprit de corps* which is fed by memories of the most prestigious successes and by coded extravagances that in the communal life of the school are taken as marks of genius.

Sartre has often admitted that when he was young he felt with particular and (among the young candidates for glory who surrounded him) even exceptional force this elitist attitude and sense of election for which the only really human beings are geniuses. In recalling the personal rites and mythology which, as "supermen on call" he and Nizan had fashioned for themselves, he specifies in his preface to *Aden, Arabie:* "There was only one difference between us: I was certain that I was one of the elect, Nizan often wondered if he was not damned" (30). Or in *The Words:* "Dogmatic though I was, I doubted everything except that I was the elect of doubt" (252). And in his last interviews: "I always thought I would win . . . ."[38] "I looked upon myself as a genius"; " . . . as I saw it, the genius and the superman were just beings who showed in their full reality as men. The mass of people who graded themselves according to figures and hierarchies were a raw material . . . which . . . was formed by submen"; " . . . the [Sorbonne] students represented beings who were not quite men."[39] And a diary entry from 1939 which was meant for only a few intimate friends and posterity is even more explicit: " . . . [I] was extremely conscious of being the young Sartre, in the same way that people speak of the young Berlioz or the young Goethe."[40]

As for his feeling of indeterminacy and its converse, his feeling of his mind's unlimited power, it is significant that they are summed up retrospectively for him, at the time his generation is being weighed in the balance, in his image of himself and Nizan as students: "Before he is led by the hand to the seat that awaits him, a student is something infinite, undefined. . . . The young elite are everything and nothing: in other words, they are supported by the state and by their families. Underneath this misty indistinctness their life burns away."[41]

Nizan, moreover, had already pointed out that one of the main ideological effects of elite schools is the intellectualist illusion: "If Alain suggests that reason and right judgment are the true saviors and that, in order to set the world right, it is necessary only that men perceive things clearly in accordance with the truth revealed by these faculties—and if he says nothing else—how could the youths interned in the Lycée Henri-IV, where they live in monastic isolation from the rest of mankind, how could these adolescents who are so fascinated by intellectual acrobatics fail to be seduced by words so flattering to their pride?"[42]

And the truth of the matter is that there are other real and symbolic isolations from the outside world which come with belonging to a distinct elite group, and with being constantly and totally immersed as academic organization requires, that tend more than boarding school and the absence of material worries do to inculcate in preparatory-school students a belief in a spiritual freedom unshackled by the constraints of everyday existence, a freedom which, like succeeding in competitive examinations, is only a question of training, self-discipline, and pure conscious effort. And the Ecole normale, which coming as it does on the heels of the *khâgne*'s obligatory asceticism seems to be the ideal embodiment of the freedom that top students deserve for passing tests brilliantly, actually does bring the sense of freedom which is produced by the complete repression of social determinants that being a student or an intellectual allows. This temporary suspension of social responsibilities—not just those of adult life but also the obligations which regulate life so strictly in preparatory classes—is the truce that elitist education grants after imposing a sufficient number of years of restraints and communal life to guarantee that this freedom will be a controlled one,[43] a homogeneous—even stereotyped—extraordinarily conformist anticonformism.[44] Even in its most audacious forms, the Ecole normale style of existence only reproduces that watered-down version of the artist's life which has been duly established by the commonplaces of legend as the traditional university life for gentlemen's sons.

Sartre fits this pattern perfectly: "For most of us, including me, the first day at the Ecole Normale was the beginning of independence. Many can say, as I do, that they had four years of happiness there."[45] Up through his final interviews, Sartre always remembers his days at the Ecole as a time of "true happiness."[46] One of the many significant signs of his total integration into university life is his participation in the school play, a characteristic ritual desacralization which shows by deriding the institution one's identification with it. Sartre is just not capable of being serious about Nizan's already evident troubles, his flight to Aden, his railing against the Ecole in *Aden, Arabie* and *The Watchdogs:* "we took his passion for mere extravagant rhetoric. As for me, I was foolishly hurt because he tarnished my memories. Since Nizan had shared my life at the Ecole, he had to have been happy there, or else our friendship was already dead at that time. I preferred to save the past. I said to myself, 'He's exaggerating.' "[47] This falling out clearly illustrates the essential difference which separates these two Ecole normale students who are so alike in their dispositions as to be "indistinguishable," and who seem to be destined for equal success. The critical distance which keeps Nizan from sharing Sartre's total investment shows a different relationship to culture and the intellectual calling which is certainly linked to Nizan's family origins: for this child of a father who has given up being a worker to become an engineer, commitment to the institutions and practices of bourgeois society, far from being something he looks forward to, is a double betrayal. As a source of contradiction, this distance makes it possible to predict even then that the strategy Nizan is struggling to develop will be less effective than that of his classmate— as a result of having been subjected by his family and school to an extraordinarily fitting education which leaves him desiring no other destiny and happiness than those which this education suggests his classmate can spontaneously adopt.

Sartre's commitment is so complete that he will never really stop thinking of man in terms of the elitist and intellectualist model this schooling holds up for him. It is true that what he has said concerning this matter in his autobiographical works has always encouraged us to think that as a result of his wartime experiences, he changed radically.[48] And his later works—his *Critique*, for example, and *The Family Idiot*— accord much more weight to the social conditioning of individual praxis than *Being and Nothingness* did. But objectively at least, whatever his intentions, he never stopped postulating the subject's power to struggle free of his "class existence." Nor did Sartre ever stop universalizing, by erecting it into a prerogative of human consciousness, the unlimited possibility of making a clean slate of things, which is the tenacious illusion of the Ecole normale student and, more generally, the professional dream of the intellectual, who is conditioned by the conditions of his work to think of himself as unconditioned. Sartre never understood that consciousness may find within itself, in the form of lasting socially formed dispositions, an inertia which limits its freedom. The man who in writing the *Critique* takes up again *Being and Nothingness*'s desperate attempt to start from scratch and think through the whole world by the sheer power of his own reflection still considers himself the phenomenological ego, with the power to effect a radical *epoche*. But the ultimate paradox for this philosopher of "consciousness without inertia" is that this same conception of man and the philosopher, when it is related to the conditions which shape its author, becomes a proof of the inertia of the habitus.

One final and indelible effect of this inertia is found in Sartre's style of life, which up till the day he dies seems stubbornly to reproduce the

Ecole normale pattern. For Sartre, these "wise stupidities,"[49] this perfectly balanced compromise between the necessary eccentricities of genius and the demands of productivity, continue to be the authentic way of life, the ideal which governs his habits. Living in hotels, rejecting marriage in favor of many "contingent loves," writing ordinarily wherever he happens to be and often in cafés, and relishing a certain excess (for example, periods of unrelenting work sustained by self-destructive use of stimulants, or the famous nights spent drinking with friends) are all characteristics of the "artist's life." Yet they are elements of a life whose work rhythms and vacations are strictly organized for the sake of production.

*But do you like this café life?*

Yes, it's my life, I've always lived like that. It isn't exactly a café life: I have a late lunch, around two o'clock, and stay at the café until four. Once in a while I have dinner with Simone de Beauvoir in a restaurant. . . .

*Why this regularity in your habits? Each week passes in the same way as the week before, each person you see has his day, his hour, always the same. . . .*

I think it comes from the fact that one needs regular habits in order to write productively. I haven't written just three novels in my life; I have written many, many pages. One cannot write a rather large book without work discipline. But having said this, I must add that I have done my writing everywhere. For example, I wrote some pages of *Being and Nothingness* on a small hilltop in the Pyrenees, when I was on a bicycle trip with Simone de Beauvoir and Bost. I was the first to arrive, and I sat on the ground under some rocks and began to write. Then the others came; they sat down next to me, and I continued to write.

Obviously, I have done a lot of writing in cafés. For example, large parts of *The Reprieve* and of *Being and Nothingness* were written in La Coupole, in Les Trois Mousquetaires—avenue de Maine—and then in Le Flore. . . .
So these habits you're talking about date from the time when I organized my life around my working hours: from nine-thirty or ten in the morning to one-thirty, and then from five or six to nine o'clock. That is how I have worked all my life.[50]

Sartre's faithfulness to the life style which made him "perfectly happy" in his youth certainly enhanced one of his most indisputable merits as an intellectual: his exceptional power to resist the seductions and pressures with which powerholders seek to ensnare intellectuals.

He refused to accept the Legion of Honor and the Nobel Prize. And strict obedience to the Ecole normale student's prime imperative—stay free of all positions—does indeed entail rejection of bourgeois respectability and all the opportunities and emblems with which adult society undermines the independence from worldly power which is the intellectual's spiritual point of honor.

# CHAPTER 6

# Sartre's Position in 1945

## 1. THE EFFECTS OF CONCENTRATION

"Sartre is what we have been waiting for, and we are sure that he will always fulfill our expectations to overflowing."[1] This is how Christian Grisoli concludes the interview he had with Sartre the day after the tumultous lecture at the Club Maintenant. As a fervent disciple, Grisoli shows the Sartre myth being born at the moment Sartre's emotional impact is at its height.

This myth is a collective belief that has nothing inexplicable or accidental about it. It is a "well-formed illusion" based on the whole set of conditions Sartre's enterprise meets and the functions it fulfills. Up till now we have analyzed these conditions and functions successively in order to bring out the specific justification for each. Now, to make clear the whole sweep and power of Sartre's position, we must stress the additional consequences of having such a concentration of titles in one single person. If the correspondence of each of Sartre's individual traits to an already consecrated tendency reminds us of a succession, all of them together constitute a veritable revolution.

Not just because Sartre is philosophy's new Bergson and literature's new Gide, the awaited heir to two thrones which have simultaneously become vacant. By combining the two roles into one, he changes their very meaning. And to this synthesis must be added the other forms of interdependence between the different kinds of symbolic capital he has accumulated. His literary activity casts its prestige onto his philosophical discourse, lending it its language and its subjects. His philosophy in turn legitimates his claim to write a metaphysical literature, slips into his novels, articulates his interpretation of his own works and—by becoming literary criticism, aesthetic manifestos, excommunications of adversaries, and clarifications of intentions—gets itself publicly accepted. For once, creator and consecrator, writer and critic, are one and the same person. Thanks to his dual function, Sartre controls two essential aspects of that collective labor, the birth of the "creator." In the same fashion, playwright and philosopher support one another. As a chronicler of the age once noted, Sartre's plays had one merit which contributed greatly to their success: "By making audiences think that they were understanding a philosopher whom everyone thought obscure, they made them think they were intelligent."[2] Conversely, Sartre's plays succeeded in getting his philosophy recognized by the less competent but more worldly public that determines who becomes famous. With equipment like this, the improvised journalism Sartre agrees to do in 1945 not only earns him no discredit (as it would if he made it a profession); it makes his position all the more striking: the philosopher shows that he can make direct interpretations of the passing scene, and in lending intellectual dignity to reporting, wins the recognition of journalists.

There is one other form of capital which plays a not unimportant role in the process of consecration: the possibilities of information, cooptation, and publicity which go with living perfectly in place and in tune at the heart of the intellectual world. Of course we must avoid considering such mechanisms a consciously pursued strategy or a sufficient reason for success. For the person in the right place with the right competences, they are opportunities which open up spontaneously. All we need to do is keep in mind the other factors which also come into play in the production of Sartre's image and of his works themselves. His interest in Husserl and his stay in Berlin stem from a conversation with his "little buddy" Aron. It is thanks to the support of his friends Charles Dullin and Pierre Bost that Gallimard accepts the manuscript of *Nausea*. Dullin, furthermore, is an invaluable connection for a beginning playwright: it is he who makes it possible to stage *The Flies* during the Occupation. And the theater opens the doors for Sartre to the most influential circle of the Parisian intelligentsia of the day.[3] Through his frequent hobnobbing with artists and writers who also constitute the elite of current producers and public, his life and even the image of his life begin to change. Sartre's life becomes the most famous symbol of intellectual nonconformism. It is the life called for by his works.

Sartre's position, a symbiosis of all dimensions of intellectual excellence, can explain the echo Sartre awakens in his public. He plays in all registers, sounds all chords. He is simultaneously an intellectual, moral, and political guide and a symbol of revenge against all forms of power. He regains for philosophy the sovereign prestige which it seemed to have irrevocably lost, freeing it from its academic monopoly and breathing new life into it. As the living image of the free man who—

like Orestes, Mathieu, and Hugo—is "without ties or roots," Sartre
produces in both the character of his life and the lives of his characters
a flattering epic of the hero as intellectual. He is an ideologist articulating
and exalting the intellectual worldview.

It is this ubiquity which makes Sartre unbeatable in the lists where
at the Liberation, in the open situation of a social slate wiped clean by
the War and by the disappearance or decline of the dominant pre-War
generation, a small number of contestants are struggling to win the field.
The complete intellectual brings out the flaws of his competitors. His
closest rival in literature, Camus, is a philosophical amateur in comparison to the author of *Being and Nothingness*. And his only serious
philosophical competitor, Merleau-Ponty, is only a philosopher. Aron,
who of all the members of his class seemed up till the War to be the
most likely candidate for the most brilliant position, finds himself at the
Liberation in a position which diverges from—and thus loses out to—
the definition of legitimacy which is personified by Sartre. The triumph
of commitment alone would be enough to put Bataille and Blanchot out
of play, without even considering other glaring defects, notably philosophical ones. Other figures who are even less suited to the prevailing
definition of legitimacy are a fortiori out of the competition.

Sartre's contemporaries commonly refer to this image of the "total"
intellectual to indicate his incomparable greatness: "Philosopher, novelist, playwright, critic, and journalist, able to express himself with equal
facility in all these modes, Sartre stands there, cordial and uncompli-
cated, open to everyone's questions, his mind abounding with ideas
which his clear, curt speech immediately weaves into a seamless web,"
as Grisoli describes him in the aforementioned interview.[4] And it is
thanks to this "coherence," as another admirer notes, that everything
Sartre does seems legitimate: "His use of such personal language is
legitimate because it is intellectually coherent, in contrast to rhetoric
like that of Georges Bataille or Maurice Blanchot."[5]

# 2. THE IMPORTANCE OF A REVIEW

We would be forgetting one of the main conditions of Sartre's original
and continuing success if we failed to consider *Les Temps Modernes*, the
review he founds in 1945, just as the rage for existentialism breaks out.
In founding it he puts in place an updated version of the apparatus Gide
and the *Nouvelle Revue française* set up between the wars: the combination of a writer who has reached the heights of his consecration and
a review. Of course Paulhan's presence on the editorial committee and

the choice of Gallimard as publisher show that Sartre's position as new ruler succeeds to and is continuous with the past ruler's position in the field. But what is most important is that throughout this change in style there is one unchanging element, the review: from this time forward, this institution plays an essential role in the struggle to win and hold symbolic power. Witness the fact that in post-War French culture the stars are generally backed by some group, and these groups are usually identified by some common publication.

Camus, for example, next to Sartre the most fashionable writer of the day, edits *Combat*, the most famous daily born of the Resistance, without considering the objective ties which, until 1952, link him to Sartre and his review. By occupying very similar positions in different spaces—that of dailies and that of reviews—the two staffs can assure themselves of mutual profit from the dual presence gained by constantly exchanging coworkers, articles, reviews, and interviews.

Simone de Beauvoir gives us an idea of the extent of this exchange: "Bost wanted to become a journalist; Camus had read the manuscript of the book he had written during the war about his experiences as an infantry private, *Le Dernier des métiers;* he took an option on it for the series *Espoir* which he was editing for Gallimard and sent Bost to the front as a war correspondent. Whenever you asked Camus for a favour, he would do it so readily that you never hesitated to ask for another; and never in vain. Several of our younger friends also wanted to work for *Combat;* he took them all in. Opening the paper in the morning was almost like opening our mail. Towards the end of November, the United States wanted its war effort to be better known in France and invited a dozen reporters to the States. I've never seen Sartre so elated as the day Camus offered him the job of representing *Combat*."[6]

Among all the other personalities occupying an intellectual stage which had been profoundly altered by the War, the deportations, the Resistance and the purges, there is not a single one without institutional ties. Upon his return to Paris, Gide, who since 1944 had tried to break free of his isolation by giving help from Algiers to Jean Amrouche in founding a new review, *l'Arche*, backs a new venture, *Terre des hommes*, a daily edited by Herbart. Most of the big names belong to one or another of the reviews which—whether they are older ones like *Cahiers du Sud* and *Esprit* or ones started during the War, and even if they are exclusively literary reviews—all won their prestige during the Resistance by publishing antifascist writers under the Occupation: *Fontaine, Messages, Poésie, Confluences, la Nef*, and the most famous one, the actual organ of the Comité national des écrivains (which sits in judgment during the harsh purges of intellectuals that took place at the Liberation), *les Lettres françaises*.[7]

To understand this tendency to form groups and the privileged role that founding a review seems to play in institutionalizing groups, we need only think of cultural life as a field of forces governed by competition, in which one can exist and assert one's existence only by winning recognition from the field, making a name for oneself. The logic of the market leads to concentration and accumulation. Having recourse to a review as a constituent operation of an overall enterprise accords with the logic of one special form of capital, intellectual capital, which can only be converted from an individual property to a collective patrimony through a symbolic operation capable of producing and imposing the image of a collective reality. In bringing different names together under a single cover, the review makes them a precise and visible group, a structured and structuring whole, a source of acceptance and rejection, a place which marks out and consecrates. This transformation is especially necessary for a prophetic position such as the one Sartre embodies. For the intellectual who takes it upon himself to deal with all the major problems of his day, it is indispensable to have a reliable tribune at his disposition.

The creation of *Les Temps Modernes* produces a major change in Sartre. It is a change in his nature, and not just his power, because the review itself functions as a real field in and through which the properties Sartre has accumulated achieve expanded reproduction, but only at the ultimate cost of a decisive redirection and restriction of its editor's trajectory.

This perspective will enable us to avoid the impasses characteristic of philosophical definitions of existentialism. On the one hand, doctrinal criteria prove to be incapable of defining the phenomenon, as is shown by the wide variation among classifications made on this basis; on the other hand, such criteria do not explain the fact that among these varying classifications there is unanimous agreement on the names of Sartre and Merleau-Ponty, the only two whose inclusion seems self-evident to all.

It is on the basis of doctrinal criteria that definitions of existentialism have been proposed which are so vague that they identify it with philosophy itself, as Mounier does in his *Introduction aux existentialismes* (Paris: Denoël, 1947). At a time when existentialism is *the* philosophy, Mounier has all the interest in the world in establishing a usage broad enough to include his own personalist position. But in doing so he ends up encompassing practically the entire Western spiritualist tradition.

M.-A. Burnier, in contrast, gives the title of *The Existentialists and Politics* to a book which is in fact concerned exclusively with the group at *Les Temps Modernes*. Although he speaks of the group's "philosophical kinship" as justification for choosing them, he actually considers only the fact that they all worked at the same review, whose "common spirit" he invokes but does not even try to define philosophically.[8]

It could probably be said of all phenomena labeled "cultural movements" that an affinity of ideas is one of the necessary conditions but not the basic source of their identity as movements. In the case of existentialism, it is the review which produces and accounts for the apparent, and apparently sudden, transubstantiation which in 1945 transforms Sartre's personal success into a collective event, a "school of thought."

Our analysis of *Les Temps Modernes'* position among intellectual reviews will confirm this hypothesis. A comparison of their contents will bring out the continuity between them all—even those which the protagonists and their contemporaries saw as far from, if not incommensurable with, one another—by showing how all are related and, at least in their approach, outdated. The differences of doctrine in terms of which individuals and groups distinguished themselves from one another and justified their exclusions or alliances do not actually distinguish them unless they are connected to the characteristics which contrast them and their functions *as* groups.

Similar considerations explain why an analysis of Sartre's position at the time it becomes dominant turns out to be inseparable from an analysis of *Les Temps Modernes*. Of course Sartre's continuing dominion could not be explained by his review alone without considering the ongoing harmony between his activities and historical events: the problems of reconstruction, the Cold War, the dramatic events of decolonization in first Indochina and then Algeria all help maintain a social demand for prophetism. But the power and very form of Sartre's hegemony can only be explained by his review.

# PART TWO

Sartre and *Les Temps Modernes* during their hegemonic phase

The triumphal phase of *Les Temps Modernes* ends with the crisis of 1952–53 and the departure of Merleau-Ponty, at which time signs of the review's inability to adapt and concurrent signs of phenomena which will prove hostile to existentialism start to become evident. Consecration is a double-edged process which establishes the review's position and in so doing destines it to fall from this position by rendering it incapable of staying on top of the changes in the intellectual field. The editorial changes within the review between 1953 and 1962 show that these years mark the beginning of a period which we do not intend to analyze here: from this time on *Les Temps Modernes* is no longer the sensitive and faithful expression of the state of the field.

# CHAPTER 7

# The Position of *Les Temps Modernes* in the Field of Reviews

Within the field which is structured only in terms of groups identified as reviews, the position of *Les Temps Modernes* is defined by its relation to them. Thus it is essential to begin by establishing its supremacy to other reviews, so that we may then treat it as a system which is relatively independent of other positions yet also best represents this stage of the field's history.

## 1. THE FIELD OF REVIEWS AND ITS EVOLUTION

We cannot possibly consider all the intellectual reviews circulating in France during the existential era. But to reconstruct the field structure of this time, we need only observe the positions which contribute most to defining it.

A first comparison of the trajectories of the most influential reviews— on the basis of criteria such as the period in which they are influential and the content and composition of their editorial staffs—will enable us to make out certain tendencies which in their difference they share.

In 1945, the landscape about which the pre-War intellectuals still on the scene are scattered is the one which took shape during the Occupation. It does not last very long. During the next five years the field is fundamentally restructured. This upheaval alone is enough to establish *Les Temps Modernes'* dominance, since its appearance proves to be the source of the upheaval, and its model the ruling paradigm of all the other changes in the field.

To begin with it is significant that nearly all the names still extant in 1945 disappear one by one. With the exception of *Les Cahiers du Sud*, a review which is too local and peripheral to be subject to the repercussions of the Parisian market, the only reviews which survive are two politically militant ones—*Esprit,* which is the voice of committed Catholicism, and *les Lettres françaises,* over which the C.P. won control when the underground ended—whereas the small independent reviews which were led into the capital city by the Liberation—*Fontaine, Confluences, l'Arche, la Nef*—or which (like *Terre des hommes*) had just been founded at the Liberation, all die.[1] Their inability to compete with *Les*

### THE EVOLUTION OF THE FIELD OF REVIEWS

| Model \ Year | . . . 1939 40 41 42 43 44 45 46 47 48 49 50 51 |
|---|---|
| Literary | *Fontaine* <br> *Messages* <br><br> *Confluences* <br> *Les Lettres* <br> *françaises* <br> *l'Arche* <br> *La Nef* <br> *Terre* <br> *des Hommes* |
| Philosophical | *Deucalion* |
| Hybrid | *Cahiers* <br> *du Sud* <br><br> *Critique* |
| Committed | *Esprit*     *Action* <br> *T.M.** <br> *Liberté de l'esprit* <br> *La Table ronde* <br> *La Nouvelle Critique* |

*\*Les Temps Modernes*

*Temps Modernes* is easy to understand. As a result of its unprecedented concentration of capital in its editor and its editorial staff, which includes representatives of all the different forms of legitimacy recognized at the time, Sartre's review is a pole which irresistably attracts "free" intellectuals, those with no ties to any orthodoxy. The model it offers—a model which seems to combine literary and philosophical excellence, freedom and commitment, close reasoning and the capacity to think about everything—sharply devaluates the currency of all the other reviews which during the War had freely proliferated in the void left by the *N.R.F.*'s disappearance behind the cloud of its collaboration. All these pretenders—whose understandable propensity to simply reproduce the characteristics of their predecessor's twenty-year reign has enabled them to hold the literary ground that the *N.R.F.* once held—suddenly seem no more than flawed outmoded copies of a reality which is itself outmoded in relation to a position which seems both to preserve the past and move ahead.

An analogous effect that *Les Temps Modernes'* appearance has on the philosophical field explains the minimal success of *Deucalion*, the review founded in 1946 by Jean Wahl, who also tries to revive a pre-War model, that of the avant-garde philosophical review embodied during the thirties in *Recherches philosophiques*. In claiming to realize "pure" philosophy's highest aspirations by moving to open it up to the whole of experience, the existentialists seem paradoxically to be reducing it to no more than an academic exercise. Wahl and his review had been an important source for Sartre during his philosophical beginnings, as he will subsequently admit in his *Search for a Method:* "At that time one book enjoyed a great success among us—Jean Wahl's *Toward the Concrete.*"[2] Now this relationship between the two positions is reversed, as we can see by comparing the attention *Deucalion* pays to Sartre[3] with the existentialists' carefree unconcern for it. Their only reaction to Wahl's criticisms is two amused lines in Simone de Beauvoir's journal.[4] Simply comparing this change to the one we have seen taking place in Sartre's relationship to the *N.R.F.* sums up the meaning of the concentration that *Les Temps Modernes* has achieved: by reabsorbing into a single position the two previously separate positions in which he himself first made himself known, Sartre eliminates them both.

The evolution of the field of reviews is characterized by another phenomenon which shows that *Les Temps Modernes* has assumed a hegemonic role. From the time the review first appears, we begin to see a general tendency of intellectuals to pool their efforts in committed or at least hybrid forms which are closer to the existentialist model. This tendency is evident in the main steps intellectuals begin to take around 1950. The "free" intellectuals, those without orthodox ideological ties, are almost completely monopolized by *Les Temps Modernes*. The few who are not, those who for one reason or another occupy positions which are objectively incompatible with that of *Les Temps Modernes*, gather at least for a time at *Critique*, the review Georges Bataille founds in 1946. The men already associated with Bataille before the War are gathered there: Blanchot and Klossowski, Koyré and Kojève, Ambrosino and Eric

Weil, Wahl and other representatives of academic philosophy—Vuille-min, Lévinas, and Jankelévitch. The first to be kicked out of *Les Temps Modernes*, Aron and Paulhan, will pass through *Critique* on the way to finding a place which suits them better. Even though *Critique* is not a committed review, it is close to the *Temps Modernes* model, and since it is not tied to any particular profession, it too opposes the traditional model.

The new definition of legitimacy also puts pressure on intellectuals who are either Communists or close to the C.P.: *la Nouvelle Critique*, founded in 1948, shows both by its choice of editors and by its format that it is trying to be a Communist counterpoint to the existentialists' review. *La Pensée* and *les Lettres françaises*, it is true, continue to uphold the old separation between literature and philosophy. But only the loyalty of their militant readers assures their survival. The main foci of the Catholic intelligentsia—*Esprit*, the weekly *Témoinage chrétien*, *le Centre catholique des intellectuels français* (C.C.I.F.)[5]—also agree with *Les Temps Modernes'* conception of culture as enlisted in the cause and fighting on all fronts. But the clearest sign of a general tendency is the trajectory of conservative intellectuals. The rare segments who were not compromised during the Occupation gradually group around interdisciplinary and militant reviews whose archetype is recognizably *Les Temps Modernes*. The Gaullist version, *Liberté de l'esprit*, does not hesitate to publish those who speak for a more aggressive right. François Mauriac and Raymond Aron, those pillars of the *Figaro*, go one to *la Table Ronde* (1948), which unites traditional conservatives, the other to *Preuves*, which is created in 1951 as an organ of the French section of the Congress for Cultural Freedom, an international movement of liberal inspiration start-ed in 1950. But the dominance of the Sartrean model seems even more absolute if one considers that during this period the entire discussion of the social sciences is reduced, so to speak, to the highly restricted space granted it by reviews such as *Esprit* and *Les Temps Modernes*. Specialized journals are rare prior to the end of the fifties, when *Sociologie du travail* (1959), *Archives européennes de sociologie* (1960), and *Communications* (1961) appear.

Throughout this restructuring movement of the field of reviews, the decisive external source of change remains the political situation. Po-litical pressure on culture takes the form of either forcing intellectuals to make a commitment or leading them to make a choice among positions which are chiefly those that have been politically legitimated by the Resistance—the Communists, the Catholics, and the Gaullists. But the field's internal hierarchy has a weight of its own, as is shown by the fact that its hegemonic position is not occupied by the intellectuals who are members of the C.P., the strongest organization politically, but by *Les Temps Modernes,* which is not only committed but has the most intellectual capital.

## 2. STRUCTURED RELATIONS

On the basis of the foregoing analysis of field tendencies, we can identify (along with *Les Temps Modernes*) *Esprit, la Nouvelle Critique,* and *Critique* as the reviews which demarcate the realm of significant positions in the period under consideration. The reason why *Esprit* and *la Nouvelle Critique* are chosen over *la Table ronde* or *Preuves* from among committed reviews is that right-wing publications are less representative in an era when legitimate intellectuals are on the left. It may seem arbitrary in this perspective to include a noncommitted review like *Critique.* But we shall show that at this time, and in relation to *Les Temps Modernes,* it represents another, shadowy side of the avant-garde. Although it is in its unsettling erudition too esoteric to achieve high consecration, it nevertheless embodies a direction which will subsequently come to the fore.

Without claiming to establish exhaustively the objective characteristics of such a complex system, we can begin by reconstructing the systematic relationships among the reviews in question from their book reviews, polemics, and attacks, and on this basis establishing the hierarchy of their different positions.

The first thing we notice is that all the reviews have a practically unilateral relationship to Sartre's group. By devoting essays, articles and quotations to it, they show a lively interest in it which it does not reciprocate, and its freedom to ignore them is a sure sign of its hegemony.

But a hierarchy does emerge from the totality of these relationships. *Critique*'s constant interest in *Les Temps Modernes* and its scrupulous criticisms of it suggest that it holds the position of an obviously declining review which must always be concerned with the position of the dominant review, yet can still oppose it with its own model of excellence.

The editor of *Critique,* Bataille, had not stopped being concerned with Sartre's existentialism, from the time Sartre savagely attacked his *L'expérience intérieure* [in "Un nouveau mystique," *Cahiers du Sud* 260 and 261 (1943), reprinted in *Situations I].* He had first defended his position against Sartre's criticisms, with a care which showed he had been deeply wounded, in a "Reply to Jean-Paul Sartre" published as an appendix to *Sur Nietzsche.* In very short space he brings out a whole string of articles in *Critique:* "Le surréalisme et sa différence avec

## THE RELATIONSHIPS AMONG *LES TEMPS MODERNES* (T.M.), *ESPRIT, CRITIQUE,* and *LA NOUVELLE CRITIQUE* DURING 1949

The relationships (reviews, attacks, exchange of writers) established during a year can show in a significant way the structure of relations.

\* = attacks; O = reviews; s = exchanges of writers

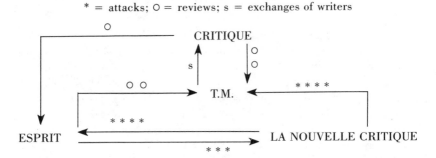

*T.M.* (*Les Temps Modernes*)
Has relations only with *Critique*. One of *Critique*'s regular writers, Klossowski, publishes in *Les Temps Modernes* an article about another *Critique* writer, Maurice Blanchot [40 (Feb. 1949)].
*CRITIQUE*
Relationships with *Les Temps Modernes:* two reviews: R.-P. Caillois, of G. Varet, "L'ontologie de Sartre" [37 (June 1949)]; V. Craste, of Merleau-Ponty's *Sense and Non-Sense* [36 (May 1949)].
Relationships with *Esprit:* one review: G. Bataille, in "La souveraineté de la fête et le roman américain," talks about *L'âge du roman américain,* by C.-E. Magny, who writes for *Esprit* [39 (Aug. 1949)].
*ESPRIT*
Relationships with C.P. intellectuals: two entries opposing the C.P.'s cultural politics and one direct attack on the staff of *la Nouvelle Critique:* in 2 (Feb.), a note on *la Nouvelle Critique* in the "Journal à plusieurs voix"; in 5 (May), J.-M. Domenach, "Le P.C.F. et les intellectuels"; 12 (Dec.), a note in the "Journal à plusieurs voix": "Parti des peintres et peintres du Parti."
Relationships with *Les Temps Modernes:* two favorable reviews in 12 (Dec.): M. Beigbeder, "Théâtre philosophique? Sartre," 924; J.-M. Domenach on *The Second Sex* (1005).
*LA NOUVELLE CRITIQUE*
Relationships with *Les Temps Modernes:* four attacks: in 6 (May), A. Wurmser, in the "Chronique des antis," attacks Sartre's position on the Kravchenko affair; in 7 (June), G. de Arboussier ("Une dangereuse mystification") condemns Sartre's "theory of négritude"; in 8 (July-Aug.), J. Kanapa, in "Les communistes ont un plan," takes a hostile stand in the debate over *The Second Sex;* in 10 (Nov.), M. Mouillaud speaks aggressively against *Entretiens sur la politique,* by Sartre, Rousset, and Rosenthal.

Relationships with *Esprit:* four attacks: 5 (April), Wurmser on Izard concerning Kravchenko; 7 (June), M. Mouillaud responds to Domenach [see *Esprit* 5 (1949)] in "Liberté de l'ésprit et esprit de parti"; 9 (Oct.), J.-T. Desanti, "Scrupules et ruses d'Emmanuel Mounier"; 10 (Nov.), P. Daix attacks *Esprit* for its position on the Rajk trial.

---

l'existentialisme" 2 (1946); "Baudelaire mis à nu" 8/9 (1947) (in which he comments admiringly on Sartre's *Baudelaire,* although criticizing it for being not so much a critical study as a moral judgment); "De l'éxistentialisme au primat de l'économie" 19 (1947) and 21 (1948), in which he lets his aggressiveness show: "Modern existentialism is a compromise. . . . This slide involves a cancerous growth of the intellectual enterprise. . . . Understanding as an academic exercise goes beyond all normal bounds (above all in Sartre's writing). . . . This philosophy's language is laborious, it is gluey. It seems to me to show a basic uncertainty. Existential thinking is always trying to keep from thinking without ever succeeding in eliminating thought. As a child in the grip of an urgent need dances around on the same spot without being able to reach a decision, this style of thinking, stricken with its own morose virtuosity, steals away but will not die. . . . Sartre says that all he wants to do is tell the truth in his time. I have difficulty believing it: how could a *philosopher* who wanted to do this fail to make a searching analysis of the limits he meets in the course of his investigations?" (520ff, passim and note); and "Vue d'ensemble: l'éxistentialisme" 41 (1950). If we add to these the articles that other *Critique* writers devote to Sartre, the very favorable commentaries that Merleau-Ponty's works draw from R. P. Caillois [22 (1948)] and V. Craste [36 (1949)], and the critical but careful reviews S. de Beauvoir receives [J. Bousquet 1 (1946) and G. Bataille 44 (1951)], we get an idea of the attentive concern with which *Critique* follows the existentialists.

The enthusiastic "Sartrism" of some of those who write for *Esprit,* on the contrary, and the attempt others make to challenge the dominant review, show admiration. This is true not only of Jeanson, who goes over to *Les Temps Modernes,* but of Claude-Edmonde Magny. Domenach too always shows respectful recognition of existentialism. He launches cooperative ventures with existentialists, such as the "Appel à l'opinion internationale en faveur d'une Europe socialiste," which is published in November 1947 by *Esprit* alone, but is readied in numerous meetings with representatives of *Les Tempes Modernes, Combat,* and *Franc-Tireur.* Moreover, when *The Second Sex* is published he devotes a very positive review to it [12 (1949)]. Mounier chiefly attacks Sartre's atheism, thereby shifting his confrontation with existentialism from philosophical grounds onto the more favorable grounds of value. (See, for example, his "L'éspoir des désespérés.") Jean Lacroix, *Esprit*'s philosopher, does the same thing. [See *Marxisme, existentialisme, personnalisme* (Paris, 1951).] Another of *Esprit*'s writers, Marc Beigbeder, is fascinated by Sartre, to whom he pays aggressive attention: in addition to an essay, *L'homme Sartre* (Paris: Bordas, 1947), he writes a commentary on Sartre's plays in *Esprit* 12 (1949).

The accusations and insults with which *La Nouvelle Critique* constantly, aggressively attacks *Les Temps Modernes* express its impotent animosity. There is practically no issue which does not take the existentialists to task. During its first year of publication, for example, the following major articles appear: 1, Desanti violently attacks Merleau-Ponty for *Humanism and Terror*; 3, the same Desanti writes one article against Sartre and Lukács writes another; 6, Sartre is denounced as an anti-Communist for his stand on Kravchenko; 7, Sartre's "theory of negritude" (in his preface to an anthology by Senghor) is called a "dangerous mystification," and Bottigelli labels the existentialists "new Dührings"; 8, Kanapa takes aim at *The Second Sex* and all its reviewers; 10, Sartre's turn: he is attacked for his role in the R.D.R. and the "Entretiens sur la politique."

The meaning of these differences becomes clear when we look at the relationships that the three reviews which write about *Les Temps Modernes* have to one another. *Critique* pays no attention to *la Nouvelle Critique* or *Esprit*. *La Nouvelle Critique* constantly attacks *Esprit* but says nothing about *Critique* (a noncommitted review does not bother Communist intellectuals). *Esprit* also pays no attention to *Critique*, but sometimes engages in outright polemics against the Communists, although it generally prefers to keep things on the theoretical level of discussions of Marxism. In sum, although *Critique* seems isolated, *la Nouvelle Critique* shows its illegitimacy by having its attacks on the other groups go generally ignored, and *Esprit* shows a certain weakness in its constant attention to the existentialists and the Communists.

The positions of the reviews can be mapped even more precisely in terms of the goings and comings of their writers. These show the marginal position of *la Nouvelle Critique*, the only review which seems to be completely excluded from their circuit. There is on the contrary a relation of contiguity between *Les Temps Modernes*, *Esprit*, and *Critique*, whose staffs are tied together by occasional contributions as well as by migrations. Yet in this same respect, *Esprit* shows that it is less legitimate than the other reviews: its exchanges with them are the exception, whereas the relationship between *Les Temps Modernes* and *Critique* is very close.

In the exchanges between *Les Temps Modernes* and *Critique, Critique*'s regular writers (such as Blanchot, Klossowski, de Schloezer, Craste, Laude, Alquié, Renou, C. Chonez, and Kahnweiler) contribute more often to *Les Temps Modernes* than (with the exception of Queneau and André Masson) the reverse. But it is significant that after Paulhan, Aron, and Ollivier break with *Les Temps Modernes*, they all gravitate (at least for a time) toward *Critique* (Aron and Ollivier even becoming members of the editorial board): *Critique* is the only acceptable place during these years, besides *Les Temps Modernes*, for "free" intellectuals. Exchange between *Les Temps Modernes* and *Esprit* is more rare, practically limited to Jeanson's case (which can be understood as an exceptional promotion for special merit: Sartre authorizes his interpretation of *Being and Nothingness*). There is also a single, remarkable case of exchange between *Critique* and *Esprit*, that of Albert Béguin, who will become *Esprit*'s second editor, and who often writes for *Critique*. He is in fact the only unquestionable authority on culture whom *Critique* can claim as its own. Leibowitz's is a representative case: an *Esprit* writer before the War, he leaves it after the War for *Les Temps Modernes* and *Critique*. Furthermore, even though his friendship with Bataille, who hid him in his house during the Occupation, is much closer than his relationship to Sartre, it is Sartre he asks to write a preface to his book, *L'artiste et sa conscience*—which is Sartrean even in its title.

# 3. THE CONSENSUS OF THE TIMES

Since the common denominator of all these reviews is their determination to deal with every single vital question or important issue of their times (the title of *Les Temps Modernes* is symbolic), and since it is the same times all are writing about, the common topics they tackle are especially clear and undeniable. For the first time, intellectuals are directly, openly analyzing their own times. That is why their reviews provide such an exceptional catalog and inventory—and reflection—of those harmonious-disharmonious relationships which in other periods of history are shrouded by masks and censoring, and thus less readily perceptible. No doubt the commitment which is existentialist culture's point of honor is also its weak point: it lays it open to exaggerating philosophy's relationship to "contingency," to social roots, which even on the lofty heights of "pure" philosophy is never absent but is just so euphemized (according to the rules of a form or discourse which can become eternal only by making itself seem timeless and self-engendered) that efforts to establish its objective presence become difficult, inconvenient, and subject always to facile refutations.

Merleau-Ponty, the existentialist who as a result of his academic position had the most reason to anticipate the objections of "pure" philosophers, recognized this truth in his preface to *The Adventures of the Dialectic:* "We need a philosophy of both history and spirit to deal with the problems we touch upon here. Yet we would be unduly rigorous if we were to wait for perfectly elaborated principles before speaking philosophically of politics. In the crucible of events we become aware of what is not acceptable to us, and it is this experience as interpreted that becomes both thesis and philosophy. We are thus allowed to report our experience frankly with all its false starts, its omissions, its disparities, and with the possibility of revisions at a later date. By doing so we manage to avoid the pretense of systematic works, which, just like all others, are born of our experience but claim to spring from nothing and therefore appear, at the very moment when they catch up with current problems, to display a superhuman understanding when, in reality, they are only returning to their origins in a learned manner."[6]

What is happening politically and socially directly determines, for the most part, what appears in reviews, with the result that their chronology could be superimposed on that of current French and international events (of course with intervals and gaps which we shall see are significant). The history of the post-War world unfolds through the successive order of their articles: in the aftermath of the Liberation, meditation on the conflict and projects for reconstruction; purges, nationalizations, reforms of the army, the school system, the press; discussions of the Constitution; the Nuremberg Trials and the revelations of Nazi war crimes; the fears aroused by atom bomb tests; the war in Indochina; the Marshall Plan and the Atlantic Pact; the Lysenko case, the Kravchenko trial, the denunciation of Stalinism and the crisis of the peoples' democracies, Titoism; and then the Korean War, the uneasiness stirred by the Algerian situation; McCarthyism. . . .[7]

Even *Les Temps Modernes'* characteristically sweeping essays on the relationships between morality and politics, which might seem to be an existentialist bow to one of the sacrosanct topics of traditional philosophy, reveal their contingent roots (and their function of providing a secular morality for deracinated intellectuals) when they are related to their contexts: discussions of the purges, the importance taken on by the Communist Party, revelations about Stalinism. And comparing *Les Temps Modernes* to the other reviews confirms the close ties all have to their times by showing that they all devote space to the same subjects. Simone de Beauvoir's "L'existentialisme et la sagesse des nations" [*Les*

*Temps Modernes* (Dec. 1945)] complements Lacroix's "Les catholiques et la politique" [*Esprit* (June 1945)]; "Témoinage et efficacité," another article by Lacroix [*Esprit* (Dec. 1945)], complements de Beauvoir's "Idéalisme moral et réalisme politique" [*Les Temps Modernes* (Nov. 1945)]. If Simone de Beauvoir speaks of a "morality of ambiguity," Mounier entitles one of his articles "Les équivoques du personnalisme" [*Esprit* (Feb. 1947)]. Bataille writes essays for *Critique* with very indicative titles: "La morale de Miller" (June 1946), "Le sens moral de la sociologie (ibid.), and "La moral du malheur" [on Camus (June-July 1947)]. And Weil joins the debate with "Raison, morale et politique" (June 1948). If we note further that during the same period Merleau-Ponty revises *Humanism and Terror* and Sartre is busy writing his *Morale*, and if we take the post-War Camus the moralist into account, we cannot ignore the weight of this conjuncture, of that call for a reconstruction of moral philosophy about which we have already spoken in recalling the historical conditions of existentialist prophetism.

Once one leafs through the other reviews, the question of the correct relationship to the Communist Party loses its appearance of a typically Sartrean problem and shows itself to be the obsession of an entire generation. There is not a one which is not polarized by it.[8] The proliferation of articles and special issues on certain countries such as the United States, Germany, and Indochina is explained by the fact that these are countries in which international equilibrium hangs in the balance. One can see especially how much the ambivalence toward America which is so evident in Sartre's highly critical attitude toward U.S. policy and his concurrent fascination with the country is typical of all the French intelligentsia. Think of the enthusiasm with which French intellectuals go visit America right after the War, and of the interest in it shown in the reports they publish in *Combat* and *le Figaro*.[9] The investigative balance sheets these reviews draw up on French institutions and democracy take on their full meaning when they are related to the efforts made at the Liberation to renew French society. And their constant debate about colonialism is tied to a France gripped by problems of decolonization.[10]

This convergence of the reviews also reveals differences which are significant because they are relatively constant. *La Nouvelle Critique* publishes no special issues on foreign countries; it is behind the times in noticing problems of decolonization; and its specialized criteria of choice limit its *aggiornamento* almost exclusively to French, even Parisian, realities. As far as the timing of the articles that different reviews devote to the same questions is concerned, *Les Temps Modernes* and *Esprit* are neck and neck ahead of the rest, and on certain fronts *Esprit* beats out *Les Temps Modernes:* it is *Esprit,* for example, which sounds the alarm about North Africa; it also publishes the first of the big sociologically inspired inquests; and it is *Esprit,* finally, which breaks the taboo against anti-Communism honored by all left intellectuals since the Liberation by denouncing, at the time of the Rajk affair, Stalinism's "scholastic Marxism." And the reviews also have observable differences of genre: investigations are characteristic of *Esprit,* big sweeping syntheses of *Les Temps Modernes,* erudite overviews of *Critique,* and inquisitions of *la Nouvelle Critique.*

Thus textural characteristics—what is said and when and how it is said—do not suffice to explain the observed hierarchy and relations of reviews: *Les Temps Modernes'* domination, *Critique's* originality and isolation, *la Nouvelle Critique's* lot of being given little or no consideration, and *Esprit's* low-key legitimacy. The contrasts and conflicts among the reviews can only really be explained by the characteristics of the groups whose beliefs they express.

# 4. A SYSTEM OF STRATEGIES

In saying that differences of product relate to differences of producer, I am not thinking of a cause-effect relationship. A person's "capital" gives form and value to his practices through a sort of transposition of its constituent elements[11]—both objective social elements such as material possessions, titles, and fame, and individually embodied elements such as the habitus, with its systems of schemes for classifying what is perceived and evaluated. The relation these elements have to the possibilities offered by a person's specific field of play, here the intellectual field, directs his strategies. According to this hypothesis, the objective affinity, which ties a group's different practices together (without any explicit intention on its members' part) and distinguishes them from the objective affinity that ties the practices of other groups together, is explained by the practical tendency of individual agents to group together on the basis of an affinity of habitus. Since I am only concerned here with explaining the practices of intellectuals, I shall consider only those characteristic intellectual practices of each group in question which have relevant consequences in the intellectual field. To understand fully how they affect the field, we must look at them as a system of relations, even though we must break them down here for the sake of analysis. As for the agents themselves, we shall consider only the most important ones: the official editors and the writers who are the most assiduous coworkers at the review and the most closely associated with its image.

# 4.1 Esprit

*Esprit*'s model is the closest to the existentialists' review. It is even in some respects undeniably a historical precedent. For it was *Esprit* which, in company with other reviews of "non-conformist"[12] groups, invented in the thirties the basic principle of committed reviews: the philosophical and political essay grafted onto major topics of current interest, the taste for "authentic" documents, and the stress on ethical concerns. Yet when *Les Temps Modernes* appears on the intellectual scene, it is *Esprit* which has the air of a tarnished, inferior copy of the original.

If we consider the producers' capital, the personalists as a group prove to have less of it than the existentialists in three such decisive dimensions as social class origin, geographical origin, and academic titles. In the French intellectual field, moreover, being stamped "Catholic" at this time is a negative factor. And the individual probability of these disadvantages favoring a trajectory and practices which are less legitimate than those of *Les Temps Modernes* is heightened by their cumulative effect.

If we compare the biographical data of the founders of *Les Temps Modernes* with the biographical data of the chief producers of *Esprit* at the Liberation, the difference in the endowment of the two groups is both systemic and striking. The first were born in Paris or grew up there in families of bourgeois intellectuals (Sartre, Aron), military men (Merleau-Ponty), or liberal professionals (Simone de Beauvoir). They attended the most prestigious Parisian lycées (except Simone de Beauvoir, who until she enrolled at the Sorbonne went to private schools, as was customary for well-brought-up young ladies), studied at the Ecole normale, and were all *agrégés*. Even before *Les Temps Modernes* was founded, they all already held a recognized position in intellectual space.

The nucleus of *Esprit* come from the provincial lower-middle and middle class. (Mounier comes from Grenoble; Lacroix, Fraisse and Domenach from Lyon; Touchard from Mans; Madaule from the Pyrenees; and Marrou from Marseille.) They are militant Christians, usually Catholic, occasionally Protestant. They have the same sort of academic capital as the existentialists, but not of such a high quality: they do their studying in the provinces; although most are *agrégés* (Mounier, Lacroix, Madaule), only one among them, Marrou, attends the Ecole normale, and only one, Fraisse, has his doctorate—and he got it at Lyon, not Paris. They have no recognized capital in French cultural life besides that which is associated with their review and which they earned working there. Some of them are long, even lifetime, lycée teachers: Lacroix teaches philosophy at the *khâgne* in Lyon, Madaule ends his career as a history and geography professor at the lycée Michelet, and Touchard is first a tutor at the lycée Henri-IV and then a professor at the Ecole alsacienne before becoming a top-level bureaucrat in the theater. There is not a single consecrated writer among them, and those of them who are university professors (Fraisse, Marrou) are far from having won the fame of a Merleau-Ponty or an Aron.

The particular conjunction of dispositions which characterizes the personalists—who are first-generation intellectuals, Catholics, and sons of the salaried and rising provincial lower-middle and middle class—explains their characteristic group ethos: an ascetic and meritocratic, spiritualist, and elitist moral rectitude.[13] This class ethos must be seen as the chief source of the differences which both on the level of literature and in the realm of politics almost systematically divide *Esprit* and *Les Temps Modernes*.

The literary dimension, which is almost nonexistent in *Esprit* from its inception in 1932, is of basic importance to *Les Temps Modernes*. The literary capital Sartre accumulates is further augmented by that of Simone de Beauvoir, Queneau, and Leiris, as well as by the capital of new authors which the existentialists' review is able, thanks to its authority, to attract and consecrate. Its prestige, the special place it reserves for literature, and the care it takes to make sure that the texts it publishes are "written" make it the most important literary tribune of the day.

The literary prestige of *Les Temps Modernes* falsifies Mounier's claim that it is because the current generation chose to reject literature that he has omitted it from *Esprit*. Recalling the founding of *Esprit*, he writes: "A whole era was coming to an end, the dazzling era of post-World War I literary flowering; Gide, Montherlant, Proust, Cocteau, Surrealism—this display of fireworks was falling back silent on its own ashes. It had sprung forth as a marvelous expression of its times. It had not brought to mankind the torch of a new destiny. The sense of disappointment which followed these guides without a guiding star, set to the music of Wall Street's distant rumblings, led their successors to reflect on the destiny of a civilization which seemed capable of brilliance but only at the price of some sort of underlying decay. The thirties' generation was going to be a serious, solemn generation concerned with problems and uneasy about the future. Literature at its most gratuitous had dominated the preceding generation. The one which followed was to commit itself more intimately to spiritual, philosophical and political quests."[14]

But the different example of *Les Temps Modernes* gives grounds for thinking that *Esprit* rejected literature not in response to a generational attitude but as a result of a "necessary choice"—a choice in which the personalists' social characteristics undeniably play a part. Their stress on ethics over aesthetics, content over form, and "substance" over "show" corresponds to the habitus of a class which is not granted the detachment from material problems and their practical urgency which in the privileged classes favors the development of the aesthetic attitude. In this sense, the inferior social and intellectual legitimacy which distinguishes Mounier and his contributors from the literary lords of the preceding generation as well as from the existentialists is an important key to understanding their differences in their relationships to literature. When Mounier contrasts the value of the "serious" to the "gratuitousness" of formal concerns, he is just rationalizing. The distinction between "serious" and "gratuitous" at the core of his writing is one of those fundamental systems of classification which would not constantly recur in cultural history if they did not translate class relationships, "embodied social structures."[15] The verbal distinction expresses the social class distinction between those dominant ones who possess the easy familiarity with literature characteristic of legitimate heirs and those whom they dominate, who are tied to a functional conception of literature which is implicitly ethical rather than aesthetic. By their very insistence on the "serious," the personalists "class" themselves and in so doing give us the key to their unhappy relationship to literature: their social class ethos.

We meet this ethos again at the source of the group's ethical and political choices. And in this case, morality is a privileged field of observation: not only has the social crisis brought the discussion of values and the ethical approach in general to the fore, but in this context the ethos of a group like *Esprit,* whose main distinguishing characteristic is its ethical disposition, shows forth in its pure state. The "spirit of seriousness" which is the source of *Esprit*'s aversion for the "playful seriousness" of literary exercises is no more than one manifestation of the moral rectitude which governs all other manifestations of this sector of the intellectual field, and which becomes particularly evident in ethical questions. The cardinal virtues of personalist morality are prudence, hard work, competence, and discipline. If we include fidelity to Catholicism, we can see that this morality is bound to seem, in spite of its prudent openings, basically conformist in comparison to the radical questioning of all moral laws and their foundations which the existentialists are proposing. Tied as it is to a creed, *Esprit*'s morality has neither the stamp of universality nor the unprecedented air inherent in *Les Temps Modernes*' prophetism.

We can effectively illustrate the difference between *Esprit* and *Les Temps Modernes* in this respect by comparing their attitudes toward the watershed issues of sexuality, women, and family. *Esprit* maintains a total silence concerning the topic of homosexuality, which is most obviously associated with *Les Temps Modernes* through Genet, whom Sartre's important essay consecrates. As for women, *Esprit* shows no concern for them except when it gives a sympathetic reception to *The Second Sex* (Domenach)—that is to say, except when it is dragged into the question on the initiative of *Les Temps Modernes*—and has no women at its central core, whereas the role of women such as Simone de Beauvoir and Colette Audry helps define the structure of *Les Temps Modernes'* capital. There is a particularly striking difference between the open morality of the couple upheld by Sartre and Simone de Beauvoir—an anti-institutional morality which rejects exclusive relationships, marriage, and procreation—and the patriarchal model of the Châtenay-Malabry community, which by having its families live in the same place, physically cements the work and friend relationships that Mounier and his closest collaborators have to one another. These ethical differences surface in systemic differences between two ways of living and thinking about ethics: the one stressing authenticity, freedom, breaking rules and breaking out of roles, and "situations"; the other adopting as its values seriousness, discipline, asceticism, and brotherhood.

The political values of the two groups have the same structural basis and show analogous differences. *Esprit*'s prudent progressivism corresponds to the group's fundamental dispositions—desire for order, respect for hierarchy, trust in competence and merit—just as "critical fellow travelling" with the Communist Party is the only form of commitment possible for *Les Temps Modernes*. In contrast to *Les Temps Modernes'* noisy struggles against every form of established order, *Esprit* significantly opposes the "established disorder," that is to say (in "third force" language), the evils produced by the anarchy of "liberal capitalism": "ineffectual" and "corrupt" parliamentarianism and "collectivism," the concept of "the power of the masses." These aversions put *Esprit* on the side of moderate, classical conservative or neoconservative political forces, with which the review openly maintains relations. Two of *Esprit*'s coworkers—Jacques Madaule, M.R.P. mayor of Issy-les-Moulineaux from 1949 to 1953, and Francis Goguel, a professor and influential person at the Institut d'études politiques and a personal adviser to de Gaulle who in 1971 became a member of the Conseil constitutionnel after having held a series of high positions in national administration—symbolize the two extremes of the review's political position: a traditionalist pole, marginal but never rejected, and a "progressive" pole which plays an important role in the construction of a technocratic utopia which will be the new social philosophy of the dominant class.

It is this combination of what post-War France is demanding and what it is rejecting which accounts for Goguel's collaboration with *Esprit*, as it does for that of other public figures such as André Philip and Roger Leenhardt, whose social characteristics as members of the Protestant big bourgeoisie of Paris contrast sharply with those of the review's central core. Relations such as these, coupled with episodes in the review's history such as its relationship with the Ecole des cadres d'Uriage,[16] show that although *Esprit*'s original combination of ideologies has led some to call it nonconformist, it is actually in profound conformity with what is required for legitimacy in the "enlightened" sectors which become the new ruling class of post-War France.

## 4.2 Critique

While existentialism is at the height of fashion, *Critique* is read by only a narrow, essentially academic public: its format does not conform to what the field demands. The review's failure to conform is a consequence of its producers' capital. When we look at Bataille and other men like Blanchot, Klossowski, Kojève, and Koyré who have a lot to do with *Critique*'s image, we see the outlines of two main models, two ways of deviating from the normal intellectual's career: the foreigners' model and the model of Frenchmen such as Bataille, Piel, and Blanchot, as well as of the Swiss Klossowski, who was born and educated in France, and whose itinerary and practices merge with the Frenchmen's more than with those of the foreigners Weil, Koyré, and Kojève. It is true that unlike these Frenchmen, who come from modest and provincial beginnings, Klossowski is born into the upper and European intellectual bourgeoisie: Rilke and Gide are his godfathers.[17] But like the Frenchmen at *Critique*, although for the different reason that he is a foreigner and an autodidact de luxe endowed with a noninstitutional cultural and social capital, he lacks the course of studies of a legitimate heir.

The socially and geographically remote origins of these men, their irregular or atypical studies, and their particular encounters and experiences help shape a heretical ethos which thrusts them into unclassifiable combinations of interacting suggestions from all the important avant-gardes of between-the-wars French culture: Surrealism, the ethnologists who gravitate around Mauss and the Musée d'ethnographie; the circles evolving between the exotic and the esoteric which draw France's attention to Hegel, Kierkegaard, Nietzsche, Husserl and Heidegger; the most unorthodox and mystical fringe groups of Christianity; and the so-called "non-conformist" groups who in the thirties invent, along with the "third way," an original form of political opposition which is both anti-capitalist and anti-Marxist.

Bataille's complex trajectory alone is enough to outline the position of the atypical family gathered at *Critique*. Born in 1897, by the time he founds the review in 1946 he already has behind him a curriculum with which that of Sartre or Merleau-Ponty pales in comparison.

The first thing his biography suggests is a "difficult" adolescence: a geographically peripheral place of origin (Auvergne), a blind and paralyzed father, an episode (expulsion at sixteen from the lycée at Reims) which suggests an already "deviant" adolescent, and before he is twenty, traumatic service during World War I. The Ecole des chartes (1918–22) assures him work as a librarian which he does until he dies: from 1922 till 1942 in Paris and from 1951 till 1962 at the Bibliothèque municipale in Orléans. But unlike the Ecole normale, it does not represent the royal road to the kingdom of the ruling intelligentsia, only the necessary condition for a career as an intellectual civil servant. Thus Bataille wins access to the world of "creators" by warding off destiny on the strength of his own efforts, leading the lifelong double life of his regular job and his secret, scandalous research. His habitus as an intellectual irregular pushes him toward often innovative experiments with alternatives to established culture, and at the same time keeps him on the fringes of things in a position of his own which is never identified with any of the groups he frequents. Thus even though his encounter-confrontations with the Surrealists show his affinities with their positions (in 1928, he joins other Surrealists in signing the anti-Breton manifesto, *Un cadavre*; he subsequently becomes Breton's ally in Contre-Attaque[18]; and long maintains friendly and cooperative relationships with former Surrealists, especially Leiris), he is never a Surrealist. Nor an ethnologist, in spite of many friendships and ventures which show an important web of relationships to the beginnings of the "new ethnology" in France: a reader and admirer of Mauss, a friend of Leiris, Métraux, and G.-H. Rivière, Bataille founds *Documents*,[19] *Acéphale*,[20] and the Collège de sociologie,[21] and writes for *Minotaure*[22]—all of them fleeting elitist ventures emblematic of an intellectual climate in which interest in ethnology is of major importance—as well as writing would-be theoretical essays of his own such as *La part maudite* and *L'érotisme*. A tireless "discoverer," he knows and uses Freud, hobnobs with Freud's French disciples, has himself psychoanalyzed in 1927, and even takes part (in 1938) in the inauguration by the pioneers of French psychoanalysis (Allendy, Borel, and Paul Schiff) of a rapidly disbanded "Société de psychologie collective."[23] And we know that Bataille's curriculum even includes being present at the top spot for Parisian insiders in the thirties: Kojève's lectures on Hegel at the Ecole des hautes études.

Bataille's political trajectory, that "love of dissidence" which is the common element of all the seemingly contradictory stands he takes, can be understood as a consistent translation of his ethos as an original. Eternally against the current, Bataille sides with the most miniscule of minigroups, with the minority of the minorities, and often on highly equivocal ideological grounds. The basis of all his choices, even the most obviously "revolutionary" ones, is in fact that ambiguous "a-theology"—more in the tradition of Nietzsche and de Sade than of Marx— in which Benjamin already saw the danger of a "proto-fascist aestheticism."[24] Thus we see him supporting the Cercle communiste démocratique and, with Boris Souvarine, the review *Critique sociale* in a period when the Communist Party itself, which has only reached a membership of 30,000 in 1932–33, can be considered an isolated minority; then with Breton founding Contre-Attaque—which considers itself "leftist" opposition to the Popular Front—at the moment all the established intellectuals—and first of all Gide and Malraux—are Communist sympathizers, and finally abandoning politics altogether when, during and after World War II, commitment becomes an indispensable component of intellectual excellence.

Bataille's trajectory combines in one single position characteristics which are also found in part, although in different combinations, in the trajectories of Klossowski, Blanchot, and Piel. In Klossowski's, we find a sui generis mysticism which draws him for a time into the orbit of *Esprit* (along with other heretical public figures of the day such as Paul Landsberg, Marcel Moré, and Denis de Rougemont[25]) and even leads him to enter a monastery. His name is associated with Bataille's most esoteric ventures: Contre-Attaque, the review *Acéphale* and the secret society of the same name, and the Collège de sociologie. Like Bataille, he has ties to *Recherches philosophiques*, the review sparked by Wahl and Koyré which plays a major role in introducing phenomenology and "philosophies of existence" into France, and he attends Kojève's lectures. Like Bataille also, he frequents the tiny circle of France's first psychoanalysts: in 1933, he publishes a "psychoanalytic study" of de Sade in the *Revue française de psychanalyse*.[26] The recurrence in Klossowski's trajectory of almost all the places which identify Bataille's position shows how close the two are. Their closeness translates into their having largely the same tastes and interests, claiming the same forebears (above all Nietzsche and de Sade), having similar eroticotheological obsessions, sustaining a friendship which for the younger Klossowski becomes veneration (in the 1947 edition of his book, *Sade, mon prochain*, he dedicates pages to Bataille which he will himself subsequently characterize as "apologetic" and eliminate), and sharing a critical destiny which unites them with the other progenitors of "philosophies of desire."

The affinities which link Blanchot to Bataille are less evident, less direct. It is a matter of an objective proximity of their positions in intellectual space, and of the analogous characteristics upon which it is based. Blanchot too is an "outsider." Like Bataille, he comes from the provinces, and like Bataille's studies, his prepare him for nothing in particular (his biography speaks vaguely of "university studies"): a pre-War Action française sympathizer and editor of Jeune Droite reviews (*la Revue française, Réaction, Combat*) before becoming the head of Jeune France (a cultural association patronized by the Vichy régime), he begins during the War, with the publication of *Thomas l'obscur*, a career as a writer and literary critic which steers clear of politics and any form of commitment.

It is Blanchot's position as an irregular in the intellectual field which makes probable both his encounter with Bataille and the contiguity we can see between their stands and practices. *Combat*'s far right is not so far from Contre-Attaque's far left, as their shared sympathy for Ordre nouveau shows. Thus the anti-Stalinism and antidemocratic views of Blanchot's articles for *Combat* have an undeniable affinity with the "superfascism" which Bataille proposes in Contre-Attaque and subsequently in *Acéphale*. Shortly afterwards, both men slip from their virulent extremism into total political noncommitment. Even on the strictly intellectual level they are united by their nonconformity, especially in a radically problematic relationship to literature, on the edge where the literary object self-destructs, which leads them in innovative directions.[27] For Bataille, "the only way to redeem the sin of writing is to annihilate what is written" (*L'abbé C.*). For Blanchot, literature, like death, separates us from things and from being, yet is the only experience which keeps us from falling into absurdity and nothingness. This link between the disposition of an irregular and a break with the established rules of writing is also found in Klossowski. "Novels" of his such as *La vocation suspendue*, and his trilogy *Les lois de l'hospitalité*, in which fiction is attacked and fragmented by a complex play of mirrors, are a part of this process, characteristic of the avant-gardes of the time, of undermining particular genres and writing itself.

Jean Piel's lesser-known trajectory is overshadowed by Bataille and his heritage, as is shown symbolically by the fact that Piel takes over as editor of *Critique* when Bataille dies. Beginning in the thirties, Piel is closely associated with Bataille's main ventures, and with building the core of his future works around the concept of "waste." During the War, he also establishes ties to Blanchot, and in these relationships a basic component of *Critique* is forged.[28]

The ethos of the *Critique* group may be summed up as a general propensity to question norms and concepts of normality. This characteristic is one of the review's two main poles, the one which leads it to explore everything new, different, and forbidden, and to approach and investigate all things magical, sacred, primitive, exotic, esoteric, unconscious, erotic, insane, and violent as openings to a "different" reality which by its very existence challenges the reasoning, values, and order that Western society has established.

*Critique*'s other pole is personified by its influential group of foreign contributors: in addition to Eric Weil, who along with Bataille founds the review and plays a major role in it, figures like Koyré and Kojève. This pole's connecting axis with the other is established in the thirties, as the close relationships between the *Recherches philosophiques* team and the Collège de sociologie attest.[29] The connection may be explained as a meeting of irregulars: those who live on the most disturbing, "unclassifiable" fringes of Parisian culture and those foreigners who gravitate around the Ecole des hautes études.[30] Because the Ecole pratique des hautes études is loosely organized and relatively marginal in the academic field, it offers foreigners the easiest access to advanced teaching, and as a consequence provides teaching which is cosmopolitan, noncanonical, and more often innovative than the Sorbonne's.[31] But a significant contrast in the relations between the two poles is already evident. Whereas Bataille and Klossowski are deeply influenced by Kojève's rising star, Kojève shows reservations about, and criticizes to the point of clear divergence from, the position taken by the leading lights of the Collège, especially Bataille.

Something Caillois says gives an indirect indication of what separates the two groups: "We [the Collège de sociologie] had tried to get support from Kojève, who as you know was the top interpreter of Hegel in France. Kojève had an extraordinary intellectual grip on our generation. I must say that our project got no support from him. I remember. It was at Bataille's, on the rue de Rennes, that we laid out our project to Kojève. . . . Kojève heard us out, but he rejected our plan. In his view, we were putting ourselves in the position of a magician who wanted his sleight of hand to make people believe in magic."[32] In sum, what separates Kojève and—judging by their philosophizing—Koyré and Weil from Bataille is their attachment to logic, rationality, and rigorous thinking.

This claim is confirmed by a letter to the Collège de sociologie from Jean Wahl, who, as a member of both *Recherches philosophiques* and the Collège, is a significant indicator of relationships between the two teams. In this letter he writes that in hearing Caillois evoke "everything irrational which haunts him into investigations which are perhaps too or not sufficiently rational," and in seeing in him and Bataille "the secret motives which led them toward what they believed to be science," many in the audience "had some doubt . . . about the rigor of the positive results [these investigations] produced."[33]

The roots of this difference most probably lie in a more general difference of philosophical habitus between the German and French cultures in which the two groups were formed. Traditionally, the different intellectual attitudes of the two nations are described as a difference between "culture" and "civilization"—between Germanic profundity and seriousness, on the one hand, and on the other hand, the brilliant superficiality of "French genius." And this traditional distinction, as Norbert Elias has shown, corresponds to an objective difference that has been perpetuated by the conditions under which the intelligentsia of the two countries are educated and coexist.[34]

There is no doubt that it is the erudite and cosmopolitan, yet rigorous and profound character of the philosophizing of men like Koyré, Kojève, and Weil which in the context of Parisian intellectual life most clearly distinguishes them from not just the model embodied in Bataille and his group but from the brilliant Ecole normale graduates at *Les Temps Modernes*, who even at the height of their consecration are far from enjoying a comparable reputation for seriousness. The work of these masters consistently combines scrupulous documentation with a high degree of precision in its approach, subject matter, and research methods which a simple comparison of pre-War *Recherches philosophiques* and post-War *Critique* reviews will show is in sharp contrast to the eclecticism and constant intermingling of perspectives that make Bataille's work an ineffable hybrid impossible to classify as a genre or discipline. The attention these foreigners pay to scientific developments and the philosophical questions they raise is significant in this respect: it has nothing in common with Bataille's carefree use of hypotheses suggested to him by the human sciences. For him, the objective method of science is not adequate for understanding "human reality," since understanding "the whole" presupposes in his view emotional involvement.

Together with Caillois and Leiris, Bataille writes an Introduction to the Collège de sociologie which is published in July 1938 in the *N.R.F.* His own contribution is an article-manifesto entitled *L'apprenti sorcier*, in which one reads: "The man whom fear has stripped of the need to be human has placed supreme faith in science. He has renounced the *total* character [in italics in the text] which his acts had insofar as he willed to live out his destiny. For the scientific act must be autonomous, and the scientist represses all human interests except the desire for knowledge. Any man who assumes the burden of science has traded his concern for living out his human destiny for a concern to discover the truth. . . . All human knowledge is a result of such deliberate self-deception, which in widening the realm of the human has left human existence crippled." And later on he says that myth is "living human reality" (D. Hollier, *Le collège*, 40ff and 55). As Hollier points out (note, 55), the expression "human reality"—and we would add, the insistence on a "totality" which sets "life" and "science" in conflict—is a "linguistic muddle" which is typical "in 1938" and is a symptom of "existentialism's penetration to the left bank of the Rhine" and "its establishment as a full-time occupation on the Left Bank of the Seine."

Yet *Critique*'s work of providing information and cultural criticism makes it an invaluable introduction to the newest and most fertile intellectual experiments taking place at the time, for the most part on an international scale, in all fields, from philosophy to theoretical physics. Although it does not neglect literary and philosophical exegesis, it is far from giving it the preponderant role it once had in the traditional intellectual review and still has in the existentialists' review. *Critique* pays particular attention to the most recent developments in the human sciences, above all in the fields of linguistics and anthropology.[35]

With its two poles of science and "transgression," the review foreshadows the combination which will characterize the cultural climate of the 1960s: the scientific flavor common to different incarnations of "structuralism" and to avant-gardes such as *Tel Quel*, which openly admit, moreover, that they see themselves in Bataille's preoccupations: in his references to de Sade and Nietzsche, slogans such as "consummation" and "transgression," and in what is thought to be the impossible relationship to writing of that "unemployed negativity," the intellectual. And certain of *Critique*'s younger writers, such as Barthes and Foucault, are destined to play major roles on the intellectual stage. But it is understandable that for the moment the review should remain in the shadows. It combines a number of characteristics which the intellectual public at large does not recognize as marks of legitimacy. It represents a systematic break with the principal traits of the dominant model, as can be seen by comparing it to *Les Temps Modernes*. Its very title excludes fictional works. This may seem to be a strange choice for an outfit which includes undoubted writers such as Bataille himself, Blanchot, and Klossowski. But it becomes perfectly comprehensible when we realize that it is only in the field of criticism—only in terms of their common disposition to absorb, discuss, and inventory all forms of knowledge without exception—that there is any objective possibility of a meeting of the minds between two groups who are so different in their concerns and habitus, so distant from each other in the "secret motives"[36] for their interest in science. To make clear the loss of potential capital which this renunciation of "creativity" involves, we need only recall that Blanchot and Klossowski end up submitting the most ambitious of the literary texts they publish at the time to *Les Temps Modernes*. *Critique* is also absent from the plane of ethics, which is so important to the success of the existentialist model. Bataille's strange, tormented quest is no equal of *Les Temps Modernes'* prophetism: it is a desperate, unreasoning religion which does not meet the demand for a rationalization of reality characteristic of the demand for prophecy. Whereas the existentialists' nonconformity is a profoundly ethical scandal, an ethics which sees itself as more authentic than the "wisdom of nations," the attitude Bataille suggests lays itself open to seeming no more than deviant. And finally, *Critique*'s lack of commitment—the detachment implicit in meditating on texts but never directly on events, in taking up a position on the neutral ground of exegesis and scientific discourse—makes it seem rear echelon in relation to the image of a front-line fighter of current battles which *Les Temps Modernes* has won for itself by its briefs, inquests, eyewitness reports, and earsplitting stands on current problems.

## 4.3 La Nouvelle Critique

When positions which are farthest from the center of the field are related to its overall state and functioning, they themselves show themselves in a new light. This is true of *la Nouvelle Critique*, created as the offensive spearhead that the C.P. (having since 1947 abandoned its self-imposed political isolation) brandishes at "bourgeois" culture. We can understand why this project fails once we recognize that political legitimacy is not enough to assure the success of a cultural operation: intellectual capital—which the C.P. does not have—is also necessary. Although for the duration of the Cold War the C.P. continues to be an obligatory political touchstone for intellectuals, its prestige in cultural matters is based almost entirely on figures such as Picasso and Eluard whose position owes nothing to the directives and the recognition of the Party. This poverty of the C.P.'s militant culture, which Communist historians themselves admit to, requires explaining in turn. But to hold

Communist tradition and strategy responsible would be to mistake effect for cause. The Party line relates to the sociological profile of the persons who produce it. In a field in which freedom is an essential component, the agents who have the most to gain by identifying themselves with a party and accepting an orthodoxy are those who, having few gifts, have few objective hopes of winning a prestigious position in cultural space through their own efforts. In itself, joining the Party implies a relationship to culture which negates legitimate dispositions by putting culture in the service of a cause. The indigent rigidity of the C.P.'s cultural policy and official cultural production is thus explained by its intellectuals' lack of capital. The true source of party culture, and the Party's ideas about culture, comes down to a sort of spontaneous adjustment of positions and dispositions, usually lived in good faith as a calling.[37]

*La Nouvelle Critique,* "the militant Marxist review" (as its subtitle proclaims), is an exemplary fruit of party culture, whose functioning and characteristics it expresses to the extreme.[38] It is as much the characteristics of its producers as it is of their products which reveal a position that judged by the dominant criteria of intellectual legitimacy is weak and inferior. The weight politics has in the enterprise is indicated by the presence on the editorial committee of two mouthpieces of the machine such as Victor Leduc and, above all, Victor Joannès, who has been a Party member since 1933 and a member of the Central Committee since 1945, and is superintendent of the "ideological" section of the instructional and educational sector. The authority of Zdanov, which is made explicit from the introduction to the first issue, governs the stands taken by the review and the directives frequently published there by Casanova, Aragon, and other Party authorities. The primacy of politics is also indicated by the presence on the editorial committee of Jean Fréville, a militant since 1927, a self-taught polygrapher, the author of realist novels, poems, and essays on the most disparate subjects, and *Humanité*'s literary chronicler: militant faith is all it takes to make up for mediocre cultural merit.

It is the other editors who, with their degrees in advanced studies in philosophy and literature, put *la Nouvelle Critique* forward as the rival of "bourgeois" intellectual reviews. But as soon as their capital is compared to the existentialists, this challenge seems a mockery.

Pierre Daix and Annie Besse (later known as Annie Kriegel) are trained in literature; Jean-Toussaint Desanti, Jean Kanapa, and Henri Lefebvre are philosophers; but none of them has titles equal to Sartre's or Merleau-Ponty's. Desanti (who as an Ecole normale graduate, an *agrégé,* and later a *docteur-ès-lettres* is the best "equipped") is at this time still a lycée instructor headed for a lackluster university career.

Kanapa, the editor-in-chief, is a young *agrégé* and student of Sartre's. His career is a paradigmatic illustration of the chance for rapid advancement that the Party offers young persons without capital but capable through their iconoclastic fury of playing the roles which the ideological offensive holds in store for them. Edgar Morin speaks in *Autocritique* of "kanapism."[39] The same is true of Annie Besse, who during the years she is becoming an editor of *la Nouvelle Critique* and a member of the fédération de la Seine is still competing for the *agrégation* in history (1948) and working to finish her studies at the Ecole normale de Sèvres (1945–49). The same is true of Pierre Daix: the same age as Kanapa, brought to the fore by the Resistance, only a *licencié de lettres*, he becomes assistant editor of the Editions Sociales in 1947, at only twenty-five, and in 1948, editor-in-chief of *les Lettres françaises*. Owing everything to the Party, he is a perfect machine politician: for him, the interests of the machine and his personal interests are one and the same.

Even the review's most important coworkers have relatively little capital, which explains their relation to the Party and the intellectual field. This is true of Lefebvre, a Sorbonne graduate from the provinces who his whole life long has to try to measure up to the Ecole normale elite of his generation. His savage attacks on Sartre, Nizan, and Friedmann—all of them Parisians and Ecole normale graduates—may be read as the surly rivalry of a less fortunate classmate; his longtime obedience to the Party as the search for a compensatory authority; and his inability to win the Party's recognition and confidence—in spite of his oft-demonstrated zeal in self-criticism and denunciation of former comrades such as Nizan and Friedmann—as the consequence of the mistrust he arouses by his profound affinity for his former schoolmates, an affinity evidenced by the youthful intersections of their trajectories as members of the group *Philosophies* (1925) and of *la Revue marxiste* (1929–30). As a man who is out of place both in the Party and in the intellectual field, Lefebvre embodies the contradictions of Communist culture.

The insignificance of *La Nouvelle Critique*'s capital in relation to the capital of the *Temps Modernes* team accounts for the signs of weakness which characterize its entire strategy: its constant recourse to the authority principle and, what is worse, to an illegitimate (that is, political rather than cultural) authority such as texts on culture by Lenin, Stalin, and Casanova; its substitution of denunciation, insult, and anathema for criticism; and finally, its unconscious reference to a dominant model which is evident in the characteristics it actually has and which contradicts those it means to have.

There is no doubt that *La Nouvelle Critique*, like *Les Temps Modernes*, intends to be synoptic. Everything is discussed, and discussion is for everyone. Yet it is above all the young champions who talk: the Kanapas and Daixes and Desantis whose course of studies, comparable to that of the existentialists, gives them a sort of competence by right. As it does at *Les Temps Modernes*, the effect of the chief editors' training makes itself felt in the space given to literature and in the tendency to a philosophical approach, although movies, drama, and painting are also discussed; current political events are commented on; stands are taken on affairs which divide the French intelligentsia during those years (Lysenko, Kravchenko, Rajk, Soviet camps, the Korean War); room is made for "authentic" documents, exposés, and eyewitness accounts (which are frequently solemn self-criticisms); and as at *Les Temps Modernes*, when the occasion arises attention is paid to the sciences, especially the social sciences. It is significant in this regard that like *Les Temps Modernes, la Nouvelle Critique* is interested above all in economics, which in the post-War period begins to benefit sooner than sociology from the social demand which is tied to the policy of a planned economy.[40] During *la Nouvelle Critique*'s first year, there is a voluminous brief devoted to refuting Keynes which corresponds to the discussions sparked by Uri and Domarchi in *Les Temps Modernes* of the shape of the world economy. And we see the same condescending attitude toward science that we see in the existentialists, who as philosophers take it upon themselves to establish the grounds of scientific debate and pass final judgment on it. Consequently, it is the philosopher Kanapa who opens and closes the brief on Keynes. Like *Les Temps Modernes, la Nouvelle Critique* clearly aspires to prophecy, presenting itself as a complete guide, simultaneously cultural, moral, and political.

But the common ground which *la Nouvelle Critique* shares with *Les Temps Modernes* is just what marks its actual distance from its ideal model. It lacks the necessary qualities which make *Les Temps Modernes'* synoptic ambition seem legitimate. To begin with, literary "creation." Although *la Nouvelle Critique* is concerned with literature, it produces none, and limits itself to judging and prescribing. It says what socialist literature must be; it exalts Aragon but condemns Kafka, and it absolves Balzac in the manner of Lukács, who makes him a socialist *malgré lui.* Instead of the prestigious unpublished manuscripts which *Les Temps Modernes* is in a position to publish thanks to its power to attract the literary avant-garde, the "militant Marxist review" offers norms and condemnations.

It is in an equally worn and faded form that *la Nouvelle Critique* unfurls that other blazon of existentialist prophecy, the capacity to transform each event—from the most banal everyday experience to history's still unfinished dramas—into a reflection which combines all the marks of high philosophical consecration. As the spokesman for orthodox Marxism, *la Nouvelle Critique* is almost the negating opposite of this combination. It not only invents nothing, it reveals an already invented mode of thought which has all the rigidity of orthodoxy (the repulsive side of dogmatism) and which is moreover, in the French philosophical field, the illegitimate philosophy par excellence. Its discourse thus seems not prophetic but simply apologetic, the vulgate of a "vulgar" way of thinking. This series of contrasts—between those who have title to nobility and those who do not, between those who create and those who repeat, between those who inquire and those who furnish rules—explains why *la Nouvelle Critique*'s Marxist prophetism seems an outworn caricature, and why its attacks do not harm, but by their implicit recognition help, their intended victims.

*Les Temps Modernes'* absolute supremacy to all other intellectual groups provides the key to understanding its polarization of French intellectual life and the veritable monopoly of legitimacy it seems to establish. The tendency toward concentration inherent in capitalist economies holds true also for their symbolic phenomena. As workers "separated from the means of production," "free" intellectuals who are not tied to associations incompatible with their intellectual calling find *Les Temps Modernes* an almost obligatory route to consecration. But the reason why the existentialists seem to suck dry the intellectual field is not simply that they swallow up its resources. By putting the spotlight on themselves, they cast all positions beside their own into shadow, where they remain invisible and thus for all practical purposes nonexistent. This explains the existentialist era's silence, forgetfulness, and indifference concerning productions which today, through a retrospective projection of current interests and values, may seem interesting and important. And since monopolistic concentration characteristically reproduces itself, this damping effect keeps operating as long as the conjunctural conditions of existentialist success remain unchanged.

# CHAPTER 8
# The Field of *Les Temps Modernes*

## 1. ITS FUNCTIONAL PRINCIPLES

*Les Temps Modernes'* monopoly of legitimate culture throughout the period under consideration makes it a relatively autonomous system. To explain its systemic character, and its evolution during the period, we must focus above all on the way that it functions. There would be no use looking through the texts published in it for specific intrinsic characteristics we could say incontestably distinguish it from other reviews. To see that this is true, we need only recall the many, sometimes radical changes which changing conditions of legitimacy successively produce in the image of authors such as Nathalie Sarraute, Jean Genet, and Michel Leiris (to mention only the most striking cases) who have either accepted a Sartrean interpretation of their artistic project or adopted one on their own. It is not the presence of shared intrinsic characteristics which unites them but the absence of any distinguishing political or cultural marks incompatible with the main coordinates of the commitment model. *Les Temps Modernes* functions to express the views of intellectuals who have their own individual reasons for participating in society's life, and as such it confronts us with the fascinating paradox of *free commitment*. At one extreme, the review rejects any literature or science which in its claim to be "pure" is not "responsible"; at the other, any compromise with the powers that be or any party commitment which might bind "choices" to orthodoxy.

This position in itself assures a certain consistency in the contents of *Les Temps Modernes*. The review's political line, throughout its different phases and expressions, never strays from certain guidelines: play the role of critical consciousness, uphold the taboo against anti-Communism, and at the same time keep your distance from the Communists and the U.S.S.R. The consequences of this stand become evident at the time of the Korean War, when the break between Sartre and Merleau-Ponty leaves a void in its political leadership. Thanks to the review's inertia as an institution, existentialist prophetism is able to maintain its continuity by means of often ad hoc, temporary replacements who—from Claude Bourdet to Dzelepy, an American who occasionally comments on U.S. policy during the Korean War—may seem in terms of their trajectories to be wholly incompatible with the review.

On the strictly cultural level, the first thing that defines the limits of *Les Temps Modernes'* repertoire is the times' characteristic indifference to, or suspicion of, formal research and scientific truth. But this general characteristic is reinforced by the specific dispositions of the review's chief coworkers, which reproduce the Ecole normale culture's traditional reservations about, and antagonism toward, science and empirical research. Thus the sciences rarely get a chance to speak, and when they do (whether they be physics or economics and anthropology), only on condition that they submit to an existentialist reading.[1] Philosophy reserves for itself the right to establish the theory of scientific practice, to make clear to science the ontological foundations of the phenomena which it must be content to simply observe. We recognize here the traditional attitude which enables philosophy to acquire the prestige of science and at the same time affirm its own sovereignty.

In maintaining that the selective principle governing the texts chosen for publication in *Les Temps Modernes* is not to be found among criteria of form or content but must be sought in the review's position in the intellectual field, I am not denying that existentialist culture has its own style, not trying to reduce it to a sum of realities whose only common characteristic is what they all reject. If in addition to this external principle we consider another, internal, one—the competition among the review's producers—we shall have the means we need to explain the review's characteristics and evolution as a structured system of intellectual strategies. Far from being simply the result of interacting forces, the review according to this hypothesis functions as a laboratory which through a constant and spontaneous collective adjustment produces its own coherent structure and overall orientation.

## 2. THE STRUCTURE OF *LES TEMPS MODERNES'* INTERNAL FIELD RELATIONSHIPS OF FORCE

To represent *Les Temps Modernes* as a field of forces whose confrontations and combinations define the existentialist model is to presuppose the existence of a hierarchy in which the importance that each individual member of it has in shaping the review depends upon the position he occupies in the hierarchy at each moment. That is why we must first distinguish, within *Les Temps Modernes'* total population, with its informal family air, the objective structure that each position in the hierarchy has in terms of its rank and function before we give each individual agent the attention that his relative importance to the enterprise demands. In this way, we can bring out the logic of the field, which governs both the relationships between those who act within it and the evolution of its contents.

Certain indications allow us to establish (in what must obviously be an approximate way) the circle of cohorts at *Les Temps Modernes* who are during the period under consideration essential to its image and its function. In the first rank of essential personnel are the members of the original editorial board, as well as those who are members of subsequent ones and are prior to 1953 already working with the review and noted as regularly attending its meetings.[2] Close behind them are other contributors who can be identified by a combination of criteria—the nature, length, and importance of their contributions,[3] and their personal relationships with the main agents—as being especially close to the inner circle. In this way we can establish some summary groupings:

The original editorial committee, consisting of Sartre, Merleau-Ponty, Simone de Beauvoir, Leiris, Aron, Paulhan, and Ollivier.

The inner circle of coworkers who attend the meetings: Bost, Pouillon, Pontalis, Jeanson, Gorz, Lefort, Colette Audry, Cau, Erval, Guyonnet, Renée Saurel, J.-H. Roy, Stéphane, Todd, Péju, Lanzmann, Chambure. Many of these will show up on subsequent editorial committees.

Those most closely related to the review:

among academics, if we consider those who make a large number of contributions[4] or write a column for a while, there are few names we can quote: Etiemble, Uri, Domarchi, Belaval, Vuillemin, Auger;

among those writers and artists whose contributions are generally few, the distinguishing criterion is friendship with Sartre, which is generally evidenced by his having prefaced one of their works. In terms of this criterion we can establish a group of authors who were associated with the review during this period, such as Vian, Nathalie Sarraute, Genet, Queneau, and Wright;

among the figures who handle the art criticism and literary criticism, the following are distinguished by their fame and frequent contributions: Leibowitz, Limbour, Masson, Nadeau, Antonina Vallentin, and Dort;

finally, certain political journalists such as Dalmas, Guérin, Bourdet, and Rousset deserve notice for the importance and frequency of their contributions, and for the status granted them.

The difference between the founders of the review and all the other agents is not a merely formal one. They come together already endowed with valuable capital which, cumulatively, is what makes the enterprise itself possible. Objectively considered, their relationship is both an alliance for the sake of accumulating symbolic power and a probable antagonism, since each one of them tends—according to his disposition and the interests inherent in his position—to shape the review's still fluid and open reality to his own individual advantage.

None of the other close collaborators of *Les Temps Modernes* finds himself in this situation—then or later. The first disciples, such as Bost and Pouillon and Pontalis, are at the Liberation untitled neophytes. And by the time the editorial committee finally gets some new blood, *Les Temps Modernes* will already be an established institution dominated by Sartre and identified with his position: Sartre's *imperium* will have impregnable frontiers which rival coworkers cannot cross; henceforth, the review's editors will no longer be Sartre's competitors but his friends, disciples, and epigones.

In retrospect, we can see within the original editorial committee a hierarchy which was scarcely visible in 1945. Even today it is not evident at first sight, but only if one objectifies the complex relations between the different kinds of capital possessed by the agents and the norms of legitimacy in force. Unlike Sartre's relationship to his epigones, it is not a matter of the evident distance between still unknown disciples and the most highly consecrated French intellectual. It is a difference between models of excellence all of whom are prestigious enough to seem at first sight equal. This accounts for an editorial makeup which might seem surprising in the light of the subsequent trajectories of its members. "[In] those days, none of these names clashed,"[5] and a common undertaking seemed possible, precisely because their hierarchy was not evident but was hidden by differences which had not yet become divergences heightened and strengthened by the very logic of competition.

The first difference to be noted is between the group of editors of the same age, all *agrégés* in philosophy bound together since their university days (Sartre, Aron, Merleau-Ponty, Simone de Beauvoir), and the rest, each of whom represents a different world in the culture of the time: Paulhan, Leiris, Ollivier. Since the ties that the members of the latter group have to those of the former—and even to one another—are not based on any deep affinities of habitus acquired during a common course of studies, they are objectively speaking conjunctural and fragile. Paulhan, the oldest, has his adventuresome beginnings behind him,[6] followed by a long period (the whole between-the-wars period) of association with the *N.R.F.* His prestige, the merit of having been in the

Resistance since 1941 and having been with Decour the founder of *les Lettres françaises*,[7] and his friendly relationship with Sartre and Simone de Beauvoir all account for his presence in this review of commitment. Leiris's path is also special. He goes through the most tumultuous and most fruitful avant-garde experiments of the between-the-wars period: Surrealism, with its language games and concern for the unconscious; the "new ethnology," which gravitates around the Musée de l'homme and Mauss; and Bataille and the Collège de sociologie. Ollivier, who comes to *Combat* from the ranks of *Jeune France*,[8] has a still different position, that of political journalist. He is the only one who has no personal ties to Sartre: his presence cements the alliance between *Les Temps Modernes*, Camus, and *Combat*.

The progressive elimination or annexation of these positions is inherent in the weakness they reveal, retrospectively, in comparison to the position of the Ecole normale graduates on the review. Paulhan's prestige, based on the *N.R.F.* and pushed even farther back into the past by the very success of the existentialist enterprise, shows inexorable signs of age. Leiris's capital must wait for the changed context of the sixties to be reevaluated: in all its aspects, from its literary preferences to its interest in ethnology, it is alien to the existentialist temper.

But there are also significant differences within the group of *agrégés*. Aron's differences with Sartre are just beginning to develop. Consequently, each of the two men underestimates them, as is shown by the role comparable in importance to Sartre's and Merleau-Ponty's that Aron plays in the first two issues.[9] In fact, their divergence may even now seem to be minor in relation to the long period in which the two travel almost parallel paths. More precisely, Aron seems to anticipate before the War the main steps in Sartre's development. Ranked number one in the competition for the *agrégation* which Sartre fails, he precedes Sartre as lecturer in Berlin, and it is he who arouses Sartre's interest in phenomenology,[10] although his own interests take other directions, among which Weber's thinking is the most important. His doctoral thesis, *Introduction to the Philosophy of History* (1938), is the first important philosophical work in his generation to have taken up the approach which will subsequently characterize existentialism: the concern with the meaning and rationality of history. At the end of his life[11] Aron was still trying to make it clear that his book had preceded *Being and Nothingness* and—as Sartre himself had recognized—had influenced it. And Aron suggested that his precociousness handicapped his work, since it came out in an intellectual climate which was not yet as favorable to these concerns as it would be at the time of Sartre's success. The gap between these two parallel lives widens further during the War, which as a result of the different experiences it brings to them precipitates the divergence of their dispositions. Aron moves counter to the dominant direction the field is taking at this time, whereas Sartre is the one who best sums up and articulates that direction. As the age turns toward philosophy, Aron prefers sociology, a discipline which is looked down upon and is just showing its first timid signs of reviving on the fringes of the University.[12] Whereas Sartre voluntarily abandons his career as professor for the highly prestigious career of free writer, Aron long compromises his career (he is not hired by the Sorbonne until 1956) by working as an editorial writer, a job which wins him a place on the heights of journalism but discredits him as an academic. Moreover, he is anti-Communist at a time when for French intellectuals anti-Communism is the most unforgivable of sins. Austere and withdrawn, he even differs from the existentialist model in his style of life.

Simone de Beauvoir's position differs from all the others in that it is not antagonistic but complementary to Sartre's. Her role is a hybrid one in relation to the two positions we have noted: that of Sartre's allies, who have independent capital, and that of his disciples, who owe their legitimacy to him. Unprecedentedly for a woman, and a young woman at that, de Beauvoir already possesses sufficient titles in 1945 to join the most prestigious editorial staff of the day without shocking anyone. She is an *agrégé* in philosophy; Gallimard has published a novel of hers, *She Came to Stay*, which has been given a flattering reception;[13] and she has written essays and made her first sally into the theater. And yet her success and her trajectory are inseparable from her relationship with Sartre. She is an invaluable alter ego whose presence on the editorial committee alone shows Sartre's absolute dominion over the enterprise, since he alone has a "double."

We still have to specify Merleau-Ponty's position, to make clear what it is about his capital which predisposes him to be the only member of the original editorial committee who, in terms of both his central role and his intensely dialectical relationship with Sartre, can be considered, along with Sartre and Simone de Beauvoir, the real nucleus of the review. In 1945, Merleau-Ponty is certainly the figure nearest Sartre in French intellectual space. He shares with him not just the overall course of studies that Aron also shares, but more specific characteristics. The same philosophical orientation: phenomenology, and existential philosophy, and the same political outlook: that sympathy for Communism which makes them at the Liberation new "fellow travelers." In both areas, Merleau-Ponty's personal reputation is quiet but solid, since it is based on the judgment of competent peers: his doctoral theses, *The Structure of Behavior* and the *Phenomenology of Perception* (1945), have made him the most esteemed representative of existentialism in uni-

versity circles, which look instead on Sartre's work with perplexity at
the "worldliness" it brings to philosophy.[14] Politically speaking, Merleau-Ponty's activities during the Resistance, his direct acquaintance
with the writings of Marx and Marxists (unusual among intellectuals of
that day, even Communist), and his relationships of mutual esteem with
Communist intellectuals legitimate his position as a model of intellectual
commitment.

Merleau-Ponty's dual prestige makes him an invaluable, irreplaceable ally for Sartre during the whole delicate stage in which the review
must consolidate its hegemony and define its image. To begin with,
he assures limited but important support from both the review's coworkers and its public: his being a part of the academic world that
Sartre has abandoned functions as a symbol of legitimacy and also as
a means of making effective personal contacts. Furthermore, Merleau-
Ponty is able to give commitment a political content which Sartre is far
from having elaborated in 1945. He is the only member of the editorial
committee who can actually influence the review's line and development, and as such is Sartre's only serious opponent. And yet there is
every reason to expect that in case of conflict Sartre will win, and to
see the superiority he will always enjoy over Merleau-Ponty. In comparison to the "total" intellectual, Merleau-Ponty is only a philosophy
professor, a figure who evokes the grizzled pedant. Even his university
career proves a handicap. It associates him with institutions, which are
antiprophetic, whereas Sartre's independence favors charisma. In addition, it implies censorship and above all—as a result of internalized
norms—self-censorship, which contrast sharply with the clamorous logic
of intellectual success.

The disparity between the two public figures is also measured by
the capital that their relations to the other members of the review give
them. Most of those who work for *Les Temps Modernes* are recruited by
Sartre and gravitate around him. Among those who go to the meetings—
the inner circle—there is only one disciple of Merleau-Ponty: Lefort.
The vast majority of those around Sartre are not headed for the academy
but for essay writing and journalism. Sartre can also better guarantee
them the legitimacy they need than Merleau-Ponty can. And it will
be their weight which tips the balance in favor of Merleau-Ponty's departure from *Les Temps Modernes*, for by improving their positions on
the editorial committee, they will end up directing the review toward
tendencies, expectations, and interests which objectively diverge from
Merleau-Ponty's position and make his presence a hindrance.

Sartre is equally the dominating center of the circle of the most
regular and most important outside contributors to the review. Among
the various kinds of contributors constituting this external source of

inside capital, Merleau-Ponty's only connections are with academics.[15] The other kinds of connections—with writers, artists, critics, and journalists—are all Sartrean friendships, discoveries, or alliances. This difference in recruiting is only an image writ large of the difference in form and volume of the two chief editors' capital. Academics, furthermore, are a minority of the *Temps Modernes* population and have little influence on its form or contents.

Thus it is understandable that *Les Temps Modernes* ends up reproducing the characteristics of Sartre's position.[16] In the highly centralized, tightly knit world of Parisian intellectual life, the central, multifaceted character of Sartre's position makes it the operant determinant of the probable, almost necessary meetings which lead to most of the external collaborations with the review. Inasmuch as Sartre is the only one in this intellectual world who can fully express it, he is also the one who can most fully dominate and control it. Whereas Merleau-Ponty's professional restraint keeps him on the fringe of Saint-Germain-des-Prés, Sartre is very much a part of it, indeed, the heart of it. This explains the sort of "preestablished harmony" which seems to govern his friendships and acquaintances. He not only spends most of his time with writers, artists, and journalists (as Simone de Beauvoir's memoirs show); the figures he spontaneously takes up with are the elite of this world. It is a matter of an affinity or homology between avant-gardes who are already consecrated or about to be consecrated in their respective sectors, such as Camus, Queneau, Masson, and Giacometti. And in the case of authors still unknown outside the Latin Quarter—such as Vian and Genet—it is a matter of Sartre's position having a dual, and convergent, effect. Sartre is the contact, the filter, and the interpreter of the emerging moods of his milieu, and what is more, he has the power to make his preferences legitimate. It is these mechanisms, and not some mysterious flair, which make *Les Temps Modernes* the place where most of the new names are discovered and made known.

This ability Sartre has to polarize the intellectual field is the key factor in his power. On the one hand, his consecration is heightened by the success of the new authors made known by *Les Temps Modernes*, by a preface he has written,[17] or simply by being befriended by him. On the other hand, the very concept of intellectual excellence which Sartre embodies is reinforced by works of literature, essay writing, and journalism that follow channels first marked out by him and are read as Sartrean works. This can be said, for example, of the works of Nathalie Sarraute or Jean Genet. It is true that both probably owe their literary recognition to Sartre.[18] But his interpretation of their writing— since it is based entirely on his own categories of bad faith, authenticity and inauthenticity, freedom, choice, and existential project—manages to obscure the most novel and experimental aspects of their works, the ones which will subsequently lead people to speak of the "new novel" and the "new theater."

Sartre's statement of purpose for writing an "existential psychoanalysis" of Genet is very explicit on this point: "I have tried to do the following: to indicate the limit of psychoanalytical interpretation and Marxist explanation and to demonstrate that *freedom* alone can account for a person in his *totality;* to show this *freedom at grips with destiny,* crushed at first by its mischances, then turning upon them and digesting them little by little; to prove that genius is not a gift but the way out that one invents in desperate cases; to learn the choice that a writer makes of himself, of his life and of the meaning of the universe, including even the formal characteristics of his style and composition, even the structure of his images and of the particularity of his tastes; to review in detail the history of his liberation."[19]

The same approach shows through the lines of Sartre's short introduction to *Portrait of a Man Unknown:* "Nathalie Sarraute has a horror of the *tricks* [*mauvaise foi*] of the novelist, even though they may be absolutely *necessary.* . . . Nathalie Sarraute seeks to safeguard her *sincerity* [*bonne foi*] as a storyteller. . . . I believe that by allowing us to sense an intangible *authenticity,* by showing us the constant coming and going from the particular to the general, by tenaciously depicting the reassuring, dreary world of the *inauthentic,* she has achieved a technique which makes it possible to attain, over and beyond the psychological, human reality in its very *existence.*"[20]

Our analysis of the internal force relationships of *Les Temps Modernes* shows Sartre's supremacy to his collaborators and the gravitational pull he exercises on all sectors of them, from the center to the periphery. We have identified a nucleus constituted by Sartre, Simone de Beauvoir, and Merleau-Ponty. Alongside this nucleus, the other members of the original editorial committee, who are associated with *Les Temps Modernes* more out of their need for concentration of symbolic capitals than any real affinities, are seen to be no more than a predictably short-lived administrative council. The fact that they have capital of their own, however, distinguishes them from a third group of collaborators who owe their legitimacy primarily to Sartre.

In light of these relationships, the history of *Les Temps Modernes* during this period can be seen to be a complete sequence whose beginning and end are summed up symbolically in the editorial committees of 1945 and 1953, a sequence which seems to confirm the analogy between the logic of symbolic power and the logic of economic or political power. For it is a sequence which may be described as a process of concentration and institutionalization analogous to that which characterizes the formation of capitalist enterprise. In this process, the independent producers are progressively eliminated to the benefit of those agents who do not question Sartre's sovereignty. And this is the way the review's phase of accumulation and definition comes to an end.

In order to reconstitute this history in greater detail, we must analyze the trajectories of the review's most significant coworkers in order to make clear the specific contributions each segment of them makes. As we shall show by relating the characteristics of their positions to their practices, the basic principle which objectively governs their strategies and enables us to understand them is the symbolic capital they possess.

## 3. THE "ADMINISTRATIVE COUNCIL"

The objective differences which separate the other members of the editorial committee from its nucleus very soon become apparent. Ollivier, Aron, and Paulhan leave the review within a year. Leiris stays on, but in a subordinate position. As a result of the status all these editors enjoy, and of the differences of role which come to light as soon as the differences in their positions are taken into account, their relations with *Les Temps Modernes* are no less significant for being short-lived or unhappy.

It is significant that the first to leave, Ollivier, seems from the start to be the most alien. He is the only member of the editorial committee Simone de Beauvoir does not refer to when she remembers *Les Temps Modernes'* original team.[21] His only appearance in *Force of Circumstance* is through the hostile picture painted of him by Bost, Sartre's disciple whom Camus has hired at *Combat*: "[Bost] told us a lot about *Combat*, about the passion Pascal Pia was bringing to the task of killing the newspaper and himself with it, about Ollivier, whom everyone loathes and who knows it, about Aron, who's also getting himself disliked by understanding *Combat* so intensely and insisting on saying so. . . . Bost says Aron and Ollivier couldn't care less about the way people have to live, about their exhaustion, their hunger; the problem just doesn't exist for them."[22]

Ollivier's difference from the rest is confirmed by his only two contributions to the review. The first article, devoted to Camus' *Caligula*,[23] shows his position as Camus' spokesman on *Les Temps Modernes*. In his other contribution about Saint-Just,[24] Ollivier stands up symbolically for the non-Communist members of the Resistance by calling on Jacobin revolution, as they like to do, in order to imply opposition to Communist revolution.[25]

Jean Paulhan also seems isolated. His prestigious presence is far more important than anything he actually does, which is little. He gives some technical advice: "Paulhan, who had edited the *N.R.F.* for many years, gave us the benefit of his experience; he usually made up most of the numbers, and he taught me the technique," Simone de Beauvoir writes.[26] He continues his reflections on literature and publishes some articles which have no relation to the review's position: a meditation on rhetoric[27] and some high-flown "Morceaux choisis" pseudonymously signed "Maast." "Paulhan has put together a very nice collection of texts: extracts from his own work, from Léautaud and from baroque manuscripts. I went to thank him. In his office, ten people dipping into a box. 'We were looking at photos of all the places Rimbaud visited,' Paulhan told me. 'Would you like to have a look?' But I went to collect some proofs. . . ."[28]

Aron's collaboration with *Les Temps Modernes* reveals a more complex relationship to the enterprise. At the outset, it is intense (two articles in the first issue and one in the second),[29] but then abruptly stops, ending with an open polemic against Sartre.[30] Aron's antagonism to Sartre's position can be seen in the first pieces he writes. In opposition to Sartre's prophetism, Aron presents a clearheaded analysis of the problems French society faces in the aftermath of the War, and modestly reformist proposals concerning specific aspects of current economic, political, and social reality. He supports the Atlantic Pact, whereas even at the height of the Cold War, *Les Temps Modernes* will continue to advocate neutrality. In this review which is about to become the spearhead of anticolonialism, Aron talks about preserving French Africa.[31] He advocates breaking up the current tripartite government and isolating the Communist Party, urging socialists and radicals to give up their "unnatural" alliance with the Communists and come over to the camp of the Mouvement republicain populaire–Rassemblement du People français, whereas *Les Temps Modernes* suggests, as Merleau-Ponty puts it, supporting "the line of the F.C.P." Proletarian revolution, which is an indisputable goal for Sartre and Merleau-Ponty, is for Aron a threat to be warded off by the characteristic means of a liberal economy.[32] But Aron's quasi-systematic opposition is yet another (implicit and negative) way of acknowledging Sartre's position at the center of things. This relationship is so forcefully imposed on Aron that even after he has left *Les Temps Modernes*, he keeps on following and criticizing the various stages of Sartre's "imaginary Marxism," and in this way remains tied to the characteristic approach of his generation.[33]

Michel Leiris's case illustrates another way the dominant model has of putting its stamp on others. Even though his profile as a former Surrealist, a poet, and an ethnographer is the farthest from Sartre's, he sticks with the review and supports commitment. It is a true case of conversion: the texts he publishes in *Les Temps Modernes* show him severely questioning his personal past with all the characteristic feelings of guilt which at the time weighed so heavily on intellectuals with revolutionary penchants.

This conversion process is particularly evident in the text *De la littérature considérée comme une tauromachie*. Published in *Les Temps Modernes* in 1946,[34] it has all the earmarks of a convert's typical rereading of the past in the light of his new convictions. It is in fact a preface to *L'âge d'homme* (published in 1939), which in its aims as well as its assumptions is a Sartrean work: "literature as tauromachy" means "writing a book which is an act," and the action proper to literature is to reveal the truth. Leiris compares this form of action to a toreador's because it involves the writer in a difficult, dangerous struggle with himself against the narcissism and search for complicity which broods over the sincerest of confessions.

In the light of this attitude, certain writings which might otherwise seem to be literal records of free associations take on a different look and reveal an unmistakable guiding thread. Take for example "Dimanche," the beginning of a new autobiographical cycle, *La règle du jeu*,[35] which Leiris has just undertaken. His new preoccupations account for this work's air of existential summing up; its concern for truth (in accordance with Leiris's concept of commitment); its approach (the meaning and justification of intellectual work); and its self-condemnation: "Every man who has the leisure to enjoy a certain material well-being must be considered guilty, no matter what he does, in respect to those who are poorer than he."[36] Beneath its air of wandering where the spirit listeth, "Dimanche" actually follows a plan which makes it resemble Sartre's biographies, insofar as it is concerned to reconstitute the history of a "calling" conceived of as the history of one's discovery of one's individual social truth and as a metanoia. Leiris sees the desire to escape the conditionings of ordinary experience as the source of his choice of literature and ethnography as professions: "The eternal outsider, that is the image of myself I tended to shape in willing myself a poet."[37] ". . . Do not practice any of those too easily admissible professions which brand the man condemned to forced labor with a number he will bear until he dies."[38] The title, "Dimanche," alludes to the scansion of time in terms of working days and holidays which is in fact one of the constraints characteristic of normal professions. But Leiris now sees these constraints instead as guard rails which held him safe from the dizzying brink of the empty page, the nothingness, the death with which an eternal Sunday threatens him. His conclusion is also Sartrean: to be legitimate, intellectual labor must be assimilated to revolutionary action. Both seem to Leiris to be attempts to ward off time and death through a transformation of reality which must take into account the material conditions of its realization.

Yet the power of the field is made still more evident by the fact that conversion to commitment is not an advantageous strategy for Leiris. He goes so far as to sacrifice, or at least downplay, an important part of his activity which does not seem to fit into his new program. It is undoubtedly no accident that his poetic and ethnographic production come to an almost complete stop until the sixties. His contributions to *Les Temps Modernes* are above all sections of his autobiographical work which can be more easily converted into usable material. The poetry and the "imagined stories" to which his fame is chiefly due shrink down to one single piece.[39] The two articles he devotes to ethnography consist in criticisms of colonialism in ethnographic studies[40]: yet another questioning of his past stemming from his commitment. Too radical to succeed, conversion in Leiris's case means above all mutilation. Simone de Beauvoir's laconic comment on his role in the review is revealing: "Leiris was in charge of poetry, and our tastes rarely coincided."[41] And the fact is that although he is recruited as a poet and a poetry expert, he is destined to disappoint the group's expectations by proving to be as powerless to get them to share his tastes as he is to turn himself into a committed writer.

# CHAPTER 9

# The "Nucleus": Sartre, Simone de Beauvoir, Merleau-Ponty

The strategies of Sartre, Merleau-Ponty, and Simone de Beauvoir can be analyzed as a microsystem of the system, with a relatively autonomous logic of its own. These coworkers are distinguished from all the others by their position as co-protagonists. Their paths and their symbolic interests are so closely linked that they cannot help constantly confronting one another. To account for their trajectories, we must consider this mutual reference. Even those developments which seem at first sight most independent shine with a different light when they are analyzed in terms of these reciprocal interrelations.

The place and importance given to this triumvirate's respective contributions to the review are in themselves a clear sign of their authority, as well as of the differences in the roles each plays within it. Sartre, Simone de Beauvoir, and Merleau-Ponty have exclusive rights to the lead articles. High prophecy, reflection on the tasks and destiny of contemporary man, is reserved for them, whereas it is up to their disciples to handle the routine tasks of critically analyzing current political and cultural events. The supremacy of the triumvirate is so clear that all the other coworkers at *Les Temps Modernes* accept it as self-evident, as is evidenced by Boris Vian's "Chronique du menteur," a parody for internal consumption only in which characters with eloquent names (Pont de Beauvarte . . .) despotically monopolize the pages of a review.[1] As a result of this quasi-monopoly, the review is identified with its three chief editors. The different uses each makes of his individual space only heighten our sense of their collective domination. These differences can be seen as a sort of diagram of the distribution of power among the three. There is a clear quantitative spread between Merleau-Ponty's contributions [among which there are only two long essays: "Le Yogi et le prolétaire" (1946)[2] and the long excerpt from *The Prose of the World* with which he takes leave of the review[3]] and those that Sartre and Simone de Beauvoir make during the same period.

Simone de Beauvoir publishes much of what she writes as she gets it written: to begin with, her essays on ethics, then *America Day by Day, The Second Sex,* and her essay on de Sade.

In addition to the Introduction to the first issue (and to mention only his main works) Sartre publishes up through 1952 *Anti-Semite and Jew,* his essay on Baudelaire, *Materialism and Revolution, What Is Literature?, Dirty Hands,* "Entretiens sur la politique," *Black Orpheus, Troubled Sleep,* "Drôle d'amitié," his essay on Genet, *Lucifer and the Lord,* and *The Communists and Peace.*

Thanks to *Les Temps Modernes,* Sartre's exceptional fruitfulness is transformed into an irresistible hegemonic apparatus. It is as if from his permanent place in the foreground—with the support of Simone de Beauvoir, who seems to have acted as mediator—he shoves off onto the less productive Merleau-Ponty the dirty work of running the review: from choosing and revising manuscripts to correcting proofs and making contacts with contributors, the publisher, and the printer.

# 1. THE ROLE OF SIMONE DE BEAUVOIR

Simone de Beauvoir's trajectory is conditioned more than anyone else's by her relationship to Sartre. It reflects the traditional sexual division of labor. Sartre develops existentialism's philosophical, aesthetic, ethical, and political principles. His companion applies, disseminates, clarifies, supports, and administers them.[4]

Sartre's ambition to combine philosophy, literature, theater, and journalism is also evident in the polyphonic range of Simone de Beauvoir's production. And no matter what the genre in which she tries her skills, we see that Sartre is guiding her—as she usually acknowledges. Accepting Sartre's ideas about the relationship between technique and metaphysics, she presents her novels as an effort to realize an existential literature. It is Sartre's success on the Parisian stage at the Liberation which encourages her to try writing a play on her own, *Les bouches inutiles,* which is Sartrean even in its conception, insofar as she uses the theater to illustrate a philosophical approach.[5] And she follows Sartre's example again in venturing into the field of the philosophical essay with *Pyrrhus et Cinéas* and *Pour une morale de l'ambiguité.* As we know, ethical reflection is the main preoccupation of Sartre and the Sartreans after the War.[6] Similarly, Simone de Beauvoir finds justification for the autobiographical interests which run through her most commonly praised works—her novels and her memoirs as well as her reporting and her investigations of the situation of women—in Sartre's conviction that the committed intellectual's responsibility is to set out from his own experience to think about the present. Moreover, she has said that the latent desire to tell the story of her own life was the source of her most famous books: *The Second Sex*, which made her the pioneer of contemporary French feminism, and *The Mandarins*, which earned her the Prix Goncourt. And her memoirs tell how decisive Sartre's encouragement and theoretical support were in helping her follow her inclination to talk about herself.

> My essay was finished, and I was asking myself: What now? I sat in the Deux Magots and gazed at the blank sheet of paper in front of me. I felt the need to write in my fingertips, and the taste of the words in my throat, but I didn't know where to start, or what. "How wild you look!" Giacometti said to me at one point. "It's because I want to write and I don't know what." "Write anything." In fact, I wanted to write about myself. I liked Leiris' *L'Age d'homme*; such sacrificial essays, in which the author strips himself bare without excuses, appealed to me. I let the idea begin to take shape, made a few notes, and talked to Sartre about it. I realized that the first question to come up was: What has it meant to me to be a woman? At first I thought I could dispose of that pretty quickly. I had never had any feeling of inferiority, no one had ever said to me: "You think that way because you're a woman"; my femininity had never been irksome to me in any way. "For me," I said to Sartre, "you might almost say it just hasn't counted." "All the same, you weren't brought up in the same way as a boy would have been; you should look into it further." I looked, and it was a revelation: this world was a masculine world, my childhood had been nourished by myths forged by men, and I hadn't reacted to them in at all the same way I should have done if I had been a boy. I was so interested in this discovery that I abandoned my project for a personal confession in order to give all my attention to finding out about the condition of woman in its broadest terms. I went to the Bibliothèque Nationale to do some reading, and what I studied were the myths of femininity.[7]

Simone de Beauvoir's review of *The Elementary Forms of Kinship*[8] shows signs of another characteristically Sartrean activity: taking it upon oneself to show science what its observations really mean. She presents Lévi-Strauss's book as "a book which frees us from the factual, which establishes a method, and which suggests speculations"; and of course what we are to understand by "speculations" is Simone de Beauvoir's philosophical reading of the book, which sees "correlations between certain descriptions of his and existentialist themes."[9] Her calm annexation of an intellectual position which is destined to make itself known by opposing and dethroning existentialism is significant.

It is also in light of Simone de Beauvoir's relationship to Sartre that her exchanges with Merleau-Ponty take on their full meaning. Sartre seems to delegate to his companion the responsibility of replying to the writings devoted to him by his most famous coworker. Thus in the first months of the review Merleau-Ponty publishes a text on *Being and Nothingness* and in return Simone de Beauvoir rewards him in the same issue with an article on the *Phenomenology of Perception*.[10] And once again it is she who takes it upon herself to reply when Merleau-Ponty moves to the attack against Sartre in *The Adventures of the Dialectic*.[11] This same delegation of authority is found in the role Simone de Beauvoir plays in the review. By taking on a sizable number of editorial tasks, she allows Sartre to control *Les Temps Modernes* without taking time off from his intellectual production.

## 2. SARTRE AND MERLEAU-PONTY DURING THE FIRST TWO YEARS OF THEIR COLLABORATION

Merleau-Ponty is the only coworker at the review who is capable of challenging Sartre's position by opposing it with an alternative version of the committed existentialist intellectual. Their confrontation is decisive for the history of the review. Consequently, we shall give it special attention. We shall begin with an analysis of their respective positions during the first two years of the review and we shall show that the contrast and conflict between the creator and the professor correspond to two different ways of understanding and doing intellectual work— two styles—which give the first phase of existentialism its richness and ambiguity, and its tension between the expectations of the intellectual public at large and a new, more demanding conception of philosophy.

### 2.1 Sartre, 1945–1947

During these two years, the enticements of fame seem to dominate Sartre's production. It is only in 1947 that he manages to begin the works which at this time he considers the essential, indispensable extension of his creative, philosophical, and literary project: the *Ethics* that he promised at the close of *Being and Nothingness* and volume three of *The Roads* to Freedom, which he announced in the insert for The Age of Reason and The Reprieve as the conclusion of the cycle. The pressure of immediate tasks seriously compromises the realization of this program by delaying its execution and thus making it progressively out of date.[12] The only two essays Sartre publishes during this period which (as applications of ideas developed in his philosophical anthropology) relate directly to his philosophical program—his Baudelaire and Anti-Semite and Jew—are actually edited before 1945. Strapped by countless commentaries, attacks, and requests, Sartre at this time turns himself into a polygraph fully employed in the tasks of the moment.[13] He enlists his prestige in the service of his friends—writing prefaces, introducing exhibitions, protesting Communist slanders of Nizan and wrongs done to Dullin. But above all he devotes himself to specifying, further developing, and defending his position, in response to the avalanche of criticisms which lay bare the gaps, the obscurities, and the fluctuations in his first manifestos on existentialism and commitment. He increases the number of interviews he gives to the papers and on the radio. The direction he takes is the one visible already in his Introduction to Les Temps Modernes and in his lecture, Existentialism Is a Humanism. It is a matter of bolstering these ideas and beginning to illustrate them. The "Tribune of Les Temps Modernes," a short series of radio broadcasts entrusted to Sartre under Ramadier's ministry and turned into a series of commentaries on current politics, seems to Sartre to provide an opportunity to put into practice the form of political action he thinks a writer should take. And even in the two plays he writes at this time, The Victors and The Respectful Prostitute, which are devoted to the subject of torture and the subject of racism respectively, what he has in mind is clearly a committed art capable of reminding audiences of disagreeable realities. Developments in his philosophical doctrines are left to the main texts he is currently writing, which he publishes serially in Les Temps Modernes: "Materialism and Revolution" and What Is Literature? These take up again the tasks which since 1945 have been the two complementary sides of Sartre's concerns: criticizing Marxism and justifying literature as an inherently revolutionary activity.

These two essays are the most significant reflection of the effects success tends to have on Sartre's works. To begin with, an undeniable loss of rigor. Sartre has never given in so much to the temptation to make bold syntheses, never has he been so little concerned to specify his subjects, bring supporting arguments to bear, avoid approximations. These are flaws his most faithful commentators have come to recognize, as he did implicitly himself by subsequently restating what he states here. His casualness is particularly disturbing in his text on Marxism, in which "dialectical materialism" is reduced to the view of it currently presented by French Communist philosophers inspired more by Lenin's *Materialism and Empiriocriticism* than by Marx. On the basis of this wholly approximate view, Sartre rejects the whole of Marxism as a "hasty, provisional construction" shot full of holes, and as a "myth" which cannot be effective since truth alone is revolutionary.

In the second place, never in Sartre's writing has its function of self-legitimation been as preponderant as it is in these texts. The philosophy of the subject and of freedom is proclaimed the only "coherent philosophy which [is] superior to materialism in being a *true description of nature and of human relationships.*"[14] And in *What Is Literature?* commitment is erected into the essence and norm of all literature, thereby producing what is probably the most important manifesto of literary prophetism in history.

The peremptory formulas of *What Is Literature?* condense the credo of an entire generation: literature is an "unconditional" appeal that one freedom, the writer's, makes to another, the reader's; the literary work is an act of generosity which always presents "the world as a whole"; aesthetic pleasure is the recognition of a value, a "transcendent," "absolute" end, the world itself, which creative activity offers "to human freedom as a task"; a book is a "categorical imperative." "To write is thus both to disclose the world and to offer it as a task to the generosity of the reader. It is to have recourse to the consciousness of others in order to make one's self be recognized as *essential* to the totality of being; it is to wish to live this essentiality by means of interposed persons; but, on the other hand, as the real world is revealed only by action, as one can feel himself in it only by exceeding it in order to *change* it, the novelist's universe would lack thickness if it were not discovered in a movement to transcend it."[15] "We no longer have time to *describe* or *narrate . . . we must reveal* to the reader his power, in each concrete case, of doing and undoing, in short of acting."[16]

Sartre's propensity for erecting a particular conception of literature into a universal law accounts for excesses in this text such as his condemnation of "pure art" and the essential difference he establishes between prose and poetry, between communication, in which words are only signs, and poetic language, in which they are objects: "Since words are transparent and since the gaze looks through them, it would be absurd to slip in among them some panes of rough glass."[17] "We know very well that pure art and empty art are the same thing and that aesthetic purism was a brilliant maneuver of the bourgeois of the last century. . . ."[18]

Sartre's concern to define his own positions, coupled with the confidence success brings, accounts for a final change we can see in these two essays: an apparent relaxation of his previously intense effort to update his work. In "Materialism and Revolution," Sartre does no more than develop the conclusion of *The Transcendence of the Ego*: "It has always seemed to me that a working hypothesis as fruitful as historical materialism never needed for a foundation the absurdity which is metaphysical materialism." He continues to be concerned above all with showing Marxism's "absurdity," rather than with exploring its "fruitfulness." The result is like the many "refutations" of Marxism his generation had already produced in the thirties on the basis of the same underlying resistance (itself based on the education they had received) to a view which makes physical and social matter the explanatory principle of reality. Sartre picks up on the favorite accusations of the so-called "non-conformists": "materialism is the opiate of the revolution"[19]; it is a "myth"; it does not ask whether socialism is possible, but "adheres to an unbending law of evolution and accepts the absolute constraint of facts"[20]; it leaves no room for freedom. Above all, and this is no accident, Sartre's essay reminds us of certain texts of Simone Weil's, who more than any other French intellectual of her time had developed a spiritualist critique of Marx's thought.[21] But Sartre is far from dwelling on Marx with the attentiveness which enabled Simone Weil to recognize, with what was at that time extraordinary lucidity, not only the most serious limitations of Marx's theory of revolution but also the fact that in spite of their limitations Marx's works are a prime source for any scientific understanding of society.[22]

*What Is Literature?* represents no innovation in Sartre's work either. Its conception of the writer's role repeats ideas already put forth in the Introduction to *Les Temps Modernes*, and turns out to be very close to the view of France's first theorists of "socialist realism": Nizan and the Aragon who produced "For a Socialist Realism" and the inquest, "For Whom Do You Write?" which was published in *Commune* beginning in 1933. The approach to literary history which made *What Is Literature?* seem when it first appeared to be so much more original than the established models is scarcely more innovative. At the time, Sartre seemed to be combining precision and simplicity by providing a theoretical key capable of reducing to a clear scheme a literary patrimony which was very old, very rich, and as far as its recent history was concerned, still confused and controversial. The truth is that his determination to establish the universality of his theory leads him to elaborate a dialectical schema which is rather close to those produced by Marxist theoreticians in the twenties and thirties. Starting out from the same aim of showing that literature is always related to social structure, Sartre ends up conceding much more to Marxist thinking than he does in "Materialism and Revolution," although he does salvage the primacy of the subject by proclaiming that the writer, as one who is always free to take on or dodge his historical tasks, is always responsible for his works. Sartre's brilliant formulations, suggestive hypotheses, dramatic vivacity, and correct insights mask the reductive poverty of the lesson he draws from Marxism. The Good Book which surfaces in this novel about literature's imminent shotgun wedding to the proletariat is the most teleological version of the Marxist vulgate, derived from Marxian texts which reproduce the vices of Hegel's philosophy of history. The cycles of literary history are scanned in terms of the stereotyped reductionist triad of class relationships: dominant class as thesis, rising class as antithesis, and that incarnation of Objective Spirit, the intellectuals, on hand to bring about the synthesis. Sartre is able to justify all his judgments concerning writers because his criterion for success—their capacity to oppose the dominant class and recognize the rising class of their day— is so vague. Thus he absolves the classical period with the argument that true art is always committed, but accuses Flaubert, Gide, and the Surrealists of having missed the potential public, the proletariat, that history offered them. As in the *Phenomenology of Spirit*, history here is a self-sustaining progressive process whose implicit highest stage is Sartre's existentialism in Sartre's France: the logical and chronological conclusion of history in *What Is Literature?*'s retrospective view of it is the position of the man who is writing the book, the chosen one who can at last decipher the mission of history and bring it to its conclusion.

The apparent paradox that a "philosophy of the subject" should end up rejoining and naturally incorporating this sort of Marxism is perfectly comprehensible. There is a resemblance between the two which must be imputed more to habits inculcated by traditional philosophical training than to the often improbable or undemonstrated influences of philosophical schools which are temporally and spatially remote from one another. It is this training that encourages vast and apparently systematic syntheses which treat history as a process of realizing some ultimate end. Marxist philosophers are only reproducing this way of thinking when they treat abstractions whose function is to denote complex collective realities—the Proletariat, the Bourgeoisie, the Working Class, Capitalism—as the anthropomorphic subjects of History.[23] We can see why upon closer inspection *What Is Literature?* reminds us particularly of the approach and limitations of some of Lukács' analyses. Sartre and Lukács are both pursuing the same aim of interpreting literature in terms of Marxist categories, and both run into the same problems, which stem from the education they have received. Thus both tend to find the subjective in the objective by slipping from metaphor into the personification of concepts. From abstraction to abstraction, from generalization to generalization, both end up erecting their personal view into a universal schema for interpreting and evaluating literary phenomena. Although such apriorist dogmatism does allow for suggestive insights, it does not actually account for the complexity and diversity of actual practices but sizes them up and judges them in terms of a vision of what they ought to be which is embodied in its idealistic dialectic of symbolic functions. This objective proximity of the two men is perhaps the main reason for the virulence of the confrontation between the one's "free" version and the other's Communist version of an intellectual style and philosophical approach which both deeply share.

## 2.2 Merleau-Ponty, 1945–47

At this time, the chief differences between the intellectual styles of Merleau-Ponty and Sartre undoubtedly stem in part from the different demands of their two trajectories, which diverge in a radical way as a result of Sartre's success at the Liberation. Whereas Merleau-Ponty pursues the brilliant academic career open to a model Ecole normale graduate, Sartre's royalties—especially what he gets from his plays—give him a material independence which enables him to give up teaching forever. With this institutional constraint, a barrier to the worldliness that fame tends to impose falls, and the motive for precision and depth, which Merleau-Ponty, as a professor, still has, disappears. The latter cannot forget that his articles are read by his academic colleagues, who are stern judges—especially of one whose very collaboration with a profane enterprise such as Les Temps Modernes makes suspect.

The contrast between the two men's attitudes stands out when we compare the "political" writings Merleau-Ponty publishes at this time in Les Temps Modernes to "Marxism and Revolution," which may be considered the result of Sartre's political reflections during this same period. Merleau-Ponty's analyses are more circumscribed, more precise in defining their topics, more bolstered by arguments. If he talks about domestic politics, he specifies persons and situations.[24] In his essay on Stalinist terror,[25] he studies in detail the book by Koestler which gives rise to his reflections, and he sets to work distinguishing the U.S.S.R. in 1947 from the circumstances at the time of the Purge Trials in the thirties. Perhaps it is just this concern to be precise which helped make his stands seem more radical than Sartre's and create the image of an "ultra-Bolshevist" Merleau-Ponty.[26] Yet the fact is that he always puts forth the positions he adopts as provisional hypotheses which he qualifies with explicit conditions. Thus his most famous statement—"support the C.P. line"—is only ad hoc advice in a situation which calls for a choice.

Merleau-Ponty's position concerning Marxism is based on a close reading of Marx and is much more thoughtful and subtle than Sartre's concurrent formulations.[27] In his 1945–46 writings, Merleau-Ponty outlines the task of synthesizing Marxism and a philosophy of the subject which Sartre will take up more than ten years later in his *Critique of Dialectical Reason*, when being a Marxist had come to be a form of conservatism which was already threatened by the vogue for structuralism. As Sartre will later, Merleau-Ponty proclaims Marxism an unsurpassable paradigm that existentialism is not claiming to surpass but only to integrate by making explicit the philosophy of man which in Marxism remained implicit.[28] But his sympathy for Marxism is more prudent. Whereas Sartre proclaims Marxism "the philosophy of our age," a "science," and "a totalization," Merleau-Ponty values its "concrete analyses" and its hypotheses, and stresses the "Marxist uneasiness" which springs from its discovery of the contingency of history and which leads Marxists to struggle to make it rational without being sure that a rational history is possible.[29] Commitment for him comes down to exacting work; it is a matter of "[taking] stock of this century and the ambiguous forms which it offers us," while always being prepared to question all choices.[30] Merleau-Ponty is far from transforming his personal opinions into dogma. Thus he does not hesitate for example to consider and partially approve of a position which in 1946 is completely beyond the pale of established intellectual legitimacy: that of Thierry Maulnier, a former Maurassian and current writer for the *Figaro*.[31]

But the fact that Merleau-Ponty and Sartre are allies shows that they are not completely opposed to one another. Instead of considering Merleau-Ponty's model as competing with Sartre's, we should think of it as a more rigorous variant of existentialist prophetism, and of the relation between the two models as a tension between conflicting demands. Merleau-Ponty too succumbs to the temptation to prophesy, especially in *Humanism and Terror*, the most ambitious of all the essays he devotes to politics and history. The temptation is evident in a tendency toward sweeping synthesis which contrasts with his concern for objectivity and with the subtlety of his reasoning. His anguished questioning as to the meaning and rationality of history betrays, in spite of his denials, the temptation to think of history in terms of ultimate ends, to search for finality in the historical process. With his hypothesis of a "Historical Reason," Merleau-Ponty rejoins the millenarian Marxist tradition which has given a mythical personification, the Proletariat, the task of realizing the classless society. No doubt the times themselves favored the success of this naive philosophy of history. But is is equally certain that what counted for the intellectuals was that it satisfied their ambition to reduce the complexity of empirical reality to a universal principle of intelligibility and an ultimate logic. This impatient love of theory is basically what Merleau-Ponty shares with Sartre. That is why *Humanism and Terror*, which is strong with precise and pertinent observations, concludes by drawing up an abstract balance sheet. The criterion in terms of which Merleau-Ponty proposes to measure the success of the U.S.S.R. is the "progress" which the Proletariat, as the "regulator of History," has made in its political consciousness and its capacity for struggle.

We find this same oscillation between intellectual rigor and the pretense of looking on from "God's standpoint" when we follow Merleau-Ponty into other areas he investigates. He is undoubtedly more sensitive than Sartre to new tendencies which are beginning to develop in the intellectual field, and more prompt to see the philosophical problems these changes are going to produce. He is one of the first to relate the works he is studying—the investigations of Gestalt psychology, the works of Saussure and Guillaume, certain pages[32] of Marcel Mauss—to a new cultural paradigm based on the concepts of structure, system, and relation. He does not fail to see the heuristic, synthesizing power that this way of thinking has in comparison to the existing division of scientific labor. He thus ends up with an original philosophical project which tends to reconcile the new ideas he has drawn from the human sciences and biology with the typical preoccupations his generation has with history, politics, and the conditions of knowledge and action—preoccupations structuralism will repress. But his aim is objectively ambiguous, his cognitive interest merges with his desire to reaffirm philosophy's superiority to the sciences. The fact is that he shares Sartre's pretense to justify the methods and results of the sciences without ever having used those methods to produce scientific results. His express ambition is to give philosophy the sovereign role in relation to contemporary thought that it was granted in ancient Greek civilization.[33] His writings show that by 1945 he is already thinking of an ontology whose aim and truth criterion would be its capacity to understand all the hypotheses and experiments contemporary culture offers for thought, and to find the point of intersection between Marxism and epistemology, and between phenomenology and the human sciences: a theory of being which would admit its own historical nature without despairing of being true. And the texts Merleau-Ponty publishes in *Les Temps Modernes*, even those which may seem at first sight to be the farthest from such concerns, show that he does not stop at the planning stage. They show a constant labor of progressively readapting reflections aroused by the most disparate encounters.

Thus even the philosophy of history at work in a political essay like *Humanism and Terror* looks different in the light of Merleau-Ponty's overall philosophical project. Here he conceives of the historical process as the tortuous articulation of an "objective meaning" which can be better read by the retrospective gaze of the historian who can see the whole picture than by the historical actors themselves who, as players in the game, never fully grasp its meaning. Marx alone cannot account for this view, which is fed by a multitude of sources, including Husserl's theory of intentionality, Heidegger's ontology, and the concept of "structure." If the latter is understood as "a new way of looking at being," it provides a way of going beyond the traditional subject-object distinction by considering both as two structural aspects of being. But Merleau-Ponty, on the contrary, whether he is talking about metaphysics, the human sciences,[34] art, or the cinema,[35] means to correct the traditionally neutral perspective of epistemological and aesthetic discourse by taking into account the lesson he has learned from Marxism about the social and political function of cultural phenomena. A typical example of this synthetic tension is the 1947 article, "The Metaphysical in Man," in which for the first time he explicitly gives the philosopher the job of articulating the "implicit metaphysics" of current science. To show how the most diverse cultural experiments are converging in the hypothesis that the "subjective" and the "objective" are inherently related, he not only cites developments in biology and the human sciences, he also considers an eminently political example, the Russian Revolution, as if to show that philosophy and politics cannot be separated but reciprocally imply one another.[36]

This philosophical project springs from the need to reconcile commitment and truth, metaphysics and science, and because it tries to hold divergent trends together seems to be a hybrid, intrinsically fragile strategy. Whereas Sartre concentrates any symbolic capital he can accumulate which enriches the prophetic model—and only such capital—Merleau-Ponty risks seeming both a failed prophet and a failed professor in trying to hold together reciprocally invalidating virtues. His effort to be exact, the problematic nature of his cultural interests, and their esoteric novelty are not easily reconciled with the demands of prophetism. What enhances the prophet's success is felicity of phrase, clarity of systematization, and capacity to satisfy an already present, urgent, and widespread demand. In this perspective, paradoxically, the risks of fame which threaten Sartre, such as delay and oversimplification, become assets. It is no accident that at this time, Merleau-Ponty's most novel ideas and most subtle distinctions pass unseen before the review's readers, who chiefly retain his most radical formulations, divorcing them from the truth conditions their author has established.

It is a significant fact that even for Sartre the lesson of the early Merleau-Ponty can be summed up in a few peremptory statements. Thus it is no exaggeration to see the outlines of the stand which will be defended theoretically in *The Communists and Peace* in sentences such as "What we must do with respect to communism is to define a practical stance of comprehension without adherence, of free study without disparagement,"[37] or "support the C.P. line." Just as the Sartre of the *Critique* develops, in reference to Marxism, the most extreme statements of *Humanism and Terror*: "It is still valid as a critique of the present world and alternative humanisms. In this respect, at least, *it cannot be surpassed. . . .* On close consideration, Marxism is not just any hypothesis that might be replaced tomorrow by some other. It is the simple statement of those conditions without which there would be neither any humanism, in the sense of a mutual relation between men, nor any rationality in history. In this sense Marxism is not a philosophy of history; it is *the* philosophy of history and to renounce it is to dig the grave of Reason in history. After that there can be no more dreams of adventures."[38]

Thus the manner in which an enterprise like *Les Temps Modernes* conceives and carries out its intellectual task of living up to the expectations of a wide public of nonspecialized readers plays right into Sartre's hands. On the other hand, Merleau-Ponty is too close to Sartre's position to fully represent professorial excellence. His disdain for documentation and the labors of empirical research; the careless hermeneutic grace with which he links together phenomena of different epochs, cultures, and disciplines; and the insouciance of his critical and biographical techniques all make him seem instead to be a brilliant essayist. And since he is a metaphysician, his way of thinking does not correspond either to the antimetaphysical bias which will dominate French philosophy after 1960.

The ambivalence of Merleau-Ponty's position is equally visible in his writing. He rarely indulges in the outbursts and theatricalities which give life to Sartre's prose, or in the lexical and syntactical tricks which give it its tone of imperious truth. Yet the richness of metaphor, the allusions, the connotations, the frequent flights of pure association, and the restrained but never absent emotional vibration of his language make it highly evocative and far from the hypotheticodeductive method and the unequivocalness of meaning characteristic of scientific discourse.[39] But the very personal, seductive style this tension produces is not enough to win him the literary reputation which distinguishes Sartre's position.

## 3. FIELD EFFECT IN THE EVOLUTION OF SARTRE AND MERLEAU-PONTY

Although the relationship between Sartre and Merleau-Ponty seems to be a one-sided, discontinuous one in which Merleau-Ponty pays attention to Sartre but Sartre only concerns himself with Merleau-Ponty in the posthumous homage he pays him in "Merleau-Ponty,"[40] the truth is that from 1948 on their interdependence plays an essential role in the trajectories of both men.

Merleau-Ponty begins writing about Sartre in 1936 with a review of his *Psychology of Imagination [Journal de psychologie normale et pathologique* 9–10 (1936): 756–61]. His tone is friendly but not entirely flattering, with reasoned reservations surfacing here and there. Next, he writes a very favorable article about *The Flies [Confluences* 25 (1943): 514–16]. Having become Sartre's ally in the *Temps Modernes* venture, he supports him heatedly against his adversaries with two articles which show great admiration: "The Battle over Existentialism" [*Les Temps Modernes* 2 (1945)] defends the importance and novelty of *Being and Nothingness* against its Catholic and Marxist critics; "A Scandalous Author" [*Le Figaro littéraire* (Dec. 6, 1947)] defends Sartre's literary and moral virtues. Then, after a ten-year silence, Merleau-Ponty devotes a long chapter in *The Adventures of the Dialectic* to him: "Sartre and Ultrabolshevism," a stern indictment which marks a profound turning point in respect to the past. And he will speak of him one final time in his Preface to *Signs*, where he gives a more subtle version of the criticism Sartre made of himself in the Preface he wrote for Nizan's *Aden, Arabie*.

What stays with us above all in this relationship is the end of it, this radical break which is hard to understand if we try to reduce it to merely political differences. Analysis will bring out a far deeper relationship, whose main lines we must now summarize. Everything happens as if Sartre were tending toward a form of militant commitment which in a basic way is an extension of the political position Merleau-Ponty stated during the two preceding years. Sartre draws progressively closer to the Communists, up to the culminating point at which he writes *The Communists and Peace* (1952–53). In everything Merleau-Ponty writes during this same period, on the contrary, there are signs of a growing pessimism about "real" Communism and the political effectiveness of intellectuals at the height of the Cold War, as well as a searching examination of the Marxist philosophy of history. But he seems above all to be treading on Sartre's grounds, for up until 1952 his interest shifts from politics to elaborating a theory of expression—especially artistic and literary expression—which can be understood as a response to *What Is Literature?* This partial role reversal is expressed symbolically by the fact that *Les Temps Modernes* publishes in the same issue the results of Merleau-Ponty's reflections on artistic and literary expression, "Indirect Language and the *Voices of Silence*," and *The Communists and Peace*, the fruit of Sartre's new political course. But the force of this reciprocal reference can be measured only in relation to the period which follows. Merleau-Ponty devotes himself to a radical revision of his ideology which produces *The Adventures of the Dialectic* (1955). The book concludes with a reply to *The Communists and Peace*, as if each new development in Sartre's position systematically provoked a counterpoint from Merleau-Ponty: one now to the Sartre of 1952, the political philosopher, as previously to the Sartre of 1947, the literary theorist. Even the orientation and ontology of Merleau-Ponty's final period may be seen as a response to Sartre: Merleau-Ponty does not think he has settled old scores until he has measured himself against the task Sartre confronted him with in writing *Being and Nothingness*. But Sartre in turn continues to draw on the Merleau-Ponty of *Humanism and Terror*, in the process of drawing nearer to Marxism which leads him to the *Critique*.

For expository reasons we shall look at the two trajectories in succession, first Sartre's, then Merleau-Ponty's, but we shall look at them as the two terms of a relationship which is really what we are analyzing as the explanatory principle of the two men's practices. At the same time, we shall be concerned to show how the developments in this relationship—especially Merleau-Ponty's break with Sartre and *Les Temps Modernes*—are tied to changes in the broader system it is a part of: the intellectual field and, as a field within this field, the review.

## 3.1 *Sartre from the R.D.R. to* The Communists and Peace

Everything Sartre does between 1948 and 1952–53 may be related to his attempt to get away from the indirect, vague commitment through literature which he had theorized about in the preceding period, and especially to take up a position in respect to the Communist Party. Sartre goes on examining this problem, either directly or through his characters, in *Dirty Hands*, his brief experience with the R.D.R.,[41] the "Entretiens sur la politique," *Troubled Sleep*, "Drôle d'amitié," his Preface to Dalmas' *Communisme yougoslave* (1950)[42] and the other one he wrote the same year for Stéphane's *Portrait de l'aventurier*,[43] and *Lucifer and the Lord*. But it is a problem which seems to him both inescapable and insoluble, for in spite of appearances, his social worldview is basically unchanged. Think of the dilemmas wracking characters such as Hugo and the heroes of *The Roads to Freedom*. It is always the same choice between the intellectual's pure and unadorned but ineffectual rebellion and adhering to the course of history as it really is, an opaque and impenetrable reality embodied in the Communist Party. Sartre continues to establish an absolute dichotomy between the imperatives of conscience and the imperatives of action, between ethics and praxis, between the intellectual and the masses. In choosing to "get his hands dirty," to accept the discipline of the organization that the masses see as their organization, the intellectual gives up his abstract freedom and impotent lucidity without any hope of making others forget his bourgeois origins, of doing away with his difference, or of succeeding in understanding a form of action which is not the fruit of decisions but of the blind force of circumstance. As a "necessary" expression of this force, the Communist Party may justifiably take stands which put the militants' loyalty to a rugged test by putting efficiency ahead of principles. For Sartre, the Communist Party's attitude at the time of the Nazi-Soviet Pact is an exemplary instantiation of this logic, which produces a tormenting conflict in a person who sees Communism as the embodiment of history's objective meaning yet grants transparent consciousness alone the power to make sense out of the world. The conflicts which troubled Communist militants in 1939, as Sartre lived them through Nizan, function in the works he wrote at this time as the symbol which crystallizes his approach and as the scheme which structures the plot of his novels. Say the story of Brunet and Schneider-Vicarios, which in Sartre's projection was to form the central core of *The Last Chance*, the final, uncompleted volume of *The Roads to Freedom*. Or the conclusion of *Dirty Hands*, where the Party's unexpected reversal of its line leads Hugo to commit suicide. And the Preface to *Aden, Arabie* shows that even as late as 1960, Sartre has not changed his point of view about what political action requires: in his judgment, Nizan's break with the C.P. in 1939 was, for a militant who understood the Party's logic, an emotional, irresponsible reaction.

Everything Sartre does at this stage is tied together by his desire to overcome this contradiction. In all his imaginary heroes (in Matthieu and Brunet, in Hugo and Goetz), in the hopes which lead him for a time to spark the R.D.R., in the two prefaces we have referred to already, in his manuscript on ethics, and in *Saint Genet*,[44] we find the same ideal of an action which is effective yet still "pure"—that is, free and self-aware. Sartre imputed the pessimistic conclusion of his quest to circumstances: the Cold War, the R.D.R.'s failure, the Korean War, the rigidity of Stalinist Communism. He articulates this historical pessimism in *Saint Genet*, where he declares that ethical action "is *for us* inevitable and at the same time impossible."[45]

There is no doubt that Sartre's idea that a concrete ethics was a "nontranscendable impossibility" was justified by the Manichean context of the Cold War. But it is significant that for Sartre there was only one "historical situation" in his whole life which embodied his ideal of action—the Resistance. Significant because the Resistance had not actually "synthesized Good and Evil": in its spontaneous unanimity, and in the weight it gave to individual choice over organizations and parties, it had instead simply done away with Evil by concentrating it all in the occupier. As early as 1945, in the first issue of *Les Temps Modernes*, Merleau-Ponty had pointed out the reasons why intellectuals had been fascinated by their experiences during the Resistance: "The Resistance was a unique experience for them, and they wanted to preserve its spirit in the new French politics because this experience broke away from the famous dilemma of being and doing, which confronts all intellectuals in the face of action. . . . [The] Resistance experience, by making us believe that politics is a relationship between man and man or between consciousnesses, fostered our illusions of 1939 and masked the truth of the incredible power of history which the Occupation taught us in another connection."[46]

From the moment organizations once again become more important than individuals, political life, Sartre thinks, falls back into the old "choice between what is effective and what is human," which Merleau-Ponty saw in 1945 as the false dilemma typical of intellectuals confronted with the need to act. For those who define fully human action as a choice made by a subject who transcends his "situation," the organization is "Evil." Sartre has written the following revealing words about this feeling he had during those years of an insurmountable contradiction: "The contradiction was not one of ideas. It was in my own being. For my liberty implied also the liberty of all men. And all men were not free. I could not submit to the discipline of solidarity with all men without breaking beneath the strain. And I could not be free alone."[47]

In *The Communists and Peace*, Sartre does not modify this attitude, only the conclusions he draws from it. The book marks a change which is explained by the greater and greater pressure that the field puts on Sartre to go beyond the general commitment to which he had heretofore limited himself and adopt in the pages of *Les Temps Modernes* the line of free alliance with the Communist Party that Merleau-Ponty had formulated in the early days of the review and that had become the symbol of its politics. In "Merleau-Ponty," Sartre himself recognized the force of this pressure. He recalled how increasingly impatient his coworkers had been to break the silence Merleau-Ponty had decided on after the Korean War and to reestablish—if need be, in opposition to Merleau-Ponty—the political image Merleau-Ponty himself had created. Sartre's narrative gives us a glimpse of how strongly, if confusedly, the little world that revolved around *Les Temps Modernes* felt that the survival routine instituted in 1950 just would not do any more. To avoid going under, there had to be a striking rebirth, a prophetic public stand comparable to *Humanism and Terror*—and only Sartre had the authority needed to pull it off. He certainly felt, as did those who were pressuring him to remain faithful to the ethics of commitment, that he was being faced individually with a historical responsibility that he must not fail to meet. Yet the fact remains that the review itself—and especially its new recruits, young people without capital who expected everything of it—was objectively faced with a vital need for renewal which was defined much more by the logic of the intellectual field than by the logic of the political field, the Korean War, or Jacques Duclos' arrest. In fact, even though Sartre himself does not interpret the matter in this way, he provides all the arguments needed to support such an interpretation. He describes the review as contradicting its own conception of the writer's role. He shows with horror that the subject who appeals freely to the readers' freedom has been replaced by an institution which must simply reproduce itself to meet the expectations it has itself aroused. At the same time, the resignation of Merleau-Ponty, who is trying to resist these institutional restraints, is shown to be the consequence of a divergence more profound than mere political disagreement: a divergence of strategies, a difference of intellectual posture.

Even as Sartre provides what is needed for an objective understanding of this parting of the ways, he is led to misunderstand it by ideological defense mechanisms which are interesting to observe. He justifies the stand he takes in 1952 as a more opportune choice for left intellectuals than Merleau-Ponty's neutralism, concerning which he writes: "I can't decide whether this idea was late or early in 1950. One thing only is certain. It was not on time."[48] Sartre represents the review's evolution as fate, a tiny institution's inevitable submission to the force of history: "What may be of interest in this adventure—which each of us lived painfully—is that it shows the sources from which discord may spring in the heart of the most loyal friendship and closest agreement. New circumstances and a disintegrating institution—our conflict had no other causes."[49] Projected against the background of history, the episode takes on a tragic grandeur: it is absorbed into the epic's basic theme of conflict between human will and inexorable collective destiny. This notion of the indifferent power that circumstances have over people—"We were all victims . . ."[50]—should be stressed, for it shows the continuity between the early Sartre and a text written later than the *Critique*. For the philosophy of freedom, there is only an apparent contradiction, a characteristic paradox, in saying that subjects are powerless in the face of objects they have themselves created, "caught in the gears." Sartre's radical dualism, in assuming a rupture between men and things, grants only one freedom to the subject, the freedom to accept its destiny. Consciousness' relation to the world is that of an onlooker, a lucid gaze which presupposes the spectator's absolute otherness: "That goes without saying. Once we are caught in the gears, we are dragged in all the way. The little freedom left us is resumed in the instant where we decide whether or not to put our finger in. In a word, our beginnings belong to us. Afterwards we can only will our destiny."[51]

If we analyze *The Communists and Peace*, we can understand why Merleau-Ponty considered this alleged revival of the "critical fellow travelling" that he himself had advocated at the Liberation a double and doubly unacceptable distortion. In its fundamentally different context, it took on a different meaning, and in addition Sartre was justifying it in terms of his worldview: "I thought that while I was being faithful to his thought of 1945, he was abandoning it. He thought he was remaining true to himself and I betraying him. I claimed to be carrying on his work, he accused me of spoiling it."[52]

And the truth of the matter is that although Sartre takes the position Merleau-Ponty held in 1945 as the key source of his essay, he only takes its best-known formulas, which for him are the essence of it, and which having become in the interim the institutionalized trademark of that position, are for *Temps Modernes* readers an instant evocation of the old line. All Sartre has to do is do away with the nuances and eliminate the conditional character of Merleau-Ponty's Communist sympathizing, denying the necessity and even the possibility of historical verification, to turn the program of *Humanism and Terror*—"What we must do with respect to communism is to define a practical stance of comprehension without adherence, of free study without disparagement"[53]—into the line of *The Communists and Peace*: "[The] purpose of this article is to declare my agreement with the Communists on precise and limited subjects, reasoning from *my* principles and not from *theirs*. . . ."[54] No matter that at the height of the Cold War, and after all that has become known about Soviet camps and the Korean War, the strategy of unity of action with the Communists, which was realistic at the time of tripartite rule in France, has become an abstract position. The difficulties of the Communist Party and the confusion of the times become ideal conditions for an alliance between intellectuals and the Party. For a man who conceives of "pure" action as infinite transcendence, action in defiance of reality is the closest thing to purity. As for the "principles" Sartre appeals to in his defense of the Communist Party, we can let Merleau-Ponty speak of them. He above all others who have an interest in disavowing this so-called alignment with the Party subjects *The Communists and Peace* to a closely reasoned criticism.[55] And naturally enough, as a philosopher criticizing another philosopher, he sticks chiefly to refuting Sartre's principles. He shows how far Sartre is in this respect from the "authentically dialectical" Marxism to which *Humanism and Terror* was referring, and to which Sartre—judging by his quotations from Marx, by the weight he gives to historical and economic evidence, and by his wide use of Marxist terminology—is claiming to refer.

Sartre seems to be becoming a Marxist and adopting Marxist terminology, Merleau-Ponty says, but he is actually just as close to his same old philosophy as always—and just as far from Marx as he was at the time of "Materialism and Revolution." He still establishes an absolute dichotomy between consciousness and physical, social and historical reality. Sartrean freedom asserts itself in negating reality, in a never-ending struggle: the world is an inert, opaque reality whose meaning can never be definitively established. Facts in themselves are senseless; only "the solitary heroism of consciousness" makes any sense out of them. Truth is either self-evident or there is no truth; it must be ceaselessly captured and recaptured from the essential ambiguity of facts by the creative power of the self. Since Sartre's philosophy takes consciousness to be the source of the "genesis of meaning," it cannot give the concepts of praxis, history, and revolution the meaning that they have for Marx. For Marx the only reality is "the equivocal reality of facts"; human history is made—and makes the sense it makes—without any absolute certainties; it is an ongoing adjustment to the probable. But in Sartre's philosophy, the probable is inconceivable: facts can never be the basis for action but must be only limiting conditions, a resistance to be overcome. The only thing that counts and that can be known is the choice subjects make. History as process disappears. It is this "purely subjective" philosophy, Merleau-Ponty stresses, which leads Sartre to his "purely activist Communism—which no longer believes in truth or revolution or history," and which conceives of the Party in terrorist fashion as the infallible interpreter of the will of the proletariat—leads him, that is, to justify the Stalinist pragmatism which Stalinism itself justifies on the entirely different grounds of its "purely objective philosophy." Stalinism's naturalistic conception of the historical process, Merleau-Ponty argues, is already implicit in certain of

Marx's formulations and in Lenin's conception of the relationship between the Party and the working class. For it is the concept of the
historical mission of the proletariat, and of the Party as its historically
and politically conscious vanguard, Merleau-Ponty now[56] believes, which
legitimates Stalinism's "state of frenzy belonging to the leader alone"
(A.D., 129). And he shows how the "folly of the Cogito" paradoxically
leads Sartre to analogous conclusions, making an absolute of the Party
and doing away with historical verification. If the meaning of history is
recreated at each instant by the choice of conscious subjects, and if the
proletariat as a mass of alienated and divided individuals is headless,
then it is only through its Party that it can attain the consciousness and
dignity of a subject and begin to exist as a class for itself. Merleau-
Ponty considers Sartre's insistence on thinking of social class as a subject to be a "methodical mythology" which is inevitable for a man who
can only conceive of human relations as relationships between consciousnesses. For such a thinker, history will make sense only if it comes
down to a series of "signed and dated acts," to a duel whose protagonists
are the proletariat and the bourgeoisie personified. ". . . [E]xtreme per-
sonalism makes history into a melodrama, smeared with crude colors,
where the individuals are types. There is only a single monotonous flight,
ended and begun at each moment, with no acquisition, no truces, no
areas of abatement" (A.D., 147–48). In Sartre's language, Merleau-
Ponty points out, the masses, like a woman, "condescend to surrender
themselves, they wait to be forced, to be taken" (A.D., 149). The Communists and Peace is an exchange of glances between the most "disinherited," whose accusing presence reveals the truth about society, and
Sartre, who responds from afar by reading that truth in their eyes. "We
are (Merleau-Ponty comments) in the magical or moral universe" (A.D.,
154).

   In asking us to see this subjectivism as the continuing basis of Sartre's
entire work,[57] Merleau-Ponty does not ignore the aspects of that work
which would seem to contradict this interpretation: Sartre's special attention to, his fascinated horror at, those ambiguous, disturbing phenomena which are neither men nor things and do not even have any ontological status. "The apparent paradox of [Sartre's] work is that he
become famous by describing a middle ground, as heavy as things and
fascinating for consciousness, between consciousness and things—the
root in Nausea [sliminess] or situation in Being and Nothingness, here
the social world—and that nonetheless his thought is in revolt against
this middle ground and finds there only an incentive to transcend it
and to begin again ex nihilo this entire disgusting world. . . . The paradox
is only apparent, since it is necessary to have another background—the

transparency of consciousness—in order to see the root, the [slimy], or history in their obscene evidence" (*A.D.*, 137–38 and note 78, 138).

The stakes at risk lead Merleau-Ponty to go beyond the bounds of philosophical commentary. Consequently, he touches on an explanation of the myth of the transparent subject and its absolute freedom: Sartre's profound ambivalence toward physical and social reality, and the intellectual education which shaped this ambivalence into a radical subjectivism. Furthermore, Merleau-Ponty had learned from personal experience and from Sartre's intolerance of Lefort's criticisms of *The Communists and Peace* the symbolic violence to which such a philosophy can easily lead.[58] "The certainty that one has the truth makes one dizzy. It is in itself violence," he writes concerning the "narcissism," the mandarin pride implicit in the role of society's consciousness and interpreter of the will of the disinherited which Sartre bestows on himself (*A.D.*, 178) in his claiming to legitimate the Communist Party in the name of principles which are inconsistent with its history and doctrine—and in which it does not recognize itself. At the very moment Sartre seems ready to join the Party and the proletariat, he maintains an impassable distance from them: joining is fine for the "subhuman" workers who have not yet acquired the dignity of subjects, but makes no sense for that subject par excellence, the intellectual, who possesses the truth about the proletariat and the Party. Contrary to appearances, Merleau-Ponty argues, Sartre's Communist sympathizing is still his means of neutralizing the Other rather than accepting it, of asserting himself rather than working to transform society, a transformation Sartre judges ontologically impossible (*A.D.*, 193ff).

Merleau-Ponty's bitterness about his still recent break with Sartre makes him harsher than usual, and makes him underestimate the strength of Sartre's solidarity with the dominated of the earth, which has never weakened. But Merleau-Ponty does have the merit of lifting the veil which shrouds the most forgotten aspect of commitment, which its supporters reduce to sheer generosity and its detractors to a series of mistrusts and misunderstandings. He shows how much an attitude which on the political level was utopian (and often proved to be impracticable or to lead to unintended consequences) made sense on the level of intellectual success. Defying political realism never stopped being a profitable investment for Sartre, even when he did not mean it to be, even though he was never an opportunist. And this double logic, which makes lost but lofty causes symbolic coups as well, is particularly evident in the case of *The Communists and Peace*. This passionate defense of the Communists is both insanely generous in respect to the Communist Party's political isolation at the time and a vigorous revival of a *Temps Modernes* in crisis. To fail to see this duplicity would be to dis-

honor Sartre's courageous labors of self-criticism: he himself recognized
the "ideological interest" which was inextricably bound up with his
political passion, unmasking "loser wins" as the renunciation of effectiveness and temporal power which is for the intellectual the sign that
he is chosen.[59]

## 3.2 Merleau-Ponty's evolution

Merleau-Ponty's trajectory after 1948 seems to be governed by two
chief concerns which are in many ways divergent: one is his relationship
to Sartre, the other is coming to terms with the new tendencies in the
intellectual field—structuralism and, in politics, neutralism—which are
beginning to challenge the existentialist model. Merleau-Ponty is in a
good position to see these developing tendencies before anyone else
does. It is essential that we understand these aspects of his situation if
we are to understand the direction taken by his research, which follows
two parallel but interlocking paths. On the one hand, he begins a process
of criticism and self-criticism of the equivocations of commitment, and
of the dogmatic Marxism which fed them. When we pull this research
out of its accompanying philosophical commentary, which tends to make
it seem self-contained, it turns out to be a veritable crossroads where
all the important new currents of the period meet. So it is worth our
while to stop and consider it in order to clarify everything it owes to the
effects of Merleau-Ponty's position in the field.

## 3.2.1 His redefinition of his philosophical project and his theory of expression

For Merleau-Ponty, *What Is Literature?*, which was published in *Les
Temps Modernes* in 1947, is a powerful catalyst. It leads him to compare
Sartre's themes with similar themes of his own which up until then had
been marginal in his work. We know that in 1948 or 1949 he puts together
a long résumé of Sartre's essay, to which he appends his own highly
critical comments. He sees Sartre's celebration of the "transparency"
of prose, and of literature as the power to "unveil" or "create" pure
and absolute meanings, as one more expression of the gap between man
and the world which he had thought at the time Sartre would be able
to overcome. A concluding note to his comments shows that Merleau-
Ponty originally intended to limit them to literature.[60] But his basic
concern is to disassociate himself from this Sartrean manifesto which,
because it appeared in *Les Temps Modernes*, directly implicates him.

And in pursuing this aim, he brings in other longstanding or new concerns which gradually expand his project into a theory of expression.
The chief longstanding concerns are his studies of painting and of the
works of Saussure and Vendryès. The new ones are two recent readings:
Malraux's *Voices of Silence* and Blanchot's article, "Le musée, l'art et
le temps." The upshot of this project is *The Prose of the World*, the
posthumous text published by Lefort, and "Indirect Language and the
Voices of Silence," the reworked extract from this text which he publishes in *Les Temps Modernes* in 1952. To tell the truth, the latter is
offered chiefly as a reply to Malraux and contains no explicit allusions
to *What Is Literature?* But everything about it—from the claims it defends to its dedication to Sartre and the circumstances under which it
is published (it is Merleau-Ponty's final contribution to *Les Temps Modernes* and it comes out at the same time as the first part of *The Communists and Peace*)—everything shows that Sartre is the man it is meant
for.[61]

Merleau-Ponty's report for Martial Gueroult, who was backing his
candidacy to be a member of the Collège de France in 1952, shows that
he subsequently increased the scope of his project. His study of language
becomes the first panel of a diptych in which he means to display all
his previous investigations against the new ground of a philosophical
"theory of truth." In moving from a theory of literature to a theory of
expression and a metaphysics, Merleau-Ponty has managed to outline
the program which for the rest of his life he will work ceaselessly to
complete, the program which will produce "Eye and Mind" and *The
Visible and the Invisible*. And it is just because he has such a well-
defined program of his own that we are struck to see how much weight
he still gives to Sartre in the report that he submits to Gueroult. His
allusion to Sartre is particularly evident in his constant opposition to
the concept of the transparency of language, and to the ontological
dualism on which this concept is based. It is as if Merleau-Ponty's
original intention—"I must produce a sort of *What Is Literature?*"—
had broadened to become, "I must produce a sort of *Being and Nothingness*,"[62] as if his conviction that Sartre had failed were encouraging
him to have a try himself at the most ambitious of all philosophical
undertakings, developing a theory of being. Opposition to Sartre's proud
"I think," to the Sartre who "forgets he has a body," can be read between
the lines of the text submitted to Gueroult.[63] Thus Merleau-Ponty sum-
marizes his program by stating that on the basis of his discovery of the
body as a "symbolic power," he means to establish "a concrete theory
of the mind which will show the mind in a relationship of reciprocal
exchange with the instruments which it uses."[64] And in explaining why

it was that in realizing this project he began with a book on literary language (*The Prose of the World*), he writes: "In this area it is easier to show that language is never the mere clothing of a thought which otherwise possesses itself in full clarity. . . . Communication in literature is not the simple appeal on the part of the writer to meanings which would be part of an a priori of the mind . . . The writer's thought does not control his language from without. . . ."[65] Statements like these, which he seems to have arrived at by reversing Sartre's most famous ones, are alone enough to show the obsessive presence of Sartre in a program which, since Merleau-Ponty never quotes him, might otherwise seem to be governed by purely speculative concerns.

The other source of Merleau-Ponty's program that we must consider if we are to understand it is his relation to the intellectual field. His taking it upon himself to become a theorist, that most prestigious of philosophical tasks, is certainly encouraged by his joining the Collège de France and—even more so—by his need to respond to the rise of the human sciences. And thanks to his position, Merleau-Ponty precociously feels the pull of the latter.[66] It is significant that beginning in 1948 Claude Lévi-Strauss is one of the main people he is talking to,[67] so that without ceasing to refer to Sartre, the reigning world champion, he is already keeping his eye on the main challenger for champion of the new mode. This Janus look is an excellent symbol of Merleau-Ponty's intellectual position, always at the intersection of opposite poles, eternally threatened by ambiguity, dominated by the problem of establishing unity and equilibrium between conflicting tensions. Torn between the academic and the prophetic, the human sciences and philosophy, Lévi-Strauss and Sartre, Merleau-Ponty's undertaking is constantly dual. And there is no doubt that this ambivalence limits his philosophy, which exhausts itself trying to defend the dialectical unity of being against conflicting temptations. In "Merleau-Ponty," Sartre gave a good description of this obsession with synthesizing, whose prime target he was and whose paralyzing consequences he had seen first hand. Yet it must be granted that in a man like Merleau-Ponty who found himself trapped between Sartre's radical subjectivism and the equally radical objectivism of the new dominant thinkers, such concerns are fully justified.[68]

We can already see in *The Prose of the World* and "Indirect Language and the *Voices of Silence*" how much Merleau-Ponty's work is governed by his opposition both to Sartre's philosophy and to the philosophy implicit in the new structuralism. In insisting that all human activities are interwoven in one seamless symbolic web—expression—which is always historical, corporeal, and contingent, Merleau-Ponty is not just challenging Sartre's idea that meaning is a pure, transparent creation

which transcends the signs, techniques, and materials it makes
of in making the sense it makes—transcends, that is, material reality
as it has been produced, "worked up," and given meaning by history—
he is also denouncing the illusion of generative grammar: the temptation
of structural linguistics to study spoken language as a universal logic
immanent in speech acts whose generative "laws" the linguist deci-
phers. Merleau-Ponty includes a chapter on mathematics in *The Prose
of the World* in order to show a fortiori—in respect to the most formalized
mode of expression—that there is always, "between the institutionalized
signs and the *true* significations they designate, an instituting speech
which is the vehicle of everything." In opposition to the "objectivist
illusion" Merleau-Ponty reminds us that mathematics too is a construction, as its historical evolution proves. Mathematics does not refer to
some absolute, preexisting meaning which it simply expresses, but to
a contingent, historically conditioned field of meanings: "Culture . . .
never gives us absolutely transparent significations; the genesis of meaning is never completed. What we rightly call our truth we never contemplate except in a symbolic context which dates our knowledge."[69]

In opposition to the concept of an always renewed creation *ex nihilo*,
and in opposition to a scientific naturalism which assumes that truth is
always already there in things themselves, Merleau-Ponty draws on
historical examples from the arts and sciences, as well as on primitive
gestures and naive perceptions, to show that the most elementary human
activity is already symbolic, since it is "in a relationship of exchange
with the body," with things, and with those other things, institutions.
Institutions, and bodies fashioned by institutions, make communication
between persons possible, even persons of different epochs and cultures. It is institutions which assure continuity in the different historical
manifestations of the human. Each expression reawakens or transforms
already instituted symbolic fields: human activities, in any and all of
their manifestations, are distinguished from one another and make the
sense they do as "differentiations" of a "structure" of "possibilities."
Although Merleau-Ponty is primarily concerned with "continuity," this
scheme of his nevertheless enables him to account for different modes
of expression as well. It is the mediation of instituted structures which
enables him to explain how expressive forms are specified as singular
fields, styles, and acts. Generalizing Saussure, he argues that every
human act is a "spread" in relation to an already established language,
a "coherent deformation" of a structure. But in contrast to Saussure,
he does not ignore the restructuring power of this "deformation" and
the overall historicity of the structure itself. It is thanks to this dialectical
conception of the relationship between the instituting and the instituted

that he is able to explain, for example, how it was possible for a "universe of painting" to be constituted historically as an open yet culturally distinct field, or how values are transformed from epoch to epoch, so that even the most diverse artists of a given period and society (his examples are Delacroix and Ingres) actually have an affinity to one another which distinguishes them from artists in other periods with other concerns.

These are undeniably important insights. Merleau-Ponty's concept of a relationship of exchange between subject and object, mind and body, persons and institutions suggests a way of accounting for human reality which does not, as Sartre does, reduce it to absolute creation or, as Lévi-Strauss does, to an autochthonous process. Yet these pages on expression show the inconveniences of counterthinking. On the one hand, both Merleau-Ponty's competition with Sartre and his reaction to the cult of empiricism and to the formalism of the new structuralist masters tend to heighten his synoptic, prophetic aspiration. On the other hand, his need to keep abreast of developments in the human sciences and his need to distinguish himself from Sartre combine to sustain—in conflict with his aspiration to prophesy—his aspiration to be scientific.

The consequences of this twofold opposition can also be seen in the increasingly clear direction Merleau-Ponty's philosophizing takes. His antagonism toward Sartre, and his aim of making the human sciences conscious of their implicit philosophy, drive him toward ontology. And his chief concern with stressing the subject-object dialectic which he criticizes Sartre and Lévi-Strauss for subverting tends to immure his thinking in a labyrinth with no exit. Thus his final work, *The Visible and the Invisible,* is an ontology in which the interplay of opposites that he depicts in his pursuit of being becomes so exacerbated that we can see justification for Sartre's calling it a "fixation." Henceforth, Merleau-Ponty insists to the point of paroxysm on the continuum which unites the two poles of any dialectical relationship, rather than on the differences between them. He wants to show that there is no radical break between naive perception and science, between ordinary language and literary language, between pictorial expression and poetic expression, and between the "wild-flowering thought" growing out of our embodiment in action and reflective thought. He sees the key to the functioning of all reality in the psychological unity effected by the simplest perception. He tries to reduce all phenomena to this perceptual relation by noting homologies, echoes, and correspondences. This approach does allow him to bring out affinities and unsuspected patterns, but by neglecting differences, it leads him to founder in the indistinct. Experiments, cases, theories—all become mere signs and indices of the unity of Being. Through its failure to deconstruct and articulate the movement

of the dialectic, his philosophy is reduced to a multiplication of metaphors meant more to suggest and to mime than to define. In the late
Merleau-Ponty, the truth of Being resembles the ineffable truth of mys-
tics, and requires the language and procedures of a negative theology.

What sets Merleau-Ponty's anthropology in opposition to the implicit
intellectualism of Sartre's "pure" consciousness is its idea that "naive"
perception is linked to reflective language by an unbroken chain of
meanings. And yet this idea itself reflects another common form of
intellectualism. In order to establish the dignity of all expressive forms,
Merleau-Ponty reduces them all to more or less developed modes of
conscious thought.[70] *Non*reflective activities end up seeming *pre*reflective to him, and reflective thought the "highest point of a tacit and
implicit accumulation." This is a form of intellectualism different from
Sartre's and like structuralism's insofar as it conceives of human activities according to a linguistic model as communication and exchange.
On this point Sartre, who bases intersubjectivity on "the struggle to the
death between consciousnesses," is, by way of Hegel, the better student
of Marx. Whereas conflict based on the ontological egotism of the for-
itself is obsessively present in Sartre's thinking, Merleau-Ponty never
considers material or symbolic interests irreducible sources of conflict
in his explanations of human actions. If for example he is explaining
relationships of rivalry between artists and schools in the history of
painting, he speaks of unawareness, blindness, false perception. In
opposition to Malraux's "cruel history," he sets a "cumulative history,
in which paintings join each other by what they affirm."[71]

"There are thus two historicities. One is ironic or even derisory, and
made of misinterpretations, for each age struggles against the others as
against aliens by imposing its concerns and perspectives upon them.
This history is forgetfulness rather than memory; it is dismemberment,
ignorance, externality. But the other history, without which the first
would be impossible, is constituted and reconstituted step by step by
the *interest* which bears us toward that which is not us and by that life
which the past, in a continuous exchange, brings to us and finds in us,
and which it continues to lead in each painter who revives, recaptures
and renews the entire undertaking of painting in each new work."[72]

For Merleau-Ponty, the human interest that underlies the continuity
of human history is the interest in solidarity, "a response to what the
world, the past and the completed works demanded . . . accomplishment and brotherhood."[73] It is significant that he calls the break he is
making with Sartre at the same time he is writing these words a "philosophical" break, specifying that it is "as personal and as general as
possible."[74] Even then he thinks the conflict has arisen from a difference

of ideas, from intellectual errors, as he had argued in "Indirect Language" was the case for those other "rival contemporaries," Ingres and Delacroix.

## 3.2.2 *The revision of commitment*

Because it has gone wholly unnoticed that Merleau-Ponty's redefinition of his philosophical program toward 1948 involved a revision of his conception of commitment, it has been hard to understand the crisis brought about by the Korean War and his break with Sartre. This blindness is understandable, since what is involved is a gradual process which does not occasion any explicit project. Merleau-Ponty's revision of his conception of commitment is only the objective meaning that can be drawn from his public interventions during this period: his brief, infrequent publications in *Les Temps Modernes* after 1948, and *The Adventures of the Dialectic*. In introducing the latter, which was published in 1955, Merleau-Ponty refers to his experience at *Les Temps Modernes* in such an allusive way that it is hard to realize that this reference is essential to understanding his book: "In the crucible of events we become aware of what is not acceptable to us, and it is this experience as interpreted that becomes both thesis and philosophy. We are thus allowed to report our experience frankly with all its false starts, its omissions, its disparities, and with the possibility of revisions at a later date."[75]

In "Merleau-Ponty," Sartre makes no mention of *The Adventures of the Dialectic* except as an indication of Merleau-Ponty's tendency to "decapitate" the dialectic, paradoxically turning back against his former friend the very accusation the latter had always made against him: that he resisted the synthesizing stage of the dialectic. But since Sartre was more deeply involved than anyone in Merleau-Ponty's crisis, it is scarcely surprising that he too failed to realize that this book published in 1955 represented an attempt to rationalize the crisis which itself resolved the crisis. Since such a reading would have required a painful reexamination of their relationship, we must believe that repression probably played a role in Sartre's blindness. Yet to understand not just Sartre's but the critics' shortsightedness on this score we must consider a further explanation.

The only way to see the course Merleau-Ponty took between 1945 and 1955 as a revision of the "commitment" which first he and then Sartre embodied in the pages of *Les Temps Modernes* is by establishing the objective meaning that commitment has as a phenomenon with concrete defining characteristics and conditions of possibility: only, in short, by understanding commitment as its meaning has been brought out in all the work of reconstruction which this book has so far accomplished. We must understand commitment as the French intellectual field's response to that mythical Communism which brings together as different aspects of a sole reality the Revolution, the proletariat as the universal class which is destined to realize it, the U.S.S.R. as the land of socialism, the Communist Party as the incarnation of the proletariat, and Marxism as the doctrine which articulates the meaning of this "objective" historical movement. We must remember that even though commitment never wholly worships these dogmas, it does partake deeply of them. We must especially remember that for committed intellectuals (and here too Sartre and Merleau-Ponty are representative), the historical evolution of "actually existing Communism" was a sort of practical verification of Marxist hypotheses, that the falsification of these hypotheses seemed to them to prove decisively that history could not be made rational, and that it was precisely Merleau-Ponty who was in 1945–46 the most famous spokesman for this position, the man who had even given it its name of "Marxist wait-and-seeism." It is only in this framework that Merleau-Ponty's post-1948 ideological trajectory can be seen as a critique of the myths of commitment. The questions he raises correspond to characteristic problems of commitment: the evolution of French and Soviet Communism, the aporias and contradictions of Marxist and Marxian philosophy of history, the political responsibility of intellectuals. Merleau-Ponty continues to define himself in relation to these axes, but by reversing his earlier approach: thus his earlier revolutionary enthusiasm is followed by disenchantment (which is marked above all by three episodes: the Rajk trial,[76] the discovery of Soviet labor camps, and the Korean War); his acceptance of dogmatic views of social class, the Party, and "historical reason" by their liquidation; and his rejected models (Lenin, Trotsky, and the orthodox self-criticism of Lukács) by his identification with contrasting models (Montaigne, Machiavelli, Weber, and the young Lukács). Since this framework is often no more than implicit, we must make clear its presence in Merleau-Ponty's public interventions after 1947, beginning with the "political" texts he published in Les Temps Modernes.

In an article Merleau-Ponty wrote about Montaigne in December, 1947,[77] we can read between the lines a revealing self-portrait of what preoccupied its author at the time. In his preference for the ambiguous "self"—Montaigne's "mixture of mind and body"—over Descartes' consciousness-as-mind, we recognize Merleau-Ponty's objections to Sartre's philosophy. In this connection, the attention he pays to Montaigne's attitude toward politics becomes significant: it expresses the tormented interest in this problem that Merleau-Ponty always has, but at a moment when he never explicitly confronts it. He identifies with the difficult combination Montaigne embodies. With his pessimism: "there is a witchcraft in social life" (*Signs*, 204). With the awareness that after all we are involved in the social world, which functions according to laws of its own that it would be folly to ignore or refuse to obey. He approves of Montaigne for having "entered the bewitched realm of public life" (208); and for having written: "*life is a material and corporeal movement, an action that by its own essence is imperfect and disordered; I occupy myself with serving it as it is*" (210). In company with Montaigne he denies that a good—that is, rational—State is possible. He agrees with him that "the State [is] among those external devices we find ourselves joined to by chance and ought to use according to their law without putting anything of ourselves into them" (204). With this, Merleau-Ponty bids farewell—in an implicit but peremptory way—not only to the myth of the U.S.S.R. but more generally to the myth of the State as privileged bearer of historical rationality.

An article Merleau-Ponty publishes in *Les Temps Modernes* in July 1948 enables us to see what his position is one year later.[78] This time he is dealing with a current topic: a polemic over posthumous falsifications and manipulations of Trotsky's thinking. Here Merleau-Ponty makes his point of view explicit. He assumes that the development of the U.S.S.R. proves that the decay of capitalist society can give rise not to socialism but to a new—bureaucratic—form of domination and exploitation (259–60).

Since Merleau-Ponty's definition of commitment is tied to the hypothesis that Soviet Russia represents the transition to socialism, this rejection of the hypothesis also lays the definition open to question. From this point on, Merleau-Ponty will reject (although at this point still indirectly) his program, "support the C.P. line." Not only the C.P. (Merleau-Ponty argues, considering only those political movements which intellectuals support) but the Gaullists and the Trotskyites condemn their supporters to a "paranoid" politics because they are afraid to face the truth. The analytical labors needed to get at the truth are henceforth only possible outside political parties.

The "Note on Machiavelli" which is published in *Les Temps Modernes* one year later (Oct. 1949) also seems to be an autobiographical projection which is completely dominated by the same concerns.[79] Since "one hundred years after Marx, the problem of a real humanism remains intact", we can reread with profit a Machiavelli who "formulated some of the conditions of any serious humanism" in showing that good politics is not made with principles alone but also requires moral action (223).

A few months later (Dec. 1949), Merleau-Ponty offers Lukács' post-1946 development and the difference between the Rajk trial and the 1937 Moscow Trial as proof of the decay of "actually existing socialism": "Thus communism goes from historical responsibility to naked discipline, from autocriticism to repudiation, from Marxism to superstition."[80]

These articles published in *Les Temps Modernes* betwen 1947 and 1949 show that Merleau-Ponty's ideological revision, although quiet, is a public one. Its successive episodes—his denunciation of Soviet camps in the January 1950 issue,[81] his silence after the Korean War begins, and his break with Sartre and the review—do not seem at the time to mark a sudden, incomprehensible turn on the part of one who had argued at such length in defense of the 1937 trial, but to be the consequence of a progressive erosion which had undermined point by point the axiomatic system upon which his position in 1945 had been based.

*The Adventures of the Dialectic* is the culmination of this line of thinking, as is shown to begin with by the story of how Merleau-Ponty came to write it. According to Lefort's account, when *The Communists and Peace* comes out in 1952, Merleau-Ponty stops working on the book he is writing, *The Prose of the World*. Except for the courses he is giving at the Collège de France (which bear on the theory of expression), everything he has been doing takes a different turn: "He reread Marx, Lenin, and Trotsky and accumulated considerable notes on Weber and Lukács which were part of his next project, *Les Aventures de la dialectique*. . . ."[82] The fact that Sartre's essay seems urgent enough to lead Merleau-Ponty to interrupt a work he has almost completed, a work into which he has put his whole philosophical ambition, shows how much it means to him. We know it seems to him like a double betrayal: of his current ideas and of the old ones Sartre claims to uncover. He must reply without delay if he is to reestablish the truth about the way he used to think and specify his current criticisms of that previous way of thinking. The book's contents bear out this aim. It is this aim which makes clear how the organization of its five chapters—which are devoted successively to Weber, the early Lukács, Lenin's thought, Trotsky's experience, and Sartre's "ultrabolshevism"—constitute a coherent framework. This road is the same one Merleau-Ponty traveled in the opposite direction in his attempt to go back to the conditions of possibility underlying the dogmas of commitment and, inseparably, Stalinist dogmas. Weber and the Lukács of *History and Class Consciousness* stand out in his book as the key sources he encountered in his investigations.

The psychological explanation of Merleau-Ponty's retreat from commitment which Sartre gives in "Merleau-Ponty" is not satisfactory, chiefly because it fails to consider the evolution of the intellectual field. Sartre suggests that Merleau-Ponty is reacting to the climate of the Cold War:

the man who has never stopped yearning for the lost paradise of childhood cannot bear the fall of utopia. But this account does not explain
why the Rajk affair, the revelation of Soviet camps, and the Communist
attack in Korea shake a faith in the U.S.S.R. which has survived events
such as the Moscow Trials and the Nazi-Soviet Pact that in other famous
crises such as Nizan's are decisive. Furthermore, although the dead
Merleau-Ponty cannot respond to Sartre's interpretation, a year before
he dies he seems to anticipate and indirectly refute it in the Introduction
he writes to *Signs*, where he comments on the analogous explanation
Sartre offers concerning Nizan's case: "One can understand, then, the
objections Sartre makes today to the Nizan of 1939, and why they are
without weight against him. Nizan, he says, was angry. But is that anger
a matter of mood? It is a mode of understanding which is not too
inappropriate when fundamental meaning-structures are at stake. For
anyone who has become a Communist and has acted within the Party
day after day, things said and done have a weight, because he has said
and done them too. In order to take the change in line of 1939 as he
should, Nizan would have to have been a puppet. He would have to have
been broken, and he had not become a Communist to play the skeptic"
(*Signs*, 32).

In defending Nizan's reasons for acting the way he did, Merleau-
Ponty stresses one factor which undoubtedly counted heavily for Nizan
in 1939 as it did for Merleau-Ponty around 1950: commitment for both
men is a "fundamental" choice. Although their experiences are distinguished from one another by the times in which they live and by the
way in which they live them, as existential choices they are analogous:
for Merleau-Ponty as for Nizan, they are the hinge on which a crucial
period turns. In the 1930s image of Nizan as one of the most brilliant
hopefuls of the French intellectual world of the day, the writer cannot
be separated from the Communist, just as the Merleau-Ponty who in
1945 becomes (along with Sartre) the prophet of French existentialism
cannot be separated from the inventor of *Les Temps Modernes*' political
line. Both Merleau-Ponty and Nizan have hopes for Communism and
the U.S.S.R. which are not just social and political but intellectual and
personal as well. To both, the meaning of Marxism, political action,
existence, and human history seems to hang on the decisive test of the
success or failure of the Soviet experiment.

Merleau-Ponty's account has the merit of suggesting that the reason
why the destruction of such hopes is so serious for Nizan—and for
himself—is that it is not just the private matter Sartre reduces it to:
Nizan and Merleau-Ponty had hitched their public figure, their image,
and their intellectual prestige to these hopes.

Yet even this account is inadequate if we ignore the collective dimensions of the phenomenon. We cannot understand its "objective meaning" unless we understand that the course Nizan took and the course Merleau-Ponty took are two exemplary tokens of the type of life history into which each respectively falls: that of Communist intellectuals between the wars and that of "fellow travelers" at the Liberation. It is only in this perspective that we can go beyond Sartre's undeniable but far too general diagnosis of a utopian syndrome and explain the specific modalities—the course and content—of each case. Consequently, we must compare Merleau-Ponty's trajectory to other intellectual trajectories which in company with his will let us retrace the history of commitment after the Liberation.

Think first of Sartre's development, which lags behind the avant-gardes as the dominant position characteristically does. In the first phase of his commitment, from Socialism and Liberty to the R.D.R., Sartre reminds us of the "third way" attempts of the thirties. In 1952, he adopts the "critical fellow traveling" whose antecedents are to be found even before Merleau-Ponty in the Gide and Malraux of the mid-thirties. If we consider other versions of commitment in the post-1945 French intellectual field, such as that of *Esprit* and that of intellectuals who joined the Communist Party during the period of the Resistance and the Liberation, we notice that between 1948 and 1950 a reverse movement starts to surface. The first step in *Esprit*'s disenchantment is its November 1949 issue (in June of that same year Mounier is still writing, "Anti-communism is death"): taking off from the Rajk case, the review announces the "crisis of the peoples democracies." In subsequent issues, it takes a stand on the Yugoslav schism, in December publishing an article by two well-known "fellow travelers," Cassou and Vercors, with the significant title, "The People Must Not Be Deceived," and in the February 1950 issue, an eyewitness account in which three members of the review who have returned from Yugoslavia clear Tito of Communist calumnies. Furthermore, in January, François Fejtö, Rajk's rehabilitator, brings up the case of another dissident, the Bulgarian Kostov. These same events lead to the first important resignations of C.P. intellectuals: those of Duvignaud, Clara Malraux, Antelme, Mascolo, and Morin.[83] Thus Merleau-Ponty's evolution follows a collective trajectory: that of intellectuals who are drawn into—or to the side of—the C.P. around 1945 and who withdraw as a result of events which seem to banish their utopian dreams beyond all hope of return. Sartre's different way of responding to these same events becomes comprehensible once one considers the difference in his trajectory: at this point he has *not yet* bet on the U.S.S.R. and the C.P. And yet his position in turn influences that of Merleau-Ponty, who is still settling accounts with him and thus joins him—at least in his approach to the problem—on his own ground.

We can determine the characteristics which distinguish the Merleau-Ponty of 1955 from the Merleau-Ponty of 1945—and from Sartre—as well as the characteristics the two men still have in common, by analyzing *The Adventures of the Dialectic.* If we consider the time at which Merleau-Ponty is writing it—just after personally significant events such as his being named to the Collège de France and his break with *Les Temps Modernes*—we can understand one aspect of it: its more forceful opposition to Sartre and its tendency to put stock in academic virtues. Competence, rigorousness, and the search for "truth" seem increasingly to Merleau-Ponty to be the only justifiable definition of philosophical commitment. This line of thinking is evident in *In Praise of Philosophy,* his inaugural lecture at the Collège de France, a text which is significant because it is the solemn declaration of a man who feels he is at a decisive turning point in his life.

But the most remarkable novelty in *The Adventures of the Dialectic* is its new authority, the thought of Weber. Once again Merleau-Ponty is tapping into the transformations of the field as soon as they begin and making them his own: Weber, or more specifically, *The Protestant Ethic,* is just beginning to enter French culture, which at the time is polarized by another late discovery, Marxism. And Marx, especially a Marx who is little and poorly understood, seems a priori to be incompatible with Weber, who, even less known, is reputed to be the "Marx of the bourgeoisie" and the exact opposite of Marx himself.[84] But the chief reason for stressing this French encounter with Weber is the catalytic role it seems to play in a crisis which simultaneously undermines intellectual, political, and existential certainties. On each of these levels, Weber contributes greatly to encouraging and orienting Merleau-Ponty's evolution, as we can see from the following quotation from his *In Praise of Philosophy,* a text which is wholly Weberian, even in its language: "Today, when it is hard to uphold values and at the same time meet needs, we're asked to choose one or the other. But in any society which is worth our while, we must have both. We must reject the ultimatum: we must hang on to both. This is our common fate, the fate of political man. Political man no more follows the course of events than he simply obeys his conscience. His greatness comes at the moment he says, 'This far, and no farther,' and stands his ground and waits for the wave to break or carry him beyond the barrier. This uncertain moment in our lives and in our world is where we learn true courage. But someone has to be there to talk about it. This chatterbox is the philosopher."[85]

This explains why the opening chapter of *The Adventures of the Dialectic* is devoted to Weber. It shows both the tradition which the book is adopting and the code in terms of which it must be read. It is also the author's indirect way of presenting his own views, since he clearly identifies with Weber, recognizing a complete "kinship of choice" with him. He sees himself not just in Weber's thought but in the ethical dilemmas Weber faced, in his ill-starred political efforts, and in his struggles with commitment's equivocations. It is as if Merleau-Ponty wanted to use his sketch of Weber to give his readers an idea of not just the intellectual history but all the history behind his book: his experience with commitment, the reason he had been "so easily expelled" from it and had "returned so quickly to his studies," the principal ambiguities that he saw—and rejected—in commitment (its "dogmatic philosophy of history" and its pretense of deriving a course of action from that philosophy), the "hidden weakness" of Stalinist violence, and the "hidden violence" of the "ethics of ultimate ends" to which Sartre succumbed in *The Communists and Peace* (*A.D.*, 27).

In any case, the newest and most interesting aspects of *The Adventures of the Dialectic* come as we said from Merleau-Ponty's encounter with Weber. He does not simply discover him, he freely elaborates on his teachings. Thus he has no hesitation in speaking of a "Weberian Marxism," that is to say, in bringing out the affinity and convergence between Weber's conception of the historical process and that of the young Marx. Of all the Marxists, it seems to Merleau-Ponty, only the Lukács of *History and Class Consciousness* has succeeded in developing this Marxian conception, even though it is the most precious heritage Marx has left us, which we must take as our basic referent even as we criticize it.

We can understand why Merleau-Ponty reaches this synthesis of Marx and Weber. The course he has taken itself suggests and establishes the possibility of his doing so insofar as, having encountered Weber after Marx, he does not see him as opposed to Marx but on the contrary as close and complementary to him in his concerns and hypotheses: that is to say, insofar as he easily and spontaneously manages to reconcile the two in his own thinking, to follow Weber without betraying Marx.

This seemingly heretical view of Merleau-Ponty's—which combines the investigations of Weber and Marx with his own in the "symbolic matrix" of the dialectical conception of history—must be seen as the faithful fruit of Weber's teaching. The influence of Weber—who reads Western history as the contingent development of an "objective meaning," "rationalization"—is present especially in Merleau-Ponty's way of understanding dialectic as a worldview which has been produced historically and is subject to historical dissolution and disappearance. "[These intelligible nuclei of history] appear at the point where man and the givens of nature or of the past meet, arising as symbolic matrices which have no preexistence and which can, for a longer or a shorter time, influence history itself and then disappear, not by external forces but through an internal disintegration or because one of their secondary elements becomes predominant and changes their nature" (*A.D.*, 16–17).

Thus the very aim of *The Adventures of the Dialectic* is Weberian: to reconstitute the development and transformations of a symbolic form. In the light of this aim, Merleau-Ponty's choice and ordering of themes become more comprehensible. The introductory chapters are devoted to showing how the idea of the dialectic takes shape in the works of Marx, Weber, and Lukács. The remaining chapters, to showing how it degenerates in "having its nature changed" by a "secondary element"—the "dialectic of circumstances"—which reduces it to a "second nature," and how beginning with Lenin this degenerate form of the dialectic becomes dominant in the Communist tradition.

In Weber's thinking, Merleau-Ponty argues, the concept of the dialectic of history is no more than a postulate implicit in his way of writing history and in his concern to get beyond the antinomies of the subjective and the objective, of knowledge and action, and of morality and efficacy which haunt him. Weber never succeeds in formulating this implicit postulate explicitly, because he is still "dominated by the idea of an unconditional, disinterested truth." Marx and Lukács do succeed by relativizing the concepts of subject and object in a history they conceive of as a seamless web, a "relationship among persons which is mediated by things." Having historicized truth, they are able to discover "an absolute in the relative" without falling—at least in their first formulation of it (Marx in his pre-1850 writings and Lukács in *History and Class Consciousness*)—into the concept of a principle inscribed in the historical process itself. And it is this authentically dialectical Marxism that Merleau-Ponty compares to the thinking of Weber, the Weber who shows how history manifests a contingent meaning which can no more be reduced to the intentions of subjects than it can to the development of an immanent logic.

Merleau-Ponty thinks that the common and essential insight of Marx and Weber which makes their conception of history truly dialectical is their recognition of the symbolic dimension of human existence. In this insight he sees a still implicit affirmation which is the explicit center of his own ontology, the insistence that the body is never sheer inertia and the mind never perfect lucidity. He says concerning Marx: ". . . The meaning of history appears in what he calls 'human matter,' an ambiguous setting . . ." (*A.D.*, 33); ". . . This order of 'things' which teaches 'relationships between persons', sensitive to all the heavy conditions which bind it to the order of nature, open to all that personal life can invent, is, in modern language, the sphere of symbolism, and Marx's thought was to find its outlet here" (*A.D.*, 65).

It is this idea that the symbolic has a weight of its own in the production of reality which is the source of the basic thesis of *The Adventures of the Dialectic*: the reason why "actually existing Communism" has failed, both on the level of its theoretical capacities and on the level of its political and social results, is that it has betrayed the dialectic which inspired it by naturalizing it and turning it into the inevitable logic of the historical process. Merleau-Ponty offers the historical examples of Lukács' trajectory after *History and Class Consciousness* and Trotsky's life history as the best illustrations of the respectively intellectual and political consequences of this doctrinal degeneration. It is because Lukács believed in a historical truth embodied in the proletariat and the Communist Party that he was led to give in to Leninist orthodoxy and, through increasingly serious concessions to it, to compromise the coherence of his thought. He did not succeed in either reconciling the theory of reflection with the autonomy he granted to culture or meeting the demands of the Party apparatus with his self-criticisms. In Merleau-Ponty's judgment, this same dogmatic conception of the Party accounts for a troubling aspect of Trotsky's life history: his refusal, at the time Stalin is rising to power, to denounce the maneuverings of a Central Committee which is determined to eliminate him. And the reason why Trotsky is incapable even later of understanding why he failed is that in his theory of permanent revolution he preserves the concept of a "continued negation immanent in the internal mechanism of history" (*A.D.*, 89).

Weber's influence also plays a considerable role in Merleau-Ponty's critique of Sartre's concept of commitment. What Merleau-Ponty condemns Sartre for is his equation of thought and action, of the writer's function and the function of the political man. He explicitly argues—and he had never done so before—that these are two distinct roles, each with its own governing rules. This is the characteristic position of Weber, who argued for the relative autonomy and the specificity of human activities, and in particular of those two professions, intellectual work and political work, upon which his personal experience had led him to meditate more directly. Merleau-Ponty's imputing to Sartre's worldview the ambiguity of his commitment is also Weberian. For Merleau-Ponty,

Sartre's way of conceiving of action stems from his conception of freedom as pure and always renewed creation present "in every action and
in none, never compromised, never lost, never saved, always similar"
(*A.D.*, 190). Whether it be an "act of unveiling," as in *What Is Literature?*
or a political intervention, as in *The Communists and Peace*, commitment
for Sartre can never be anything but an apparent and—in the last analysis—indifferent action which is led by circumstances to adopt an
"involuntary line": an action which remains consistent with itself in
becoming "different," and which is free to proclaim, just after it has
denounced the Soviet camps, "The U.S.S.R. is the proletariat's only
hope." In Sartre's thinking "as in Descartes' [Merleau-Ponty says iron-
ically], the principle of changing oneself rather than the order of things
is an intelligent way of remaining oneself over and against everything"
(*A.D.*, 193). Neither criticism nor action, Sartre's allegedly radical freedom leads to radical submission to "the established order." In the name
of the "magical *fiat*" of "the slave in irons," one deludes oneself into
believing that in letting oneself be dominated by the world, one is dominating it. *The Communists and Peace* itself is for Merleau-Ponty one
instance of the imaginary action to which Sartre's philosophy of the pure
subject is condemned, an action which takes place only in thought and
which is no less dangerous when it thinks it is speaking for the
disinherited.

And yet, judging by certain things Merleau-Ponty says, the concept
of commitment he offers at the close of his self-criticism is not as far
from Sartre's as he claims. He writes for example: "Commitment was
at first the determination to show oneself outside as one is inside, to
confront behavior with its principle and each behavior with all the others,
thus to say everything and to weigh everything anew, to invent a total
behavior in response to the whole of the world. *Les Temps Modernes*
demanded of its founders that they belong to no party or church, because
one cannot rethink the whole if one is already bound by a conception
of the whole. Commitment was the promise to succeed where the parties
had failed; it therefore placed itself outside parties, and a preference
or choice in favor of one of them made no sense at a moment when it
was a question of recreating principles in contact with facts. Yet something already rendered this program null and void and announced the
avatars of commitment: it was the manner in which Sartre understood
the relation between action and freedom."[86]

In these overarching aspirations ("to say everything . . . to weigh
everything anew . . . to invent a *total* behavior in response to the *whole*
of the world . . . [to] rethink the whole"), we see again the Merleau-
Ponty whose influence was decisive in turning the commitment of *Les*

*Temps Modernes* toward prophetism. The continuing affinity of his intellectual style to Sartre's is evident in the very construction of *The Adventures of the Dialectic*: in its taste for syntheses which bring out an overall meaning in a vast array of phenomena by ordering them in terms of a coherent framework which, like a drama, has its beginning and its end. Although the book announces history's contingency, it is undeniably an anthropomorphic reading of history which treats the "adventures of the dialectic" as biographical episodes. By fitting experiences which are actually very different into this uniform framework, it inevitably forces their meaning. Thus the Marxian philosophy of history seems to follow and complete Weber's thinking, which is treated as predialectical. Stalinism risks seeming to be chiefly the result of ideological degeneration. And the chapter on Sartre remains incongruous, for it is not connected to the others by any philosophical link but by the special and difficult relation between intellectuals and the Communist Party which gave rise to commitment. And Merleau-Ponty's continuing ambivalence toward precision and prophetism is also revealed in the language of *The Adventures of the Dialectic*, which even when it is setting forth the most abstract of concepts is studded with metaphors and tempted by the siren call of lyricism.

Merleau-Ponty's departure is a heavy loss for the review. In losing him it loses a capacity for innovation which is essential to maintaining its hegemony, especially the hegemony of existentialism, which has staked its honor on its modernity, its capacity to be always at the forefront of things. In losing him it loses the only editor capable of tempering the effects of Sartre's monopoly, a loss which tends to crystallize the already consecrated format of the review. A new phase dominated by simple reproduction begins: at Sartre's side in the foreground gather coworkers who cannot be considered either his peers or his competitors but only his disciples or his staff—in short, his epigones.

# CHAPTER 10
# The Epigones

Up until 1948, the "epigones"[1] play a modest part in the history of *Les Temps Modernes*. This is the period in which the nucleus of the review—Sartre, Merleau-Ponty, and Simone de Beauvoir—is most active. Their writings are often veritable manifestos. Essays such as *Humanism and Terror, What Is Literature?*, and *The Ethics of Ambiguity* define the *Temps Modernes* line in all fields of existentialism: politics, ethics, and literature. The nucleus takes direct charge of the work of the review: it goes after contributions, chooses the ones the review will run, and does a large part of the editorial work. As the essential vehicle of existentialism's recognition and success, a powerful if still precarious mechanism, *Les Temps Modernes* polarizes the attention and resources of its founders. Yet even at this time we see men who stand out from the crowd of occasional contributors[2] because they are close friends or disciples destined to make a difference in the subsequent history of *Les Temps Modernes*: Jacques-Laurent Bost, Jean Pouillon, Jean-Baptiste Pontalis, Claude Lefort, Francis Jeanson, André Gorz.[3]

Changes start to come in 1948. The role of the nucleus diminishes: Sartre and Simone de Beauvoir spend less and less time running the review, which they leave to Merleau-Ponty, who having entered at this time the period of his great philosophical and ideological crisis, reduces his own production to rare and widely scattered texts. A phase in which their place is taken by many others opens—showing, by the way, the solidity of the enterprise. *Les Temps Modernes* has become such an established, consecrated place that anyone who writes for it becomes established and consecrated. We see Lefort commenting more and more often on current politics, as well as Pouillon and Jeanson, who were previously limited to literary and philosophical commentary. And yet for the moment it is not this group of close friends who fill the void left by Merleau-Ponty's increasing absence but journalists, who are distinguished from disciples by their greater autonomy. Some carry out the menial but indispensable tasks of eyewitness reporting. For example, Dzepely, an American who follows the Korean War, or Elena de la Souchère, who does reports on the Spanish, Portuguese, and Latin American situation. But the most important figures are the ones who replace the existentialists in their prophetic role: Roger Stéphane, the author of a series of provocative articles on domestic politics; Claude Bourdet, who leads the fight against the War in Indochina; Daniel Guérin, who publishes essays on the American situation; or again Louis Dalmas, who offers an analysis of Yugoslav Communism at the time of the Tito schism.

Between 1952 and 1953, when Merleau-Ponty resigns from the review, this cycle ends. It is indeed a turning point: a new category of actors establishes itself and will play a decisive role. This is clearly indicated by the editorial board which is established in December 1953: it is not made up of the earliest disciples or of the chief coworkers of previous years but of the men who supported Sartre in the difficult phase which led to *The Communists and Peace*: Jean Cau, Claude Lanzmann, and Marcel Péju.

We must wait till 1961 before this organization in turn enters its crisis stage. With Péju eliminated, and Cau already gone in 1956, the Sartreans from the early days finally inherit the review, as is shown by the new managing committee of June 1962, in which their names appear alongside those of Sartre, Simone de Beauvoir, a new name, Bernard Pingaud, and the only one left from the previous editorial board, Claude Lanzmann.

# 1. PROPERTIES AND TRAJECTORIES OF THE DIFFERENT SEGMENTS

The first disciples were recruited by Sartre (Bost, Pouillon, Pontalis) or Merleau-Ponty (Lefort) during the short time they taught in *lycées*. To these must be added two who were disciples by choice: Jeanson and Gorz. All are just coming on the intellectual scene. Like their masters, they are trained philosophers, although their university curriculum is generally less prestigious. Only Pontalis and Lefort, the two Parisians in the group, have taken their *agrégation* and their doctorate; none is an Ecole Normale graduate. They either are just beginning to publish or have not even yet begun to write. With the exception of Lefort, who plays an important role in *Socialisme ou barbarie*,[4] and Jeanson, who keeps up his connection with *Esprit*, belonging to *Les Temps Modernes* is the only capital they can bank on for recognition. The differences between them and their masters at the time they join the group—differences of age (from ten to twenty years in relation to Sartre), title, and consecration—show the review's obviously hierarchical structure. Above all, these men who are just starting out identify their success with Sartre's success. To understand the near unanimity which long seems to characterize their relationship to Sartre, we must be aware of this identification of their interests with Sartre's, which spontaneously produces an admiring consensus without their master's ever having had to make explicit use of his power. The peculiar emotional intensity of this relationship is also explained by the high degree of reciprocal dispositions upon which it is based, with the youngest disposed to feel the charm of scarcely older teachers who in their fame maintain the unorthodox ways and scandalous aura of the bohemian life, and with Sartre and Simone de Beauvoir disposed to make their earliest disciples—who recognized them before they were highly consecrated—the trusted lieutenants they need in order to maintain and defend the position they have won.[5]

In 1948, when the directorial crisis requires new people to take up the slack, this element is not yet ready to do it. Forced to seek coworkers from outside the group, the review turns spontaneously to men who are close enough to its line not to disrupt its coherence but far enough from it not to envisage taking over the enterprise. Stéphane, Dalmas, Guérin, and Bourdet are distinguished from the original disciples by the relative independence of their positions. Even the youngest, Stéphane and Dalmas, are already known when they start to work for *Les Temps Modernes*. Furthermore, their trajectory points to a strategy which clearly differs from the prevailing strategy among the major and minor prophets of existentialism. All, for example, are far from the characteristic curriculum of the *Temps Modernes* model: Bourdet graduates from the Ecole polytechnique in Zurich, Guérin from the Ecole libre des sciences politiques, and Dalmas and Stéphane are only college graduates. What makes their autonomy and distance from *Les Temps Modernes* possible is not just their having capital of their own and connections with other intellectual centers but their having different social positions—a different language and worldview—which makes them unassimilable. Even Stéphane, whose assiduousness in attending the meetings and doing the work of the review makes him most a part of it, is far from being a member of the cult. His position can be symbolized by the book he publishes in 1950, *Portrait d'un aventurier*. Sartre's preface has nothing in it of the master bestowing his grace on his disciple. He writes as an influential friend going bail for the book, but he barely touches on its subject; instead he takes it as a pretext for dealing with a problem he thinks is central, that of the relationship between the man of action and the militant. But the heroes Stéphane is fascinated by are the figures he portrays in his book: Lawrence, Malraux, and von Salomon.[6]

In 1953 it becomes clear that the review must without further delay get back to the prophetism which had distinguished it and start it up again. Over the years it has entrusted its prophetic function to outside agents who lack the power to elevate denunciation or protest to the dignified level of a philosophy of events, and now there is no doubt that it must fall back on the names the public clearly identifies with *Les Temps Modernes*. But in assuming responsibility for this task, why does Sartre base his efforts on recent coworkers such as Lanzmann, Cau, and Péju rather than on the original disciples who are bound more closely to him and seem at first sight to have the same basic qualities as the others?

The new editors are the same age as—and even younger than—these disciples. Like them they have majored in philosophy, and they too are unknown beginners when they first swim into Sartre's orbit. Yet we notice significant differences between the two groups: although the original capital of the newcomers is more modest than that of the original Sartreans, they seem to be, if not more ambitious, at least more impatient to become known. Certain signs which become evident when they first meet Sartre suggest an imbalance between their hopes and their objective possibilities of success: academic failures and signs of failure, jobs taken just to survive, and open repudiation—in the name of new intellectual models or an irritated politicization in which social resentment surfaces—of goals to which they once aspired. All these signs presage a trajectory in which a gap between aspirations and resources tends to produce disappointments, conversions, and reconversions: the inevitable revision of hopes that this gap requires is going to be disguised as the change of plans by which we transform our inescapable failures into deliberate rejections.[7]

Cau and Lanzmann, who come from the provincial petty bourgeoisie, arrive in Paris at twenty to prepare for entrance exams to the Ecole Normale—at the cost of what waverings between hopes and fears, between visions of the possible and intimations of the probable, we can get an idea of from the indications we gather from different sources. We must quote one passage from Olivier Todd[8] in which we can see that these affinities between this second wave of Sartreans (Lanzmann, Cau, and Todd himself) are anchored in significant childhood ties among sons of the same marginal intelligentsia: "Sometimes, on Saturday evening, my mother and Claude Sernet[9] take me to Mony de Boully's, a former Surrealist who also had become a bookseller. He strikes me as more dazzling than Achille Ouy. He talks about Jean Paulhan. He tells stories about masturbating dogs or pigeons. Young people flock around him and his wife, Paulette, who is a warm woman who stutters—except when she is reading a poem aloud. Paulette's children, Claude and Jacques Lanzmann, are frequently there with their sister, Evelyne. She is living with a certain Rezvani. Claude, it goes without saying, wants to be a combination of Malraux, Proust, and Vailland. He is preparing for, or has prepared for, a certain Ecole normale supérieure on the rue d'Ulm. I do not have the slightest idea what that means. Claude is often there with one of his buddies, Jean Cau, who has a mushy Southern accent. Jacques Lanzmann, Jacquot says, paints. He cut off his ear to make sure he was a genius."[10]

Simone de Beauvoir adds a few more characteristics: "On his return from America, Sartre had received a letter from a *khâgneux*, Jean Cau, asking help in finding work; he was preparing for the Ecole Normale entrance exams, though this was his first attempt and he hadn't much hope; after the exams his parents would insist that he go back to live with them in the country. Sartre replied that he would look around for him. He fell ill, went to Switzerland, and didn't look around. In June, Cau—who had addressed similar letters to other writers without success—came to see him; the academic year was almost over. 'All right,' said Sartre, 'be my secretary.' Cau accepted. . . .'"[11] Note the anticipation of failure ("he hadn't much hope") and the alternative he had invented: to enter by the service entrance the world in which he dreams of living—as a famous man's secretary—because the front door is barred to him. Lanzmann and Péju have been through the same experience by the time they join *Les Temps Modernes*. They have had to accept jobs as intellectual laborers (as rewriters for a big newspaper).

By the time Cau, Lanzmann, and Péju meet Sartre, he can no longer seem to them to be the reigning model he was for the original Sartreans, all of whom begin their careers by following the trail blazed by the master. In *Temps et roman*, Pouillon elaborates on Sartre's ideas about temporality in the novel. In *Le dernier des métiers*, Bost seems to provide an illustration of the sort of parajournalistic novel Sartre hoped would flourish.[12] Pontalis's "calling," psychoanalysis, is one of Sartre's basic interests. Pontalis, moreover, continues to be fascinated by writing; he starts working for *Les Temps Modernes* as a critic and author,[13] and he is working on a novel at the time.[14] In *la Nouvelle revue de psychanalyse*, psychoanalysis and writing go hand in hand, and in 1980 Pontalis will end up publishing a novel.[15] The first books Jeanson and Gorz write have to do with Sartre's philosophy, and each is devoted to ethical thought, the task Sartre's ontology leaves unfinished.[16]

The editorial board which takes over *Les Temps Modernes* in 1953 immediately demonstrates its rejection of the Sartrean model by its striking departures from it. Cau's "notes" and the book he publishes in 1951, *Le coup de barre*, toss commitment out of literature and literary criticism.[17] Lanzmann and Péju, on the contrary, seem to turn their backs completely on philosophy and literature by dedicating themselves henceforth to politics.[18] To Sartre they seem to speak for a position independent of his own and so close to that of the proletariat as to make them its credible spokesmen. In this period in which Sartre is drawing near to the C.P. himself, Péju's and Lanzmann's pro-Communism[19] no doubt seemed to him to be the stimulus and assurance he needed. The stimulus to go farther by following them in their passionate identification with the party of the dominated; the assurance that he was on the right track.[20] He sees these young people who speak his language and share his views as not only the essential support he needs at a difficult time but invaluable replacements.[21] He is also able to delegate power to them as a result of their ambiguous position of dependence in independence which makes them objectively much more staff workers than allies. Their lack of capital of their own makes them, in spite of their apparently powerful position, actually subject to Sartre's authority.

The editorial staff's new arrangement between 1961 and 1962 takes on its full meaning if we consider the time it is taking place: the period between the publication of Sartre's *Critique* and the end of the Algerian War when the decline of his hegemony becomes evident.

A series of signs indicates that the state of the intellectual field has changed and the existentialist model has been challenged. Around 1960 it is no longer possible to ignore the central place that the human sciences have taken in the field, and the influence they are having in changing the requirements for intellectual legitimacy. The creation of a degree in sociology in 1958 symbolizes this discipline's new departure and the impetus given to it by the increased social demand for it in the phase of economic expansion accompanying De Gaulle's return to power and the birth of the Fifth Republic. Following the establishment of sociology as a university major, there is a rapid proliferation of public and private centers, funding, heads of institutes, chairs and students, production, and specialized reviews. The latter take information and discussion about the social sciences away from intellectual reviews such as *Esprit* or *Les Temps Modernes* that used to be the ones which received most of it and could thus better control it.[22]

The beginning of the vogue for structuralism can be dated as 1958 with the publication of *Structural Anthropology*. The new stars who begin to shine in the philosophical field (Barthes publishes his *Mythologies* in 1957, Foucault's *Madness and Civilization* comes out in 1961) also invoke the authority of the most strident characteristics of structuralism: antihumanism, antihistoricism, the "decentralization" or even "dissolution" of the subject, the objectivist metaphysics, and the conflict between scientific neutrality and commitment's voluntarism.

This readjustment is spurred by a series of episodes. In 1957 J.-F. Revel's broadside *Pourquoi des philosophes?* proclaims the end of philosophy's historic role, ridiculing especially philosophy's characteristic procedures and results, and its metaphysical, ontologizing pretentions. And it is above all the "philosophers of existence"—Husserl, Heidegger, Sartre, and Merleau-Ponty—who bear the brunt of his sarcasm. The current interest in the challenge set forth in *Pourquoi des philosophes?* is measured by the scope of the debate it provokes. Lévi-Strauss considers it in *Structural Anthropology*, as does Goldmann in an article published in *Les Temps Modernes* in 1957 (13: 237–45) and later reprinted in *Recherches dialectiques*.

Sartre's *Critique of Dialectical Reason* itself, and the reactions it provokes, can be seen as an eloquent sign of the crisis of Sartrism. The book reads like an attempted counteroffensive in which Sartre is trying to reestablish the culture of commitment by bringing anthropology back to its theoretical "prolegomena."

The responses that Sartre's feat draws from men like Lévi-Strauss and J.-D. Reynaud, who may be considered the respective representatives and champions of the new structuralist and empirical sociological tendencies, are also significant. What is common to the pages of *The Savage Mind* which are devoted to the *Critique* ("History and Dialectic," 245–69) and the article Reynaud devotes to it in the *Revue française de sociologie* in 1961, "Sociologie et raison dialectique," is the irreverence with which Sartre's theoretical terrorism is henceforth treated. Nothing better indicates the position of strength from which the representatives of the human sciences now address themselves to Sartre than this summary rejection, which does not even bother to prove that "analytic reason" is autonomous and superior to dialectical reason.

To this we must add that the social and political conditions which commitment once expressed have disappeared. The recovery of the economy, the consolidation of Gaullism, the termination of the Algerian War, the Cold War, and the complementary collapse of utopian Communism, which after Budapest and the Twentieth Party Congress of the Soviet Union is stripped of its mobilizing myths, all conspire to overthrow existentialist prophetism, which is a crisis culture presupposing the post-War problems of French society and international tension, as well as the prestige of the revolutionary cause as the dominant concept of an eschatological discourse on the meaning of history. The times are ripe for a new optimistic social philosophy which is inclined to believe that economic mechanisms have an inherent tendency to rationality, and that science is better able than politics to facilitate the automatic progress that modernization seems to promise.[23]

This climate of a politically demobilizing intellectual field is worsened by the crisis of the left. Although the events of 1956 shake its Communist wing, the Socialists also come out of the Algerian War shattered. The left becomes an indefensible ally which Sartre begins to draw away from with "le fantôme de Staline." This essay is *Les Temps Modernes'* expression of a crisis in the relationship between intellectuals and politics. If we also consider that the deaths of Camus (1960) and Merleau-Ponty (1961) follow on one another's heels, we can imagine the loneliness of the mandarin who has managed to survive the crisis only to find himself challenged on the intellectual as well as the political level.[24]

In this perspective, the editorial changes which took place between 1961 and 1962 look like a strategy of reinforcing *Les Temps Modernes'* "unshakable values." The new editorial committee reidentifies the review with the people it has incorporated in the course of its history: the original disciples and Lanzmann, who through the relationships he has established with Sartre and Simone de Beauvoir can be assimilated to the "family." They are distinguished from the rest by their total support of the master. This explains the elimination of Péju,[25] who had remained a "staff worker" destined to fall by the wayside when the staff work to be done and the titles required to do it change with the changing situation. The time of Sartre's "sons" has arrived: from this time forth they are the ones likely to succeed him and free themselves from him without, however, questioning the sovereignty over *Les Temps Modernes* of this man who for them represents the primitive myth upon which they have built their careers.

## 2. THE INDIVIDUAL STRATEGIES

To give a more complete idea of the contributions which different segments made to the evolution of *Les Temps Modernes*, we must specify the conflicts which divide individual agents within each group.

In the group of disciples, Lefort stands out from the rest as Merleau-Ponty's sole follower. The difference between his position and that of the Sartreans is analogous to the difference between their respective masters. From the time of his first contributions to *Les Temps Modernes*, Lefort proves to be a vanguard thinker whose insight into certain points is even ahead of Merleau-Ponty's. But he shares the latter's conception of philosophy as an activity of laying foundations which is coextensive with contemporary social reality and scientific knowledge. And like Merleau-Ponty, Lefort distinguishes himself from Sartre and his disciples by political and cultural choices which anticipate the field's evolution. Thus in 1946, when Sartre is still biased against politics and his disciples are just beginning to take an interest in it, Merleau-Ponty and Lefort are deeply involved in the confrontation with Marxism. The first is in touch with the orthodox members of *Action*[26] and is writing *Humanism and Terror*; the second is one of the leading spirits of Socialisme ou barbarie. Both have rejected as deterministic the Bolshevist conception of the revolution and the Party which the Fourth International revived,[27] and having discovered Weber,[28] are heading toward a libertarian radicalism[29] at the time when Sartre is entering in 1952 his phase of maximum accord with the Communists and interest in Marx's thought. Lefort and Merleau-Ponty both like to join reflection on politics and history to reflection on literature and art.[30] Like Merleau-Ponty, Lefort understands the challenge that the new flourishing of the human sciences at the beginning of the fifties represents for philosophy. As soon as Lévi-Strauss's first works appear, Lefort points out both the importance and the aporias of Lévi-Strauss's thinking with an acuteness which is not unrelated to his concern to master a position which endangers philosophy's primacy.[31] The parallel paths taken by Lefort and Merleau-Ponty make it inevitable that both will break with Sartre when *The Communists and Peace* is published.

But Lefort's positions are always more radical than Merleau-Ponty's. A Trotskyist while his master is more of a Leninist, he pronounces the failure of the Soviet experiment before Merleau-Ponty does and more decisively than he does. Whereas Merleau-Ponty recognizes the need for, and the effectiveness of, institutions, the guiding thread of Lefort's tumultuous political trajectory is his rejection of organizations.[32] This difference comes out clearly in their break with Sartre, which is immediate and resounding on Lefort's part but delayed and attenuated into a "philosophical difference" on Merleau-Ponty's.

The relationship which another of Merleau-Ponty's disciples, Tran Duc Thao, established with Sartre and *Les Temps Modernes* was too short-lived and irregular to make a difference in the review's history, but it is significant as a result of its analogies with Lefort's case. Thao also shows resolute autonomy. He starts out with *Phénoménologie et marxisme dialectique*, a work which develops an approach which the master has as yet scarcely begun to envisage. He takes part in *Les Temps Modernes* by taking peremptory political stands: he and Lefort are the only disciples to provoke reservations from the directors, who keep their distance from certain articles that the two write by presenting them as mere "opinions."[33] Having persuaded Sartre to participate in a series of interviews which are to be published later as a book, he does not hesitate to bring suit against him for stopping publication.[34]

Sartre's disciples, we might say, have the opposite problem: freeing themselves from an identification with Sartre which threatens to become a serious handicap. Their history at the review can be read as the story of different outcomes resulting from differences in the capital each had been able to accumulate. In this perspective, there is a significant relationship between their initial position, their success, and their termination of their relationship with Sartre. The ones endowed with resources of their own in addition to their relation to the master are the ones who assert themselves most as independent individuals and, in varying degrees, emancipate themselves most easily.[35]

The oldest disciples, Bost and Pouillon, are from the outset the most dependent on Sartre: they have no other capital when, at around thirty, they join the editorial staff of *Les Temps Modernes* at the Liberation. Things are different for the others. Jeanson, when he first makes contact with Sartre in 1946, already has a past in the Resistance and what will later prove to be decisive experience in Algeria, and is working for *Esprit*. Pontalis's relationship with Sartre is above all a friendship, parallel to a model academic career which stretches up through the *agrégation* and a doctorate in psychology to an eminent position in French psychoanalysis. Gorz does not really start to take part in the activities of the review until 1961, when he is already well-established as a journalist specializing in the economy and as the author of *The Traitor*, an original book which, by the way, is praised by Sartre in one of his most brilliant prefaces, "Rats and Men."

It seems that for the youngest disciples, the greater their initial autonomy, the greater their success, and the greater their success, the greater their subsequent autonomy—up to the point at which they break with Sartre and the group.

Jeanson has a falling out with Sartre in 1956 when he criticizes the manner in which Sartre condemns the Soviet invasion of Hungary. Although he has been listed since 1951 as a manager of *Les Temps Modernes*, he has long since stopped working for the review. His struggles at the side of the Algerian N.L.F., and his 1955 book, *l'Algérie hors la loi*, have made him one of the leaders of the intellectuals' opposition to the Algerian War. Thus what seems to be a matter of Sartre coming to the support of Jeanson in his clandestine struggle against the War by taking part in the 1960 "Jeanson trial" is actually the result of an exchange: by associating himself with his disciple, the master recaptures a role in the political avant-garde which is slipping away from him.

Similarly Pontalis, who thanks to the authority he has attained[36] is independent by the time the review publishes a "psychoanalytic dialogue" accompanied by a commentary from the hand of the master ("A Psychoanalytic Dialogue, with a Commentary by Jean-Paul Sartre"), can publicly decry the ambiguity of Sartre's relationship to psychoanalysis.[37]

The position Gorz occupies at the end of the sixties as a world famous political theorist[38] shows the real meaning of his (long unaccepted) resignation in 1974 after a disagreement among the editors about an issue of the review devoted to the far-left Italian group, Lotta Continua: his resignation was a test of strength.

This relationship between independence and success is confirmed by the trajectories of Bost and Pouillon, the only ones who never challenged their tie to their master. Without thinking in the least of rejecting Sartre, Pouillon becomes Lévi-Strauss's student toward the middle of the fifties. His position as mediator between existentialism and structuralism is symbolized by his taking charge in 1966 of putting out a special issue of Les Temps Modernes on structuralism.[39] Although he plays an important role in the operation of Les Temps Modernes and of Lévi-Strauss's review, l'Homme, he stays out of the limelight. His own works are always presented as products of his academic studies: in the footsteps of Sartre, the youthful work Temps et roman; in those of Lévi-Strauss, the ethnological works.[40]

Bost's trajectory also confirms the inextricable link between career and relationship with the master. Up to the very end he is still Sartre's confidential advisor, the filter who chooses, comments on, and evaluates books, events and persons. Along with Simone de Beauvoir, Bost is Sartre's obligatory mediator with the world.[41] And his absolute dependence on Sartre in this role seems to perpetuate the initial state of symbolic penury which made the role possible to begin with. Introduced into journalism by Sartre, he goes from Combat to Express, then to the Nouvel Observateur, without ever winning a top-level post.[42]

There is something tragic about the fate of the original disciples. Constantly confronted with an image of sovereign excellence, they are continuously challenged to reproduce it even though Sartre, unlike Durkheim or Lucien Febvre, has left them no method, no way of thinking or "mental tools," which would enable them to escape the dilemma of either trying to mimic him—knowing in advance they must fail—or resigning themselves to silence.

Before we look at the second group of editors, we must pause for a moment at the journalists who kept *Les Temps Modernes* going between 1948 and 1952. We need only consider the most important ones: Stéphane, Bourdet, Guerin, and Dalmas.

They play rather different roles in *Les Temps Modernes*. For Stéphane, the review is for a time the main pole of his activity. He takes part in the meetings, he regularly publishes articles, he takes editorial stands on current politics. The others limit themselves to furnishing contributions on particular subjects. The difference in their relationship to the review corresponds to a difference in the degree of autonomy they enjoyed when they began working for it. Although Stéphane is not without titles when he joins *Les Temps Modernes* in 1948,[43] he is still an unknown. He only acquires personal status in 1950 by founding the *Observateur*, which will in time become the *Nouvel Observateur*, a new model of weekly for intellectuals. Daniel Guérin and Claude Bourdet, on the other hand, already have a solid reputation when, in 1950 and 1951 respectively, they start to work for *Les Temps Modernes*; and Dalmas, although he is the same age as Stéphane, already has made his name in journalism when, in 1950, he publishes his essay on Yugoslav Communism in *Les Temps Modernes*.

Guérin makes himself known before the War with an essay on fascism (*La peste brune*, 1933) and as a founder of the Centre laïque des auberges de la jeunesse. His interpretation of the French Revolution as a failed proletarian revolution in his 1946 book, *La lutte des classes sous la Ire République*, had widespread repercussions in the French left, which was living the Liberation as a revolutionary era.[44]

Bourdet is also a top-level figure at this time. As a managing editor of *Combat* since 1942 who had been deported to Buchenwald, he is one of the intellectuals in the public eye at the Liberation, as well as the vice-president of the Assemblée consultative and the general manager of Radiodiffusion française. He takes part in the founding of the *Observateur* in 1950 and becomes its co-manager.

Dalmas probably owes his rapid advancement to his aristocratic and powerful family (he is the son of a Polignac who is president and general manager of the Pommery champagne company and is related to the princes of Monaco): just a college graduate in 1946, at twenty-five he becomes news editor of *France-Dimanche* and, in 1950, when he publishes *Le communisme yougoslave*, he is already vice-president of the Association des journalistes scientifiques.

If we compare the overall political trajectories of these journalists, another dividing line appears. Dalmas joins Stéphane in opposition to

Guérin and Bourdet. The latter remain loyal to their respective positions on the left: Guérin within the unorthodox Communist tradition which is anti-authoritarian and critical of Leninism, Bourdet within the non-Communist left which is the core of first the New Left and then the Parti Socialiste Uni. Stéphane and Dalmas instead abandon the revolutionary politics of their youth to end up one as a Gaullist and the other as wholly uncommitted.

We should probably look for the origins of this difference in differences of both generation and acquired dispositions. Bourdet and Guérin belong to the intellectual generation of Sartre, whose ideological history is dominated by its guilt feelings concerning the proletariat and the revolutionary cause. They also share with Sartre an intellectual habitus doubly anchored in their family origins (they are sons of intellectuals[45]) and in their highly esteemed scholarly capital.[46]

Stéphane and Dalmas belong to a generation which is ten years younger and reached maturity in a period of revolutionary disenchantment, Cold War, and disclosures of Stalinist misdeeds. Born into a sector of the dominant class which was richer in economic than in cultural capital,[47] and having become journalists without even beginning graduate studies (their social position allows them to forget about academic titles), they express through their choices the ambivalence of their dispositions, which are divided between the pole of intellect and the pole of power. Each publishes, toward the age of thirty, his most ambitious—and most radical—book, prefaced by Sartre, one to become a television producer, the other the head of his own news service. This double shift from revolutionism to conservatism and from aspiration for intellectual success to that of running a business coincides with growing old. It is as if, having once been drawn close to the dominated classes by the uncertainty of their chances for success, they were led by success to profound solidarity with the class from which they sprang.

In spite of the great similarity of their main characteristics, the members of the review's second group of editors also show significant differences. The first thing we notice is the difference between the position of Péju and Lanzmann, who act as Sartre's political advisors, and Cau's position. The latter's publications in *Les Temps Modernes* are reviews, literary experiments, and meanderings which have no profound effect on the review's image, whose nature shows that the reason for his having been made an editor—to lend legitimacy to Sartre's personal secretary and spokesman—is entirely different from theirs. But Cau's dependence on Sartre, which is material as well as symbolic, gets repressed and transfigured into friendship. And it is probably this ambivalence in their relationship which makes it fail. Cau's resistance to identifying himself with Sartre is evident in what he produces. This accounts for his break with Sartre and the subsequent savagery with which this former secretary will cry out in the pages of *Paris-Match* an ideological counter chorus to all Sartre's positions.

Todd writes in his book: "Was this a case of a son rejected by his father? At any rate, Cau had the merit of liberating himself completely from Sartre, of completely severing his umbilical cord" (111). "Cau was not treated like a member of the family. When Mme Mancy spoke of him she did not call him 'Jean' or 'Cau' but 'the secretary.' He was not intellectual and philosophical enough to suit the family. He did not speak their lingo" (110). But the almost systematic opposition to Sartre which Todd sees in Cau's attitude shows that Cau's tie to Sartre, although negative, is far from being broken: "There was a time when it seemed that no matter what the subject, all one had to do was know what Sartre thought about it and adopt the diametrically opposed viewpoint to be able to imagine in advance what Cau would write in *Match*. The more 'progressive' the one became, the more 'reactionary' the other" (110ff).

The difference between what happens to Péju, who is kicked out and carries on a public polemic with Sartre,[48] and to Lanzmann, who is adopted into the family, shows the really profound underlying difference between two members of the editorial staff who initially seem very much alike and almost interchangeable in their function of lending Sartre ideological backing. The key to this difference undoubtedly lies in the difference in weight and independence of their respective positions in the review. Péju is top secretary from December 1953 to December 1961. After *The Communists and Peace*, he is the main one who gives *Les Temps Modernes* a place in current politics, succeeding Merleau-Ponty in a function for which Sartre is little suited. Even though he does not stick his neck out when it comes to political theory, he cannot be said to be Sartre's mouthpiece. Schooled in existentialism's outlook and lingo,[49] he develops analyses, interpretations, and new departures, writing peremptory editorials in which he takes intransigent stands—even going to far as to declare his support for Ben Bella and maintain (in spite of Sartre's perplexity) that "Evian is Brest-Litovsk."

Thus it is Péju who determines the stand *Les Temps Modernes* takes on all the major issues of the day: Indochina, the E.E.C., German rearmament, and French behavior toward the two superpowers.[50] He is the one who takes a stand on Mollet, Mendès France, and De Gaulle, and in an article on Mendès France, even runs the risk of formulating (for the first time in the review's history) a precise line on the problem of the State and parties.[51] And it is Péju, finally, who in 1957–58 opens a phase of intense relations between *Les Temps Modernes* and Polish Communism.[52]

Péju's political disagreement with Sartre concerning Algeria seems to be not the real cause of their break but a revealing episode which lays bare what has become intolerable to Sartre: the power Péju has gained over the review, which threatens to upset the balance established after Merleau-Ponty left. Péju is the only one of those kicked out who will bring his case before the bar of public opinion. The others creep away quietly without making a scene, implicitly recognizing that Sartre is *Les Temps Modernes*, and that it is useless to dispute his sovereignty.

Lanzmann for his part seems to win the position of one of Sartre's close "family," with its inseparable combination of dependency and intellectual and affective symbiosis.

Simone de Beauvoir, in her portrayal of Lanzmann, retraces a difficult history of a search for identity rooted in an experience of being doubly excluded as a Jew whom anti-Semitism traps into defining himself abstractly as a Jew, and as an intellectual whose success never reaches the level of his original ambition: "When, at the age of thirteen, he discovered anti-Semitism, the whole world was shaken, nothing survived intact. . . . [Reduced] to the abstract notion, a Jew, he felt expelled from his own being. . . . He had been torn apart, the world had been given over to chaos: he tried to make himself whole again and rediscover order in the world. At twenty, he believed in the universality of culture and he had worked zealously to make it his: he had the feeling it didn't quite belong to him. . . . In his childhood, by forcing him to renounce either his 'Jewishness' or his individuality, the world had stolen his Self: when he said *I* he always felt like an impostor. . . . Lacking any frame of reference, he adopted very easily the viewpoints of people he respected . . ." (*F.C.*, 294–96)

Many of those who become official members of the editorial staff after 1953 fashion careers with newspapers. Gorz, Bost, Péju, Lanzmann, and Cau become journalists. If we also consider the role played by Guérin and Bourdet, we can judge the growing influence of journalism within the review. It is true that it already had influence in the first editorial committee, which included Aron and Ollivier, both at the time editorial writers for *Combat*. But in those days journalism was marked with the stamp of academic excellence which distinguished Merleau-Ponty, Sartre, and Aron himself (who embodied the review's synthesis between the two positions). In those days, *Les Temps Modernes* could seem an original model of intellectual excellence which combined the loftiest philosophical tradition with a presence on the current scene. In losing Merleau-Ponty, the review loses this important initial bipolarity, a loss further aggravated by the fact that it also involves a loss of some of its other university people, names which recurred frequently in the earlier days; Lévinas, Vuillemin, Uri, Belaval, Auger, and one of the first and most regular contributors, Etiemble, who will explain his reasons for breaking off with the review in a "Lettre ouverte à Jean-Paul Sartre sur l'unité de mauvaise action."[53]

The growing separation between the review's two poles, and the growing isolation of its surviving university people, is evident in the journalists' open hostility to them. Here is Todd's description of the two university people who came to editorial meetings, Merleau-Ponty and Pontalis: "Maurice Merleau-Ponty, with his Roman nose and haughty air, took the attitude of I-don't-talk-just-for-the-sake-of-talking and How-can-I-be-here-on-equal-footing-with-these-clods. An important man, he often imposed on others, even on Sartre himself. Sartre respected him more than he liked him. . . . In that rather Bohemian crowd of mavericks, Merleau-Ponty stood out in his conventionality. Pontalis the psychoanalyst, as pompous as Merleau-Ponty but straitlaced in professional silences, punctuated his interrupted pauses with brief vague comments that recalled responses to his patients: Which reminds you of . . .? And . . .? All right, and then . . .?"[54]

Around 1968, *Les Temps Modernes* has been taken over by a majority who are oriented toward essay writing and journalism. Led by Gorz, who in the sixties had succeeded Péju as political editor, the review adopts positions which mark the triumph of an anti-institutional spirit. Its attacks on the university and on psychoanalysis provoke the resignations of two other members of the editorial staff, Pontalis and Pingaud.

Here is Simone de Beauvoir's account of the matter: "When Kravetz, and others after him, called for 'the Sorbonne for the students' in numbers 64 and 65, and made a violent attack upon official university lectures, Pontalis and Pingaud were strongly opposed to his propositions. They did not make this publicly evident, but in private they did not conceal the fact that they were shocked and distressed by some of the positions adopted by the magazine. They openly stated their disapproval when Sartre published the 'psychoanalytical dialogue' and explained why he thought the document fascinating—an opinion shared by all the other members of the committee. . . .

"In a note, Pontalis objected that the Censier watchword 'Victims of analysis, rise up!' implied a radical rejection of psychoanalysis. Pingaud felt that the tape-recorder man's 'move into direct action' did not provide a suitable opportunity for calling psychoanalysis into question. *Both in the one and the other there was to be seen the same tendency that had caused them to defend the tradition of official lectures.*

"The matter went no farther. But as the magazine—spurred on primarily by Sartre and Gorz—more and more deliberately adopted a left-wing line, Pontalis and Pingaud left in 1970. It was Gorz's 'Destroy the University,' the leading article in the April number, that made up their minds. 'The position, signature and form of this article make it appear to define the collective opinion of the *Temps Modernes* team. As we cannot accept these propositions, we have regretfully decided to leave the editorial committee,' they wrote. We too regretted their departure; but our intellectual and political disagreements had become too grave for friendship to overcome them. . . ."[55]

This development draws *Les Temps Modernes* even closer to journalism, as can be seen by its relations with first the *Observateur* and then the *Nouvel Observateur*. The trajectory of Bourdet, who goes from the governing board of *Combat* to that of the *Observateur*, is an indication of these relations. Several of *Les Temps Modernes*' coworkers (Stéphane, Bourdet) take part in the founding of the *Observateur* in 1950, and several more (Gorz, Bost, Todd) in the founding of the *Nouvel Observateur* in 1964. The *Nouvel Observateur* becomes Sartre's favorite tribune—and that of his review—for making himself heard when there is an urgent need to. In all likelihood, the audiences for the two publications largely overlap.[56] And the weekly follows and comments on the doings of Sartre and his disciples with a watchful eye.[57]

In losing its academic component and going over to the side of journalism, the review loses some of its legitimacy, finding itself stripped of the essential difference which formerly distinguished it from its competitors. In addition, this internal transformation coincides with the tranformation of the political and social climate and the concurrent weakening of existentialism. Thus the two basic determinants of the history of *Les Temps Modernes*—internal competition and social demand—combine to assure its decline. The first seems to operate as a perverse mechanism which leads Sartre to centralize power in his own hands only to deprive himself in so doing of his most prestigious allies. The second renders obsolete the image of Sartre which gives the review its image, the image he himself saw and asked others to see in his works. The very correspondence between what he had to say and what his contemporaries were looking for which accounts for yesterday's success makes that image seem irretrievable today, and makes those who try to remain loyal to him end up threatening the survival of his works. This accounts for the fact that today's readings of his works spontaneously agree in repudiating the model which enabled him to conquer his times. Instead they rediscover aspects of his work which were overshadowed by the prophet of freedom whom a triumphant Marxist humanism had thrust into the foreground in 1945: they put the stress on his least famous, least noted texts—above all the unpublished ones. Thus Geneviève Idt draws a contrast between the "witness to the truth" and the disturbing fantasies and mimetic skill which allow her to speak of a "baroque" and "carnavalesque" Sartre. Michel Sicard looks at Sartre in the perspective of a "modernist aesthetic" which he finds implicit in Sartre's study of Tintoretto, rather than in terms of the principles set forth in *What Is Literature?* Today's critics retrace Sartre's path and go back from the *Critique* to the "negative" Sartre, the "metaphysician of the void" and the disciple of Heidegger. And it is not Sartre the public figure they prefer but the young Sartre revealed by the wartime letters and *War Diaries*, cocky to the point of arrogance and in his amorous relationships far from the new "transparent" morality to which he aspires.

In losing ground on all fronts—above all on the philosophical, theatrical, and political ones—Sartre also loses the image of a total intellectual which constituted the power and originality of his position in 1945. The titles he has accumulated tend to decrease the value of his capital instead of enhancing it: his outmoded characteristics tend to make his other characteristics obsolete too. This tendency is evident by the time *The Family Idiot* comes out: his undertaking arouses much attention, but almost entirely from the literary field, whereas the book is meant to be his most synoptic work and the crowning glory of his entire intellectual trajectory. The philosophical anthropology which underlies the method he applies to Flaubert, and the aim which governs his investigation—to show how Flaubert became this writer who wrote these words—are based on an approach which in a context dominated by the structuralist mood seems unrelated to today's world. *The Family Idiot* is seen above all as a literary feat; its theoretical intentions are ignored.

The phase of reassessment which began with Sartre's death shows that henceforth his oeuvre can only expect partial and diminished recognition. Even his most zealous supporters no longer dream of preserving it in its entirety. From now on the domination on all fronts which defined the excellence that Sartre embodied is a thing of the past.

# NOTES

## Abbreviations

A.D.      Maurice Merleau-Ponty, *The Adventures of the Dialectic*, trans. Joseph Bien (Evanston: Northwestern, 1973).

B.N.      Jean-Paul Sartre, *Being and Nothingness*, trans. Hazel E. Barnes (New York: Philosophical Library, 1956).

F.C.      Simone de Beauvoir, *Force of Circumstance*, trans. Richard Howard (London: Penguin, 1968).

H.T.      Maurice Merleau-Ponty, *Humanism and Terror*, trans. John O'Neill (Boston: Beacon, 1969).

L.P.E.      Jean-Paul Sartre, *Literary and Philosophical Essays*, trans. Annette Michelson (New York: Collier, 1955).

O.R.      M. Contat and M. Rybalka, *Sartre, Œuvres romanesques* (Paris: Gallimard, 1981).

P.L.      Simone de Beauvoir, *The Prime of Life*, trans. Peter Green (London: André Deutsch, 1962).

W.L.      Jean-Paul Sartre, *What Is Literature?* trans. Bernard Frechtman (New York: Philosophical Library [1949]).

W.S.      *The Writings of Jean-Paul Sartre*, 2 vols., comp. Michel Contat and Michel Rybalka, trans. Richard C. McCleary (Evanston: Northwestern, 1974).

243

# Introduction

1. See especially Pierre Bourdieu, "Genèse et structure du champ religieux," *Revue française de sociologie* 12 (1971): 295–334; and the Preface to *Le sens pratique* (Paris: Editions de Minuit, 1980).

2. Bourdieu has set forth explicitly his conception of the intellectual field and its function. See, for example, "Champ intellectual et projet createur," *Les Temps Modernes* 246 (Nov. 1966): 865–906; "Le marché des biens symboliques," *L'Année sociologique* 22 (1971): 49–126; "Champ du pouvoir, champ intellectuel et habitus de classe," *Scolies* 1 (1971): 7–26; "La production de la croyance," *Actes de la recherche en sciences sociales* 13 (Feb. 1977): 3–44. Elements of a more general theory of social space may be found in *La distinction* (Paris, 1980), *Le sens pratique* (Paris, 1980), *Questions de sociologie* (Paris, 1980), and *Ce que parler veut dire* (Paris, 1982).

3. Cf. P. Bourdieu, "Sartre," *London Review of Books* 2 (Nov. 20-Dec. 3): 11–12.

# Part One

1. Simone de Beauvoir, *Force of Circumstance*, trans. Richard Howard, (London: Penguin, 1968), 46 (hereinafter *F.C.*).

2. " 'La nausée' de Jean-Paul Sartre," *Alger républicain* (Oct. 20, 1938), and A. Camus, *Essais* (Paris: Gallimard, 1965), 1417–1419.

3. *Alger républicain* (March 12, 1939), and Camus, *Essais*, 1419–22.

4. *Aux Ecoutes* (July 30, 1938).

5. "Les Romans de Sartre," *L'Arche* 10 (Oct. 1945): 121–34. Reprinted in *La part du feu* (Paris: Gallimard, 1949), 195–211.

6. See F. Mauriac, *Bloc-notes* (Paris: Flammarion, 1958–71), 5 volumes: *Memoires politiques* (Paris: Grasset, 1967).

7. Provoked by a statement Sartre made ["The reason Céline supported the Nazis' socialist planks was that he was in their hire," in "Portrait de l'antisémite," *Les Temps Modernes* 3 (Dec. 1945): 442–70], Céline fires back with a violent broadside, *A l'agité du bocal* (P. Lanauve de Tartas, 1948).

8. See J. Wahl, "Essai sur le néant d'un problème," *Deucalion* (Paris: Ed. de la revue Fontaine, 1946): pp. 41–72. See also Chapter 7 below for the relationship between Sartre and Wahl.

9. Marcel was an attentive critic of the early Sartre: of *Being and Nothingness* [see *Homo viator* (Paris: Montaigne, 1944)], of Sartre's plays [see *L'heure théatrale* (Paris: Plon, 1959)], and of his novels [he reviewed *The Wall* in *Carrefour* 4 (June-July 1939): 85–86, and *The Age of Reason* in *la Nef* 13 (Dec. 1945): 130–33].

10. Merleau-Ponty's relations with Sartre will be analyzed in Chapter 7 below.

11. See the series of articles, "A propos de l'existentialisme," published in *Confluences* in 1945, two of which are devoted to Sartre: 5 (June-July): 531–38; 6 (Aug.): 637–42. Concerning the success of Beaufret's lectures, see Simone de Beauvoir's account in *La force des choses*, 68.

12. See Alain Touraine, *Un désir d'histoire* (Paris: Stock, 1977), 22ff. Among Alquié's numerous responses, we may mention an article on *Being and Noth-*

*ingness* in *les Cahiers du Sud* (1945): 648–62 and 807–16, a debate with Naville published in *la Revue internationale* in March 1946 (cf. Simone de Beauvoir, *La force des choses*, 68), and a lecture at the *Collège philosophique*, "Humanisme surréaliste et humanisme existentialiste," in *L'homme, le monde, l'histoire*, Cahiers du collège philosophique (Paris: Arthaud, 1949).

13. Among the articles he writes on Sartre, see his report on the Club Maintenant lecture ("Les conférences. L'existentialisme est un humanisme," *Fontaine* (Nov. 1945) or his commentary on Sartre's *Baudelaire* in *Fontaine* (April-May 1947), reprinted in *Le sadisme de Baudelaire* (Paris: Corti, 1948).

14. See the long review devoted to the first two volumes of *The Roads to Freedom*.

15. See the review of *The Age of Reason* and *The Reprieve*, "Le tourment existentiel," in *Combat* (Oct. 23, 1945), and the section devoted to Sartre in *Le roman français depuis la guerre* (Paris: Gallimard, 1970).

16. See *le Monde*, Oct. 17, 1945.

17. See the article, "Comment parlons-nous?" in *le Figaro* (Nov. 3, 1945).

18. *Le Figaro* took note of all Sartre's novels as soon as they came out: *Nausea* (May 28, 1938), *The Wall* (March 4, 1939), *The Age of Reason* and *The Reprieve* (Oct. 20 and 27, 1945), and *Troubled Sleep (le Figaro litteraire*, (Oct. 22, 1949).

19. With a review of *Nausea* [Jean Daniélou, 237 (Oct. 1938): 140–41] and of the first two volumes of *The Roads to Freedom* [Louis Beirnaert, 247 (Nov. 1945): 272–73].

20. For *Esprit's* position, see Chapter 7.

21. For Mounier's position, see his *Introduction aux existentialismes*, Collection Idées, new edition (Paris: Gallimard, 1962) and *L'espoir des désespérés* (1953).

22. See his review of *The Age of Reason*, *Esprit* 13 (Dec. 1, 1945): 969–71. *Sartre and the Problem of Morality*, trans. Robert V. Stone (Indiana, 1980), prefaced by a laudatory letter from Sartre (Paris: Editions du Myrte, 1947), is the first of a series of books on Sartre, as well as an itinerary within which Sartre continues to be an essential landmark.

23. *Le problème moral et la pensée de Sartre* (Paris: Editions du Myrte, 1947), prefaced by a laudatory letter from Sartre, is the first of a series of books on Sartre, as well as an itinerary within which Sartre continues to be an essential landmark.

24. See the essays that were published when these works of Sartre came out and reprinted in *Essai sur les limites de la litterature* (Paris: Payot, 1968) and in *Litterature et critique* (Paris: Payot, 1971).

25. See Pierre Boutang, Jean Pingaud, "Sartre est-il un possédé?" *la Table ronde* (1946).

26. See "J.-P. Sartre et le suicide de la littérature," *la Table ronde* (Feb. 1948): 195–210.

27. See "Un faux prophéte, Jean-Paul Sartre," *Les Lettres françaises* (Dec. 28, 1945).

28. See "Existentialisme et marxisme," *Action* 40 (June 8, 1945) and the book, *L'existentialisme* (Paris: Editions du Sagittaire, 1946).

29. See *L'existentialisme n'est pas un humanisme* (Paris: Editions Sociales, 1947).

30. See *La sainte famille existentialiste* (Paris: Editions Sociales, 1947).

31. Georges Blin, "Les conferences."

32. The burlesque of this impact which Boris Vian gives in *L'écume des jours*, Chapter 28, is itself an indication of the deep impression this unprecedented secularization of philosophy made.

33. "Un auteur scandaleux," *le Figaro littéraire* (Dec. 6, 1947).

# Chapter 1

1. See V. Karady, "Normaliens et autres enseignants á la Belle Epoque," *Revue française de sociologie* 13, 1 (Jan.–March, 1972): 35–58. Karady's observations concern the beginning of the century, but since there had been no basic change in the social and institutional foundations of a teaching career, they apply to the thirties as well. It must be added that the prestige of the Ecole normale supérieure was also due to its image as the school for future rulers. The image did not quite fit the reality, but it was fed by certain famous cases such as those of Jean Jaurès and Léon Blum, and by a tenacious legend which originated at the time of the Dreyfus Affair and was crystallized by such pamphlets as Charles Péguy's *Notre jeunesse*, A. Thibaudet's *La république des professeurs*, and J. Benda's *La trahison des clercs*, and by Hubert Bourgin's book, *De Jaurès à Léon Blum, L'Ecole normale et la politique* (London: Gordon and Breach, 1970—a reprint,with a new introduction by D. Lindenberg, of the original edition, Paris: Fayard, 1938). Concerning the latter, see V. Karady, "Trois études sur l'Ecole normale supérieure," *L'Année sociologique* (1973): 223–33.

2. According to Raymond Aron (interview with the author, 1979).

3. See J.-L. Fabiani, "Les programmes, les hommes et les œuvres," *Actes de la recherche* . . . 47/48 (1983): 3–20.

4. See V. Brombert, *The Intellectual Hero, 1880–1955* (Philadelphia: Lippincott, 1961), 21–40.

5. In addition to J. L. Fabiani, "Les programmes," see V. Karady, "Les professeurs de la République," *Actes de la recherche* . . . 47–48 (1983): 90–112.

6. E. Zola, *Une campagne* (Paris: G. Charpentier, 1882), 247–50, quoted in Alain Peyrefitte, *Rue d'Ulm* (Paris: Flammarion, 1977), 368.

7. See C. Charle, *La crise littéraire à l'époque du naturalisme* (Paris: Presses de L'Ecole normale supérieure, 1979).

8. Concerning the groups which, at the end of the last century, succeed one another at the summit of consecration (indicated by admission to the Académie), see R. Ponton, "Programme esthéthique et accumulation du capitale symbolique, le Parnasse," *Revue française de sociologie* 14, 2 (1973): 202–20, and R. Ponton, "Naissance du roman psychologique," *Actes de la recherche* . . . 4 (1975): 66–81.

9. See V. Brombert, *The Intellectual Hero*.

10. Cf. E. Zola, *Une campagne*, in A. Peyrefitte, *Rue d'Ulm*, 368–69.

11. See C. Charle, *La crise*, 17 and 175.

12. See J. L. Fabiani, "Les programmes."

13. See V. Karady, "Les professeurs de la République," 90–112.

14. See J.-L. Fabiani, "Les programmes," 19.

15. See G. Boillat, *La librairie Bernard Grasset et les lettres françaises* (Paris: Champion, 1974); A. Anglès, *André Gide et le premier groupe de la N.R.F.* (Paris: Gallimard, 1978); P. Assouline, *Gaston Gallimard* (Paris: Balland, 1984).

16. See the 1974 interviews in S. de Beauvoir, *Adieux*, trans. Patrick O'Brian (New York: Pantheon, 1984), 133, 137.

17. *Sartre*, script of a film by A. Astruc and M. Contat (Paris: Gallimard, 1977), 48.

18. "From 1920 to 1930, especially as lycée students, we were indistinguishable." Preface to P. Nizan, *Aden, Arabie*, trans. Joan Pinkham (New York: Monthly Review Press, 1968).

19. See "Une idée fondamentale de la phénoménologie de Husserl: l'intentionnalité," *la Nouvelle Revue française* 34 (1939): 129–31.

20. At this time Sartre had already published, in addition to his youthful writings, *Imagination* (1936), *The Transcendence of the Ego* (1936–37), *Nausea* (1938), and *The Wall* (1939). In the articles drawn from the first important interview Sartre granted, Claudine Chonez stresses the author's dual activity in presenting him. See C. Chonez, "Jean-Paul Sartre, romancier philosophe," *Marianne* (Nov. 23, 1938), and "A qui les lauriers des Goncourt, Femina, Renaudot, Interallié?", *Marianne* (Dec. 7, 1938).

21. M. Blanchot, "Les romans de Sartre" in *l'Arche* 10 (1945): 121–34, quoted in M. Contat and M. Rybalka, *Sartre, Œuvres romanesques* (Paris: Gallimard, 1981), 1925 (hereinafter abbreviated *O.R.*).

# Chapter 2

1. As Sartre put it in the interview he granted C. Chonez, "Jean-Paul Sartre, romancier philosophe," quoted by Contat and Rybalka in *O.R.*, 1696.

2. Here is Sartre's description of the chief protagonist of "The Angel of Morbidity": "He was a mediocre man. . . . He looked for unconventonal ideas with that patient application of the little-minded. . . . His buddies . . . took for a genius the odd monster they had made by grafting their own unsuccessful 'superman' maxims onto his mediocrity." Michel Contat and Michel Rybalka, *The Writings of Jean-Paul Sartre* (hereinafter, *W.S.*), trans. Richard McCleary, vol. 2, *Selected Prose* (Evanston: Northwestern, 1974), 4.

3. The classic in this genre is P. Roussel's *Le petit normalien*, quoted by A. Peyrefitte, *Rue d'Ulm*, 330–33.

4. See S. de Beauvoir, *The Prime of Life*, trans. Peter Green (London: André Deutsch, 1962), 71 (hereinafter, *P.L.*).

5. See S. de Beauvoir, *Memoirs of a Dutiful Daughter*, trans. James Kirkup (New York: World, 1959), 364 (hereinafter, *Memoirs*).

6. G. Idt, Preface to *O.R.*, xix.

7. See S. de Beauvoir, *Memoirs*, 363ff.

8. See Contat and Rybalka, *O.R.*, xliiiff.

9. S. de Beauvoir, *P.L.*, 89.

10. The book was turned down by the publisher Rieder, to whom Nizan had shown it. Only an excerpt from it appeared in *Bifur* (1931), thanks to Nizan, who wrote for this magazine edited by Georges Ribemont-Dessaignes.

11. See the 1974 interviews in S. de Beauvoir, *Adieux*, 208.

12. See G. Idt, in *La nausée* (Paris: Hatier, 1971), 7; G. Raillard, *"La nausée" de Jean-Paul Sartre* (Paris: Hachette, 1972): 22–24; Contat and Rybalka, *O.R.*, note 1722ff. See also Sartre, *The War Diaries of Jean-Paul Sartre*, trans. Quintin Hoare (New York: Pantheon, 1984), 272: "I was living dissociated from myself, like M. Teste" (hereinafter, *War Diaries*).

13. See Contat and Rybalka, *O.R.*, 1720.

14. Concerning these functions of the narrative device in *Nausea*, see G. Idt, in *La nausée*, 51ff and G. Raillard, *"La Nausée" de Jean-Paul Sartre*, 42ff.

15. See S. de Beauvoir, *P.L.*, 89–90, and the comments of Contat and Rybalka, *O.R.*, 1662.

16. See the account of N. Frank, *Les années 30 où l'on inventait aujourd'hui* (Paris: P. Horay, 1969), 90–91, and S. de Beauvoir, *P.L.*, 45, who recalls that she and Sartre "ate up detective stories."

17. See Contat and Rybalka, *O.R.*, 1724.

18. See S. de Beauvoir, *P.L.*, 127 and 213. These are techniques which G. Idt and G. Raillard have pointed out and analyzed in their respective commentaries on *Nausea*.

19. See S. de Beauvoir, *P.L.*, 45, 114–115, and 117, and *Memoirs*, 356. On *Nausea* and Proust, see Contat and Rybalka, *O.R.*, 1663.

20. There is abundant commentary on these mediations in S. de Beauvoir's *The Prime of Life*.

21. *O.R.*, 1666.

22. S. de Beauvoir, *P.L.*, 112–13.

23. Between 1931 and 1933, Sartre gives a lecture at Le Havre on Joyce's interior monologue.

24. For her analysis of *Nausea*, see *La nausée*, 52ff.

25. S. de Beauvoir, *P.L.*, 92.

26. He subsequently formulates the governing principles of this new genre in analyzing Kafka's techniques in an essay on Blanchot's *Aminadab* [*Cahiers du Sud* 255 and 256 (1943); reprinted in *Situations 1*, and in Jean-Paul Sartre, *Literary and Philosophical Essays*, trans. Annette Michelson (New York: Collier, 1955), 60–77 (hereinafter *L.P.E.*)].

27. S. de Beauvoir, *P.L.*, 151.

28. Jean-Paul Sartre, *Nausea*, trans. Lloyd Alexander (New Directions, 1964), 10.

29. Ibid., 135.

30. See S. de Beauvoir, *P.L.*, 237.

31. See the essay on Blanchot referred to in note 26 above and concerning Camus, "Explication de *L'étranger*," *Cahiers du Sud* 253 (1943), reprinted in *Situations 1* and in *L.P.E.*, 26–44.

32. In *W.S.*, I, 52–53.

33. See "A propos de John Dos Passos et de 1919," *N.R.F.* 299 (1938): 292–301. Reprinted in *Situations 1* and in *L.P.E.*, 94–103.

34. See *P.L.*, 114.

35. See *Nausea*, 101. As for Faulkner's influence, see Sartre, "*Sartoris* par William Faulkner," *N.R.F.*, 293 (1938), reprinted in *Situations 1*, and "A propos de *Le bruit et la fureur*: la temporalité chez Faulkner," *N.R.F.* 309 and 310 (1939), reprinted in *Situations 1* and in *L.P.E.*, 84–93. See also *P.L.*, 149–50.

36. Sartre, *Nausea*, 39–40.

37. See G. Idt, *La nausée*, 57, and the Preface to *O.R.*, xxiv.

38. *Le Temps* (July 14, 1938), quoted in *O.R.*, 1706.

39. See *P.L.*, 40–41. On the various occurrences of the tree in Sartre's works, see Contat and Rybalka in *O.R.*, 1783.

40. G. Idt, "Modèles scolaires dans l'écriture sartrienne," *Revue des sciences humaines*, 174 (1979): 83–103.

41. J.-P. Sartre, *The Words*, trans. Bernard Frechtman (New York: Braziller 1964), 159.

42. J.-P. Sartre, "Une idée fondamentale de la phenomenologie de Husserl: l'intentionnalité," *N.R.F.*, reprinted in *Situations 1*, 31.
43. *Situations 1*, 32.
44. As G. Idt has recognized in *La nausée*, 62.
45. *Nausée*, 170–71.
46. Sartre, "Une idée fondamentale," 32.
47. Ibid.
48. See the article devoted to Blanchot, in Cahiers du Sud 255, 226 (1943): 130ff and "M. François Mauriac et la liberté," *N.R.F.* [305 (1939)]: 212–32, reprinted in *Situations 1* and *L.P.E.*, 7–25.
49. *Les Nouvelles littéraires* (June 18, 1938), quoted by Contat and Rybalka in *O.R.*, 1703.
50. Quoted in *O.R.*, 1704.
51. Contat and Rybalka, "Notice sur *La Nausée*," in *O.R.*, 1667. As for the alterations which divide the factum from *Nausea*, see S. Teroni Menzella, "Da 'Melancholia' alla 'Nausée,' note su un manoscritto sartriano," *Studi francesi* 68 (1979): 253–70.
52. See G. Raillard, *"La Nausée" de Jean-Paul Sartre*, 30ff.
53. See *P.L.*, 290–91.
54. Quoted in *O.R.*, 1696ff.
55. J.-P. Sartre, "François Mauriac and Freedom," reprinted in *Situations 1*, 41–52, and in *L.P.E.*, 15–17 and 24. (I have underlined the normative aspects of Sartre's judgments.)
56. February 15, 1939.
57. 306 (March 1939).
58. See the interview in *France-Soir* ( Feb. 28. 1969), quoted by Contat and Rybalka in *W.S.*, 66–67, where the polemic Sartre's article stirred up is reconstructed.
59. "A propos de *Le bruit et la fureur: la temporalité chez Faulkner*," reprinted in *Situations 1*, 66, and in *L.P.E.*, 84–85.
60. *Situations 1*, 24; *L.P.E.*, 103.
61. *Situations 1*, 34; *L.P.E.*, 7.
62. *Situations 1*, 52; *L.P.E.*, 24.
63. The most famous of these "refutations" is an essay by J.-L. Curtis, in *Haute école* (Paris: Julliard, 1950), followed by other comments in *Questions à la littérature* (Paris: Stock, 1973). On Sartre as a critic, see also G. Prince, *Métaphysique et technique dans l'oeuvre romanesque de Sartre* (Geneva: Droz, 1968); M. Sicard, *La Critique littéraire de Jean-Paul Sartre* (Paris: Lettres modernes, 1980); S. Briosi, *Sartre critico* (Bologna: Zanichelli, 1980).
64. *Situations 1*, 44; *L.P.E.*, 14.
65. *Situations 1*, 48; *L.P.E.*, 21.
66. See *P.L.*, 254ff and passim.
67. Ibid., 257.
68. These three books, written respectively by Jules Romains, Arthur Koestler, and Antoine de Saint-Exupéry, were published between 1938 and 1939. When he is called up, Sartre will accord each an important role in his evolution toward commitment during the "Sitzkrieg." See the letter he sent to Simone de Beauvoir from the front on December 4, 1939, in *Lettres au Castor* (Paris: Gallimard, 1983), vol. 1, 458, J.-P. Sartre, *War Diaries*, 56 and 65ff.
69. *Ce Soir*, May 16, 1938, quoted in *O.R.*, 1702.

70. *Etudes* 237 (Oct. 1938): 140–41; quoted in *O.R.*, 1709.

71. It was written during the spring and summer of 1938.

72. See the "insert" composed by Sartre, *W.S.*, 1, 63.

73. See G. Idt, *"Le Mur" de J.-P. Sartre* (Paris: Larousse, 1972), an analysis which is invaluable both for its formal qualities and for the references and contexts for the stories which it establishes.

74. Such as the first lost effort, "Soleil de minuit," which was inspired by a Norwegian cruise, and "Dépaysement," an "atmospheric" story conceived during a stay in Naples and originally thought of as the starting point for a collection of stories of the "impressions of cities" type. See *O.R.*, Appendix I, and *W.S.*, 2.

75. See *P.L.*, 106ff, 168ff, 201ff, and Contat and Rybalka, "Brief Comment" on "The Room," "Brief Comment" on "Erostratus," and notes, in *O.R.*, 1834–1843.

76. *Situations 1*, 22; *L.P.E.*, 101–102 (my italics).

77. A. Cohen-Solal points this out in *Paul-Yves Nizan, communiste impossible* (Paris: Grasset, 1980) (written with Henriette Nizan), 130.

78. See G. Idt, *"La Mur" de J.-P. Sartre*, 182ff. For Sartre's position concerning psychoanalysis, see also J. Pacaly, *Sartre au miroir* (Paris: Klincksieck, 1980), Chapters 1 and 3, and S. Sportelli, *Sartre e la psicoanalisi* (Bari: Dedalo, 1981).

79. See *Situations 1*, 23, 34, 52, 71, 73ff; *L.P.E.*, 7, 24, 91ff, 102.

80. C. Chonez (Sartre interview), "Jean-Paul Sartre, romancier philosophe," quoted in *O.R.*, 1697.

81. *O.R.*, 1697.

82. *War Diaries*, 78.

83. In a letter he writes to Jean Paulhan about the story, "The Wall," Gide calls it a "masterpiece" (quoted by Contat and Rybalka in *O.R.*, 1824, note 3.

84. See G. Idt, *"Les chemins de là liberté, les toboggans du romanesque,"* *Obliques* 18–19 (1979): 75–94, for Sartre's relation to Gide and a complete analysis.

85. See Contat's accounts of the two novels in *O.R.*, 1891 and 1967.

86. Interview in *L'Avant-scène* 402–403 (1968): 33–34, quoted by Contat and Rybalka in *W.S.*, 1, 88.

87. *War Diaries*, 182.

88. See P. Bourdieu, "L'ontologie politique de Martin Heidegger," *Actes de la recherche* . . . 5–6 (1975): 109–56.

89. See the letter to S. de Beauvoir, October 26, 1939, in *Lettres au Castor*, vol. 1, 377.

90. Letter to S. de Beauvoir, January 9, 1940, ibid., vol. 2, 27.

91. Letter to S. de Beauvoir, April 23, 1940, ibid., vol. 2, 180ff.

92. Jean-Paul Sartre, *The Reprieve*, trans. Eric Sutton (New York: Bantam, 1968), 326. Sartre will come back to this interpretation more broadly in *What Is Literature?* (in those passages M. Contat very appropriately recalls in his "Brief Comment" on *The Reprieve* in *O.R.*, 1963–1971), where even though he speaks in generalities, he further articulates the theory of his practice. See *Situations II*, 242ff, 252ff, 327ff.

93. *Les Lettres françaises* 15 (1944): 8, insigned; quoted in Contat and Rybalka, *W.S.*, 94.

94. P. Lorguet, "Jean-Paul Sartre ou l'interview sans interview," an interview feature in *Mondes nouveaux* 2 (1944): 3; quoted in Contat and Rybalka, *W.S.,* 107.

95. C. Grisoli, "Entretien par Jean-Paul Sartre," *Paru* 13 (1945): 5–10.

96. See Chapter 4, section 3.2 below.

# Chapter 3

1. Jean Hyppolyte, *Figures de la pensée philosophique* (Paris: P.U.F., 1971), 232.

2. The title, from a book by Maritain which Simone de Beauvoir adopted ironically for a book she wrote in the thirties to take a particular kind of education to pieces: *Quand prime le spirituel* (Paris: Gallimard, 1979).

3. See Politzer's *La fin d'une parade philosophique: le bergsonisme* (1929), Nizan's *The Watchdogs* (1932), and their *Revue marxiste* (1929–39).

4. Jean-Paul Sartre, *Search for a Method*, trans. Hazel E. Barnes (New York: Vintage, 1963), 17–21.

5. See the reconstruction of the period which S. Moravia has made in the chapter from *La ragione nascosta* (Florence: Sansoni, 1969), which he devotes to French culture between the wars.

6. See the account given by Raymond Aron in *La sociologie*, and C. Bouglé's preface to *Les sciences sociales en France. Enseignement et recherche* (Paris, 1937), a report gotten up for the 1937 Exposition which provides a valuable reconstruction of the current state of the social sciences. See also Claude Lévi-Strauss, "La sociologie française," in G. Gurvitsch, *La sociologie au XXᵉ siecle*, vol. 2 (Paris, 1947).

7. For his own account, see Preface, *Les sciences sociales en France* and *Les maîtres de la philosophie universitaire en France* (Paris, 1938).

8. See the account of S. Pétrement, *La vie de Simone Weil* (Paris: Fayard, 1973), or of another Ecole normale student at the time, Clémence Ramnoux, who admits in an unpublished interview (1978) that he was turned away from sociology by Bouglé's "mediocrity."

9. See V. Karady, "Naissance de l'ethnologie universitaire," *l'Arc* 48 (1971): 33–40.

10. An expression of M. de Unamuno's which Sartre uses to define the mood of his generation at the time in *Search for a Method*, 19.

11. See V. Descombes, *Le même et l'autre* (Paris: Ed. de Minuit, 1979).

12. C. Malraux, *Voici que vient l'été (Le bruit de nos pas*, vol. 4) (Paris: Grasset, 1973), 59ff.

13. *Revue philosophique de la France et de l'étranger* 1 (1924).

14. C. Malraux, *Voici que vient l'été (Le bruit de nos pas*, vol. 4), 60.

15. Ibid.

16. Jean Wahl, "The Present Situation and the Present Future in French Philosophy," *Philosophic Thought in France and the United States*, ed. Marvin Farber (Albany: State University of New York Press, 1968), 38.

17. *La théorie de l'intuition dans la phénoménologie de Husserl* (Paris: Alcan, 1930).

18. *Etude sur la phénoménologie* (Faculté de lettres de Nancy, 1931).

19. See S. de Beauvoir, *P.L.*, 112.

20. For the role played by German phenomenology in phenomenology's penetration of French thinking, see Jean Hering, "Phenomenology in France," in *Philosophic Thought in France and the United States*, 67ff.

21. J. Wahl, "The Present Situation and the Present Future of French Philosophy," in *Philosophic Thought in France and the United States*, 39.

22. "Sur un certain front unique," *Europe* (Jan. 1933), reprinted in *Pour une nouvelle culture* (Paris: Grasset, 1971), 53–58. For the growing influence in France of phenomenology and philosophies of existence, see R. Diaz's documented history, *Les cadres sociaux de l'ontologie sartrienne* (thesis, Paris: Lib. A. Champion, 1975), especially for Kierkegaard, 244ff, and Heidegger, 254ff, where it is said that *Being and Time* "is the work which is most frequently checked out of the Ecole normale library from 1928 to 1934."

23. "Premières confrontations avec Hegel," *Critique* 195–96 (1963).

24. S. de Beauvoir, *P.L.*, 253: "Meanwhile Sartre was writing a treatise on phenomenological psychology which he entitled *La Psyché*, and of which in the end he published an extract only, calling it . . . *The Emotions: Outline of a Theory.*"

25. In the "insert" for the 1940 edition of *The Psychology of Imagination*, he emphasizes: ". . . I showed that 'the imaging function of consciousness would have its origin in the nihilating power of Mind, which is another word for its total freedom.' " Quoted in Contat and Rybalka, *W.S.*, vol. 1, 73.

26. *The Psychology of Imagination*, trans. Bernard Frechtman (New York: Philosophical Library, 1948), 266.

27. Ibid., 272. In the "insert," he specifies that he wanted to "avoid using the old term 'image,' " which is still so muddied by empiricism and positivism."

28. *The Transcendence of the Ego*, trans. Forrest Williams and Robert Kirkpatrick (New York: Farrar, Straus and Giroux, 1972), 98–99.

29. *War Diaries* 134.

30. J.-P. Sartre, *Imagination*, trans. Forrest Williams (Ann Arbor: Michigan, 1962), 4.

31. In the "insert" for *The Psychology of Imagination*, quoted in Contat and Rybalka, *W.S.*, vol. 1, 73.

32. *The Emotions: Outline of a Theory*, trans. Bernard Frechtman (New York: Philosophical Library, 1948), 9 (hereinafter, *The Emotions*).

33. Ibid., 94.

34. Ibid., 46–47.

35. Jean-Paul Sartre, *Being and Nothingness*, trans. Hazel E. Barnes (New York: Philosophical Library, 1956) (hereinafter referred to as *B.N.*).

36. *The Emotions*, 5–6.

37. *The Transcendence of the Ego*, 105.

38. In *The Adventures of the Dialectic*, trans. Joseph Bien (Evanston: Northwestern, 1973) (hereinafter referred to as *A.D.*). See also below, Part Two, Chapter 9, Section 3.1.

39. In "La liberté cartésienne," the Introduction to a volume of selections from Descartes. Republished in *Situations 1* and in *L.P.E.*, 180–97, as "Cartesian Freedom."

40. The *War Diaries* show that Heidegger's thinking is the starting point and main source of Sartre's basic ontological concepts.

41. Farber, ed., *Philosophic Thought in France and the United States*.

42. Jean Wahl, "La situation présente de la philosophie en France," in *L'activité philosophique contemporaine en France et aux Etats-Unis*, ouvrage coll. dirigée par M. Farber, Vol. 2, *La Philosophie française* (Paris: P.V.F., 1948), 40.

43. "The Battle Over Existentialism," in Maurice Merleau-Ponty, *Sense and Non-Sense*, trans. Hubert L. Dreyfus and Patricia Allen Dreyfus (Evanston: Northwestern, 1964) (hereinafter *S.N.S.*).

44. Jacques Havet, "French Philosophical Tradition Between the Two Wars," in *Philosophic Thought in France and the United States*, 26; J. Beaufret, "A Propos de l'existentialism," (3) *Confluences* 6 (Aug. 1945): 637; R. Campbell, "Existentialism in France since the Liberation," in *Philosophic Thought in France and the United States*, 138ff.

45. C. -E. Magny, "Système de Sartre," *Esprit* (March-April 1945), reprinted in *Littérature et critique* (Paris: Payot, 1971); M. Tournier, *Les Nouvelles littéraires* (Oct. 29, 1964); A. Gorz, *Le Traître* (Paris: Seuil, 1958), 243.

46. J. Beaufret, "A propos de l'existentialism," 642.

# Chapter 4

1. Jean-Paul Sartre, *Nausea*, 133.
2. Contat and Rybalka, *W.S.*, vol. 1, 63.
3. Sartre, *B.N.*, 627.
4. See *War Diaries*, 77ff, and *Sartre*, the film script, 48ff.
5. See the already quoted review by E. Jaloux, for whom this chapter is "the only mistake in the book, for we have heard a hundred times since Octave Mirabeau this hateful satire of the big bourgeoisie." *Les Nouvelles littéraires* (June 18, 1938), quoted in *O.R.*, 1703.
6. Insert for the 1938 edition of *Nausea*, in *W.S.*, I, 52.
7. Jean-Paul Sartre, "Materialism and Revolution," *L.P.E.*, trans. Annette Michelson, 229 (my italics).
8. See P. Bourdieu, "L'invention de la vie d'artiste," *Actes de la recherche en sciences sociales* 2 (1975).
9. Geneviève Idt, "Sartre mythologue," in *Autour de Sartre* (Paris: Gallimard, 1981).
10. Ibid., 136.
11. Concerning this whole paragraph, see P. Bourdieu, "Le marché des biens symboliques," *l'Année sociologique* 22 (1971): 49–126, and "Champ de pouvoir, champ intellectuel et habitus de classes," *Scolies* 1 (1971): 7–26.
12. Quoted in M. Winock, *Histoire politique de la revue Esprit* (Paris: Seuil, 1975), 239.
13. Simone de Beauvoir, *F.C.*, 4.
14. S. de Beauvoir, *F.C.*, 8. In his *Conflits, pouvoirs et société à la liberation* (Paris: U.G.E., 1980), G. Madjarian shows how illusory this national unity was at the time of the Liberation, and how Gaullism served as a bulwark against acute social conflicts which could have led to a real political revolution.
15. Edgar Morin, *Autocritique* (Paris: Seuil, 1975), 76.
16. "In 1952, in *The Communists and Peace*" (note in the text).
17. De Beauvoir, *P.L.*, 6–7.
18. Ibid., 7.

19. Jean-Paul Sartre, "A More Precise Characterization of Existentialism," 155–60 of Contat and Rybalka, *W.S.*, vol. 2.

20. Jean-Paul Sartre, *Situations 2* (Paris: Gallimard, 1948), 26.

21. J.-P. Sartre, "The Humanism of Existentialism," in *The Philosophy of Existentialism*, Wade Baskin, ed. (New York: Philosophical Library, 1965), 51.

22. *Situations 2*, 12.

23. Ibid., 13.

24. Ibid., 15.

25. Ibid., 16

26. A lecture, "On Humanisn," given at the intellectuals' congress, "In Defense of Culture," held in 1935 in Paris; in J. J. Brochier, *Paul Nizan, intellectuel communiste*, vol. 2 (Paris: Maspero, 1979), 36.

27. S. de Beauvoir, *Adieux*, 376–77.

28. Sartre, "The Humanism of Existentialism," 37.

29. Sartre, "Presentation des *Temps Modernes*," 16.

30. Ibid., 22–23.

31. Ibid., 28.

32. Ibid., 27.

33. Contat and Rybalka, *W. S.*, vol. 1, 85.

34. Ibid., 115, and in an interview Sartre gave to Christian Grisoli in *Paru* (1945), which is reprinted in *O.R.*, 1915.

35. See P. Bourdieu, "Genèse et structure du champ religieux," *Revue française de sociologie* 12 (1971): 295–334, to which I am referring in the whole parallel which follows.

36. Ibid., 324.

# Chapter 5

1. There is a revealing confession in the *War Diaries:* "It has taken the war, and also the assistance of several new disciplines (phenomenology, psychoanalysis, sociology)—as well as a reading of *L'Age d'homme*—to prompt me to draw up a full-length portrait of myself."

2. *B.N.*, 574.

3. J.-P. Sartre, *L'idiot de la famille* (Paris: Gallimard, 1971), vol. 2, 2074–2075.

4. J.-P. Sartre, *The Family Idiot*, vol. 1, trans. Carol Cosman (Chicago: Chicago, 1981), 528.

5. *L'idiot de la famille*, vol. 2, 1142, note 1.

6. Ibid., 2106. It is significant that Sartre has recourse here to the same quote he has already used in *The Words* (248) to evoke the sense of a religious calling he had himself felt as a child concerning his own vocation.

7. Conversations with Simone de Beauvoir in 1974; *Adieux*, 214–15.

8. *The Words*, 9.

9. Which he may be considered insofar as he was brought up by a grandfather who taught liberal arts.

10. Geneviève Idt, "Modèles scolaires de l'écriture sartrienne," *Revue des sciences humaines* 174 (1979), 103.

11. *The Words*, 83.

12. Geneviève Idt's epithet in "Modèles scolaires de l'écriture sartrienne."

13. Ibid., 93–100.
14. Ibid., 85–89.
15. See P. Bourdieu, M. de Saint-Martin, "Les catégories de l'entendement professoral," *Actes de la recherche . . .* 3 (1975): 68–93.
16. *The Words*, 63. See the variations on this contrast on 159, 184, 245, and 255.
17. Ibid., 163–64.
18. Ibid., 156.
19. Ibid., 73.
20. Ibid., 76.
21. In "Modèles scolaires dans l'écriture sartrienne," 10off.
22. *The Words*, 112.
23. J. Pacaly, *Sartre au miroir*.
24. "If I relegate impossible Salvation to the prop room, what remains? A whole man, composed of all men and as good as all of them and no better than any" (*The Words*, 255).
25. Ibid., 110.
26. According to Sartre's account in his Preface to Paul Nizan, *Aden, Arabie*, 33.
27. *L'idiot de la famille*, vol. 1, 901.
28. Ibid., 946.
29. Ibid., vol. 2, 1464.
30. Ibid.
31. See J. Pacaly, *"Sartre au miroir,"* 36off.
32. Quoted in *The Words*, 165.
33. See P. Bourdieu, "Champ du pouvoir, champ intellectuel et habitus de classe," *Scolies 1* (1971), 8–9.
34. J.-P. Sartre, "The Itinerary of a Thought," in *Between Existentialism and Marxism*, trans. John Mathews (New York: Pantheon, 1974), 63.
35. In *Un désir d'histoire*, 16.
36. See *War Diaries*, 147ff and a letter to S. de Beauvoir on January 15, 1940: "There will be passages which give the 'cultured reader' a hard time. But there are beginning to be some tasty ones too: one on holes in general and another dealing specifically with the anus and love *à l'italienne*. These will make up for the others" *(Lettres au Castor*, vol. 2, 39).
37. See P. Bourdieu, "Epreuve scolaire et consécration sociale," *Actes de la recherche . . .* 39 (Sept. 1981), 36ff, for an analysis of the effects and functions of elite schools to which the observations which follow refer.
38. Jean-Paul Sartre, *Situations 10* (Paris: Gallimard, 1976),154.
39. In *Adieux*, 244, 243, 245, and passim.
40. *Diaries*, 74. Read this entire autobiographical passage, 72–88.
41. Preface to *Aden, Arabie*, 25.
42. Paul Nizan, *The Watchdogs*, trans. Paul Sittingoff (New York: Monthly Review, 1971).
43. As A. Touraine notes: "The pleasure of being there was a very simple one: the pleasure of having won a certain freedom. And that by the way is how elitist societies function: considerable restrictions are imposed on those who are destined for higher functions, after which they are granted great freedom." *Un désir d'histoire*, 32.
44. "At L'Ecole [normale] one would find manifold copies of the same disheveled portrait of Beethoven, the same plaster mask of Pascal, or the same

'pin-up girls' bursting with evident endowments; and seeing everywhere on the same walls the same Gauguin white horse unslakingly slaking his thirst from the same blue brook, one would have no trouble making out a solid shared good taste" (A. Faugatier, in A. Peyrefitte, *Rue d'Ulm*, 188ff). ". . . He no sooner opened the door to his pad than he found with delight 'an almost exact similarity of tastes, a similar way of approaching the twists and turns of language, and a peculiarly collegiate system of values which—like a filigrane—runs through and makes itself felt in every conversation" (M.-F. Guyard, quoting J. Gracq, in A. Peyrefitte, *Rue d'Ulm*, 190).

45. Preface to *Aden, Arabie*, 24.
46. See *Sartre*, film text, 33, and *Adieux*, 256.
47. Preface to *Aden, Arabie*, 24.
48. A model version of such retrospective analyses is found in Sartre's 1975 interview with M. Contat in J.-P. Sartre, *Life/Situations*, trans. Paul Auster and Lydia Davis (New York: Pantheon, 1977), 48.
49. Preface to *Aden, Arabie*, 25.
50. Interview with M. Contat, in *Life/Situations*, 35–36.

# Chapter 6

1. C. Grisoli, "Entretien avec Jean-Paul Sartre," *Paru* 13 (1945): 10, reprinted in *O.R.*, 1917.
2. G. Hanoteau, *L'âge d'or de Saint-Germain-des-Prés* (Paris: Denoël, 1965), 48.
3. The production of *The Flies* is the occasion of new friendships—with Leiris, Camus—which draw Sartre into a circle which includes Picasso, Bataille, and Queneau, and which is very different from the young, unknown "family" he has previously belonged to. See S. de Beauvoir, *P.L.*, 442ff.
4. Grisoli, "Entretien avec Jean-Paul Sartre," *Paru* 13 (1945): 5, and Sartre, *O.R.*, 1913.
5. C.-E. Magny, "Système de Sartre," *Esprit* (March-April 1945), reprinted in *Litterature et critique* (Paris: Payot, 1971).
6. S. de Beauvoir, *F.C.*, 24.
7. See concerning the movements and groupings of Parisian intelligentsia during the War, R. H. Lottman, *La rive gauche* (Paris: Seuil, 1981).
8. Michel-Antoine Burnier, *Choice of Action*, trans. Bernard Murchland (New York: Vintage, 1969), ixff.

# Chapter 7

1. *Terre des hommes* disappears in 1946, *Messages* in 1945, *Fontaine* and *Confluences* in 1947, *l'Arche* in 1948, *la Nef* in 1951.
2. *Search for a Method*, 19.
3. *Deucalion* 1 (1946) has in addition to J. Wahl's article, "Essai sur le néant d'un problème," 41–72, Alphonse de Waelhens's "Heidegger et Sartre," 13–39.
4. "At seven I met Queneau and his wife at the Pont-Royal. Georges Blin was there and took me upon the subject of *Sexualité et existentialisme*. He gave

me the best pages of a review by Wahl that's to appear shortly. Wahl's critical approach to *Being and Nothingness* is analytical in a surprising way: 'The first paragraph on page 62 is good, but the tenth line is weak'—that sort of thing. I drank two gin fizzes and was very animated. Our eighth issue is out, and people seem to think it's quite brilliant." *F.C.*, 88.

5. See, concerning the C.C.I.F., Jean Tavarès, "La 'synthèse' chrétienne, dépassement envers l' 'au-delà,' " *Actes de la recherche* . . . 34 (1980): 45–65, and "Le Centre catholique des intellectuels français," *Actes de la recherche* 38.

6. Maurice Merleau-Ponty, *The Adventures of the Dialectic*, trans. Joseph Bien (Evanston: Northwestern, 1974), 3 (hereinafter *A.D.*).

7. Remembering that the Nuremberg Trials began in 1945 is essential for example to explaining the attention focused on the Jewish problem that we see concurrently in a special issue of *Esprit* ["Les Juifs parlent aux Nations" (Sept. 1945)], in Sartre's "Portrait de l'antisémite" (Dec. 1945; the first part of *Reflections on the Jewish Question*), and in the fact that in 1945 the biographical document, "Vie," which *Les Temps Modernes* publishes in each of its early issues, is devoted two times out of three to the life of a Jew.

8. We find in *Esprit* for example Ch. Maignial's "Communistes et chrétiens" ( Feb. 1946), an investigation, "Le communisme devant nous" (April 1946), a special issue, "Marxisme ouvert contre marxisme scholastique" (Jan. 1948), articles in 1949 on the crisis of peoples' democracies, and in 1950, on Yugoslavia. The same topic appears in *Critique* in the neutralized form of theoretical discourse. In February 1947, this review publishes a discussion of Marxism; it also reviews essays on the working class [for example, Duveau's "La vie ouvrière" ( Feb. 1947)] on industrialization in the U.S.S.R. (Jan. 1948), and on Marx (Oct. 1948).

9. *Les Temps Modernes* devotes a special issue (Aug.-Sept. 1946) to the United States and publishes S. de Beauvoir's *L'Amérique au jour le jour* serially; and in 1950 publishes a long essay by Guérin on American unions and articles on the Atlantic Pact and the Korean War. *Esprit* also talks about "L'homme américain" (Nov. 1946), the Marshall Plan ( Feb. 1948), and "L'Américain de la guerre froide" (June 1949). *Critique* devotes articles to the American novel (April-May 1947), to the fortunes of Marx and Freud in the United States (June-July 1947), to the American economy (April 1948), and to the Marshall Plan (July 1948). *La Nouvelle Critique*'s articles on America are only marginal and strictly polemical. But this review generally neglects international reality: its main function is the internal one of attacking the French intellectual world in the name of the Party.

10. *Esprit* publishes a series of articles on colonialism ["Prévenons la guerre d'Afrique du Nord" (April and July 1947); "Humanisme contre guerres coloniales" (April 1950)] and an inquest, "Y a-t-il une justice en France?" (Aug. 1947). *Critique* echoes these in the January-February 1949 issue with an article by Eric Weil on the press, and with an "overview" of the colonial question in April 1949. Then comes *Les Temps Modernes* with two briefs on the press (April 1952) and on colonialism (June 1952).

11. See Pierre Bourdieu, *Distinction, a Social Critique of the Judgment of Taste*, trans. Richard Nice (Cambridge, Mass.: Harvard, 1984), above all in Chapter 2, Chapter 3, and Conclusion; and *Le Sens pratique* (Paris: Editions de Minuit, 1980), above all in Chapter 3 of Book One.

12. So baptized in L. Loubet del Bayle, *Les "non-conformistes" des années 30* (Paris: Seuil, 1969), the best-documented study of these groups.

13. Concerning the social characteristics and the ethos of *Esprit*'s personalists, see P. Bourdieu, "Les aventures d'une avant-garde," *Actes de la recherche* . . . 2/3 (June 1976): 32–38.

14. "Réflexions sur le personnalisme," *Synthèses* 4 (1947): 25, quoted by Loubet del Bayle, *Les "non-conformistes" des années 30*, 22.

15. See P. Bourdieu, *Distinction*, 319ff.

16. In this experimental "school for powerholders," which was short-lived but important as a prototype for the Ecole nationale d'administration and other laboratory schools for reproducing elites which were started after the War, Mounier and Fraisse are among the most influential ideologues, and Domenach will be a student there. See M. Winock, *Histoire politique de la revue "Esprit"* (Paris: Seuil, 1975), and P. Bourdieu, "Les aventures d'une avant-garde," *Actes de la recherche* 2/3 (June 1946): 132–38.

17. He is not yet eighteen when he is presented in Paris through a letter Rilke writes to Gide.

18. This association, which also calls itself the "Union de lutte des intellectuels révolutionnaires," and gathers a handful of intellectuals around Breton and Bataille (in Bataille's circle, Klossowski, Ambrosino, and Waldberg also join), begins with a manifesto in October 1935, and dies out less than a year later without its backers' agreement that uncompromising revolution must be its rallying cry, having sufficed to overcome their disagreements, which are more probably explained by their objective rivalries in the intellectual field than by ideological disagreements.

19. In 1920, with the poet Carl Einstein, the ethnologist G.-H. Rivière, and Griaule and Leiris.

20. Four issues come out beween June 1936 and June 1939. Ambrosino and Klossowski are coeditors with Bataille. The review supports the activities of a "secret society" of the same name which, as Bataille himself puts it, "intends to turn its back on politics and henceforth pursue only a religious (but anti-Christian and essentially Nietzschean) goal." Bataille, "Notice autobiographique," *Œuvres complètes* 7 (1976), 461, quoted in D. Hollier, *Le collège de sociologie* (Paris: Gallimard, 1979), 584.

21. Begun in 1937, it ceases its activities in July 1939. Among the "administrators," other than Bataille, who is largely responsible for its operation, there is Leiris, who is in fact rarely there. Although the Collège announces that it is more ethical than scientific, and thinks of sociology as something more than an intellectual activity (as "some sort of vertiginous contagion," "an epidemic effervescence," of a "necessarily contagious and *activist* nature," or as Caillois puts it, "virulent"; quoted in Hollier, *Le collège*, 385 and 33ff), it feeds its disconcerting beliefs on suggestions drawn from historical and social sciences.

22. A "surrealizing" review of the thirties edited by A. Skira and E. Tériade, which along with its interest in the arts includes in its program ethnography, mythology, and psychoanalysis, and which devotes its first special issue, to which M. Griaule contributes, to ethnography.

23. See D. Hollier, *Le collège*, 188ff.

24. As P. Klossowski tells it, quoted in D. Hollier, *Le collège*, 586.

25. See D. Hollier, *Le collège*, 107 and 154.

26. Concerning Klossowski's pre-War activities, see D. Hollier, *Le collège*, 249ff and 367.

27. See for example the article of July 1946, "Le terrorisme, methode de salut publique," quoted by Loubet del Bayle in *Les "nonconformistes" des annees 30*, 75.

28. See Piel's autobiographical work, *La rencontre avec la différence* (Paris: Fayard, 1982). A further confirmation of the deep ties of experience and habitus which bind this intellectual family together is found in the web of matrimonial relationships among its members. Jean Piel was Bataille's brother-in-law (and afterward, Jacques Lacan's, thanks to the latter's marriage to Sylvia Bataille: yet another example of the family resemblances of dispositions and tastes which set the stage for their encounters and alliances. Another sister of Madame Piel's married the painter Andrè Masson).

29. Bataille, Klossowski, and Caillois publish essays and articles in *Recherches philosophiques*. Wahl and Kojève are part of the narrow public which frequents the Collège, and Kojève gives one of its rare lectures not given by a member.

30. This is where Kojève teaches from 1933 on as Koyrè's substitute in the department of religious sciences. This is where Eric Weil will offer his courses after the War: it is only in 1955, after years as the recognized French expert on Hegelian philosophy, that Weil earns a post at a provincial university (Lille) with his doctoral thesis, *Logique et philosophie*.

31. Concerning the relationship between extent of institutionalization and cultural innovation, and the E.P.H.E.'s role in the French academic field, see V. Karady's observations about Mauss, "Naissance de l'ethnologie universitaire," *l'Arc* 48 (1972): 33–40.

32. An interview of Caillois which is quoted in D. Hollier, *Le collège*, 165.

33. *Ibid.*, 187.

34. See N. Elias, *La civilisation des moeurs* (Paris: Calmann-Levy, 1973). Also see, in reference to this difference in relationship to culture, P. Bourdieu, *Distinction*, especially 73ff.

35. We can get some idea of the role of cultural *aggiornamento* that *Critique* plays from some of the authors it introduces during the period under consideration: Margaret Mead ( Feb. 1946), Piaget (introduced by L. Goldmann, June-July 1947), Malinowski (April 1948), Eliade (April 1948), Dumézil (May 1948), Keynes (Dec. 1948), Wiener (Oct. 1950), Radcliffe-Brown and Evans-Pritchard (Aug.-Sept. 1951), Saussure and Troubetskoy (introduced by S. Ullmann, Nov. 1951).

36. In the words Jean Wahl uses in his already quoted letter to the Collège de sociologie.

37. Concerning this relationship between the logic of the machine and the dispositions of "machine politicians," see P. Bourdieu, "Le mort saisit le vif," *Actes de la recherche . . .* 32–33 (April-June, 1980): 11.

38. The review is enlisted in the cultural command economy inaugurated by the Eleventh Congress of the F.C.P. (June 1947); it is requested and supported by Laurent Casanova, the Political Bureau member who at the time has the greatest Party authority in cultural affairs.

39. E. Morin, *Autocritique*, Politics Series (Paris: Seuil, 1975), 92. Concerning party culture, see also Chapters 4, 5, and 6.

40. See M. Pollak, "La planification des sciences sociales," *Actes de la recherche . . .* 2/3 (1976): 105–21.

# Chapter 8

1. Thus an article Pierre Uri writes on the Marshall Plan is greeted in an editorial [34 (July 1948)] as an authentic "committed" essay on economics. And in speaking of "microscopic man," the physicist Pierre Auger suggests that confirmation of human freedom may be found in scientific discoveries. See his "Chronique scientifique" in 49 (Nov. 1949), 51 (Jan. 1950), and 54 (April 1950). Simone de Beauvoir, in her November 1949 review of *The Elementary Structures of Kinship*, sees in it a way of thinking which is not antagonistic to the philosophy of consciousness, but on the contrary close to it.

2. On the basis of oral accounts (Pouillon, Lefort) and written ones. (See above all S. de Beauvoir, *F.C.*, 147, 196, and 275.)

3. Both quantitative importance (the number and length of their contributions) and qualitative importance, as indicated by a place of honor in the abstracts, or by a particularly solemn or laudatory introduction.

4. At least seven.

5. S. de Beauvoir, *F.C.*, 22.

6. After receiving his *licence de lettres* from the Sorbonne, he goes to Madagascar in 1907, works at many jobs there, including prospecting for gold, learns Malgache, and becomes interested in the country's poetry. Back in France, he fights in World War I and writes his first story, *Le guerrier appliqué*. He becomes the secretary of the *N.R.F.* only in 1920, and manager in 1925.

7. In 1942. This is the clandestine review of the Comité national des écrivains (C.N.E.).

8. See M. Winock, *Histoire politique de la revue* Esprit, 222.

9. See concerning this matter S. de Beauvoir's account: "Aron, who had acquired much experience with *La France libre*, also gave us technical advice; he followed the progress of *Les Temps Modernes* very closely. . . ." S. de Beauvoir, *F.C.*, 55.

10. See S. de Beauvoir, *P.L.*, 112.

11. During an interview Aron granted the author. And confirmation for Aron's claim is indeed found in Sartre's *War Diaries*. In reconstructing his conversion to "historicity," Sartre writes: "Furthermore, *History* was present all around me. First, philosophically: Aron had just written his *Introduction à la philosophie de l'histoire*, and I was reading him. Second, it surrounded and gripped me like all my contemporaries, making me feel its presence." J.-P. Sartre, *War Diaries*, 185.

12. The Centre d'études sociologiques, a branch of the Centre national de la recherche scientifique, is established in 1946. Directed by J. Stoetzel, it trains the first post-War generation of sociologists (Touraine, Morin . . .). In 1947, on the initiative above all of Febvre and Braudel, proponents of the new social history (the *Annales* school), the sixth Section of the Ecole pratique des hautes études—which toward the middle of the fifties will become one of the main centers of sociological research—is established. It is only in 1958, on the initiative of Aron, who has just been named to the chair of sociology at the Sorbonne, that a degree in sociology is established. (Up until then it is tied to the liberal arts degree.) And it is only toward this time that the teaching of sociology, strengthened by a social demand for it which is increasing still more under the Fifth Republic, frees itself from the yoke of philosophy, which

has been the tutelary discipline of French academic sociology since its birth with Durkheim. See M. Pollak, "La planification des sciences sociales," *Actes de la recherche* 2/3 (1976): 105–21.

13. The first favorable review of *She Came to Stay* is by Marcel Arland in *Comoedia*. Among others, Thierry Maulnier and Merleau-Ponty ["Le roman et la métaphysique," *Cahiers du Sud* 270 (Mar. 1945), translated and reprinted as "Metaphysics and the Novel" in *Sense and Non-Sense*] will also discuss it. Public figures such as G. Marcel, Cocteau, Mauriac, and R. Fernandez flatter the author with their praise. The book is one of the leading candidates for the Prix Goncourt and the Prix Renaudot.

14. Jean Wahl, in "The Present Situation of French Philosophy," in M. Farber, ed., *Philosophic Thought in France and the United States*, speaks of Merleau-Ponty as the most interesting philosopher of his generation and gives him more space than Sartre.

15. These are connections Merleau-Ponty probably made at the Ecole normale. He had the chance as a student (1926–30), for example, to know Uri and Etiemble (who were graduated in 1929), as well as Beaufret (who was admitted in 1928). And as *"caïman"* from 1935 to 1939, Tran Duc Thao and Vuillemin.

16. Literature has the big place, the theater a small place, poetry practically no place at all. The philosophy of "events" occupies the place of honor. Science is considered suspect or is simply ignored. Literary criticism and art criticism are carefully cultivated. The presence of journalism is overwhelming.

17. From 1945 to 1953, according to Contat and Rybalka (*W.S.*), Sartre writes at least sixteen prefaces. Some become famous, such as "Black Orpheus" (1948), his preface to an anthology of Senghor's poems; those he writes for N. Sarraute's *Portrait of a Man Unknown* (1948), for R. Leibowitz's *L'artiste et sa conscience* (1950), for R. Stéphane's *Portrait de l'aventurier*, and for Dalmas's book on Yugoslav communism; or finally, such as *Saint Genet*, which was originally conceived as a preface to Genet's *Œuvres complètes* (1952).

18. Sartre encouraged both and published both in *Les Temps Modernes* when they were still unknown. See S. de Beauvoir, *F.C.,* 27ff.

19. J.-P. Sartre, *St. Genet*, trans. Bernard Frechtman (New York: George Braziller, 1963), 584.

20. J.-P. Sartre, "Nathalie Sarraute," trans. Marie Jolas, 196–202 of *Situations*, trans. Benita Eisler (New York: George Braziller, 1965).

21. S. de Beauvoir, *F.C.,* 55.

22. *Ibid.,* 81 and 86.

23. *Les Temps Modernes* 3 (1945).

24. "Miroirs de Saint-Just," *Les Temps Modernes* 6 (1946).

25. François Furet, in *Penser la Révolution française* (Paris: Gallimard, 1978), deplores the fact that for historians the Revolution is always a stake loaded with symbolic interests. And in France, referring to the French Revolution does continue to be a way of taking a stand against current adversaries in present struggles by giving a particular interpretation of past roles played by different social groups. Thus at the Liberation, every Resistance group laid claim to the Revolution. (Cf. G. Madjarian, *Conflits, pouvoirs et société à la Liberation (Paris: U.G.E., 1980), 75ff.*

26. S. de Bouvoir, *F.C.,* 55.

27. "La rhétorique était une société secrète," *Les Temps Modernes* 6 (1946).

28. S. de Beauvoir, *F.C.,* 82.

29. "Les désillusions de la liberté," *Les Temps Modernes* 1 (1945): 75–106; "Après l'évenement, avant l'histoire," *ibid.*, 153–62; and "La chance du socialisme," *Les Temps Modernes* 2 (1945): 227–47.

30. Criticized by Sartre in "Entretiens sur la politique" [36 (Sept. 1948)], Aron replies with a letter [3 (Nov. 1948)] which challenges the authenticity of the statements and ideas attributed to him. But as Aron assured me (in the interview referred to above), their disagreements had already broken out by 1947, his sympathy going to the Rassemblement du peuple français at the time Sartre is beginning to be openly anti-Gaullist (in 1947 in the radio broadcasts, "La tribune des *Temps modernes*"). See *F.C.*, 147; Contat and Rybalka, *W.S.*, 177–80; and *Pour et contre l'existentialisme* (Paris: Atlas, 1948).

31. Concerning all these stands, see "Les désillusions de la liberté," *Les Temps Modernes* 6 (1946).

32. See "Les chances du socialisme," *Les Temps Modernes* 2 (1945).

33. See *The Opiate of the Intellectuals*, trans. Terence Kilmartin (New York: W. W. Norton, 1962), *Marxismes imaginaires* (Paris: Gallimard, 1970), and *History and the Dialectic of Violence*, trans. Barry Cooper (New York: Harper and Row, 1975), a commentary on the *Critique of Dialectical Reason*. In his introduction to *Marxismes imaginaires*, Aron recognizes the tyrannical effect his intellectual adversaries have had on his works: "Perhaps it would have been better to write the book about Marxism I had been thinking about writing for forty years instead of scattering sections of it around in critical essays. But I haven't the slightest doubt that it was my philosophical interests which goaded me into carrying on controversies with various contemporary and rival sects of Parisian leftists" (9).

34. 8, 1456–1468.

35. *Les Temps Modernes* 5 (1946): 783–812 and 6 (1946): 1045–1049.

36. *Les Temps Modernes* 5 (1946): 812.

37. *Les Temps Modernes* 6 (1946): 1055.

38. *Ibid.*, 1056.

39. "D'enfer à ce sans nul échange," *Les Temps Modernes* 29 (1948): 1372–1380.

40. "Martinique, Guadeloupe, Haïti," *Les Temps Modernes* 52 (1950): 1345–1368, and "L'ethnographe devant le colonialisme," *Les Temps Modernes* 58 (1950): 357–74.

41. S. de Beauvoir, *F.C.*, 55.

# Chapter 9

1. *Les Temps Modernes* 21 (1947): 1717–1720.

2. Maurice Merleau-Ponty, *Humanism and Terror*, trans. John O'Neill (Boston: Beacon, 1969) (hereinafter *H.T.*).

3. This is the text, "Indirect Language and the *Voices of Silence*," which first appeared in *Les Temps Modernes* 80 (1952): 2113–2144 and 81 (1952): 70–94, and was reprinted in *Signs* and (in a revised version) as a chapter in the posthumous *The Prose of the World*, ed. Claude Lefort, trans. John O'Neill (Evanston: Northwestern, 1973).

4. This sexual division of labor is very evident in the realm of politics, which Simone de Beauvoir leaves chiefly to Sartre, according to the traditional

view that politics is man's business. "We always discussed his attitudes together, and sometimes I influenced him. But it was through him that these problems, in all their urgency and all their subtlety, presented themselves to me. *In this realm, I must talk about him in order to talk about us*" (*F.C.*, 12, my italics). "Practically speaking, I had little to do with it; I had enrolled in the C.N.E. on principle, but I never so much as showed my face at any of their meetings; *I thought that Sartre's presence there made mine superfluous*" (ibid., 28, my italics).

5. "I wanted very much to see *Les Bouches inutiles* put on. At the preview of *Huis clos* I had been stirred by the thunder of the applause; it was much more immediate, more intoxicating than the scattered echoes wakened by a book" (ibid., 56).

6. See S. de Beauvoir, *P.L.*, 433ff and *F.C.*, 75. Analogous considerations could even be made in the case of the "vocation" for the theater and essays evident in the post-War Camus, who was also probably drawn by Sartre's example to try his own skills in these fields.

7. S. de Beauvoir, *F.C.*, 103.

8. *Les Temps Modernes* 49 (1949): 943–49. The circumstances which interest her in Lévi-Strauss's book give a good indication of the acquaintances and contacts, characteristic of Parisian intellectuals, which contribute to the rapid dissemination of Left Bank intellectual fashions: "Leiris told me that Lévi-Strauss was criticizing me for certain inaccuracies in the sections on primitive societies. He was just finishing his thesis on *Les Structures de la parenté*, and I asked him to let me read it. I went over to his place several mornings in succession; I sat down at a table and read a typescript of his book . . ." *F.C.*, 177.

9. *Les Temps Modernes* 49 (1949): 949.

10. Merleau-Ponty, "The Battle over Existentialism," *S.N.S.*, 71–82. S. de Beauvoir, "*La phénoménologie de la perception* de Maurice Merleau-Ponty," *Les Temps Modernes* 2 (1945): 363–67.

11. See the chapter, "Sartre and Ultra-Bolshevism," in *The Adventures of the Dialectic*, and S. de Beauvoir, "Merleau-Ponty et le pseudo-sartrisme," *Les Temps Modernes* 114–115 (1955), reprinted in *Privilèges* (Paris: Gallimard, 1955).

12. Volume 2 of the cycle, *Troubled Sleep*, is not the projected conclusion (what happens to the main characters during the Resistance), which is put off to a (never completed) fourth volume, of which Sartre published only one part, "Drôle d'amitié," *Les Temps Modernes* 49 and 50 (1949). In his *Œuvres romanesques*, "Drôle d'amitié" is reprinted *in extenso* (1461–1543), whereas the other excerpts from—and projects for—Volume 4 are published in the appendix, as Sartre wished, and under the title he himself often gave, "La dernière chance." As for his *Ethics*, we know that toward 1949–50 Sartre gave the whole thing up after having written around two thousand pages, three fragments of which were published during his lifetime: "Le noir et le blanc aux Etats-Unis," *Combat* (June 16, 1949); "Sur la bêtise," *le Magazine littéraire*, nos. 103–104 (1975): 28–34; and the text presented by *Obliques*, 18–19 (1979): 249–62. The book *Cahiers pour une morale* (Paris: Gallimard, 1983) was drawn from that posthumous work.

13. As is recognized by Michel Contat, who imputes the failure of Sartre's projects during that period to this transformation.

14. "Matérialisme et Révolution," *Les Temps Modernes* 9 (1946): 1563.

15. Jean-Paul Sartre, *What Is Literature?* trans. Bernard Frechtman (New York: Harper and Row, 1965), 54–55 (hereinafter *W.L.*).

16. Ibid., 285.

17. Ibid., 19.

18. Ibid., 21.

19. Denis de Rougemont, *Politique de la personne* (Paris: Je sers, 1946), new edition, 149. See Loubet del Bayle, *Les "non-conformistes" des années 30*, 269–326.

20. G. Izard, *Esprit* 1 (1932): 140.

21. See the writings collected in *Oppression et liberté* (Paris: Gallimard, 1955).

22. See my articles: "Esperienza de fabbrica, teoria della società e ideologia in Simone Weil," *aut aut*, 144 (1974): 79–101; "Lezioni di Simone Weil," *il Progetto* 19 (1984).

23. Concerning the consequences of the inertia of the philosophical habitus, see P. Bourdieu, "Le mort saisit le vif," *Acts de la recherche* 32–33 (April-June 1980): 3–14.

24. See for example "For the Sake of Truth," *S.N.S.*, 153–71.

25. *H.T.*

26. In "Merleau-Ponty" [*Les Temps Modernes* 184–85 (1961): 304–76, reprinted in *Situations*], Sartre says that not only the progressive Americans at the *Partisan Review* but even the French intellectuals closest to the existentialists, such as Camus, were able to interpret *Humanism and Terror* as an unconditional justification of Stalinist terror.

27. See "Marxisme et philosophie," *Revue internationale* 6 (1946): 518–26, reprinted as "Marxism and Philosophy" in *S.N.S.*, 125–36.

28. See Merleau-Ponty, "La querelle d'existentialisme," *Les Temps Modernes* 2 (1945), reprinted as "The Battle over Existentialism" in *S.N.S.*, 78ff.

29. Ibid., 81–82.

30. "For the Sake of Truth," *S.N.S.*, 170.

31. "Autour du marxisme," *Fontaine* 48–49 (1946): 309–31; reprinted as "Concerning Marxism" in *S.N.S.*, 99–124.

32. See for example "La métaphysique dans l'homme," *Revue de métaphysique et de morale* (July 1947): 290–307, reprinted as "The Metaphysical in Man" in *S.N.S.*, 83–98.

33. According to Lévi-Strauss, who was tied to Merleau-Ponty by friendship but also by intellectual esteem. (*Savage Thought* is dedicated "to the memory of Maurice Merleau-Ponty," and the latter, in *Signs*, had devoted an important essay, "From Mauss to Lévi-Strauss," to the former.) See C. Lévi-Strauss, "De quelques rencontres," *l'Arc* 46 (1971): 80–87.

34. See "The Metaphysical in Man," *S.N.S.*, 83–98.

35. See "Le roman et la métaphysique," *Cahiers du Sud* 270 (1945); "Le doute de Cézanne," *Fontaine* 47 (1945); and "Le cinéma et la nouvelle psychologie," *Les Temps Modernes* 26 (1947), all reprinted in *S.N.S.* as "Metaphysics and the Novel," "Cézanne's Doubt," and "The Film and the New Psychology."

36. "The resolution to ignore the meaning which men have themselves given to their action and to keep all historical efficacy reserved for the concatenation of facts—in short, to idolize objectivity—contains, according to a profound remark of Trotsky, the boldest sort of judgment when it has to do with a revolution, since it imposes a priori on the man of action, who believes in a logic of history and a truth of his action, the categories of the 'objective' historian who has no such belief." *S.N.S.*, 91.

37. M. Merleau-Ponty, *H.T.*, 148.

38. Ibid., 153.

39. Yvon Belaval, in *Les philosophes et leur langage* (Paris: Gallimard, 1952), uses Merleau-Ponty's *Phenomenology of Perception* to "show to what degree of lyricism phenomenological description can lead."

40. *Les Temps Modernes* 184–85 (1961): 304–76; reprinted in *Situations,* 227–326.

41. The Rassemblement démocratique révolutionnaire was founded at the beginning of 1948 by journalists and militants from the non-Communist left: G. Altman, J. Rous, G. Rosenthal and D. Rousset, a former member of the Internationalist Communist Party, a Trotskyite group. Sartre was a member of the organizing committee and played an important role in it: the R.D.R. was called "David Rousset's and Sartre's movement." "Entretiens sur la politique," a conversation Sartre had with Rousset and Rosenthal which was published in *Les Temps Modernes* [36 (1948): 385–428], is the movement's manifesto. Sartre resigned with a bang in October 1949, having finally understood the pro-American and anti-Communist orientation the majority of the governing board wanted to give to an undertaking he had seen as an effort to produce a movement for revolution and democracy. For further information, see M. A. Burnier, *Choice of Action,* 54–64.

42. "Faux savants ou faux lièvres?" reprinted in *Situations 6.*

43. Le Sagittaire (Paris, 1950), 9–29; reprinted in *Situations 6.*

44. Certainly *Saint Genet* is one of Sartre's main "existential psychoanalyses." But he himself recognized, in a letter he wrote to Cocteau (Aug. 15, 1952), that Cocteau was right in saying that his dominant interest in writing the book—and even that enormous preface—is "his relationship with circumstances, with Marxism, and with the C.P." [*Le Nouvel Observateur* (Sept. 30/Oct. 6, 1983): 65].

45. *Saint Genet,* note, 186.

46. "La guerre a eu lieu," *Les Temps Modernes* 1 (1945): 64; 151 of "The War Has Taken Place," the translation of this article which is reprinted in *S.N.S.,* 139–52.

47. Unpublished notes of Sartre which Simone de Beauvoir reports in *F.C.,* 254.

48. J.-P. Sartre, "Merleau-Ponty," *Les Temps Modernes* 184–85 (1961): 282.

49. Ibid., 290.

50. Ibid., 300.

51. Ibid., 299–300.

52. Ibid., 293.

53. M. Merleau-Ponty, *H.T.,* 148.

54. J.-P. Sartre, *The Communists and Peace,* trans. Martha H. Fletcher (New York: George Braziller, 1968), 68.

55. See Merleau-Ponty, *A.D.,* Chapter 5.

56. In contrast to the position he defended in *Humanism and Terror, A.D.* is not only a criticism of this dogmatic Marxism, and of Sartre for adopting it, but a self-criticism by the author, who right after the War had supported these same myths. We shall come back to this when we look at *A.D.* in relation to the development of Merleau-Ponty's thinking. But we must make it clear now that even in *A.D.,* the abstract and mythical concept of the proletariat as "the regulator of history" is not completely abandoned. It reappears in Merleau-Ponty's distinction between Stalinism and Leninism. Leninism, ac-

cording to Merleau-Ponty, retains the notion of "a counterweight [to] historical delirium: the proletariat's agreement" (*A.D.*, 128) and "a practical [truth] criterion: whatever can be explained to and be accepted by the proletariat . . . is proletarian" (ibid.), whatever "[diminishes the proletariat's] consciousness or its power" is not proletarian (*A.D.*, 131). Stalinism simply did away with the historical verification which Merleau-Ponty considers "the essence of Marxism, the idea of a truth that, in order to be completely true, must be *evolved*, not only in the solitary thoughts of the philosopher who ripened it and who has understood everything, but also in the relationship between the leader who thinks and explains it and the proletariat which lives and adopts it" (*A.D.*, 131).

57. See the rereading of Sartre's philosophical trajectory Merleau-Ponty suggests in *A.D.*, 137ff and 188ff.

58. See C. Lefort, "Le marxisme et Sartre," *Les Temps Modernes* 89 (April 1953): 1541–1570, and J.-P. Sartre, "Réponse à Claude Lefort," ibid., 1571–1629. In his reply, Sartre attacks Lefort personally. By threatening to resign, Merleau-Ponty persuades him to eliminate a "needlessly violent" paragraph. Lefort responds in turn in a letter dated June 1953 [*Les Temps Modernes* 104 (July 1954): 157–84].

59. See the conclusion of *The Words* and the numerous self-criticisms of his late years, for example, the interview published in *l'Idiot internationale* (Sept. 1970) and reprinted in *Du rôle de l'intellectuel dans le mouvement révolutionnaire selon Jean-Paul Sartre, Bernard Pingaud, Dionys Mascoló* (Paris: Losfeld, 1971).

60. See C. Lefort, "Preface," in his introduction to M. Merleau-Ponty, *The Prose of the World*. Lefort's reconstruction provides many clarifications of Merleau-Ponty's philosophical project at this stage.

61. See the comments of B. Pingaud, "Merleau-Ponty, Sartre et la littérature," *l'Arc* 46 (1971): 80–87.

62. There is a key sentence in the Preface to *Signs* which shows in a striking way that *The Visible and the Invisible* is (at least at its inception) a counterpoint to *Being and Nothingness*: "It would be better to speak of 'the visible and the invisible,' pointing out that they are not contradictory, than to speak of 'being and nothingness'" (21).

63. Published as "Un inédit de Merleau-Ponty" in the *Revue de métaphysique et de morale* 4 (1962), and as "An Unpublished Text by Maurice Merleau-Ponty: A Prospectus of His Work," trans. Arleen B. Dallery, in *The Primacy of Perception*, ed. James M. Edie (Evanston: Northwestern, 1964).

64. Quoted by C. Lefort, Preface, *Signs*, xii.

65. Ibid., xiii.

66. In 1951, he devotes his Sorbonne course to "Phenomenology and the Human Sciences" and publishes an essay entitled "The Philosopher and Sociology" in the *Cahiers internationaux de sociologie* [10 (1951): 50–69]. We can trace an analogous philosophical development in the trajectory of Goldmann, who publishes *Philosophy and the Human Sciences* in 1952. The success this book has is enough to show that it expresses a widespread concern. We could also cite, as a sign of the increasing importance of the human sciences, the positive assessment of them set forth from 1953 on in the "Panorama de l'ethnologie" that Lévi-Strauss publishes in *Diogène*.

67. Concerning this friendship, see Lévi-Strauss's account in "De quelques rencontres," *l'Arc* 46 (1971): 80–87.

68. For a critique of structuralist objectivism, see P. Bourdieu, *Le sens pratique*, Chapter 1.

69. M. Merleau-Ponty, *The Prose of the World*, 121, and "Indirect Language and the *Voices of Silence*," *Les Temps Modernes* 80: 2116, reprinted in *Signs*, 41–42.

70. Of course he recognizes that "the man who decides to write takes an attitude in respect to the past which is his alone" (*Signs*, 79); that "[analytic] thought interrupts the perceptual transition from one moment to another, and then seeks in the mind the guarantee of a unity which is already there when we perceive. Analytic thought also interrupts the unity of culture and then tries to reconstitute it from the outside." ["Le langage indirect . . ." *Les Temps Modernes* 81 (July 1952): 75, and *Signs*, 69.] But he underestimates the conditions and consequences of this break. For him, the man who writes "destroys, if you wish, ordinary language, but by realizing it." [*Les Temps Modernes* 80 (June 1952): 2139, and *Signs*, 60.]

71. *Les Temps Modernes* 80 (June 1952): 2139, and *Signs*, 60.

72. Ibid.

73. *Les Temps Modernes* 80 (June 1952): 2137, and *Signs*, 59.

74. M. Merleau-Ponty, *A.D.*, 188.

75. Ibid., 3.

76. Rajk, the former Hungarian prime minister, is accused in 1948 of having plotted, at the instigation of Tito, to overthrow the Communist regime in his country. He is condemned to death. His case arouses strong feelings in France, where a tardy polemic over the Moscow Trials has just died down. (This polemic began with the publication of Koestler's *Darkness at Noon* in 1945. It is of particular concern to Merleau-Ponty, who makes it the starting point of *Humanism and Terror*.) As it did in the purge trials of 1937–1938, what disconcerts many intellectuals in the Rajk Trial and shakes their Communist sympathizing is the totalitarian logic—according to which to oppose is to betray—which brings the accused to accept the accusations and verdicts of which they are the victims.

77. "Lecture de Montaigne," *Les Temps Modernes* 27 (1947); reprinted as "Reading Montaigne" in *Signs*. Subsequent quotations refer to *Signs*.

78. "Communisme et anticommunisme," *Les Temps Modernes* 34 (1948); reprinted in *Signs* as "Paranoid Politics."

79. *Les Temps Modernes* 48 (1949), and *Signs*.

80. *Les Temps Modernes* 50 (1949), and as "Marxism and Superstition" in *Signs*.

81. "Les jours de notre vie," *Les Temps Modernes* 51 (1950), and in *Signs* as "The U.S.S.R. and the Camps."

82. *The Prose of the World*, xvii.

83. See E. Morin, *Autocritique* (Paris: Seuil, 1975), 94ff and 125.

84. Max Weber is spoken of for the first time in *Les Temps Modernes* in April 1952, by Lefort, in an article on *The Protestant Ethic and the Spirit of Capitalism*: "Capitalisme et religion au XVI$^e$ siècle" [*Les Temps Modernes* 78 (1952): 1892]. Even more significantly, *Critique* makes no mention of him until April 1966. There is no contradiction in the fact that Aron is an exception within this framework, since he has been a Weberian since the beginning of the thirties and his trajectory is at odds with existentialism's.

85. *Eloge de la philosophie*, iv of the cover jacket.

86. *A.D.*, 189–90.

# Chapter 10

1. Designated such without great precision, this category of co-workers has been identified by the following criteria: regular attendance at editorial meetings, the volume and weight of contributions, eventual listing on the cover, and the written or oral testimony of others.

2. Among these we may mention Claudine Chonez, E. Gabey, and Janine Bouissounouse, who are reporters, and Savin, Limbour, Leibowitz, Ménard, Scherer, and J. H. Roy, who only handle criticisms and reviews—a function which fills much space but has no influence whatsoever.

3. I have included Gorz in this group, even though he did not actually start to take part in the review's editorial life until around 1961, because from 1946 on he moves in Sartre's circle.

4. A group first formed in 1946 in association with the Trotskyite wing of the Italian C.P. which breaks with it in 1948 to found a review and a separate group of the same name. This group evolves rapidly and breaks with Trotskyism, condemning its reformist attitude toward Stalinist bureaucracy.

5. This initial relationship can account for the difference which has been noted (see Ph. Lejeune, "L'autobiographie parlée," *Obliques* 18/19) between the reverence of the original disciples—evident in the film about Sartre—and the behavior of the late disciple Michel Contat in his interviews. Lanzmann and Péju, who join the review in 1952, already adopt a more easygoing, egalitarian relationship; they come to a Sartre who is having problems and needs their help. And this phenomenon is even more evident in the behavior of the last ones to discuss matters with Sartre—Philippe Gavi and Pierre Victor (Benny Lévy)—who stand their ground stubbornly against Sartre and try to win him over to their side.

6. There are analogies between Stéphane's relationship with *Les Temps Modernes* and the relationship Todd will subsequently have with it. As in Stéphane's case, Todd's collaboration with the review will give him a spring-board to success in big journalism, without his ever having claimed to be a disciple.

7. The major realist writers often illustrated the logic of this curve in creating a category of characters of which Rastignac is the eponymous hero. See P. Bourdieu's comments in "L'invention de la vie d'artiste," *Actes de la recherche* . . . 2 (1975) on a character in *Sentimental Education,* Hussmet.

8. *Un fils rebelle* (Paris: Grasset, 1981).

9. Todd, ibid. (55) describes Sernet as a poet, a former Surrealist, and a Communist before the War.

10. Ibid., 58.

11. S. de Beauvoir, *F.C.,* 101–2.

12. In his "Introduction" in the first issue of *Les Temps Modernes.*

13. See for example "L'enfance d'un autre," *Les Temps Modernes* 5 (1946): 952ff, and "Louis n'a pas de génie," *Les Temps Modernes* 36 (1948): 479ff.

14. Advertised under the title of *Cet âge est sans pitié* in the biographical sketch in *Pour ou contre l'existentialisme* (Paris: Atlas, 1948).

15. *Loin* (Paris: Gallimard, 1980).

16. In his book, *Sartre and the Problem of Morality,* Jeanson produced a read-ing of *Being and Nothingness* very close to its author's intentions. Thanks to Sartre's

approving introduction, this book was long considered the canonical exegesis of Sartre's thought. Gorz was not so fortunate with *Fondements pour une morale*, which is not a commentary on but an original development of Sartre's thinking. When he is shown the book in 1955, Sartre does not even consider it worthwhile. (And Simone de Beauvoir faithfully reflects his judgment in dispensing with it in *Force of Circumstances* as "too Sartrean.") It will not be published until 1977—without the master's *imprimatur*. Yet Sartre approves of Gorz as a philosopher when it is his philosophy Gorz is interpreting: with his commentary on the *Critique* [see *Le socialisme difficile* (Paris: Seuil, 1967), Part 3] Gorz assumes, in respect to the second Sartre, the role Jeanson played in respect to the first. Contat and Rybalka certify the roles of each in *W.S.*

17. A. Robbe-Grillet, who reviews the book in *Critique* 49 (June 1951), sees it as a wholly formal investigation: "It is with infinite art that he tells us he has nothing to say."

18. "They both had a sound basic training in philosophy, though politics came first for both of them" (*F.C.*, 263). She says of Lanzmann: "politics seemed to him more essential than literature" (ibid., 301).

19. We can see from the subsequent political trajectory of these two that theirs was a communism born of frustration. Simone de Beauvoir has this pertinent comment about Lanzmann: "Because he had been stripped of everything, he could not stand being denied anything" (*F.C.*, 289).

20. In addition to Sartre's own recollections in "Merleau-Ponty," see Simone de Beauvoir: "They helped Sartre 'repoliticize' the magazine, and it was they more than anyone else who oriented it toward that 'critical fellow-travelling' which Merleau-Ponty had abandoned" (*F.C.*, 263–64).

21. A single example gives us an idea of the scope of the powers delegated to them: Lanzmann and Péju wrote the letter about the "baggage handlers" that Sartre read to the military tribunal at the Jeanson trial. (The letter, dated September 16, 1960, and read at the September 20 hearing, was published in *le Monde* for Sept. 22.)

22. See M. Pollak, "La planification des sciences sociales," *Actes de la recherche* . . . 2/3 (1976): 105–21.

23. See the article by P. Bourdieu and J.-C. Passeron, "Sociology and philosophy in France since 1945. Death and resurrection of a philosophy without subject," *Social Research* 24 (1) (1967): 162–212.

24. Concerning the crisis of philosophy, especially the model embodied by Sartre, and the explosion of the human sciences toward 1960, see Sergio Moravia, "La crisi della generazione sartriana," *Rivista di filosofia*, 58 (1967): 426–70, and "Filosofia e scienze umane nella cultura francese contemporanea," *Belfagor*, 23 (1968): 649–81.

25. Bost and Pouillon were the ones who warned Sartre of what they considered Péju's excessive role in the review, according to what Gorz and Pouillon himself told me in interviews, and as is suggested in Sartre's response to the letter Péju sent to *Les Temps Modernes* after he was kicked out [*Les Temps Modernes* 194 (1962): 182–89]. Objectively, this confrontation is a struggle for succession.

26. A weekly close to the Communists and headed by P. Hervé.

27. Lefort's questioning of these views can be seen in the articles he wrote for *Les Temps Modernes*. Beginning with the first, in November 1945, "L'analyse marxiste et le fascisme," he points out that the determinist theory of revolution cannot account for fascism. "Les pays coloniaux: analyse structurelle

et stratégie révolutionnaire" [18 (March, 1947)] extends this criticism to an analysis of colonial countries. "Kravchenko et le problème de l'U.R.S.S." [29 (Feb. 1948)] provides him with an occasion to announce the failure of the Soviet experiment; with "La contradiction de Trotski et le problème révolutionnaire" he challenges Trotsky's position; and in "Témoinage révolutionnaire sur l'U.R.S.S.," Victor Serge's testimony enables him to reiterate his verdict concerning the evolution of Communism.

28. See the preceding chapter, note 84.

29. Merleau-Ponty originally supports Mendès France's Comités d'action démocratiques (C.A.D.), and at the end of 1958 follows him into the Union des forces démocratiques, which brings together the entire non-Communist left opposed to the Fifth Republic. For Lefort, see below, note 32.

30. See Lefort's book, Sur une colonne absente (Paris: Gallimard, 1978), with its significant subtitle: Ecrits à partir de Merleau-Ponty.

31. See Merleau-Ponty, "Le philosophe et la sociologie," Cahiers internationaux de sociologie 10 (1951): 59–69, reprinted in Signs as "The Philosopher and Sociology," 98–113, and "De Mauss à Claude Lévi-Strauss," N.R.F. 82 (1959): 615–51, reprinted in Signs as "From Mauss to Claude Lévi-Strauss," 114–25. Lefort is one of the first to point out the implicit objectivism and antihistoricism of Lévi-Strauss's thinking. See "L'échange et la lutte des hommes," Les Temps Modernes 64 ( Feb. 1951): 1408, and "Sociétés sans histoire et historicité," Cahiers internationaux de sociologie 12 (1952): 91–114.

32. It was his rejection of existing workers' organizations which led him to found Socialisme ou barbarie in 1948. And it is because he even reaches the point of rejecting the very idea of a party that he leaves this group in 1958 to found Informations et liaisons ouvrières (which in 1960 became Informations et correspondances ouvrières), which backs "multiple centers . . . freely organizing their activities" (my italics). He is among the founders in May 1977 of the review Libre, which presents itself as "a working instrument capable of grasping the guidelines of history and the social field . . . and creating a place where one can try to think freely." To account for such an extreme "love of difference" and rejection of institutions, we must see it as a consequence of an intellectual habitus reinforced by specific biographical traits which undoubtedly lead him to radicalize the sense of social bastardy which Sartre establishes as one of the characteristics of the contemporary intellectual.

33. This is true of the following articles: Tran Duc Thao, "Sur l'interprétation trotskiste des évènements d'Indochine," Les Temps Modernes 21 (1947): 1697–1705, and "La Phénoménologie de l'esprit et son contenu reel," Les Temps Modernes 36 (1948): 492–519; C. Lefort, "Kravchenko et le problème de l'U.R.R.S.," Les Temps Modernes 29 ( Feb. 1948).

34. S. de Beauvoir, F.C., 235–36.

35. C. Charle and R. Ponton have established an analogous relation between success and emancipation in their studies of different literary schools at the end of the nineteenth century: Ponton concerning the Parnasse ("Aesthetic programs and accumulation of capital,"); Charle concerning naturalism in La crise littéraire à l'epoque du naturalisme (Paris: Presses de l'Ecole normale supérieure, 1979).

36. A member of the Association psychanalytique de France, Pontalis has an academic post divided between the C.N.R.S. and the E.P.H.E., and edits a series for Gallimard which he established, "Connaissance de l'inconscient," as well as la Nouvelle Revue de psychanalyse.

37. *Les Temps Modernes* 274 (1969).

38. See *Strategy for Labor*, trans. Martin A. Nicolaus and Victoria Ortiz (Boston: Beacon, 1967), and *Le socialisme difficile* (Paris: Seuil, 1977).

39. *Les Temps Modernes* 246 (Nov. 1966). Pouillon's introduction tends to show that Sartre and Lévi-Strauss are not only not irreconcilable but are complementary ("Un essai de définition," 769–90). And when the *Critique of Dialectical Reason* comes out and Lévi-Strauss devotes a whole semester of his seminar at the Ecole pratique des hautes études to it, Pouillon is the one who sparks the seminar.

40. Jean Pouillon, for example, initiates a collective work in honor of Lévi-Strauss, *Echanges et communications, Mélanges offerts à Claude Lévi-Strauss a l'occasion de son 60ᵉ anniversaire* (La Haye: Mouton, 1970).

41. Simone de Beauvoir continually quotes him in this function in her memoirs. See also O. Todd, *Un fils rebelle*, 12.

42. Although this destiny of Sartre's less gifted "satellites" is actually no destiny at all but is explained by the laws of the intellectual marketplace, the belief that it is feeds a whole mythology about the allegedly pernicious effects of proximity to Sartre, and Bost is one of the most frequently cited examples of it. See, for example, O. Todd, ibid., 111ff.

43. A journalist since 1938, a hero of the Resistance, he works for *Action* at the Liberation and takes part in the provisional government as special assistant to the minister of the interior, A. Tixier.

44. See G. Madjarian, *Conflits, pouvoir et société à la Libération* (Paris: U.G.E., 1980).

45. Bourdet is the son of a famous playwright and an actress, Guérin of an art critic.

46. Bourdet has a degree from the Ecole polytechnique in Zurich, Guérin from the Ecole libre des sciences politiques.

47. Stéphane is an underwriter's son.

48. In the June 1962 issue (no. 193), the managing committee of *Les Temps Modernes* announces without explanation that it has demanded Péju's resignation. Péju counterattacks in a letter to *le Monde* (June 17), to which the committee replies, in the same paper, on June 19. Péju also sends a letter to *Les Temps Modernes* which is published, along with a reply by Sartre, in the July issue (no. 194). See Contat and Rybalka, *W.S.*, vol. 1, 418.

49. His relationship with Sartre begins with an interview about *Lucifer and the Lord* (*Samedi soir*, June 2–8, 1951) in which Péju deals competently with the play's philosophical approach.

50. See Burnier, *Choice of Action*, Chapter 3 of Part 2, 122ff.

51. Marcel Péju, "Pierre Mendès France ou les ambiguites," *Les Temps Modernes* 109 (Jan.-Feb. 1955): 961–71.

52. See M. A. Burnier, *Choice of Action*, 116.

53. *Arts*, July 24–30, 1953, reprinted in *Hygiène des lettres* (2): *Litterature degagée (1942–1953)* (Paris: Gallimard, 1955).

54. *Hygiène des lettres* (2), 108 and 110.

55. Simone de Beauvoir, *All Said and Done*, trans. Patrick O'Brian (New York: G. P. Putnam's Sons, 1974), 136–37 (my italics).

56. According to an unpublished investigation by M. de Saint-Martin, 53 percent of the readers of *Les Temps Modernes* in 1966 also read the *Nouvel Observateur*.

57. Sartre, together with Mendès France, was the godfather of the first issue of the *Nouvel Observateur* in 1964.

# Index of Names

Voltaire, 1, 55, 58
Vuillemin, Jules, 115, 146, 173, 239, 261n.15

Waelhens, Alphonse de, 256n.3
Wagner, Cosima, 30
Wahl, Jean, 10, 63, 64, 65, 81, 84, 145, 146, 161, 164, 256n.1, 257n.4, 259n.29, 259n.36, 261n.14
Waldberg, P., 258n.18
Weber, Max, 1, 2, 63, 175, 213, 215, 218, 219, 220, 221, 223, 232, 267n.84

Weil, Eric, 66, 116, 145–46, 153, 159, 163, 164, 259n.30
Weil, Simone, 190
Wiener, Norbert, 259n.35
Winock, M., 258n.16, 260n.8
Wittgenstein, Ludwig, 123
Woolf, Virginia, 37
Wright, Richard, 173
Wurmser, A., 148, 149

Zola, Emile, 15, 16, 20, 50, 58, 112